A History of Early Film

Also available

A History of Pre-Cinema
Edited and with a new introduction by Stephen Herbert

A History of Early Film

Volume 1

*Selected and with a new
introduction by Stephen Herbert*

London and New York

First published 2000
by Routledge
11 New Fetter Lane, London EC4P 4EE

Simultaneously published in the USA and Canada
by Routledge
29 West 35th Street, New York, NY 10001

Reprinted 2001

Routledge is an imprint of the Taylor & Francis Group

Typeset in Times by Keystroke, Jacaranda Lodge, Wolverhampton
Printed and bound in Great Britain by TJI Digital, Padstow, Cornwall

British Library Cataloguing in Publication Data
A catalogue record for this book is available from the British Library

Library of Congress Cataloging in Publication Data
A catalogue record for this book has been requested

ISBN 0-415-21151-4 (set)
ISBN 0-415-21152-2 (Volume 1)

Publisher's note
The publisher has gone to great lengths to ensure the quality of this reprint, but points
out that some imperfections in the original material may be apparent.

CONTENTS

CONTENTS

CONTENTS

ACKNOWLEDGEMENTS

In 1915 Vachel Lindsay predicted: 'When these are ancient times, we will have scholars and critics learned in the flavors of early moving picture traditions with their histories and movements and schools, their grammars, and their anthologies.' And so it is, and I would like to thank those scholars and critics for their generous assistance with this project. The advertisements reproduced in our Victorian Cinema section were brought to my attention by Colin Harding and Simon Popple, authors of *In the Kingdom of Shadows* (Cygnus Arts, 1996), a treasurehouse of transcribed early film material. In choosing the items in this present facsimile collection, I have attempted to complement the fine selection made for that book. I would like to thank Vanessa Toulmin of the National Fairground Archive, University of Sheffield, for suggesting that I examine the unique run of *The Showman* at the Colindale Newspaper Library. Thanks also to Stephen Bottomore, a private researcher with a peerless knowledge of periodicals containing articles on early film, for providing many useful references; to Luke McKernan for his helpful and widely informed comments on the first draft of my introduction; and to John Barnes who is responsible for my interest.

The publishers would like to thank the following for permission to reprint their material:

The British Library, for permission to reprint:

W.K.-L. Dickson, 'Edison's Kinematograph Experiments', *Kinematograph and Lantern Weekly*; 'Lantern Projection of Moving Objects', *Amateur Photographer*; Alfred Angus, 'A Mutoscopic Romance', *Penny Pictorial*; Henry V. Hopwood, 'Cinematography for All', *The Optician*; 'Front Cover, September 1900', *The Showman*; anon., 'How War Films are Made', *The Showman*; 'Animated Photography', *The Showman*; 'William Clark', *The Showman*, 'Front cover, 26 July 1901', *The Showman*; T. C. Hepworth, 'Music and Effects in Cinematography', *The Showman*; 'Cinematograph Show under the new L.C.C. rules', *The Showman*; 'First in 1893' (Gaumont advertisement), *The Showman*; 'London to Johannesburg', *The Showman*; 'Animated Pictures and Elocution', *The Showman*; 'The House for Films', *The Showman*; "Sylvanus", 'Our First Kinematograph Show', *Kinematograph and Lantern Weekly*; W.H.B., 'Notes on Current Topics', *Kinematograph and Lantern Weekly*; 'Cinema Notes', *Amateur Photographer*; 'Singing Pictures at the Hippodrome', *Kinematograph and Lantern Weekly*; 'The Cinematophone' (advertisement), *Kinematograph and Lantern Weekly*; 'A Lady Kinematograph Operator', *Kinematograph and Lantern Weekly*, 'Fatal Accident at a Picture Show', *Kinematograph and Lantern Weekly*; 'The Press and the Barnsley Accident', *Kinematograph and Lantern Weekly*; Montagu A. Pyke, *Focussing the Universe*; Canon Hardwicke Drummond Rawnsley, *The Child and the Cinematograph Show and the Picture Post-Card Evil, With a note on the cinematograph by the Headmaster of Eton.*

The Science Museum Library, for permission to reprint:

'The Triumph of Colour', *The Bioscope*; 'Arrival of the Cinematograph Bill' (cartoon), *The Bioscope*; 'Market Movements' (cartoon), *The Bioscope*; 'Grand Opening of School for Lady

Operators', *The Bioscope*; 'The Faults of Non-Inflammable Film', *The Bioscope*; Arthur S. Newman, 'Standardisation', *The Bioscope*; 'Mr. M. A. Pyke's Latest', *The Bioscope*; 'Bioscope Theatres in Vienna', *The Bioscope*; 'Foreign News – France', *The Bioscope*; 'Foreign News – America; Australia [etc.]', *The Bioscope*; 'The Bioscope in India', *The Bioscope*; S. Kurimoto, 'The Progress of Cinematography in Japan', *The Bioscope*; 'Cinematography in Italy, *The Bioscope*; 'The French Cinematograph Trade', *The Bioscope*; 'Cinematography in India', *The Bioscope*; J. Ojijatekha Brant-Sero, 'A Visit to a German Picture Theatre', *The Bioscope*; 'Some Rhodesian Theatres', *The Bioscope*; 'Living Pictures and Advertisements', *The Bioscope*; 'Explaining the Pictures', *The Bioscope*; T. W. Kingston, 'Telling the Tale', *The Bioscope*; 'Music in Picture Theatres' (letter), *The Bioscope*; 'The Bioscope Parliament: The Picture Pianist' (letters), *The Bioscope*; "Souffleur", 'The Music of the Picture Theatre', *The Bioscope*; 'How Moving Pictures Help Actresses', *The Bioscope*; L. Stanford Cook, 'A Plea for the Long Film', *The Bioscope*; 'Interview with the Dramatic Critic of the Morning and Evening "Standard"', *The Bioscope*; 'Education and the Bioscope', *The Bioscope*; 'Will Moving Pictures Prevent War?' *The Bioscope*; 'The Cinematograph in Church', *Amateur Photographer*; 'Sacred Films', *Amateur Photographer*.

The National Museum of Photography, Film & Television, Bradford (The Science Museum), for permission to reprint:

Selection of Victorian film and film equipment advertisements: *The Optician and Photographic Trades Review*, *The Photographic Dealer* and *The Photogram*.

The following items have been reprinted from the author's collection, and from originals in private collections:

'Hand and Glove at the Aquarium', *Punch*; 'Our Future King at Play', *The Harmsworth Magazine*; 'Round the World for the Biograph', H. L. Adam, *The Royal Magazine*; 'Mechanical Effects and Moving Pictures', *Optical Lantern and Kinematograph Journal*; 'Phantom Players', *The Royal Magazine*; Picture postcards: 'Special Charley [*sic*] Chaplin Film'; 'Don't keep me in the dark'; 'What could be nicer?'; 'One meets such nice girls at the picture palace!'; 'At the cinema'; Margaret Chute, 'The One-Eyed Machine', *The Royal Magazine*; Vachel Lindsay, 'The Picture of Crowd Splendor', *The Art of the Moving Picture*; Colin Bennett, *The Handbook of Kinematography*; *Urban Films Catalogue*; National Council of Public Morals, *The Cinema: Its Present Position and Future Possibilities*.

INTRODUCTION

It has come then, this new weapon of men, and the face of the whole earth changes.
In after centuries its beginning will be indeed remembered.

(Vachel Lindsay, 1915)

VOLUME 1

This history of early film comprises reprints of important and interesting writings on the subject, from 1894–1917. There was much development in these early days, in both film production and exhibition. This contribution considers the actual films, the technologies that made them possible, and their exhibition in a variety of venues, seen through publications of the period.

This work is divided into the following sections:

Volume 1
- Invention
- Victorian cinema (1894–1901)
- The medium develops (1901–6)

Volume 2
- An established industry (1907–14)

Volume 3
- Critical appraisal and social concern

Many 'histories' of early film are needed, if we are to develop our understanding of the first years of motion pictures. This selection is limited to the English language, and mostly relates to early film in Britain – then important in both production and exhibition – with some reference to the USA and Europe.

The datelines for early film, or early cinema, are loosely defined. The start point is sometimes taken to be the invention of series-pictures on flexible roll film, *c.* 1888, and is usually considered to stretch to around 1913–15 and the introduction of the feature film. We have extended this cutoff date a little to include publications dating to 1917. Films, and the circumstances of their presentation, changed considerably during that time. We can perhaps divide early cinema into three periods:

(1) 1888–1901. The first sequence photographs taken on roll films were the paper and celluloid chronophotographs of the physiologist Etienne-Jules Marey (1888), the paper films of cinema visionary Louis Le Prince (1888), experiments by Wordsworth Donisthorpe, William Friese Greene (early 1890s), and many others. These inventors failed to present their films satisfactorily as moving pictures. Technical and commercial success in film presentation came with Edison's peepshow Kinetoscope launched in 1894, and audiences saw their first projected films the following year. The Lumières used the name Cinématographe for their 1895 device, giving us the term 'cinema', usually taken to involve films being projected onto a screen for group audience viewing. Despite being confined initially to a peepbox, the earlier Edison films are now encompassed in definitions of 'early cinema'. Within months of the first American and European screenings of 1895–6, moving pictures spread throughout most of the world. The main appeal of these 'animated photographs' in the first year or two was the pure re-creation of movement. As pioneer Cecil Hepworth explained in 1917 (in *The Cinema – Its Present Position* . . . p. 52):

> The films consisted in the old days of pictures of railway trains in cuttings and of omnibuses in Piccadilly – any little thing which tended to movement. There was no attempt to make a consecutive story. Any form of movement satisfied us, because it was a miracle to see moving photographs, and that was what the people were asking for.

Most films were shot in the open; a few glass-roofed studios were starting to be erected. In the UK, films were shown in variety theatres, local halls, in fairgrounds and other locations, by many types of exhibitors. The films were single-shot productions of around one minute; a programme comprised several films – perhaps ten or twelve – usually with an explanatory narration and/or musical accompaniment, and interspersed in some cases with lantern slides. The showman could select from a wide range of 'actualities' – simple documentaries showing a street scene, for example – including local views and events, sentimental child studies, lively skirt dances, sporting scenes, and very basic single-scene narratives.

(2) 1901–6. After 1900, multiple-shot productions started to appear, and film-language began to take shape. This gave more scope for narrative development, and story films became more common and more sophisticated. Quite impressive studios were built, but they were still dependent on sunlight. By 1906 a typical film was one reel – approximately fifteen minutes – in length. Though the names of regular actors were largely unadvertised their faces became familiar to the viewing public, the first stage in the 'star' system. Documentary subjects were still widely shown. In the USA, 'permanent' Nickelodeon film theatres appeared from 1905. In the UK the travelling film/slide lecturer gradually disappeared, though fairground Bioscope shows accommodating hundreds of fairgoers, with steam organs and paraders enticing the crowds inside, were very popular. In British towns rented shops were converted to show films, and the practice of exhibitors buying film prints gave way to rental arrangements.

(3) 1907–14. This third period of early cinema saw the rise of the film star. Even in Europe and the UK, audiences knew the American stars: Mary Pickford, John Bunny, Lillian Gish. Chaplin made his first film in 1914. From the start of this period documentary subjects were beginning to wane. Narrative films grew to feature-length, of around ninety minutes, although twenty-minute comedies were still popular. Studios were equipped with electric lighting. European and British film production was still important, but by 1914 Hollywood feature production had started. In the UK, American productions started to dominate the exhibition business, and from 1907 purpose-built cinemas sprang up. Musical accompaniment ranged from a lone piano to a trio, or even a small orchestra for prestigious productions in the best cinemas. By 1914 permanent cinema theatres, frequently several in competition, were a feature of every town of any size in the USA, UK and much of Europe. Films had largely disappeared from variety halls, and in Britain, from the outbreak of war, the travelling fairground Bioscope show went into decline.

Invention

Our collection begins with the period of technical invention. The story of Edison's peepshow Kinetoscope, set up in arcades from April 1894, is told by Edison's assistant W. K.-L. Dickson, who was mainly responsible for its development, and for the development of the supplying camera, the Kinetograph. Our short version of the account, 'Edison's Kinematograph Experiments' (1907), based on Dickson's 1895 book *The History of the Kinetograph, Kinetoscope & Kinetophonograph*, was published in Britain in the *Kinematograph and Lantern Weekly*, and has not previously been reprinted in this form. Subsequent research suggests that this is a loosely correct version of events, though several details are romantic enhancement.

'Lantern Projection of Moving Objects' in the *Amateur Photographer* (1896), heralds the arrival of the first screenings in Britain, arranged by Auguste and Louis Lumière, Robert Paul and Birt Acres, announcing the new medium as a progressive development of optical moving-image toys, magic lantern projection and the Kinetoscope.

Victorian cinema (1894–1901)

Boxing films were among the first to be produced, allowing lady patrons at Kinetoscope peepshow parlours to view scenes that were socially unacceptable to visit 'live'. The first projected public filmshow, by the Latham brothers in New York in May 1895, was of a boxing match. The subject of our piece, 'Hand and Glove at the Aquarium', is the popular 1897 fight between 'Gentleman Jim' Corbett and Bob Fitzsimmons; the entire fourteen rounds filmed by the large-format Veriscope camera, lampooned by *Punch* as the 'Fisticuffographic Process'.

There was tremendous international interest at the turn of the century in the Dreyfus Affair. 'A Mutoscopic Romance' (1899), from the *Penny Pictorial*, tells how Captain Dreyfus, a French Jew falsely convicted of passing on defence secrets and serving life imprisonment, was filmed in the prison exercise yard by a hidden Biograph camera. 'Our Future King at Play', *The Harmsworth Magazine* (1900) shows that the Mutoscope was not limited to cheap arcades showing risqué subjects to the masses, but reached all levels of society.

The collection continues with an evocative selection of advertisements for the earliest films and cinematographic apparatus of 1896–7. These are mainly from the scarce periodicals *The Optician and Photographic Trades Review*, *The Photographic Dealer* and *The Photogram*, indicating the industries that initially accommodated the new medium. Advertisers include Robert Paul, who made copies of Edison's Kinetoscope in the earliest days of films, and went on to be a pioneer cinema exhibitor and producer before leaving the changing industry in 1910; Maguire & Baucus, responsible for importing the films of Georges Méliès and the important American Bioscope projector, whose manager Charles Urban would become one of Britain's top film producers in the years leading up to the First World War; Baxter & Wray, Rigg, Watson, Wrench, Riley, Appleton, and other important early suppliers of film equipment; the European Blair Camera Company, and J. H. Smith (of Zurich) who were responsible for supplying filmstock to the early producers; and Philipp Wolff, and the Fuerst Brothers, who supplied film productions from many sources, including European and American producers, to the British exhibitors of the period.

The medium develops (1901–6)

In the early days of moving pictures, it was by no means certain that public audiences sitting in commercial theatre halls would be the main future of the medium. The Kinetoscope and Mutoscope peepshows, set up in rows in amusement arcades, tempted the more solitary spectator. And from the first, attempts were made to establish a domestic audience. The range of possibilities was reviewed in 'Cinematography for All', *The Optician*, (1901) by patent specialist Henry Hopwood (author of the classic 1899 technical review of moving-picture history and progress *Living Pictures*). Even at this early date, Hopwood was concerned that the professional industry had expanded as far as could be expected, and another outlet for moving pictures was needed. His review included machines using film of reduced size, and the ingenious Kinora miniature flip-photo Mutoscope. Unsure of the eventual distribution medium for their Cinématographe pictures, the Lumières had developed the Kinora (based on patents by American Herman Casler) in 1895, presumably to ensure that a domestic machine was an option if public projection was unsuccessful. With the success of their Cinématographe shows they neglected the Kinora, which was sold to Gaumont who launched it later. It had most success in Britain after 1901, with a dozen hand-turned and clockwork models available, over 600 different reels – including Lumière and Biograph films – for purchase or rent, a studio portrait option, and later even an amateur camera. The system disappeared in 1913, and home movies would have to wait until the 1920s and the introduction of narrow-gauge film systems by Pathé and Kodak, to find widespread success.

General-interest magazines of the period sometimes included articles on film-related subjects. 'Round the World for the Biograph' by H. L. Adam, *The Royal Magazine* (1901), chronicles W. K.-L. Dickson – now producing/directing for the Biograph Company – travelling with the heavy and bulky large-format Biograph camera. One scoop clearly impressed the author. 'I presume nobody', he writes, 'will be prepared to deny that the "Biographing" of [Pope] Leo XIII was the greatest thing ever accomplished in photography.'

The next articles are from the 1900–2 issues of *The Showman*, an interesting and now rare magazine for ventriloquists, magicians, singers and show people of all kinds. The importance of the comparatively new film business is reflected on the front cover of the first issue, September 1900, an advertisement for Warwick Trading Company. 'How War Films are Made' (1900) describes the 'narrow shaves' experienced by Warwick's cameraman Joe Rosenthal while filming the Boer War. 'The World's Headquarters for Animated Photography' (1902) is a cartoon advertisement for the same company, then headed by the dynamic Charles Urban: a fairground bioscope showman and his 'paraders' are having no success with the rival firms' attractions, even at 1d. admission, but are crowded out at 3d. when they switch to the Warwick Bioscope. From 1897 to the First World War, travelling bioscope shows were a major means of film exhibition in Britain. Their importance is represented by a 1901 article about 'William Clark', who adopted the name 'Colonel' during the Boer War. He was the second generation to run a Ghost Show, and by July 1897 had added films. His enterprise included engaging a local cameraman to make a short film of workers leaving a hat factory in Stockport. A front cover advertisement from the same year describes the benefits for travelling showmen of commissioning this sort of film – the genre originating with the Lumières' first success of 1895 – as the subjects would then 'come in their hundreds' to the shows. The advertisement is by Cecil Hepworth, whose father T. C. Hepworth, a long-experienced magic lanternist, wrote our next piece: 'Music and "Effects" in Cinematography' (1901). He recommends percussion to represent battle gunfire, rather than emulate one showman who 'carried realism to an absurd pitch' by firing a dozen revolvers.

'Cinematograph Show under the new L.C.C. Rules' reflects the impatience of some in the industry with the safety restrictions imposed by the London County Council, which were eventually even more stringent than this cartoon (originally printed in *The Photographic Dealer* in 1898) would suggest, requiring the projector and operator to function from inside a metal housing. The title of Gaumont's advertisement from the same year, 'First in 1893 – Foremost Ever Since' – suggesting a commencement two years before the first film screenings – indicates the importance of priority claims at that time, and refers to their 1893 Demeny 'beater movement' patent, which was not actually commercially used until 1896. 'London to Johannesburg with the Bioscope' (1901) tells of the difficulties of touring a filmshow in South Africa, where electric current was not widely available and gas cylinders non-existent.

Audiences were beginning to tire of films without a story. At a time when the single-shot actuality film was foremost and fictional narrative rare, 'Animated Pictures and Elocution' (1901) suggests the production of films 'to fit in with some of our best plays, readings, and songs', and presented with a strong vocal element, in the manner of slide presentations. 'The House for Films' (1901) describes a visit to Mr J. D. Walker, who operated one of the first film-hire services at a time when most showmen still bought films outright, relying on a fresh audience at the next town. As films got longer and more expensive, and static shows grew in number, hiring became an essential part of the business. Mr Walker and his partners Turner and Dawson had considerable success, and their firm (later the Walturdaw company) lasted for many years.

In 'Mechanical Effects and Moving Pictures' the editor of the *Optical Lantern and Kinematograph Journal* (1906), on a trip to the USA, visits a version of the popular Hale's Tours – a store is fitted out to resemble a train carriage, and projected scenery gives the effect of a journey – and a similar balloon ascent 'ride' at Coney Island.

Our first volume concludes with: *Urban Films Catalogue* (Charles Urban Trading Company, June 1905): 'We Put the World Before You'. Charles Urban was from Cincinnati, USA, and originally a travelling book salesman, who progressed to selling typewriters and other office equipment including early versions of the phonograph, then being sold for dictation. This led to an involvement with the first commercial film machine, Edison's peepshow Kinetoscope, then to film projection and finally – after moving to Britain in 1897 – film production. The catalogue offers a very wide selection of films, many produced by Urban's own cameramen/directors, others by associated individuals and companies. Urban was the UK agent for French producers Lumière and Méliès, and distributor for British filmmakers G. A. Smith, West, Williamson, Mitchell & Kenyon and others. This selection gives a good indication of the themes and subjects available to travelling exhibitors, theatre owners and operators of shopfront 'penny gaff' conversions at that period, two or three years before purpose-built cinemas started to open in Britain. (My comments on the catalogue do not strictly follow the order of the listed films, which is somewhat erratic, but particular subjects can be found in the index.)

'Sugar-coated science' was how one reviewer described the 'Natural History and Microscopic' series, comprising dozens of productions of fifty feet (less than a minute) to 500 feet (approximately eight minutes) in length, from ambitious depictions of bee culture to *Educated Monkeys in Costume*, an item of questionable educational value. Time-lapse wonders revealed *The Birth of a Crystal*. The 'Unseen World' shown by the Urban–Duncan Micro-Bioscope, under the direction of science/nature-film specialist F. Martin Duncan, provided gigantic enlargements of *Bacteria from a Water-Butt*. Glowing newspaper reviews confirm an unlikely but undoubted success, and report the 'breathless wonder' of the fun-seeking first audiences exposed to these scientific super-closeups as a 'music-hall turn' at London's Alhambra Theatre. Informing the public in a very graphic way of the 'bugs' that populated their food did not please everyone, and *Cheese Mites* prompted the cheese industry to try to get the film banned – and led to a spoof by the Hepworth company, in which the creatures are revealed to be clockwork! A listing of natural history lantern slides reminds us of the importance of mixed-media programmes at this period for certain educational lecture venues.

There is plenty of action footage in 'Races, Sports and Contests': from a *Bun-Eating Competition* – 'would make a goat laugh' – to views of a major competitor of the developing cinema, *Roller Skating in Paris*; from boat racing on the Thames to car racing in Germany, and bull fights in Spain. Other sports films include *Northern Ice Sports* as well as cricket, golf and football: Scotland v. England at Crystal Palace, 1905. In contrast, not something that would be presented as entertainment to a cinema audience today, *Hunting the Red Deer* is an 'ideal day's sport . . . "Who whoop!" cries the huntsman, as he throws the stag's entrails to the hungry hounds'. The longer productions are described shot-by-shot; useful information for archivists restoring surviving prints. The 'Music Hall' series includes cakewalkers, dancers and acrobats rather than well-known performers. 'Historic Personalities and Events' mostly feature King Edward VII and the French première Emile Loubet.

Voyage to New York – on the Mail Steamship *Kaiser Wilhelm II* – is one of several films available, whole or in part, in coloured form; the final scenes 'tinted to represent the actual glow of colour characteristic of a sunset, and the cold blue sheen of a moon-light view at sea'. This was one of many major productions exclusively presented in the UK and USA by Urban's own exhibition department, and available for sale only to exhibitors outside of those territories. This subject – unusually, shot by Urban himself – illustrates the evolution in the way that films were being sold at this time. Although still listed with individual shot descriptions, and advertised as 'Seventy Bioscope Pictures by Mr. Urban', the seventy scenes of this mega-production are supplied only as a complete compilation of 2,300 feet – advertised as forty-five minutes' duration. It would be only an exceptionally confident and successful exhibitor who would be able to afford the £57.10s. price of this particular film, but the days of showmen deciding on which shots to buy and making up their own compilations were coming to an end. Although at this time selected scenes of many subjects were still available as short sequences, this option would gradually be phased out. The increasing expense of longer films would soon lead to the film rental business superseding the direct selling from producer to exhibitor, accelerated by the establishment of fixed film-only venues, where frequent programme changes were essential.

At a time when emigration from Britain to the Colonies was still being promoted, Joseph Rosenthal's extensive series 'Living Canada' showed logging and salmon fishing, and 'The Rocky Mountains' featured spectacular Canadian Railway panoramas. *The Matterhorn* 'Conquered by the Bioscope', was filmed by Frank Ormiston-Smith of the Urban Mountaineering Expedition in September 1903: that same month he also filmed the successful *Ascent of the Jungfrau*. Ormiston-Smith was also responsible for series featuring 'Greece'; 'Turkey and Egypt'; and 'Arabia and Palestine'. Another set comprised the 'only Animated Pictures of Macedonia and Bulgarian Scenes in existence'. Further exotic scenes were captured by H. M. Lomas on the 'Urban Bioscope Expedition through Borneo', financed by the North Borneo Company and shown at its Annual Dinner – where the guests 'smoke North Borneo cigars and drink North Borneo coffee' – evidently an early form of 'corporate video'. A photograph shows Mr Lomas sitting on a platform fixed to the front of a locomotive, preparing to film one of the Railway Panoramas listed here. The term panorama was used to describe both the revealing of a landscape by a slow swivel from a fixed-camera position (hence the modern 'pan' shot), and the more dynamic travelling view – originally, and more graphically, described as a Phantom Ride – from the front of a train or other vehicle. More of these are included in the 'Railway Series'. 'Ceylon', 'India, Burmah and the Cashmere' and 'Japan' also became subjects for Urban's roving Bioscopists, as well as an extended series of the more accessible 'London'.

Other documentary subjects included 'Military and Police' and several industrial films. The interiors of *A Newspaper in Making*, showing the production of London's *Evening News*, required 'every kind of artificial lamp . . . including specially-prepared mercurial vapour lamps'. *Horse-Breaking Extraordinary* advocates forsaking the 'usual harsh and cruel methods' for – not the now fashionable horse-whispering, but the more vigorous horse-wrestling! *A Visit to the Steel Works* has interior scenes tinted 'to suitably convey the glare and orange hue from the furnaces and liquid metal on their surroundings'. *Black Diamonds, or The Collier's Daily Life*, filmed by Mitchell and Kenyon in the Midlands, included a (presumably) dramatic enactment of 'an explosion – men buried in debris – comrades to rescue' and other staged scenes mixed with the documentary shots. These arranged sequences were apparently acceptable to the Urban company, who on the next page – listing Russo-Japanese war pictures – warn that exhibitors 'should not be confounded with the disgraceful series of fakes, which have . . . misled the public and cast doubt as to the authenticity of the results obtained at great risk and expense by the conscientious Film Maker'.

At one hour and twenty minutes, 'The Tragedy of Port Arthur' series indicates the extensive coverage of important overseas events at that time – the siege had ended in January 1905 – and the public interest in such news items. 'The Great Russo Japan War' was a second series featuring this conflict, also from Urban's chief cameraman Joseph Rosenthal (who had been filming for Urban since 1898, during their days at the Warwick Trading Company, and had earlier covered the Boer War). Rosenthal, 'granted permission by the Japanese War Office to accompany the 3rd Imperial Army in its operations . . . was compelled to enter the firing line and expose himself and his instrument to many dangers . . . '. The veteran war bioscopist was not alone in filming scenes relevant to this event: the 'Naval and Marine' category includes the 'Bombardment of Port Arthur' series by marine-film specialists West's 'Our Navy' Ltd. Despite noting this as a 'Representation' of the event, not everyone would realise that it was staged and filmed off the English coast.

Although the bulk of the catalogue consists of non-fiction films, dramatic and comical productions are included. A short 'Comic Series' lists *The Meddling Policeman* who is tied with strings of sausages and deluged with flour. Fictional drama is provided by *Hiawatha*, an interpretation of Longfellow's poem in twenty scenes, performed by members of the Ojibway people and filmed by Joe Rosenthal in Canada; the period, location picture *Dick Turpin, The Highwayman* benefiting from the fact that 'All the dresses in this picture are the style of 100 years ago'; and the imported melodrama *Pierrot's Romance*.

'Spectacular and Pantomine' productions include *Cinderella*, 'in which over 35 people take part', and the 'fantastical production' *The Wonders of the Deep*, with 'personnel engaged from 17 Parisian Theatres' and 'rain produced by real water', these boasts emphasizing the theatrical origins of these Georges Méliès productions, and the proud attempts to go beyond what was possible to depict on the stage. Méliès' famous *Trip to the Moon* – with its unforgettable scene of the capsule landing in the 'pie-face' moon, one of the few icons of early cinema – is included in this category, with over 170 other Méliès films. These are mostly short, but include the more recent and ambitious twenty-five-minute space fantasy *Whirling the Worlds* (*Voyage travers l'impossible*) and Goethe's *Faust*, 'Performed in Synchronism with the principal Airs from

Gounod's Opera'. The magician Méliès had started film production soon after attending a preview of the first public Lumière show in December 1895. His particular style involved a camera position equivalent to a seat in a theatre 'stalls', from which the entire studio staging area was filmed, with liberal and ingenious use made of stop-motion, dissolve effects and superimposition. Méliès' films had originally been distributed in Britain by the Warwick Trading Company. Urban became manager of the company, and when he left to set up his own firm, Méliès' 'Star' films crossed over with him. In 1905 Méliès was still at the height of his success, but within a few years the limitations of his technique – no close-ups or moving camera, for instance – and changes in the business, particularly competition from the USA, began to tell. He abandoned filmmaking in 1913, as the period we now refer to as early cinema was coming to a close.

George Albert Smith, one-time lanternist and psychic, had been producing films at Hove, on England's Sussex coast, since 1896. Over fifty '"G.A.S." Film Subjects' are listed, ranging from *At Last! That Awful Tooth* and *Grandma's Reading Glass*, both of which make novel use of a magnifying glass, to the 1903 pantomime extravaganza *Dorothy's Dream*. The latter was one of the last significant films produced by Smith, who was by then involved in a new technical development. As we have seen, several productions distributed by Urban – in common with other producers – were available in tinted versions, with each shot given a tint in an appropriate colour. A *Grand Display of Brock's Fireworks* (at the Crystal Palace), for example, was available only in a colour-tinted version. Some films may also have been toned, a similar monochrome effect that chemically changed the black and grey elements of the picture to a particular colour, while leaving the highlights clear. More ambitiously the Méliès films were coloured by lines of women workers using tiny brushes under magnifiers to overpaint costumes, scenery, flame effects etc., with several colours within each minute frame. Within a few years, however, Smith's experiments were to result in something even more magical: 'natural colour' production. Since 1902 Urban had been financing Smith's development of this 'natural' (if theoretically somewhat limited) system of colour cinematography. Kinemacolor – commercially introduced in 1909 – was the result; a highly praised achievement with which Urban's name would be forever associated.

The catalogue continues with a selection from Smith's near-neighbour, the ex-pharmacist James Williamson, including the famous *Attack on a China Mission* – one of the earliest multi-shot narrative productions released in 1901 – and the imaginative trick film *A Big Swallow* in which the photographer is swallowed by his gentleman subject. The final list is of Lumière films. The Lumières had stopped production three years earlier, and some of these – such as *Demolishing a Wall* and *Baby's Tea* (to use the Urban-designated titles) – date back to the brothers' first filmshows of 1895, and a decade later were somewhat archaic.

Two or three years after the publication of this catalogue, the cinema was swiftly changing. The wide range of subject matter reflected in this 1905 selection would be less apparent, as fictional subjects came to prominence. Urban extended his catalogue range of fiction films the following year, with the inclusion of dramas and comedies from the important production companies of Vitagraph (USA) and Eclipse (France). Audiences in the new Electric Palaces of post-1907 demanded such story films, which were becoming longer and more lavish. By 1914, the 'classical Hollywood' format of a feature-length narrative film of an hour or more, with a supporting programme, sometimes including a newsreel, was starting to become established.

[END OF VOLUME 1]

VOLUME 2

An established industry (1907–14)

With Volume 2, we take a look at filmmaking and presentation during the latter part of the early cinema period.

In 1907, 'Sylvanus' of the *Kinematograph and Lantern Weekly*, was already looking back with romantic nostalgia to the 1890s, with 'Our First Kinematograph Show', and in 'Notes on Current Topics' a contributor to the *Kinematograph and Lantern Weekly* was reflecting on how the films then being made would be received by future generations. It was not only the trade journals that were concerned with films, they were also the subject of articles in magazines read by a wider public. A 1912 *Amateur Photographer*'s 'Cinema Notes' promoted the artistic and educational nature of the moving picture.

Technology did not stand still during these years. From the days when Edison's peepshow Kinetophone had linked Kinetoscope pictures with music cylinders, attempts had been made to popularize films accompanied by recorded sound. Despite problems with editing, synchronization and amplification, many auditoriums were fitted with sound-film equipment during the early cinema period. 'Singing Pictures at the Hippodrome' in the *Kinematograph and Lantern Weekly*, describes an eight-month run of the Gaumont Chronophone at a major London venue in 1907. A rival system, 'The Cinematophone' – from a source we have already come across, early film renter Mr J. D. Walker's company – was advertised later that same month in the same periodical. 'The Triumph of Colour' describes the public approval of Kinemacolor in 1911, with programmes running for two months at London's Scala, and 'all through the heat wave the theatre was crowded'.

Much of the discussion in the trade magazines (except where noted the following items are from *The Bioscope*) revolved around economic and commercial subjects, including expenses incurred in complying with new laws, and the damage caused by irresponsible promoters. The cartoon 'Arrival of the Cinematograph Bill' (1909) reflects the industry's concern about the commercial consequences of the Cinematograph Act which would come into effect in 1910, and 'Market Movements' (1909) illustrates the established exhibitors' concern with the 'surprising claims' of many of the newly registered businesses.

The skills required by successful travelling theatrical exhibitors are described in 'A Lady Kinematograph Operator', *Kinematograph and Lantern Weekly* (1907), and included editing films to remove 'unnecessary padding'. The woman partner of this touring couple operated the projector, such an unusual situation that her husband claimed she was 'the only lady operator in the world', although a few women, including Mr Walker's wife, had taken on this role in the earliest days. 'Grand Opening of the School for Lady Operators' (1909) is a misogynist satire prompted by the women's suffrage movement. Within a few years, lady operators (projectionists) would become a reality, as their men went to war.

'Fatal Accident at a Picture Show', *Kinematograph and Lantern Weekly*, records in detail the circumstances of a 1907 fire at a local hall, where a departing audience disturbed the gas equipment which then fired the film, causing injuries and one fatality. 'The Press and the Barnsley Accident', reported in the same paper a few months later, resulted in the deaths of sixteen children. Although this was caused by panic on the stairs and not a technical incident, the flammable nature of filmstock was a major cause of concern with those responsible for giving permission for shows in local halls, and was therefore of considerable concern to the trade. Several types of safety film were experimented with and marketed, but there were problems, described in 'The Faults of Non-Inflammable Film' (1909). However, a reasonably satisfactory cellulose acetate safety stock was soon available, and in Europe was a key selling point of the successful 1912 Pathé 'Home Cinematograph' projection system. From that date all narrow-gauge film systems intended for amateur or educational use would use non-inflammable stock, but the cinema industry would continue with mainly inflammable filmstock until as late as 1951.

Apart from the large-format Biograph (which succumbed to standard width 35mm after a few years), only 35mm (or its equivalent, 1⅜ inch) film had achieved widespread use. In 'Standardisation' (1909), Arthur S. Newman, a designer of film mechanisms since 1896, explains why films perforated – more or less – to the Edison format succeeded over the Lumière variation and became universal. Exact specifications were yet to be decided, but would be agreed later that year at a European trade convention; an important technical advance.

By 1910 the period of the shopfront 'cinema', quickly and cheaply adapted to show films, was coming to an end. Electric Theatres were opening at a steady rate throughout Britain, either converted from live theatres or other suitable buildings at considerable expense, or purpose-built. 'Mr. M. A. Pyke's Latest' in west London was quite luxurious. We shall meet Mr Pyke again later.

The UK trade press occasionally reported on film activity overseas. 'Bioscope Theatres in Vienna' (1909) mentions one equipped with 'a full set of voice imitators and noise-producing machinery'. 'Foreign News – France' (1909) reports on the success of cinemas, from the bustling boulevards of Paris to far-off mountain towns; plus details of filmmaking exploits that, typically, are probably a mixture of apocryphal stories and newspaper reports. 'Foreign News' (1910) is a world-wide roundup of moving picture news, and 'The Bioscope in India' is a report from Calcutta. 'The Progress of Cinematography in Japan' (1911) gives a brief historical account of what the writer, S. Kurimoto, refers to as 'early cinematography' in that country. (The Edison Kinetoscope mentioned was a projector, not to be confused with the earlier peepshow.) He also reveals that in 1911 two Japanese companies had representatives established in London to arrange the export of European and American films to Japan. 'Cinematography in Italy' (1911) lists the current producers, suggests that most renters' stock is 'junk', and tells of the typical cinema being 'without any comfort whatever' – with a few luxurious exceptions. 'The French Cinematograph Trade' (1911) claims a recent improvement in films after the public tired of crude productions two or three years earlier. Gaumont's talking pictures are anticipated; the lack of knowledge of the typical operator holds back the spread of technical improvement; and 'factory-gate' films are still a great draw. 'Cinematography in India' (1911) anticipates the filming of the Delhi Durbar celebrations, which were to provide Charles Urban with his major Kinemacolor success. 'A Visit to a German Picture Theatre' (1911) captures the atmosphere well. The frequent attendance of at least a portion of the audiences at 'Some Rhodesian Theatres' (1911) is suggested by the report that Bulawayo's Popular Picture Palace is considering a daily change of programme. As new cinemas open, Salisbury's earliest show – the Posada Rink and Bioscope – 'is under canvas which has seen its best days', and is about to close.

'Living Pictures and Advertisements' indicates the scarcity of advertising films in 1909, although such films were being made a decade earlier.

At a time when film language was still evolving, and explanatory captions an exception, 'Explaining the Pictures', a 1909 editorial, suggests that many dramas need either a competent lecturer or text on lantern slides to put across the information necessary for the audience to grasp the plot. Surviving films are often incomprehensible to modern archivists, who have the benefit of neither. T. W. Kingston, a practitioner of the art of 'Telling the Tale' (1909), explains that his experience of lecturing on paintings led on to 'explaining' for the films, and gives some examples of his technique.

Musical accompaniment for silent films ranged from a fair size orchestra for very special establishments, to the more usual lone pianist of variable quality. 'Music in Picture Theatres' (1911), a letter from A PIANIST of Southsea decrying the 'short-sighted policy of engaging young women at 15s. a week' started a lively correspondence, and two spirited responses, from Madge Clements of London, and Portsmouth's 'PIANISTE', are reproduced here. 'The Music of the Picture Theatre' (1911) provided further thought on the subject.

'How Moving Pictures Help Actresses' (1910) (reprinted from the *Bristol Times*) describes how 'woman's chances of earning a living have been increased by the rise of the biograph machine', an experienced actress receiving the very respectable sum of a sovereign (one pound) in cash at the end of a day's work; all expenses – even tram fares – paid. The 'Phantom Players' illustrated in *The Royal Magazine* in 1912 included the Griffith actress known to British audiences as Daphne Wayne, better known later as Blanche Sweet. 'The One-Eyed Machine' by Margaret Chute, in *The Royal Magazine*, is a popular account of filmmaking in 1912. She demonstrates the sophistication of the industry by the fact that for one drama 'ten actors and actresses were sent from New York to Ireland. Their passages were paid each way; they stayed at an Irish hotel for a fortnight, and were paid full salary all the time'. Many silent films have disappeared in the decades since their production. An unusual reason for the loss of one particular film is contained in the account of Will Barker's production of *Henry VIII*, starring Sir Herbert Tree; the twenty-four prints being burnt, as part of the contractual agreement, after a six-week run. The graphic description of this publicity stunt rather goes against the author's suggestion that Tree's appearance in this film 'guaranteed the handing down to posterity of one of the finest theatrical productions of our time', and indeed the negative has disappeared subsequently, so very probably Tree's performance has not survived. The article ends with details of the Biofix, a studio film system that delivered a moving portrait in a tin-drum miniature Mutoscope, or as a cheaper flip-book; an example appeared on the corners of the magazine's pages.

Our selection continues with a complete reprint of the second (1913) edition of a work first published in 1911, Colin Bennett's *The Handbook of Kinematography, describing the equipment, filming techniques, acting requirements, plot writing, and exhibition procedures including musical accompaniment and cinema management. Chapters on The Law and the Cinematograph.* For the subject of his Preface, the author chooses the 'invention' of cinematography, beginning, not too encouragingly: 'The history of the kinematograph is long, complex, and infinitely stodgy . . . as cheap plum duff is stodgy, with many interesting spots here and there, but oceans of plainness between.' He then races through 2,000 years of the technical history of moving images in a fairly painless five pages, patriotically crediting Friese Greene with technical success – whilst erroneously labelling Muybridge, whose chronophotographic efforts he acknowledges, an American – and crediting the Lumières for having established 'the living picture craze'. The awkward matter of Edison and his Kinetoscope, the peepshow in which moving picture films were first shown to the public before screen projection was feasible, is ignored; even though the four film-frame illustrations for this section are Kinetoscope subjects.

Explaining that some producers perforate their own filmstock, he suggests very reasonably that others will initially buy it ready-perforated, until they are 'a trifle more expert in the handling of the sensitive film rolls'. The craft element of film production continues throughout the production process to the projection print. Mood could be achieved by adding tinting and toning effects, for example: 'Weird and murder scenes . . . heightened by tinting the film faintly green in a half per cent. acid green bath'.

Persistence of vision, a physiological effect then thought to be the key process responsible for motion picture perception, is explained by the usual example of a whirling firebrand. Various intermittent movements are explained, key mechanisms being the Maltese cross – still used in cinema projectors today – and the 'dog' or beater movement, then in its last years. British projectors with evocative, long-extinct names such as Tylar's Indomitable and the Urbanora Silent Knight are described. Other brands, including Kalee and the German Ernemann, would survive for decades, and the American Simplex is still manufactured today. The French industry's importance at the cinema's beginnings is still apparent fifteen years on, the 'Pathé Lumière' projector having evolved directly from the original 1895 Lumière Cinématographe.

Projection illumination is dealt with in detail, with many ways of achieving a sufficiently bright light. Even when the operator was proficient with the electric carbon arc lamp, plugging into the 'mains' was not possible. Private generators were usually required, and were driven by various means. Steam engines were costly and bulky, but useful for travelling proprietors. Town gas was 'clean and simple'. Disadvantages of suction gas, produced by burning anthracite coal, included a 'lurking suspicion of possible explosions'. Petroleum [gas] involved 'smell (which is usually cruel)'; petrol generators were 'the order of the day'. These generators joined flammable celluloid and explosive lamps as a further danger in film exhibition, and 'Liability' mentions that in 'one case at Burnley, a visitor entered a room where the proprietors generate their own electric supply, and became entangled with the machinery with fatal results'.

Although fast disappearing as electric illumination took over, for domestic or village-hall exhibitions, limelight was still viable. Several burners are described, the most dangerous using oxgyen saturated with petrol or ether to provide a flame for the lime. A mishap, even if an explosion was avoided, would cause

> the sudden pop of the back-firing jet, the rip of bursting tube, and the nauseous escaping ether fumes permeating a darkened projection chamber, and with kinematograph audiences all on edge, as they are, for danger scares and causes of panic the prospect is not a nice one to contemplate.

The Home Secretary had recently pronounced them illegal for public shows. The author reflects: 'Many patterns of saturators now on the market seem as safe as houses, judging from their construction, but then . . . '. Perhaps he recalled the tragedy of the very early days of film, when over one hundred people were killed at the 1897 Charity Bazaar fire in France, caused by an operator attempting to re-fill an oxy-ether saturator during the show.

In a section on filming trick effects, Bennett refers to Méliès' ten-year-old production *A Trip to the Moon* as 'probably the most classic of all films', but is actually remembering a scene from a different lunar excursion. A photograph shows inventor Proszinski standing awkwardly in the back of an open horse carriage holding his 'Automatic Camera', presumably about to take a tracking shot. His popular Aeroscope was powered by compressed air, freeing both of the operator's hands to keep hold of it. The scene is more practical than it appears, since a stabilizing gyroscope was fitted.

The author warns of lip-readers in the audience, and suggests counselling actors against repetition: 'it is ridiculous in the extreme to see the frantic mother, whose child has just fallen down the well . . . exclaim, "My child has fallen – has fallen down the well – the well. – The well, she has fallen down – fallen down – my child. My child – oh, my child – my child has fallen down the well-well-"'. 'On Acting Before the Kinematograph' (meaning in front of, rather than prior to) includes performance tips from Mr Henry Morrell, of His Majesty's Theatre Haymarket. He suggests that posterity 'will be able to judge with its own eyes of the past . . . the great actors of today'. This is indeed the case for some, though Mr Morrell is not remembered as a film actor, and his own acting efforts may not have survived for posterity's judgement. In 1913 the role of director has not yet fully evolved, 'the producer acting as head stage manager, with the help of assistant manager as timer, the camera operator being also under his control. Sometimes conditions are reversed'.

Payment for filmscripts seems to have been roughly in line with that expected by jobbing journalists. 'Plots may be worth anything from 7s. 6d. for a short comic to several pounds in the case of a theme capable of being worked up into a long and powerful dramatic picture play.'

Further technical production is briefly covered with a section on micro-kinematography (including speeded-up views of flowers blooming); tele-kinematography with telephoto lenses; and general natural history filming. 'Kinematography in Colours', Bennett's pet subject, relates the history of recording colour photographically by means of filters and specially sensitized film, culminating in the successful commercial application of Kinemacolor; black-and-white film stock and revolving red-and-green filters resulting in a colour image of surprising acceptability.

Film exhibition is fully discussed. The author warns against the pianist playing well-known songs as 'the cheap seats will take up the refrains and bawl them deafeningly to the lasting discredit of any picture palace with a reputation to lose'. Instrumental solos by 'real concert artistes lend tone to a picture theatre'. Instructions are given for producing spot sound effects, including the legendary coconut shells to simulate clattering horses' hooves. More ambitious exhibitors could acquire a special sound effects machine such as the 'Andrews' Allefex'. A chapter on making song slides and topical slides of local events, is followed by further advice on 'Management of a Picture Theatre'. One of the 'best advertising wheezes' was to 'obtain the assistance of a popular individual – the mayor or local member of parliament – assisted by subordinate magnates and big-wigs. . . . to perform the cinema opening ceremony'. Ever-conscious of the need to attract audiences from all classes, Bennett suggests that 'The gaudy, bloodthirsty posters issued by some of the Continental and American makers are to be avoided in better-class neighbourhoods'. The author recommends tip-up seats, but warns of 'a kind of gaspipe arrangement which sells at four shillings'. Disinfecting is necessary to kill 'the bacteria and obnoxious putrefactive organisms always deposited where people most do congregate.' From our present perspective, where confectionery and refreshment sales are central to cinema exhibitors' income, it is interesting to see just a single sentence: 'The sale of chocolates and sweets is a profitable addition to the returns if properly managed, and the inducement of a cup of *good* tea leads many to visit the show who would not enter for the pictures alone.' Staff included the doorman, 'a huge commanding specimen of manhood'; the cashier, 'generally a lady . . . of more or less fascinating appearance and businesslike methods'. The 'seat attendants, with their electric torches . . . must be sufficiently attractive to be in keeping with the general style of the show, but not so attractive as to warrant flirtation with every youth who enters into conversation with them'. 'Self-Preservation in the Trade' warns of the bad practices and tricks rife in the exhibition business. 'The Law and the Kinematograph' reproduces the Acts relating to cinema premises and shows, in particular the safety requirements of the Cinematograph Act of 1909. The London County Council limited Sunday Cinematograph Entertainments to non-commercial (charity) events 'of a healthy and elevating character'. Music licences for all cinema music were required under the Disorderly Houses Act of 1751!

A final chapter covers copyright and censorship. The law had changed since the first edition; films were no longer protected under the Fine Arts Copyright Act of 1862, requiring the registration of the film as a sequence of photographs, which in practice meant lodging paper prints of a few sample frames. The Copyright Bill of 1911 now recognized films. Another very recent development was the appointment of a Film Censor, heading the British Board of Film Censors. Certificates were of two types: Public Exhibition ('A') and Universal Exhibition ('U'), the latter deemed suitable for children.

In 1917 a new version of Bennett's work appeared as *A Guide to Kinematography*. Ernemann projectors were dropped from the pages, but there was very little reference to hostilities, apart from melodramatic mention of a lens marketed by

> a second-rate German optician [who] up to August, 1914, was gaily wiping the floor of the English market, and gaining for his goods a reputation which, ill-deserved though it was, has taken a stream of British blood to wash away.

[END OF VOLUME 2]

VOLUME 3

Critical appraisal and social concern

Our third volume examines critical responses to early cinema, including the impassioned thoughts of one of the first film critics, the American poet Vachel Lindsay, and considers some contemporary judgements of the social aspects of moving pictures. (Items are from *The Bioscope* unless otherwise stated.)

L. Stanford Cook makes 'A Plea for the Long Film' (1911) complaining that short subjects compress good storylines, while distributors are 'deliberately setting their faces against long films'. He need not have worried; within a few years the 'modern' feature-length film would become the main part of the programme.

In an 'Interview with the Dramatic Critic of the Morning and Evening "Standard"' (1911), Mr Boyle Lawrence states that 'Personality can never be pictured', and yet expects before long 'the most competent and best known artists [actors] as ready as anybody to lend their services regularly to the cinematograph'. He presciently suggests that 'in three or four years' time a technique will have been evolved which will raise cinematography to a level with the other arts', contradicting this suggestion with doubts that film dramas will ever be subjected to serious criticism.

Four years later, American poet Vachel Lindsay has no such reluctance in praising the potential of films. Lindsay, at the height of his poetic powers, was a champion of moving pictures. He would later write of his long involvement with the new art of the photoplay, and its 'gods':

> I am the one poet who has the right to claim for his muses Blanche Sweet, Mary Pickford, and Mae Marsh. I am the one poet who wrote them songs when they were Biograph heroines, before their names were put on the screen, or the name of their director.

In *The Art of the Moving Picture* (1915), he compares what he bravely considers a new art form – moving pictures – with the established art media: 'The ripe photoplay is the art exhibition, plus action'. The introduction to the 1922 edition suggests (pp. xxiii–xiv):

> ... The book was written for a visual-minded public and for those who would be its leaders. A long, long line of picture-readers trailing from the dawn of history, stimulated all the masterpieces of pictorial art from Altamira to Michelangelo. For less than five centuries now Gutenberg has had them scurrying to their A, B, C's, but they are drifting back to their old ways again, and nightly are forming themselves in cues at the doorways of the 'Isis,' the 'Tivoli,' and the 'Riviera.'

Lindsay recognizes especially the potential of the moving picture for outdoor scenes, compared with the stage where: 'The waves dash, but not dashingly, the water flows, but not flowingly. The motion picture out-of-door scene is as big as the universe'. At the dawn of the Hollywood studio system, he promotes the unformulated *auteur* theory:

> An artistic photoplay is not the result of a military efficiency system. It is not a factory-made staple article, but the product of the creative force of one soul, the flowering of a spirit that has the habit of perpetually renewing itself.

Published just at the time when short films had largely given way to feature-length productions, Lindsay is already mourning the passing of the classic Griffith two-reeler. (By 1915, D. W. Griffith – one of the most successful directors of Hollywood's first decade – had made the legendary feature-length *Birth of a Nation*, and was in production on the epic *Intolerance*.) He categorizes three types of photoplay: pictures of (1) Action, (2) Intimacy, and (3) Splendor. The chapter chosen for reproduction here is 'The Picture of Crowd Splendor', referring to scenes showing

> ... the Sea of Humanity ... the twirling dancers in ballrooms, handkerchief-waving masses of people in balconies, hat-waving political ratification meetings, ragged glowering strikers, and gossiping, dickering people in the market-place. Only Griffith and his close disciples can do these as well as most any manager [director] can reproduce the ocean.

One past example is already revered: 'The Battle, an old Griffith Biograph, first issued in 1911. ... This one-reel work of art has been re-issued of late by the Biograph Company. It should be kept in the libraries of the Universities as a standard.' And indeed it is. Here and elsewhere in the book Lindsay complains of the growing length of film productions. 'Edgar Poe said there was no such thing as a long poem. There is certainly no such thing as a long moving picture masterpiece'. A film show had expanded from a programme of a dozen one-minute films in 1896, to perhaps an hour of ten-minute reels in 1910, to features of ninety minutes, and more.

> A one hour programme is long enough for any one. ... Six-reel programmes are a weariness to the flesh. The best of the old one-reel Biograph Griffiths contained more in twenty minutes than these ambitious incontinent six-reel displays give us in two hours.

He complains after watching the Italian epic *Cabiria*: 'Few eyes submit without destruction to three hours of film'. One of the new long features he does admire, but not without reservations about its content, concerns which have been properly voiced ever since. For Lindsay, the closer Griffith stayed to *The Clansman*, the novel on which the film was based, the less he admires the result. 'The Birth of a Nation has been very properly denounced for its Simon Legree qualities. . . . But it is still true that it is a wonder in its Griffith sections'. (Simon Legree was the slave-owner in *Uncle Tom's Cabin*.)

In other chapters the author includes some eccentric but interesting ideas – a section on Egyptian hieroglyphs is food for thought – and some foolish ones; his call for all films to be shown in silence, with only the whispered comments of the audience to be heard. And the language is sometimes overbearingly flowery. Lindsay's poetic insistence is nowhere more evident than in his description of that simple, ubiquitous sequence-framing technique of the period, the fade-in and fade-out: '. . . all things emerge from the twilight and sink back into the twighlight at last'. But the book is undoubtedly a classic, and I hope that anyone reading the chapter from *The Art of the Moving Picture* included here will search out a copy of this pioneeering work – which, unlike everything else in this compilation, is still in print.

With 'Education and the Bioscope' (1909) the suggestion of films in schools receives the highest enthusiasm from a representative of the London County Council, apparently in opposition to the proposal of that council's Education Committee that they should be excluded. Two years later *The Bioscope* regrets that nothing came of this, but praises the educational value of natural history and industrial films shown in cinemas, and asks 'Will Moving Pictures Prevent War?' (1911), suggesting that filmed reconnaissance by airship will 'materially assist in maintaining the peace of the world' – sadly, a hopeless wish.

'The Cinematograph in Church', *Amateur Photographer* (1912), records a film-producer visitor to London who tells of clergymen in the USA requiring Biblical films, though the film projector would never take over from the magic lantern in church work. 'Sacred Films', *Amateur Photographer* (1912), suggests that with religious paintings or plays the viewer makes 'unconscious allowance for the fact that . . . [they] are only representations or reconstructions' but filmmaking gives authenticity to a scene, raising objections to filming the 'central scenes of Christianity'.

Two small publications promote opposing views of the social value of the cinema. In the pamphlet *Focussing the Universe* (n.d., *c.* 1910), we meet again Montagu A. Pyke, who promotes the virtues of the new medium, set to eliminate 'racial feeling and national prejudices'. He anticipates the recording of 'every great event in the history of the world' for posterity. Audiences can 'survey all mankind from China to Peru'. Films have 'brought delight to the minds and souls of thousands upon thousands of mites in this great Metropolis . . . the one oasis in the desert of their dull and sordid lives'. Pyke tells of his determination 'to elevate, to enlighten, to instruct, and to amuse humanity'. We should not be fooled by the philanthropic evangelism of this paean to the opportunities for education with the cinematograph film; financial self-interest was the prime motivation. Film historian Nicholas Hiley tells of

> Montagu Pyke, a former commercial traveller and undischarged bankrupt who saw a chance to make some easy money. In October 1908 'Monty' Pyke established a company called Recreations Limited, whose nominal capital was £10,000 but whose assets, as he later admitted, were simply 'a very nice name plate on the

door, and some office furniture on the higher [*sic*] purchase.' Pyke approached Sam Harris [a London estate agent] for help in finding suitable premises, and Harris recalled that despite Pyke's lack of funds 'I found him two draper's shops in Edgware Road and he immediately ordered carpets, curtains, seating, everything of the best.'

(Unpublished manuscript)

Despite scepticism from most of his wealthy subscribers, Pyke managed to raise sufficient capital to open his first cinema in March 1909, and its popularity enabled him to plan a second. A substantial London circuit was quickly established, with most cinemas set up under separate companies. 'Monty' Pyke was soon enjoying a considerable annual income, and became well known for rolling up to trade events in a big car, 'with diamonds sparkling, a special cigar, and, when weather warranted, a fur-lined overcoat'.

In our second pamphlet, *The Child and the Cinematograph Show and the Picture Post-Card Evil, With a note on the cinematograph by the Headmaster of Eton* (1913), Canon Hardwicke Drummond Rawnsley recounts a music-hall fakir undergoing self-mutilation, and somewhat illogically blames the public's thirst for the horrible and sensational on the cinematograph, citing lurid text on film posters. A twelve-year-old boy tells him 'I shall never go again. It was horrible . . . I saw a man cut his throat'. Failing to find titles of specific examples of this kind of film excess, the Canon then tells of a 'friend's neighbours' who went, with their little daughter, to see Sarah Bernhardt in a cinematograph show. 'They found to their disgust the bulk of the entertainment was sensational horrors of such a character that in consequence they were obliged to sit up all night with the child, who constantly woke with screams and cries.' Having seen Sarah Bernhardt's performance on film, it is tempting to suggest that it might have been this that disturbed the child's nocturnal slumbers, though certainly sheltered children of the period were disturbed by cinema images, as recounted with rather more authority in the later report on *The Cinema*. Postcard historians have suggested that working people reduced their expenditure on picture shows in the first years of the century to spend their few pence of weekly disposable income on picture postcards. Not content to castigate only film, the pamphlet continues with a blast against the 'hardly veiled indecency' of the picture postcard, and details its censorship in various towns in Britain. In a final note on the main subject, the Headmaster of Eton concludes that, 'If the English people wish to commit race suicide . . . never has human ingenuity invented a device more efficacious for this sinister end than the moving pictures.'

The picture postcard is of interest to our story for other reasons. It brought cheap portraits of the actors and actresses to the public, and also celebrated the social pleasures of cinema-going. Five postcards on the latter theme are reproduced here.

A card featuring a cartoon Charlie Chaplin, a big star at the end of the early cinema period, introduces the idea of the cinema as a dark environment attractive to couples: 'The girlies go to the picture show because they like a lark – and if they've got a boy with them its "thumbs up" in the dark'. This is also the theme of our second card, 'Don't keep me in the dark'. 'What could be nicer?' is typical of many cards, both drawn and photographic, showing a couple in the cinema. The following two photographic cards, each set in a basic studio 'cinema front row' set, with a seduction scene on screen, illustrate more complicated scenarios: 'One meets such nice girls at the picture palace!' shows a gentleman with his arms around two women, and 'At the cinema' suggests an even more involved situation.

The Cinema: Its Present Position and Future Possibilities Being the Report of and Chief

Evidence taken by The Cinema Commission of Inquiry, Instituted by the National Council of Public Morals (1917) concludes our collection. This substantial and wide-ranging report, from the end of the early cinema period, provides a unique record of the attitudes towards the cinema by its British audiences, exhibitors, producers, the clergy and guardians of morality, and those responsible for licensing. Subjects include: lighting in cinemas – an encouragement to immoral activity; whether villainous deeds depicted on the screen influence young members of the audience to commit similar acts; and the reasons for the very high percentage of American films shown. Many interviews are reproduced verbatim, with useful facts and figures given throughout.

Part I

The purpose of The National Council for Public Morals (NCPM) was '. . . the physical and moral renewal of the British race'. Following discussion with the relevant bodies, in November 1916 a letter was sent to the NCPM by the Cinematograph Trade Council asking them to undertake 'an independent enquiry into the physical, social, moral, and educational influence of the cinema, with special reference to young people'.

The Commission, under the President, the Lord Bishop of Birmingham, included representatives of the Church, schools, Salvation Army and cinema exhibitors. Witnesses included headmasters and educationalists, eye specialists, film producers and exhibitors, police and censors. It was 'deeply concerned with the influence of the cinematograph, especially upon young people . . . '.

The commission clearly intended to be seen approaching the question with an open mind, accepting the potential for good, as well as bad, in the spread of the cinema. It considered: '. . . the possibilities of its development and with its adaptation to national educational purposes'. It was nevertheless keen to promote 'the suppression of certain evils which had thrown themselves on the cinema halls . . . '. One subject given lengthy consideration, 'The Moral Danger of Darkness', was a popular topic for the comic picture postcard of the day, which cheerfully promoted the possibilities of what a representative for the Exhibitors of London asserted was 'nothing more than the privileged manifestation of affection between the sexes'. The extent of other, less innocent, activities under cover of the darkened cinema auditoria – prostitution, indecent assault – is extensively discussed.

The commission recognized the fact that 90 per cent of films shown in Britain were American – the abundance of 'crook' films was a particular concern – and that American producers were unlikely to adapt the content of their productions for the sake of the small British market.

Many responsible witnesses spoke up for the benefits of cinemas; decreasing hooliganism had been evident in some areas, and cinemas were considered by many to be a preferable counter-attraction to public houses.

The term 'The Cinema' meant any film presentation. Mainly this involved shows in public cinemas – generally still a very mixed programme; broadly, narrative entertainments, with a smaller proportion of 'interest' films – but also films in the classroom and elsewhere. The days of audiences sitting spellbound by Urban's nature films are long past. Trade witnesses declared 'A film, however beautiful, of the life-history of a plant or insect sandwiched between a Charlie Chaplin film and a thrilling episode of the Exploits of Elaine has little chance of survival' and 'films showing manufacturing processes and natural phenomena . . . bore the audience and are tolerated in silence'. Many in the cinema exhibition trade were doubtful that the use of educational films in the cinema could be much extended, but their potential outside of the commercial cinema venue was recognized, as a development of lantern slide projection. One suggestion was the use of 'the larger instrument [standard 35mm film] and the Pathéscope [reduced-size safety film] side by side with the magic lantern . . . combining static and dynamic teaching'.

There is much discussion of 'Trade Censorship and Organisation'. The trade's own Board of Censors had been established October 1912, giving 'U' (universal) and 'A' (adult) certificates. It had only two rules: 'that the living figure of Christ should not be permitted and that nudity should be in no circumstances passed'. Attempts to make national censorship a legal requirement ended when negotiations between the Home Secretary and the Trade foundered in 1917. The NCPM study – together with a change of government in December 1916 – was very important in undermining the Home Office scheme for official censorship, and strengthened the position of the British Board of Film Censors.

The Council's conclusions and recommendations emphasized the importance of suitable lighting and projection standards in cinemas, and the condition of prints. Children should visit at a suitable hour, perhaps a maximum 'three times in a fortnight', and pictures should be 'exhilarating without leading to undue mental strain'. Acceptable conditions of censorship are outlined.

Part II

Transcripts of evidence. The Bishop of Birmingham points out that, due to the war, conditions were abnormal. 'The quiet film, the placid story, does not appeal at the moment to people whose nerves are jangled and strained by worry and loss. They seek distraction with an avidity and feverishness which is quite natural but not normal.' Visits to cinemas were roughly calculated at over one thousand million per year. Subjects discussed include juvenile delinquency, 'Love-making' in films, American products, Sunday opening, the potential danger to eyesight, and much more.

Those giving evidence included schoolchildren, aged from eleven to fourteen, who in some cases evidently said what they thought the questioner wanted to hear. One young girl volunteered 'I don't go very often, as it is very injurious to my eyes . . . '. A boy's answer to 'What do you like best at the cinema?' was the disarmingly honest: 'All about thieves'. The response to the question 'Supposing they put on some of the films you do not like, what would the boys do?' evokes the atmosphere at a children's show: 'They would grumble and shout "Chuck it off."'

The report concludes with appendices on censorship regulations in various countries, the influence of films on juvenile delinquency in New York, and reports from chief constables throughout Britain.

The report was apparently of some value, as a second NCPM cinema book was published in 1925: *The Cinema in Education: Being the report of the psychological investigation conducted by special sub-committees appointed by the Cinema commission of enquiry established by the National Council of Public Morals.* This was a detailed account of an extensive experiment in showing classes of children several different types of educational presentation – including slides/films with and without narration.

With the growth of the feature film after 1914, the early cinema period drew to a close, and the period of 'classic' Hollywood cinema arrived. Some short films would still be shown, but the varied programmes of the first two decades disappeared.

I hope that this selection of material relating to early film will be useful to the established specialist, and will indicate to the new researcher that there is much of interest to study within this complex and rewarding field.

Stephen Herbert
Hastings, January 2000

EDISON'S KINEMATOGRAPH EXPERIMENTS

AS DESCRIBED BY W·K·L·DICKSON· 15 Years ELECTRICAL ENGINEER WITH THE FAMOUS INVENTOR.

THE buildings devoted to photographic work, including the kinetoscopic experiments, are among the first things that meet the visitor's eye on approaching the grounds of Edison's works at Orange, N.J. The main photographic building is divided into several compartments. In the general work room, which is covered with sliding glass skylights and side widows, a number of cameras of different sizes, equipped with fine lenses, are idly waiting their turn to be focussed on some new object. Science and nature are so happily united that no diurnal variations are permitted to impede the development of a subject, and unfinished work is completed at night by the aid of a large group of arc lamps, giving out fifteen thousand candle-power, supplemented by several calcium light appliances. At one side of the room may be seen one of the celebrated Zeiss micro-photographic outfits, which has been of inestimable service during the many Edison lamp suits, in magnifying, to an extraordinary degree, the sectional views of the fibro-vasculae bundles used in the manufacture of the carbon filament. Many micro-photographs have also been made by the aid of this valuable apparatus in connection with Mr. Edison's bacterial researches. The processes of silvering, printing, mounting, retouching, and burnishing are carried on in this department, and the work bench and lathe, which occupy one corner, are in constant demand for kinetoscopic and kinetographic experiments.

The rooms above are devoted to copying and enlarging, as well as to the experiments in lantern projection. Around this room are stacked over a thousand negatives, to which additions are constantly made. The dark rooms are arranged in consecutive order, are well ventilated, heated by steam in the winter, and lighted by incandescent lamps, enclosed in ruby glass compartments, and softened at will by lowering the candle-power. These dark rooms greatly resemble ice boxes as to construction, the walls being filled in with sawdust to keep the temperature cool in summer. It is here that the kinetoscopic films are treated, and during their many manipulations the operators are at times forced to work in Egyptian darkness owing to the extreme sensitiveness of the film, which necessitates total exclusion of light, even to the extinction of the ruby glow.

A cursory reference has already been made to the kinetoscope and kineto-phonograph, which were born amid these mysterious surroundings, and it may be well, before seeking new fields of thought, to trace the evolutions and present status of these latest marvels of the laboratory. The initial ideas relating to the reproduction of motion are based upon the familiar toy known as the zoetrope, or wheel of life. This rude prototype contains a cylinder ten inches in width and open at the top, around the lower half of whose interior a series of pictures is placed, representing any sequence of motion it may be desired to portray, such, for instance, as wrestling, jumping, or the swift progress of animals.

These movements are seen through the narrow vertical slits in the cylinder during the rapid revolution of the little machine, and are designed to blend into one continuous impression. In the zoetrope, however, the pictures are wood cuts of rude execution, and the limited speed attainable in the production of these militate against a life-like effect, producing a series of jerks instead of the desired continuity of motion. When instantaneous photography, as evolved by Maddox and others, was utilised, superior results were attained; a degree of continuity of impression was preserved without involving the disagreeable defects apparent in the more primitive methods to which we have already referred; still with this advance certain difficulties remained but partially overcome, it seemed impossible to take pictures at sufficiently short intervals to secure the absolute blending of outline essential to a faithful portrayal of life. Matters were in this unsatisfactory condition when the resources of the laboratory were brought to bear upon the problem.

(*To be continued.*)

1

EDISON'S KINEMATOGRAPH EXPERIMENTS

AS DESCRIBED BY W. K. L. DICKSON. 15 Years ELECTRICAL ENGINEER WITH THE FAMOUS INVENTOR.

PART II.

(*Continued from Page 23.*)

AND now let us hear Mr. Edison himself on the subject : " In the year 1887 the idea occurred to me that it was possible to devise an instrument which should do for the eye what the phonograph does for the ear, and that by a combination of the two, all motion and sound could be recorded simultaneously. This idea, the germ of which came from the little toy called the zoetrope, and the work of Muybridge, Marie and others, has now been accomplished, so that every change of facial expression can be recorded and reproduced life size. The kinetoscope is only a small model, illustrating the present stage of progress, but with each succeeding month new possibilities are brought into view. I believe that in coming years by my own work and that of Dickson, Muybridge, Marie and others who will doubtless enter the field, grand opera will be given at the Metropolitan Opera House at New York without any material change from the original, and with artistes and musicians long since dead."

The synchronous attachment of the kinematograph and the phonograph was early contemplated by Mr. Edison in order to record and give back impressions to the eye as well as to the ear. The comprehensive term for this invention is the kineto-phonograph ; the dual taking machine is the phono-kinetograph ; and the reproducing machine the phono-kinetoscope, in contra-distinction to the kinetograph and the kinetoscope, which relate respectively to the taking and reproduction of moveable but soundless objects.

The initial experiments took the form of microscopic pin-point photographs placed on a cylindrical shell, corresponding in size to the ordinary phonograph cylinder. These two cylinders were then placed side by side on a shaft, and the sound record was taken as nearly as possible synchronously with the photographic image impressed on the sensitive surface of the shell. The photographic portion of the undertaking was seriously hampered by the defects of the materials at hand, which however excellent in themselves, offered no substance sufficiently sensitive. How to secure clear-cut outlines or indeed any outlines at all, together with phenomenal speed, was the problem which puzzled the experimenters. The daguerre, albumen, and kindred processes met the first requirements, but failed when subjected to the test of speed. These methods were therefore regretfully abandoned, a certain precipitate of knowledge being retained, and a bold leap was made to the Maddox gelatine bromide of silver emulsion, with which the cylinders were coated.

This process gave rise to a new and serious difficulty. The bromide of silver haloids, held in suspension with the emulsion, showed themselves in an exaggerated coarseness when it became a question of enlarging the pin-point photographs to the dignity of one-eighth of an inch, projecting them upon a screen, or viewing them through a binocular microscope. Each accession of size augmented the difficulty, and it was resolved to abandon that line of experiment, and to revolutionize the whole nature of the proceedings by discarding these small photographs, and substituting a series of very much larger impressions affixed to the outer edge of a swiftly rotating wheel or disc, and supplied with a number of pins, so arranged as to project under the centre of each picture.

On the rear of the disc, upon a stand, was placed a Geissler tube connected with an induction core, the primary wire of which, operated by the pins, produced a rupture of the primary current which in its turn through the medium of the secondary current lighted up the Geissler tube at the precise moment when a picture crossed its range of view.

The little pictures thus became visible for a fraction of a second, and, although actually in constant motion, appeared to be absolutely at rest, sharply delineated, with each succeeding image superposed upon its predecessor.

EDISON'S KINEMATOGRAPH EXPERIMENTS

AS DESCRIBED BY W. KL. DICKSON. 15 Years ELECTRICAL ENGINEER WITH THE FAMOUS INVENTOR.

PART III.

(Continued from Page 43.)

THEN followed some experiments with drums, over which sheets of sensitised celluloid films were drawn, the edge being pressed into a narrow slot in the surface, similar in construction to the old tin-foil phonograph. A starting-and-stopping device very similar to the one now in use was also applied. The pictures were then taken specially to the number of two hundred or so, but were limited in size, owing to the rotundity of surface, which brought only the centre of the picture into focus. The sheet of celluloid was then developed, fixed, and otherwise prepared and placed on a transparent drum, bristling at its outer edge with brass pins. When the drum was rapidly turned, these came in contact with the primary current of an induction coil, and each image was lighted up in the same manner as described in the previous disc experiment, with this difference only—that the inside of the drum was illuminated. The next step was the adoption of a highly sensitised strip of celluloid half an inch wide, but this proving unsatisfactory, owing to inadequate size, one inch pictures were substituted on a band one and a half inches wide, the additional width being required for the perforations on the outer edge. These perforations occur at close and regular intervals, in order to enable the teeth of a locking device to hold the film steady for nine-tenths of the one-forty-sixth part of a second, when a shutter opens rapidly and admits a beam of light, causing an image or phase of the movement of the subject. The film is then jerked forward in the remaining one-tenth of the one-forty-second part of a second, and held in rest while the shutter has again made its round, admitting another circle of light and so on until forty-six impressions are taken a second, or 2,760 a minute. This speed yields 165,600 pictures in an hour, an amount amply sufficient for an evening's entertainment, when unreeled before the eye. By connecting the two ends of the strip, and thus forming a continuous band, the pictures can be indefinitely multiplied. In this connection it is interesting to note that were the

spasmodic motions added up by themselves, exclusive of arrests, on the same principle that a train record is computed independently of stoppages, the incredible speed of twenty-six miles an hour could be shown. The advantages of this system over a continuous band and of a slotted shutter forging widely ahead of the film would be this, that in that case only the fractional degree of light comprised in the 1-2720th part of a second is allowed to penetrate to the film, at a complete sacrifice of all details, whereas in the present system of stopping and starting each picture gets one-hundreth part of a second's exposure with a lens but slightly stopped down, time amply sufficient, as any photographer knows, for the attainment of excellent detail even in an ordinarily good light. It must be understood that only one camera is used for these strips and not a battery of cameras as in Mr. Muybridge's photographs of "the horse in motion." The next step after making the negative band is to form a positive or finished series of reproductions from the negative, which is passed through a machine for the purpose, in conjunction with a blank strip of film, which, after development and general treatment, is replaced in the kinetoscope, or phonokinetoscope, as the case may be. When a phonograph record has been taken simultaneously with such a strip, the two are started together by the use of a simple but effective device, and kept so all through, the phonograph record being in perfect accord with the strip. In this conjunction the tiny holes with which the edge of the celluloid film is perforated correspond exactly with the phonographic record, and the several devices of the camera, such as the shifting of the film and the operations of the shutter, are so regulated as to keep pace with the indentations made by the stylus upon the phonographic wax cylinder, one motor serving as a source of common energy to camera and phonograph when they are electrically and mechanically linked together.

(To be continued.)

EDISON'S KINEMATOGRAPH EXPERIMENTS

AS DESCRIBED BY W. K. L. DICKSON. 15 Years ELECTRICAL ENGINEER WITH THE FAMOUS INVENTOR.

PART IV.

(Continued from Page 55.)

THE establishment of harmonious relations between kinetoscope and phonograph was a harrowing task, and would have broken the spirit of inventors less inured to hardships and discouragement than Edison's veterans. The experiments have borne their legitimate fruit, and the most scrupulous meeting of adjustment has been achieved, with the resultant effects of realistic life, audibly and visually expressed. The process of "taking" is variously performed by artificial light in the photographic department, or by daylight under the improved conditions of the new theatre, of which we shall speak. The actors, when more than one in number, are kept as close together as possible, and exposed either to the glare of the sun, to the blinding light of four parabolic magnesium lamps, or to the light of twenty arc lamps, provided with highly actinic carbons, supplied with powerful reflectors equal to about fifty thousand candle power. This radiance is concentrated upon the performers while the kinetograph and phonograph are hard at work storing up records and impressions for future reproduction. A popular and inexpensive adaptation of kinetoscope methods is in the form of the well-known nickel-in-the-slot, a machine consisting of a cabinet containing an electrical motor and batteries for operating the mechanism which acts as the impelling power to the films. The film is in the shape of an endless band, from fifty to one hundred and fifty feet in length, which is passed through the field of a magnifying glass perpendicularly placed. The photographic impressions pass before the eye at the rate of forty-six per second, through the medium of a rotating slotted disk, the slot exposing a picture at each revolution, and separating the fractional gradations of pose. Projected against a screen, or viewed through a magnifying glass, the pictures are eminently life-like, for the reason that the enlargement need not be more than ten times the original size. On exhibition evenings the projecting room, which is situated in the upper story of the photographic department, is hung with black, and provided with a single peep-hole for the accommodation of the lens. The effect of these sombre draperies, and the weird accompanying monotone of the electric motor attached to the projector, are horribly impressive, and one's sense of the supernatural is heightened when a figure suddenly springs into his path, acting and talking with a vigor which leaves him totally unprepared for its mysterious vanishing. Projected stereoscopically, the results are even more realistic, as those acquainted with that class of phenomena may imagine, and a pleasing rotundity is apparent, which, in ordinary photographic displays, is conspicuous by its absence. Nothing more vivid or more natural could be imagined than these breathing, audible forms, with their tricks of familiar gesture and speech. The inconceivable swiftness of the photographic successions, and the exquisite synchronism of the phonographic attachment, have removed the last trace of automatic action, and the illusion is complete. The organ grinder's monkey jumps upon his shoulder to the accompaniment of a strain from "Norma." The rich tones of a tenor or soprano are heard, set in their appropriate dramatic action, the blacksmith is seen swinging his ponderous hammer, exactly as in life, and the clang of the anvil keeps pace with his symmetrical movements; along with the rhythmical measures of the dancer go her soft sounding foot-falls; the wrestlers and fencers ply their intricate game, guarding, parrying, attacking, thrusting and throwing, while the quick flash of the eye, the tension of the mouth, the dilated nostrils, and the strong, deep breathing give evidence of the potentialities within.

Correction:— A name was inadvertently mis-spelt in the Gaumont Co.'s advertisement recently, Mr. Tuby of Grimsby being furnished with "Tuly" as a surname.

EDISON'S KINEMATOGRAPH EXPERIMENTS

AS DESCRIBED BY W. K. L. DICKSON. 15 Years ELECTRICAL ENGINEER WITH THE FAMOUS INVENTOR.

PART V.

(Continued from Page 93.)

THE photographic rooms, with their singular completeness of appointment, have been the birthplace and nursery of this invention; and the more important processes connected with the preparation and development of the film, together with their mechanical and scientific devices, are still carried on in this department. The exigencies of natural lighting incident to the better taking of the subjects, and the lack of a suitable theatrical stage, however, necessitated the construction of a special building, which stands in the centre of that cluster of auxiliary houses which forms the suburbs of the laboratory, and which is of so peculiar an appearance as to challenge the attention of the most superficial observer. It obeys no architectural rules, embraces no conventional materials, and follows no accepted scheme of colour. Its shape is an irregular oblong rising abruptly in the centre, at which joint a movable roof is attached, which is easily raised or lowered at the will of a single manipulator. Its colour is a grim and forbidding black, enlivened by the dull lustre of many hundred metallic points; its material is paper, covered with pitch and profusely studded with tin nails. With its flapping sail-like roof and ebon' hue, it has a weird and semi nautical appearance, and the uncanny effect is not lessened when, on an imperceptible sign, the great building swings slowly around upon a graphited centre, presenting any given angle to the ray of the sun, and rendering the operators independent of diurnal variations.

The movable principle of this building is identical with that of our river swinging bridges, the ends being suspended by iron rods from centre posts. The building is known as the Kinetographic Theatre, otherwise the Black Maria. Entering, we are confronted by a system of lights and shades so sharply differentiated as to pain the eye, accustomed to the uniform radiance of the outer air. As we peer into the illusive depths we seem transported to one of those cheerful banqueting halls of old, where the feudal chief made merry with human terrors, draping the walls with portentous black, and thoughtfully providing a set of coffins for the accommodation of his guests. And what is this mysterious recess at the other extremity, sharply outlined against the dazzling radiance of the middle ground and steeped in an angry crimson hue! Are these inquisitorial dungeons, and is that lurid glare the advance guard of the awful question? Is that gentle persuasive in process of administration, and do these half-guessed recesses conceal the hellish parapherhalia of rack and screw, glowing iron and crushing stone? Has the doom of ages overtaken our wizard at last, and is he expiating with twisted limb and scorching flesh, the treasures of his unlawful wisdom?

Ah me, that the prosaic truth must be told! No dungeons are these, thrilling with awful possibilities, but simply a building for the better taking of kinetoscopic subjects. On the platform stand the wrestlers, pantomimists, dancers and jugglers, whose motions it is destined to immortalise. Against the nether gloom their figures stand out with the sharp contrast of alabaster basso-relievo on an ebony ground, furnishing a satisfactory explanation for the singular distinctness of the kinetoscopic strips. The lurid cell at the other end resolves into a compartment for changing the films from the dark box to the kinetoscopic camera, the apparatus being run backward over a track leading from the black tunnel at the rear of the stage to this room after which the door is shut and the films renewed for a fresh subject.

IMPORTANT.—We go to Press on Wednesdays and copies are supplied to the wholesale trade on Thursday mornings. All matter, or advertisements for insertion in current issue should reach our offices not later than the FIRST POST WEDNESDAY MORNING, and if proofs are required, not not later than NOON TUESDAY.

EDISON'S KINEMATOGRAPH EXPERIMENTS

AS DESCRIBED BY W·K·L·DICKSON· 15 Years ELECTRICAL ENGINEER WITH THE FAMOUS INVENTOR.

PART VI.

(Continued from Page 103.)

WE have been sensible for some time of a disturbance in the ground beneath our feet, and are now aware that the building is slowly and noiselessly rotating on an axis, bringing into our range of vision the glory of the sun-rays westering to their close. Again we are reminded of that undesirable chain of ideas which links the past with the present, and into the commonplace of existing facts come memories of that chamber in the golden house of Nero, so arranged that "by means of skilfully planned machinery it moved on its axis, thus following the motion of the heavens, so that the sun did not appear to change in position, but only to descend and ascend perpendicularly.

We have yet to speak of the microscopic subjects, a class of especial interest as lying outside the unaided vision of man. In the treatment of these infinitesimal types much difficulty was experienced in obtaining a perfect adjustment, so as to reproduce the breathing of insects, the circulation of blood in a frog's leg, and other attenuated processes of nature. The enlargement of animalculæ in a drop of stagnant water proved a most exacting task, but by the aid of a powerful lime-light concentrated on the water, by the interposition of alum cells for the interception of most of the heat rays, and by the use of a quick shutter and kindred contrivances, the obstacles were overcome, and the final results were such as to fully compensate for the expenditure of time and trouble.

We will suppose that the operator has at last been successful in imprisoning the tricky water-goblins on the sensitive film, in developing the positive strip, and placing it in the projector. A series of inch-large shapes then springs into view, magnified stereoptically to nearly three feet each, gruesome beyond power of expression, exhibiting an indescribable celerity and rage. Monsters close upon one another in a blind and indiscriminate attack, limbs are dismembered, gory globules are tapped, whole battalions disappear from view. Before the ruthless completeness of these martial tactics the Kilkenny cats fade into insignificance.

A curious feature of the performance is the passing of these creatures in and out of focus, appearing sometimes as huge and distorted shadows, then springing into the reality of their own size and proportions.

Hitherto we have limited ourselves to the delineation of detached subjects, but we shall now touch very briefly upon one of our most ambitious schemes, of which these scattered impersonations are but the heralds. Preparations have long been on foot to extend the number of actors and to increase the stage facilities, with a view to the presentation of an entire play, set in its appropriate frame.

This line of thought may be indefinitely pursued, with application to any given phase of outdoor or indoor life which it is desired to reproduce. Our methods point to ultimate success, and every day adds to the security and the celerity of the undertaking. No scene, however animated and extensive, but will eventually be within reproductive power. Martial evolutions, naval exercises, processions and countless kindred exhibitions will be eventually recorded for the leisurely gratification of those who are debarred from attendance, or who desire to recall them. The invalid, the isolated country recluse, and the harassed business man can indulge in needed recreation without undue expenditure, without fear of weather, and without the sacrifice of health or important engagements. Not only our own resources, but those of the whole world will be at our command. The advantages to students and historians will be immeasurable. Instead of dry and misleading accounts, tinged with the exaggerations of the chronicler's mind, our archives will be enriched by the vitalised pictures of great national scenes, instinct with all the glowing personalities which characterised them.

(Concluded.)

LANTERN PROJECTION OF MOVING OBJECTS.

NO one can reasonably complain of the lack of diversion in the world of photography just now. The last few weeks have witnessed the production of a new process by Professor Herkomer; a method, also new, of photographing living bones; and several methods by which kinetoscopic pictures can be projected upon a screen in rapid succession so as to give the idea of actual movement. The wise man's axiom that "there is nothing new under the sun" for once seems to have lost its point, but those who have lived long enough under the beneficent beams of King Sol know that these apparently new things have little novelty about them. Professor Herkomer's process is almost identical with one, examples of which were shown at the Great Exhibition of 1851. The Röntgen experiments are but elaborations of those performed by Lenard, and described by him in a German periodical more than two years ago; and, as to the projection of rapidly consecutive pictures on a lantern screen, giving the illusion of motion, it was done more than thirty years ago at the old Polytechnic Institution in Regent Street. It is to this last phase of photography that in this article we wish to direct our readers' attention, for it promises to be *the* sensation of the lantern season.

FIG. 1.

As is well known, the magic lantern did not change its front name to "optical" and assume the position of a philosophical instrument until its hand-painted pictures had been superseded by photographs. This change at once transformed it from a toy into a most valuable adjunct to the lecture-hall. In the same way the lantern attachments by which successive phases of a figure in motion could be projected upon a screen had no serious application until it became possible to make the camera do the work of picture making, and the camera performs this work in such efficient fashion, and is so expeditious in its action, that forty or fifty images of a moving subject can be taken in the short space of one second.

Let us pause for a moment to consider the principle upon which such images combine upon the retina of the eye to form a continuous impression. The retina possesses a property known as "persistence of vision," which means that the image of any object looked at persists, or remains upon the retina for about the one-tenth of a second after the image itself has disappeared. The glowing end of a burnt stick moved round and round in a dark-room looks like a ring of fire, the thousands of images formed of it on the retina blending into a continuous train. The same kind of illusion gives to rockets and other fireworks their chief attraction. An old-fashioned toy took the form of a card with a different design on either side which could be twirled round by attached strings. The two separate images, such as a horse and its rider, were then presented to the retina in such rapid alternation that they coalesced and formed one distinct and complete picture. This was probably the germ of the variously named instruments which worked on the same principle and gave delight to a past generation. One of the first was the thaumatrope, or "wonder-turner." Then came the phenakistiscope, which, curiously enough, was the invention of a blind man, one Plateau. This instrument was adapted to the lime-lit lantern about forty years ago by Duboscq. It consisted of a disc of glass upon which were painted the various figures making up the design. This revolved in front of the lantern condenser, and between it and the lantern

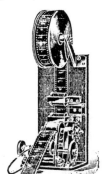

FIG. 2.

screen was a wheel containing four objectives which revolved and gave intermittent and separate light to each picture. Later on, Mr. John Beale, of Greenwich, produced his chorentoscope, so called because the design employed in it was generally that of a dancing figure. In the first form of this instrument a disc carried the various components of his picture, but in a later model the designs were painted on a slide which moved to and fro by means of a sprocket wheel (see fig. 1), exactly the same mechanism as that adopted in one of his latest forms of instrument for the projection of kinetoscope pictures.

The introduction of Edison's kinetoscope, and the wide publicity given to that instrument both in London and the provinces have set many inventive minds to work in the endeavour to project upon his lantern screen the images so beautifully revealed to the eye by means of that popular plaything. We have seen what has been done in the past, and we may now turn to what is being done now.

In Messrs. Lumiere's Cinematograph (how fond modern inventors are of long words) now being exhibited at the Marlborough Gallery, Regent

Street, we have an excellent exhibition, probably the best thing of the kind which has yet been done, if we except the apparatus shown the other night at the Royal Photographic Society's rooms by Mr. Birt Acres. In this latter contrivance the motion of treating waves was so beautifully reproduced that one had an inclination to step backward to avoid getting wet. Mr. Birt Acres has arranged to give public exhibitions of his apparatus shortly at a large hall at Piccadilly Circus; the details of its mechanism have not yet been published. In the meantime another inventor, Mr. R. W. Paul, electrician, of Hatton Garden, has shown a neat piece of apparatus called the "Theatograph," in the library of the Royal Institution, with some success, but it must be owned that in its present condition the registration of the pictures on the screen is not so perfect as in Lumiere's arrangement. Mr. Paul has not kept his method in any way secret, and he has been wise in this respect, for by courting inquiry he obtains that blessed thing called free advertisement. In fig. 2 we have a representation of the entire apparatus. The spool at the top contains some hundred feet of pictures printed on a ribbon of celluloid, which ribbon, as will be seen by reference to fig. 3, is

provided on both sides with punched apertures. A large fly-wheel, not shown here, gives motion to the sprocket wheel (fig. 1) mechanism, which it will be readily seen will cause the ribbon to be fed forward in jerks, first a downward movement, and then a pause, such movements occurring at the rate of about 15 per second. The holes at the sides of the film are to accommodate spokes in the sprocket-wheel drum which engage therewith and thus pull the ribbon forward.

FIG. 3.

It is a grave question to our minds whether this old method of solving the problem of projecting these moving images is the correct one; we are of opinion that it is wrong in principle. At any rate, we may say that the apparatus is as yet in its infancy, but will probably grow into vigorous youth before next lantern season opens. Many brains are at work upon it, much money is being spent in experiments, and the work is sure to result in something better than anything as yet available.

HAND AND GLOVE AT THE AQUARIUM.

It's wonderful! Marvellous! the reproduction of the great fight between FITZSIMMONS and CORBETT by Fisticuffographic Process at the Aquarium! They "come like shadows, so depart," and I fancy the Witches in their cave knew this trick and presented a series of "living pictures" for the instruction and amusement of *Macbeth*. By the way, herein is a hint for Mr. FORBES ROBERTSON should he wish to give this Shakspearian drama with genuine novel effects. Or, why should not the "living pictures" be given in the Play Scene in *Hamlet?* But this, by the way. *A nos mute-'uns!* For they don't speak a word! Not a sound to be heard! Except the whirring of the machinery. O my head! Never was there so dense and so silent a crowd living, moving, waving hands, and doing all that mortal men can do except speak.

Never having seen a prize-fight, I had imagined that two athletes stripped to the waist, as they appear in prints of champion pugilists, would gracefully stand up to each other until one of them could stand up no longer, the interval being occupied in "squaring up," "uitting out," "slogging," "landing" each other "one on the nut," and, in a general way, exhibiting what muscle, training, and science can effect. Consequently I was considerably astonished at finding these two champions, who seem to hate one another like poison, that is, if the refusal of FITZSIMMONS to shake hands with CORBETT is to be taken as an indication of this deadly inimical sentiment, occupying the greater part of the time taken up by the encounter in getting quite close together, and apparently hugging each other in so loving an embrace that they find the greatest difficulty in parting; in fact FITZSIMMONS seemed quite sorry to let CORBETT go, and *vice versâ*. Sometimes they dance, and kop, and hurry, and scurry round the ring, but, as it always seems, with only one aim and end, namely, that FITZSIMMONS is so deeply attached to CORBETT (or CORBETT to FITZSIMMONS, it does not matter which) as to be perpetually making for him, with a view to taking him to his arms, and giving him just another hug for old acquaintance sake, and to show that, though at the commencement he had refused to go through the formality of shaking hands, yet he was desperately attached to him, and only wanted to take him to his heart and whisper the touching truth in his ear. All this time the two champions are being followed about all over the place by a stout man in shirt-sleeves, light tie, and high collar, whom at first I took to be a kind of clergyman of some persuasion, skipping about to avoid their both hitting him or treading on his toes, and, probably, perpetually reminding them of Dr. WATTS' hymn, how, "Dogs might delight to bark and bite," and "Lions to growl and fight," but that for a couple of Christians to be engaged in a deadly pummeling encounter was not a seemly spectacle, nor a good example to set to the thousands of spectators there gathered together. However, it was soon explained to me that this stout personage, something between a genial elderly parson and a robust landlord of a public house, was GEORGE SILER, of Chicago, the referee. A nice time he must have had of it! Once he was nearly sent over the ropes with both champions on the top of him!

The fight continues. Sometimes they are in the full clear light of day, but in a steady pelt of rain or snow, at other times they are all in shadow and a heavy storm is pouring down; but whether in light or shade, all the figures, principals and crowd, are moving about under a kind of continuous Niagara waterfall, of which everyone seems utterly unconscious. It is this that makes it so weird. At last, however, FITZSIMMONS becoming annoyed at all his overtures for his amiably-intentioned hugging and em-

bracing being rejected, hits CORBETT a nasty one, when down goes the latter on his knee, and what is more, he can't get on his legs again when "time" is called; whereupon "FITZSIMMONS is," says the voice of a mysterious showman coming to us through the gloom, for the spectators are almost in darkness, "proclaimed the winner."

This verdict evidently so annoys CORBETT, that, recovering his legs just a few seconds too late, he rushes at FITZSIMMONS, who might have been taken unawares but for the rapid intervention of seconds, backers, umpire, men with fans, men with towels, men with sponges, all throwing themselves on the dangerous defeated one, and hustling him out of the ring. Then in surges the crowd, and all is muddle and jumble and jostling, when suddenly everything and everybody vanishes, the nightmare is over, the hall is once more in full light, and we, with FITZSIMMONS in one eye, CORBETT in the other, and our head aching from the silent fists of both, are staring about, dazed, wondering if "there are wisions about," whether everybody is real, whether—— "Ah! I've been a-lookin' for you, Sir!" 'Tis the voice of the cabman, I hear him complain. I had forgotten to pay him! He has been waiting for me just one hour and a half. Yes; I *am* alive; so is the cabman. It is real.

A MUTOSCOPIC ROMANCE.

THE FIGHT TO PHOTOGRAPH CAPTAIN DREYFUS IN THE PRISON YARD AT RENNES.

By Alfred Angus.   Drawings by C. Dudley Tennant.

Copyright by]   [*The Biograph and Mutoscope Co., Ltd.*

CAPTAIN DREYFUS EXERCISING IN THE PRISON YARD AT RENNES.

Captain Dreyfus is the figure in uniform indicated by the arrow in the above photograph. The picture was taken in the fortieth part of a second, and is one of several secured in the few seconds which it took Dreyfus to traverse the distance between the two doorways on the right. Having emerged from the rear one, Dreyfus is seen being hurried through the front one, the discovery having been made that photographs were being secretly taken.

TO the enterprise of the mutoscope man there appears to be no limit. When we were first privileged to witness, while seated comfortably in the stalls of London's premier theatre of varieties, a living, moving representation of the Derby as it had taken place a few hours before, we were ready to admit that the biograph was a marvellous invention. Since then we have been entertained by the vivid reproduction, at the shortest notice, of the greatest events in modern history and in social life.

But the difficulty of triumphantly reproducing such scenes sinks into insignificance compared with the feat recently successfully engineered by the Biograph and Mutoscope Syndicate. I refer to the graphic pictures of the prison life of Dreyfus, with whose name the world has long been ringing.

When the patrons of the Palace Theatre first saw the famous biographic scene, disclosing the exercise yard of the military prison at Rennes during the time when Dreyfus marched around it, they naturally asked themselves the question—"How was it possible that such pictures were procured?" I have it on the highest authority that no more difficult feat has ever been undertaken by the syndicate controlling the biograph and mutoscope rights. I have been also assured that the success of the project forms a record which it will be difficult to eclipse.

The person directly responsible for the unique mutoscopic feat is M. Orde, the manager of the French section of the marvellously successful business undertaking.

He knew that the eyes of the civilised world were at the moment fixed on that prison in Rennes; and, as a business man, he was aware that a sensational coup would prove of great pecuniary value. He set his brains to work to decide what episode in Dreyfus's prison life would lend itself best to the graphic and faithful reproduction of the biographic and mutoscopic apparatus.

After infinite trouble, he learned that at a certain hour every day Dreyfus was taken from his cell into the prison

BUILDING THE SCAFFOLD.
The scaffold on the housetop in progress of erection. It was from here that the photographs of Dreyfus in the prison yard were taken.

this course with a vigour sustained by the knowledge that every moment was of the most vital importance.

The persevering mutoscope man had noticed, as he walked by the outside of the prison yard, that immediately opposite there was a house that might be rented.

It was through the medium of this house that he intended to succeed ultimately. He sought the landlord at once, and had to make a journey to Rouen to interview him. M. Orde explained his business; that is, his wish to rent the house, for he was particularly careful, of course, not to mention the precise cause of his haste to become a tenant.

yard, where he was allowed the necessary exercise to keep him in good health.

Although he considered that his application would be scouted by the prison authorities, he felt he was bound, before taking other steps, to apply for formal permission to secure films in the ordinary way from one of the windows of the building within the prison precincts, and overlooking the prison yard. He even went so far as to request the authority of a very great French personage, whose name I am not at liberty to give. But without avail.

Knowing that it would not be of the slightest use to pursue the matter in that direction, M. Orde decided to trust to other means of securing his object, and set about

The landlord, however, was a keen man; keen enough to surmise that something was in the wind. He was also aware that Dreyfus had lately become an inmate of the prison upon which his house looked; and this fact, together with M. Orde's hurry to secure the tenancy, told him that the house was wanted, and wanted very badly. He hummed and hawed, and ended by asking a rent that would be too much for a house twice the size. References? He assured M. Orde that he was most particular on this point, as he wished to keep up the tone of the neighbourhood. M. Orde gave him the best reference he had ever had before, six months' rent in advance, and thereby made the landlord his friend. The mutoscope man came away with the agreement and keys in his pocket. Time was money with him.

The moment M. Orde arrived in Rennes he hurried to the house of which he had become a tenant in record time, and raced up the stairs to the top floor front.

Horror! He could not even see the door out of which Dreyfus and his jailers must emerge!

Ah! the roof! He got out upon the landing. There was a closed trapdoor, but no possible means of reaching it.

There was nothing for him to do but go to the house where he lodged for assistance. He drove off, found two of his men, borrowed a ladder and some tools, and returned with them to the empty house.

He and his assistants were soon through the trapdoor. But they found, after much searching, that no skylight existed, and that they must force an entrance through the tiles if they would get out into the open.

This they very cautiously proceeded to do, and in a few minutes they crept out of a square opening upon the sloping roof, where they had to exercise the greatest possible care lest they should slide down and tumble over the low parapet.

M. Orde was the first to see that even the roof was far too low for his purpose. At the highest point he could only catch a glimpse of the headgear of the guards as they moved about in the yard below.

Defeated after all!

With coats off, and covered with dust from head to foot, they pretended, while they remained upon the roof, to be artisans engaged at repairs. It would have been folly to attract the attention of anyone in authority in the prison opposite, from the barred windows of which it was possible they were being watched at the moment.

After some pretended repairing, the mutoscope men retired out of sight; M. Orde to reflect on the best plan to turn their present defeat into success.

He could plainly see that he must get to a greater height if he would make anything of the project. Reflection told him that he must, if possible, erect a scaffolding at least ten feet high upon the highest portion of the roof.

That was the next move. As quietly as possible, a carpenter was procured from a neighbouring village and sworn to secrecy. He made the necessary measurements, the timber was purchased out of Rennes, and as secretly as possible conveyed to the empty house, where each portion of the scaffolding

THE PRISON AUTHORITIES OUTWIT THE PHOTOGRAPHERS.

When the prison officials discovered what was the reason of the erection of the scaffolding shown on the previous page, orders were given for a large tarpaulin to be erected. This was done, and prevented any view of the prison yard being obtained from the scaffolding.

was cut and made ready to fit into its place, that as little time as possible might be occupied in erecting it at the proper moment.

The eventful morning arrived when the scaffolding was to be erected on the roof and the camera set in position for the great event. As early as 2 a.m., the workmen arrived and set to work, under the superintendence of M. Orde, who was now highly delighted that things had gone on so well. All day long the men toiled, and M. Orde was repaid for all his trouble and anxiety by stepping on the platform supported by the scaffolding, and finding that it commanded a splendid view of the entire yard, and he could see plainly several of the guards or jailers moving about or sitting on benches by the walls.

At an early hour next morning the camera, with its well-known accessories for its particular work, was placed in position, commanding a grand view of the entire yard, and there is no doubt whatever that the close of the exercise hour would have seen the episode transferred to the films.

But it was not to be! M. Orde was resting in one of the rooms below —now partly furnished— when a loud shout of dismay summoned him to the roof. A couple of operators stood on the platform, and they pointed with wild gesticulations to the walls of the prison.

Horror of horrors!

A crowd of workmen were busy erecting strong poles, and the presence of a coil of wire rope and a large tarpaulin told him what had happened.

The prison authorities had at last discovered, owing, no doubt, to the presence

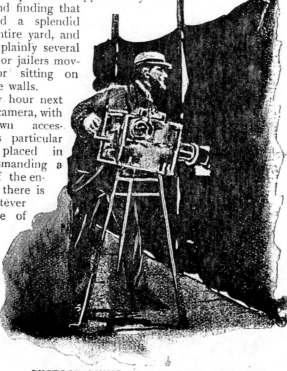

PHOTOGRAPHING THE FAMOUS PRISONER.

Following the fashion set by the prison officials, the photographer also erected a tarpaulin in front of his scaffold, and behind it waited and watched for a week in hopes of securing the much desired photographs. At the end of that time the officials, believing the quest had been abandoned, removed their screen, and the next time Dreyfus appeared in the yard he was photographed by the ever alert operator.

of the camera on the lofty platform, the purpose of the scaffolding, and were now erecting a tarpaulin screen in time to prevent Dreyfus from being photographed!

And thus it happened! For that day, at least, no photos could be obtained, and nobody knew whether it would ever be possible to accomplish the job, in spite of all the trouble and expense incurred.

But M. Orde did not despair. He, too, erected a tarpaulin screen, leaving only the small space necessary for the muzzle of the operating camera. The guards now could not see a move on the roof of the house. The operators took turns in watching for the long-looked-for opportunity to secure the films. During the possible hours of the day, a man was on the watch.

Then, at last, the patience of M. Orde was fully rewarded. After a week, the prison authorities evidently thought they had tired out the enemy, and removed the tarpaulin. Watching eagerly, the operators in an hour or two noticed some slight commotion in the yard, and presently, from the upper door shown in the accompanying photograph, there emerged, under guard, the man they had waited so long to focus. Whirr! went the apparatus, and photographic films at the rate of forty a second were being turned out. Something, however, must have occurred on the lofty platform of the house to attract the guard—possibly the camera screen was agitated by the excited movements of the operators. At any rate, Dreyfus was soon hurried in through the other door. The films secured, however, were sufficient to make the excellent living picture that so astonished and mystified the Palace patrons on the occasion of its first production.

PRINCE EDWARD, PRINCE BERTIE, AND PRINCESS VICTORIA OF YORK.

By Permission of the Biograph Studio, Regent Street, W.

"Let's sing the Anthem," said Prince Edward while in front of the camera, and the three children sang it. *See page 198.*

PRINCE EDWARD PHOTOGRAPHING HIS LITTLE SISTER.

OUR FUTURE KING AT PLAY

ILLUSTRATED BY PHOTOGRAPHS
H.R.H. THE DUKE OF YORK, AND

TAKEN BY SPECIAL COMMAND OF
PUBLISHED BY SPECIAL PERMISSION.

WE have been fortunate enough to secure permission to publish a most interesting series of photographs taken with the biograph camera of the three charming children cf the Duke and Duchess of York—Prince Edward, Prince Bertie, and Princess Victoria.

The photographs were taken on films at an amazing rate, and if our readers could see them reproduced in action by means of the mutoscope, they would be vastly entertained. They were taken in the charming gardens of Marlborough House.

These beautiful grounds make an ideal playground for children, and the young Princes and their sister enjoy the privilege of playing there almost every day, their toys being kept in a small summerhouse under some shady trees.

Princess Victoria and her brothers are inseparable companions, and she is very

THE ROYAL CHILDREN ARE GREATLY INTERESTED
IN THE MUTOSCOPE.

DRILLING THE THREE YORK
CHILDREN.

devoted to them, aspiring to be their comrade and playmate. As may be expected, they are all military enthusiasts at the present moment, and drill very prettily indeed, the two Princes taking the office of commander in turn. That this is no mere fleeting fancy of childhood is evident from the very earnest way in which these youthful soldiers go about their work.

PRINCE EDWARD SALUTES THE FLAG.

They do not use a drillbook, but know all the commands and movements off by heart. Most of our photographs represent Prince Bertie putting his brother, the future King of England, and sister through their drill, and the instantaneousness of the biograph enables it to catch the trio in the very act. They are full of life, and show how real the whole business is to the children.

On one occasion when Prince Bertie, who was acting as commander, hesitated a moment over a command, his brother and sister, who comprised his army, stood motionless in the glare of the sun

waiting for the order to move. At another time Prince Bertie gave his brother the command to "Ground arms," following it up with instructions to "Right about turn. Quick march!" Prince Edward looked up indignantly, and pointed out to his brother that he should have given the command to "Shoulder arms" first, explaining that until he had done that he could not make any movement.

That Prince Edward aspires to be a soldier is manifest in his whole bearing, and he takes as much pride in the smartness and accuracy of his every movement as the smartest man in a good regiment. It is amusing to see the earnestness with which he slaps his rifle in one of the movements of the salute. Our illustration on page 199 depicts him in the attitude of bringing down his hand to do this.

Whilst engaged in their drill before the biograph, the young soldiers heard the strains of martial music which heralded the changing of the guard at St. James's Palace

opposite. It is their particular delight to witness this ceremony every morning from a terraced walk which overlooks the palace, but on this occasion they remembered that they were before the camera, and, although wistful glances were cast in the direction of the palace, the drill was properly concluded, as outlined in the "Manual of Arms," thus displaying a power of self-control and consideration for others not common to children of their age.

The pictures of Prince Edward saluting the flag are particularly interesting, for this youthful royal hope of England is already very much attached to the English flag, and understands something of its significance. Just before the pictures were taken he planted the flag in the ground, and when it was done to his satisfaction, he walked away a few paces, and, looking at it, smilingly murmured, as though thinking aloud, "Now I can begin."

The two little Princes were very much interested in the movements of the photographers, and seeing one of them

"STAND AT EASE!"

focussing the biograph camera, they wanted it explained, and afterwards did a little focussing themselves. But the stand camera attracted them most,

"SHOULDER ARMS!"

and when for a few minutes they were left to themselves the royal trio took possession of it in the most approved fashion. The little Princess was posed in the front of the camera, and Prince Edward, constituting himself photographer-in-chief, put his head under the focussing cloth and, with a gravity beyond his years, gave

"SUPPORT ARMS!"

Prince Bertie minute instructions as to the precise moment when to squeeze the ball and release the shutter. So thoroughly engrossed were the children in this new occupation, that they did not notice that the biograph camera was again at work taking photographs of them at the rate of fifty a second. Two of these are shown at the head of this article.

"HOW'S THAT?"

After a group of the children with their nurses

"SHOULDER ARMS!"

had been taken with a hand camera, Prince Edward said, "Now that you have photographed me, let me take a photograph of you." The appeal was irresistible, and the little Prince rejoices in the knowledge that he took a photograph, and that it came out well.

Another illustration shows Princess Victoria in her little hand-carriage, drawn by one of her brothers, and a pretty story can be told concerning the

"SLOPE ARMS!" (2)

taking of it. A mutoscope had been shown to the children earlier in the morning, and the photographer promised that if they would let him take one more living picture, he would show them "the picture of a black boy" in the mutoscope. They were delighted at the prospect of seeing this black boy, and the tricycle horse and the Princess in her hand-carriage were soon careering gaily round the lawn. Something then

occurred to distract their attention, and no more was thought about the promise until the next day, when the Princess ran to meet the gentleman who made it, with outstretched hands, saying, "Good morning; where's that little black boy?"

Throughout the whole of the photographing, which extended over two mornings, the courtesy and thoughtfulness of the royal trio were most marked, and their eagerness to do just what the photographers wanted them to do made the task a pleasure. They were good

"SLOPE ARMS!" (1)

sitters, too; for, contrary to the prevalent ideas concerning royal children, they are quite unspoiled, and their demeanour is natural and unaffected.

During the second morning's photography one of them made the suggestion, "Now let us sing the Anthem." Before the photographers quite comprehended what was meant, the two boys were standing at the salute with their sister beside them. Then, after a moment's silence, three childish voices

"PRESENT ARMS!"

began to pipe in shrill treble, "God save our gracious Queen." It was a striking and touching little episode, and there was something indescribably affecting in their sweet seriousness of demeanour as they sang the grand old anthem which they must so often hear, and which to them has such a deep personal meaning.

There was just one quaint flash of humour in the little scene. The Princess raised her hand to the salute, but was speedily corrected by Prince Edward, who said, "No, you must not salute; only men do that."

A VERY QUICK MOVEMENT.

"QUICK MARK TIME!" (1)

This striking incident is shown in our frontispiece.

The day afterwards the youthful trio saw the pictures of themselves which had been taken, in life motion, in the mutoscope. Their delight is better imagined than described, and the repeated requests which they made to have "another look" testified eloquently to the fact that for a time at least they have got a new and charming source of pleasure and amusement, and their

delight may be seen by our readers depicted in the photographs on page 195.

However delightful the pictures may be to the children, they have a more serious meaning. They stand for the making of history in a new form, that of an animated pictorial record of life and personality, which grows more valuable as time goes on. In this sense they are the record of a happy childhood, and in after years Prince Edward

"QUICK MARK TIME!" (2)

and his brother and sister may be pleased to be able to call back their childhood once again, and in some degree to live over the happy mornings at Marlborough House.

An interesting incident, which appealed strongly to the embryo military tastes of Prince Edward of York, took place recently at the gardens of the Royal Botanical Society on the occasion of the St. Marylebone Carnival. A beautifully constructed model

"LEFT TURN!"

"FORWARD!"

told of Prince Edward. He was feeling unwell one day, and informed his astonished mother that he was suffering from an attack of nerves!

It may be well to point out here that the popular name of Prince Eddie, by which the little Prince is widely known to the public, is not recognised or approved by the Royal Family. The Prince is always called David by his relatives, that being the last of his Christian names. Prince Eddie was the late Duke of Clarence and Avondale.

One of Prince David's juvenile

of a field-gun, complete with ammunition-box, was a prominent feature in the parade, and was afterwards presented to Prince Edward.

It was not long before he discovered that the shells in the ammunition-box were made to open, and that the explosives with which they were filled were nothing more formidable than sweets. The little Prince set to work and sold these sweets to his friends, displaying considerable business capacity in the

"QUICK MARCH!"

characteristics is his punctiliousness in the matter of salutes. Nothing causes him greater indignation than to be passed by anyone without recognition.

With the Queen, whom he calls "Granny"—the Princess of Wales being "Grandmamma"—the young Prince is a prime favourite.

For all our photographs we are indebted to the Biograph Studio, Regent Street.

GIVING PRINCESS VICTORIA A RIDE.

matter of charging heavily for them, and has since handed over a large sum of money to the Widows' and Orphans' Fund as the result of his exertions.

At Sandringham, where he spends a good deal of his time, he lives practically in the open air, as do also his brother and sister; and it is pleasant to know that the royal children are strong and robust.

In this connection a funny story has been

PRINCE EDWARD AS TRICYCLIST.

S

FILM IN LENGTHS for Projection Work

BLAIR'S FILM is the strongest, cheapest and most reliable for making the negative and positive pictures required in the popular animated photographs. Quotations given for Strips cut to any width up to 20 inches and 120 feet in length without joins. Transparent or Matt surface.

EUROPEAN BLAIR CAMERA CO., Ltd.,
9 SOUTHAMPTON ST., HOLBORN, LONDON.
Telegrams: "HAWKMOTH, LONDON."   Factory: SIDCUP.

J. H. RIGG,
43 Skinner Lane, LEEDS.
Works: Cross Stamford Street and Telephone Street.

MANUFACTURER OF
Phonographs, Kinetoscopes, Kinematographs, Films, &c.

Telegraphic and Cable Address—"MOTOR, LEEDS.'

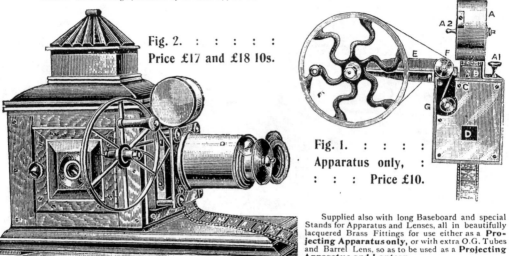

Animated Photographs!

RIGG'S (PATENTED)
Kinematograph.

Gives Best Results of any Projector on the Market.
Takes any Film with Good Results.

Cannot Damage Films. :
Always Sharp. : : ; : :
No Flicker. : : : : :
Picture Always Same Spot
   on Screen. : : : :
Bright Pictures. : : : :
No Jump. : : : : :
No Breakdowns. : : : :
Failure Impossible. : : :
Films can be taken out any
   part of its length. : :
Films can be put in in less
   than five seconds. : :

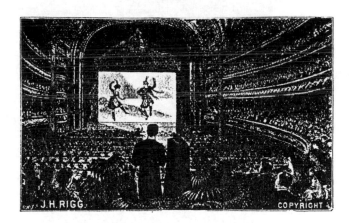

FILMS: Large Stock,
Actual Manufacturers.

Intending Buyers should see this machine. This machine is acknowledged, wherever shown, to be the BEST. This machine having been on the market for some considerable time, has every improvement that experience can suggest.

J. H. RIGG, Skinner Lane, LEEDS.

Works: Cross Stamford Street and Telephone Street.

Sole Agency for the U.S.A.:
Messrs. HAWTHORNE & SHEBBLE, 106 Chestnut Street, Philadelphia, Pa.

Animated Photography

... AND PROJECTION BY ...

THE ~
VITAGRAPH

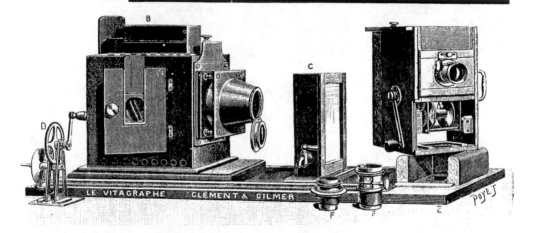

We claim the following qualities for it,
and are prepared to substantiate them.

> No vibration of pictures on screen when the films are accurately
> perforated.
> Receives Kinetoscope films and all others of same width and
> perforation.
> Does not tear or spoil the films.
> Will photograph in any weather.
> Is as small and portable as a hand camera.
> Any powerful source of light can be adapted that buyers may select.

Stock always on hand for prompt delivery.

For further information apply to the Manufacturers:

CLEMENT & GILMER,
8 and 10 Rue de Malte, PARIS.

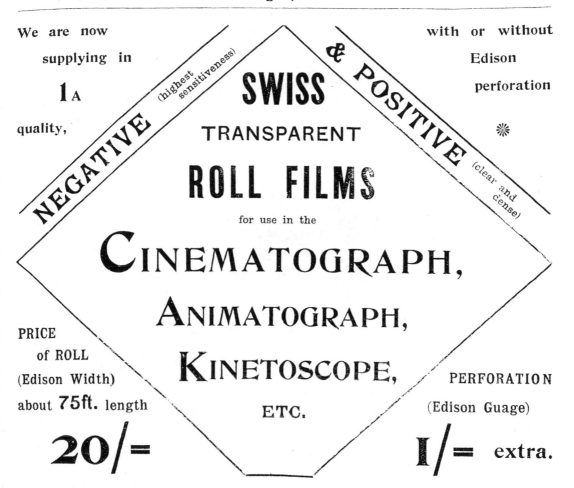

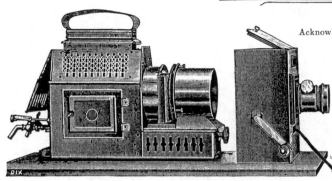

FILMS

.. FOR ..

CINEMATOGRAPHS.

Most Wonderful Subjects.

LARGEST STOCK IN ENGLAND.

MACHINES for Projection

Liberal Trade Discount.

LIST ON APPLICATION.

PHILIPP WOLFF,

BERLIN.   PARIS.

9 & 10 Southampton Street,

High Holborn, LONDON, W.C.

RIGG'S "KINEMATOGRAPH."

ROUNDABOUTS.

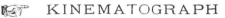

KINEMATOGRAPH
KINEMATOGRAPH
KINEMATOGRAPH
KINEMATOGRAPH
KINEMATOGRAPH

RAILWAY STATION.

ILMS.
FILMS.
FILMS.
FILMS.
FILMS.
FILMS.
FILMS.
FILMS.
FILMS.
FILMS.
FILMS.
FILMS.
FILMS.
FILMS. FILMS.
FILMS.
FILMS.
FILMS.
FILMS.
FILMS.
FILMS·
FILMS.
FILMS.
FILMS.
FILMS.
FILMS.
FILMS.
'FILMS.

THIS Machine was *one* of the *first* on the market and from practical experience contains more improvements than any other, and which can only be suggested by manufacturing and use extending over some time. We claim the following for our machine. No flicker. No *jump*. Pictures *sharp*. *Will not damage the films.* Films changed in five seconds. *Never fails.*

NOTE. We do not supply an ordinary lantern fitted with a projector but every machine is sold complete with special lantern, lenses, condensers, jets, &c., hence we get the best result to be obtained. Our machine is not a cheap machine, but from the number of repeated orders from the trade we think we have proved a cheap machine is not required but a good one at a fair price.

FILMS.
FILMS.
FILMS.
FILMS.
FILMS.
FILMS.
FILMS.
FILMS.
FILMS.
FILMS.
FILMS. FILMS.
FILMS.
FILMS.
FILMS.
FILMS.
FILMS.
FILMS.
FILMS.
FILMS.
FILMS.
FILMS.
FILMS.

TRAM TERMINUS.

For Price Lists and Particulars
write to

J. H. RIGG, 43 SKINNER LANE,

WORKS—

26, 28, 30, Cross Stamford St., and Telephone St.,

TELEGRAPHIC AND CABLE ADDRESS—
"MOTOR, LEEDS."

LEEDS.

CHILDREN LEAVING SCHOOL.

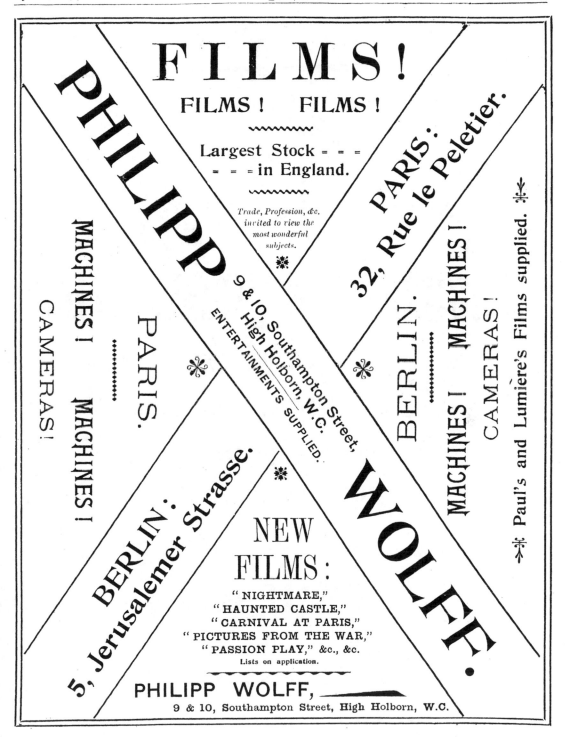

MAGUIRE & BAUCUS, LTD.,

Dashwood House, 9, New Broad St., London, E.C.

AND

44, Pine Street, New York, U.S.A.

SELLING AGENTS FOR

EDISON

PROJECTOSCOPES AND FILMS

AND

LUMIÈRE

FILMS PERFORATED TO EDISON GAUGE.

SEND FOR CATALOGUES AND TRADE TERMS.

Please mention the "PHOTOGRAPHIC DEALER" when writing.

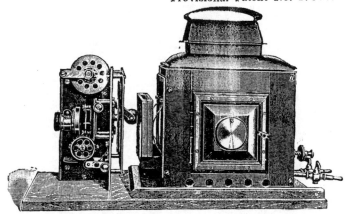

ANIMATED PHOTOGRAPH FILMS

Telegraphic and Cable Address "CALIBRATE, LONDON."

Copyright and manufactured by **ROBT. W. PAUL, 44, Hatton Garden, London, E.C.**

N.B. These Films are printed on transparent material, and are full of interest from beginning to end. They have Edison Standard perforations, and are true to gauge and steady on the screen, clear and sharp. They are delivered packed in air-tight tins, and are carefully tested, and treated to prevent stripping.

TERMS.—Cash with order. Films are not sent on approbation, but small samples can be sent when order required. All orders for Films not in stock are executed in two days.

PRICE 30s. each.   In Ordering, State Code Word.

No.	Code Word.	Description.
1	ENGINEERS,	Scene at Nelson Dock, with Smiths and Machinery at work.
2	TRAIN,	Arrival of Paris Express at Calais. Passengers disembarking.
3	BLACKFRIARS,	Traffic on Blackfriars Bridge ; beautiful detail.
4	WESTMINSTER,	Omnibuses and Pedestrians passing St. Thomas's Hospital.
5	BEACH,	Humorous scene, with persons landing from a small boat.
6	RIVER,	Exciting Rescue of a Child who has fallen overboard.
7	CHILDREN,	A beautiful domestic picture of Children and Dogs at play.
8	COLUMBIA,	Effective and artistic scene of departure of a Steamboat.
9	TWINS,	Two Infants at Tea ; very amusing and natural.
10	PELICANS,	Pelicans at the Zoological Gardens scrambling for food.
11	FIRE,	Turnout of a Fire Brigade ; a most exciting picture.
12	SHOVELLING,	Carting Snow in the Market Place, Leicester.
13	CHIMNEY,	Underpinning a Chimney-stack and the overthrow.
14	HUNT,	Meet of Lord Rothschild's Staghounds at Aylesbury.
15	PERSIMMON,	The famous 1896 Derby ; the excited crowd.
16	DERBY,	The 1897 Derby ; a fine picture.
17	RABBIT,	David Devant, the Conjurer, produces Rabbits from a Hat.
18	TRICK,	Devant produces Eggs from all parts of his body.
19	PAPER,	Numerous objects rapidly produced from a sheet of paper.
20	HAT,	Chirgwin, the White-eyed Kaffir in his humorous business.
21	PIPES,	Chirgwin plays a Scotch Reel with tobacco pipes.
22	CLUB,	Morris Cronin, the marvellous American Club Manipulator.
23	CLUBS,	Cronin, with three clubs ; a wonderful feat.
24	HENGLERS,	Sisters Hengler, specialité dancers ; suited for colouring.
25	FLAG,	the Union Jack fluttering ; nearly covers the screen.
26	DIRTY,	"The Dirty Boy" statue comes to life.
27	HAMPSTEAD,	Lively Scene at Hampstead on Bank Holiday.
28	DISEMBARKING,	Passengers arriving at Stockholm and leaving the boat.
29	FISHWIVES,	Women bringing in Fish at the Market in Lisbon.
30	BATHING,	A lively scene of Diving and Bathing in the Sea near Lisbon.
31	CADIZ,	Street Scene in Plaza del Cathedrale, Cadiz.
32	ANDALUSIAN,	Andalusian Dance, by two performers.
33	CHURCH,	After Mass, leaving the Church of San Salvador, Selville.
34	PAU,	Two men actively engaged in the Portuguese Game of Pau.
35	GRINDER,	An Arab Knife-grinder at work.
36	MONKEY,	An Arab exercising his Monkey.
37	WATER,	Women fetching water from the Nile.
38	PYRAMIDS,	A Caravan arriving at the Pyramids.
39	DRINKMAN,	A Cairo scene ; selling water from a goat skin.
40	CAIRO,	Loading Camels in a Cairo Street.
41	IRON,	Arabs at work, breaking old iron with primitive machinery.
42	BULLOCK,	An Egyptian Bullock-pump ; drawing water.
43	FISHER,	Fisherman and Boat at Port Said.
44	SAWYERS,	Egyptian scene ; a primitive saw-mill.
45	REINDEER,	A Laplander feeding his reindeer.
46	LAPLANDERS,	Laplanders arriving at their village ; a welcome home.
47	GARDEN,	Children at Play in the King's Gardens, Stockholm.
48	DERRICKS,	Derricks at work discharging coal from a steamer.
49	TROLLEY,	Electric Trolley Car coming through pine forest in Sweden.
50	GUARD,	The King's Guard marching at Stockholm.
51	ÆOLUS,	The Steamboat "Æolus" leaving Stockholm.
52	SWEDE,	A Swedish National Dance at Skansen.
53	SWEDEN,	Do. Do. eight performers.
54	SWEDISH,	Do. Do. four performers.
55	HIGHLANDERS,	The Gordon Highlanders leaving Marybill Barracks, Glasgow.
56	REVIEW,	Fire Brigade Review at Windsor, June, 1897.
57	SPORTS,	Comic Costume Scramble. Very funny.
58	CAVE,	An artistic view of a Sea Cave ; waves dashing violently.
59	RACE,	The Juvenile Plate Race, 1896.
60	SUBURBAN,	City and Suburban, Finish, 1897.
61	BRIDGE,	Traffic on the Tower Bridge.
62	DIVING,	A splendid and lively picture at Douglas.
63	DOUGLAS,	Landing Visitors from small boats. Very clear.
64	MASKELYNE,	plate-spinning by the renowned conjuror.
65	ELECTRIC,	Rottingdean Electric Railway. Very interesting.
66	LIVERPOOL,	Ferries arriving at landing stage.
67	HUSBAND,	Comic scene representing return of an inebriated husband.
68	SOLDIER,	The Soldier's Courtship. Very funny.
69	ROBBERY,	A wayfarer compelled partially to disrobe. Very laughable.
70	CAMELS,	Beautiful Egyptian scene. Very animated.
71	PRINCE,	Prince of Wales at Cheltenham, reviewing Yeomanry.
72	JEALOUSY,	Dramatic scene in Gardens, a jealous husband shot.
73	ROUNDABOUT,	A lively Bank Holiday picture at Hampstead.
74	DONKEYS,	Donkey-riding on the Beach.
75	CARPET,	Annual Procession of the Holy Carpet from Cairo to Mecca.

DIAMOND JUBILEE PROCESSION : Twelve of the Finest Views taken ; 30s. each. Complete List on Application.

FIRE PROOF IMPROVED ANIMATOGRAPHE, £10.

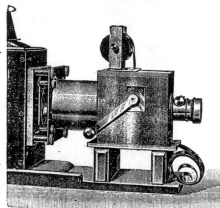
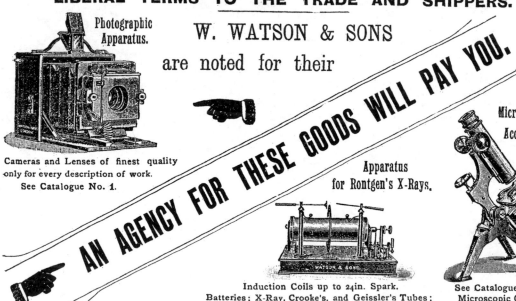

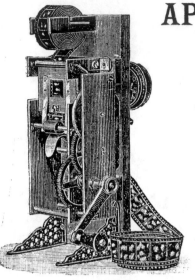
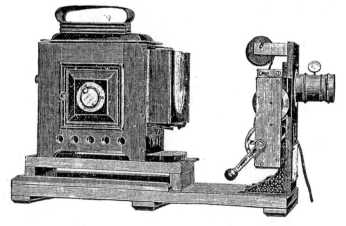

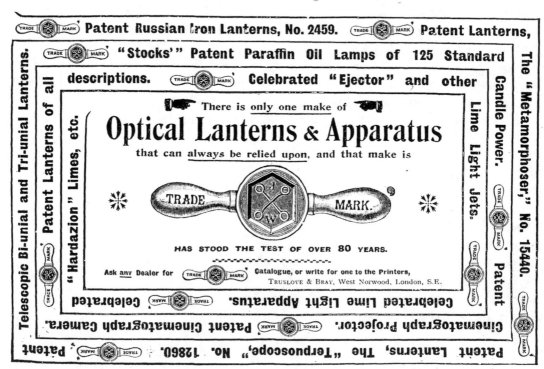

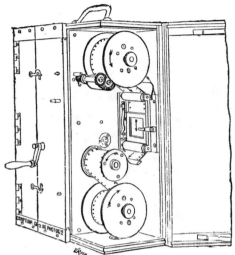
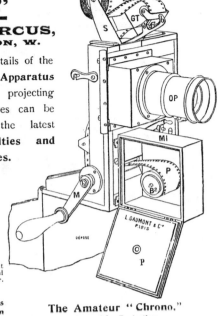
39

CINEMATOGRAPHY FOR ALL.

By HENRY V. HOPWOOD.

WHENEVER, on previous occasions, THE OPTICIAN AND PHOTOGRAPHIC TRADES REVIEW has afforded me an opportunity of dealing with matters cinematographic, I have treated mainly of generalities, history and progress.

But now I propose to deal with one aspect, and one alone, of the living picture; for I believe that the coming year will mark a very distinct stage in the commercial development and public appreciation of animated photography.

Let us consider the analogous case of photography proper. In its earlier days it well merited the name of the "Black Art." Dirty, tedious and expensive, it remained, for many years, to all intents and purposes, a professional pursuit. Certainly, many enthusiasts were found who considered their troubles well repaid by their results; but generally speaking, the amateur Photographer was a *rara avis*. With the advent of the hand-camera and cheap dry-plate the whole aspect of the matter changed. From the delight of the few, photography became the recreation of the many; to the profit of all, public and dealers alike.

FIG. 1.—" THE BIOKAM."

Turning, then, to the living picture, we find it as I see it, in the earlier, or professional stage. I know, of course, that many non-professionals have adopted it—but, broadly considered, I believe my proposition to be true. Furthermore, the success of the living picture has been so great in the exhibiting world that it seems in the course of three years to have attained a position which renders expansion difficult. I cannot conceive that its popularity should decline—as a prominent maker once said to me " the public will no more tire of living pictures than it does of the 'Illustrated Magazine '—both have come to stay."

But there does exist a field for expansion, an almost unlimited field, which so far as I can see is practically unworked. I refer to small gauge machines. I am, of course, prepared to find one or several manufacturers confronting me with a statement of the number of these small machines sold—my only reply is that I should rejoice to see that number twenty times as great.

It cannot be denied that the leading makers have fully performed their part in this matter. They have provided a most excellent choice of apparatus; different in design, moderate in price. The one thing needful is that the retailer should push the trade; and if I prove too insistent on this point the great interest which I take in the living picture must be my excuse, and I only ask that my arguments be well weighed; I believe they will prove my case.

In the first place apparatus for animated photography is a distinct line; equally distinct is the small gauge machine. They will not displace any other photographic apparatus; they are not likely to be bought except by those who already practice photography. Furthermore, the possession

FIG. 2.—" LA PETITE."

of a small machine is not likely to spoil the sale of a standard gauge one if the purchaser can afford it—if he cannot, why not sell him the one which is within his means? Anyway he may purchase later on, when the fates are propitious and his enthusiasm for the living picture is sufficiently intense.

It must be remembered that the cost of the machine is comparatively negligible. The true cost is involved in working; and while a small machine, occasionally worked, cannot be called an extravagance, a full-sized one entails such expense for films that the average amateur is apt to think once, twice, and thrice before taking the first step towards the pursuit of a hobby which cannot be qualified as other than expensive.

Yes, the small gauge machine is distinctly tempting, and many a man will buy one if its advantages are properly pointed out. The hand-camera is a constant holiday companion—the small gauge cinematograph is no more cumbersome. One would not care to take it on an ordinary excursion—but, should one day of the holiday be devoted to a regatta, would not the hand-camera be left at home and the cinematograph come out to take up the running? Five days out of six on a continental trip we should probably work in the old way—should we not be likely to devote the sixth to the actual life and motion of the streets and markets?

Is it too much to suggest that sales might easily be effected if only one of these small machines were rigged-up, ready to exhibit at short notice to any prospective customer? It only needs a light to an incandescent burner and a perfectly satisfactory display may be given on a ground-glass screen some two feet or eighteen inches square.

These small machines may be procured to suit any customer; even one who has read up the whole subject and consequently has views of his own. Of the six machines on the market two are pin-motion; two striker or dog-motion; while the remaining two possess movements which I have not met in larger machines. All of them are adapted to serve both as camera and projector, performing the latter function

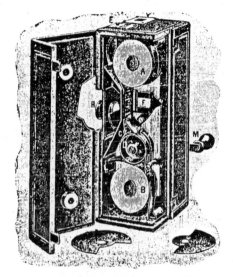

when attached to the front of an ordinary lantern in place of the objective. At the same time several makers supply lanterns specially adapted for use with their machines.

If then I confine myself to the description of narrow gauge apparatus it is because I believe that they are most worthy of attention in the coming season; the orthodox machines can well take care of themselves.

The " Biokam " is illustrated in fig. 1, which shows the complete outfit. The front part contains the intermittent motion; a very ingenious cam-disc with two grooves, one of which raises and lowers, while the other inserts and withdraws the pins which actuate the film. On this film 700 separate pictures are taken, the whole measuring some 25 ft. in length. A printing box is supplied for the purpose of making positives; these latter may also be bought in commercial subjects ready for exhibition. The film runs for quite as long as the usual 50 ft. film in larger machines, for though it is shorter, the pictures are smaller. A Voigtländer lens working at $f/7.7$ is supplied for taking negatives, its focus being $1\frac{1}{2}$ ins., and a second objective, equal in quality but of larger aperture, $1\frac{1}{4}$ ins. focus, and portrait nature is

provided for projection. Those who do not intend to take views for themselves can procure the front part of the apparatus alone, at a considerably reduced rate. This little apparatus has one special feature. It is so arranged that, when desired, it may be used as a hand camera, taking single snap-shots or even time exposures. Though these pictures are small, yet the optical arrangements are so good that the views can be enlarged to a considerable degree; in fact, the " Biokam " is specially fitted for this purpose. Thus, when out with the " Biokam " one is not debarred from taking one or more single views if occasion present itself. The compact nature of the apparatus will be seen from the fact that the front is only $3\frac{1}{4} \times 5\frac{1}{2}$ ins., the length being only 2 ins. when employed for projecting or enlarging, and a little more when used as a camera. And, as a final virtue, the complete outfit costs no more than a good quarter-plate camera, indeed, far less than many.

The other pin-motion machine is the Hughes' " La Petite," fig. 2, the pin being actuated by an eccentric. This also is a very compact little apparatus, and turns out excellent work, as I can testify from personal knowledge. Daylight-spools are employed for camera work, each film costing but half-a-crown. The separate views are $\frac{1}{2}$ inch by $\frac{3}{8}$, and leave nothing to be desired on the score of sharpness and detail. The degree of possible enlargement is great; a good

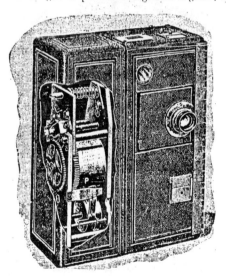

oil-lamp will give a two to three-foot picture, while with lime-light even nine feet may be attained. I can claim this machine as an old acquaintance, having handled it before it came on the market, and one of the experimental films which I then saw brings another advantage of the small gauge machine to my mind.

I suppose there are few, comparatively speaking, who go in for home portraiture, who have not had, at some time or another, lucky shots of which they are inordinately proud.

One gets the children into the garden, spoils about a dozen plates, and at last by a combination of fortuitous circumstances arrives at a happy result. I am not throwing stones, for I "live in a glass house" and speak from my own experience. Now, home portraiture of the cinematographic variety is not only very effective in itself but has the advantage that a choice may be made from a large number of exposures. Among the six or seven hundred views repre-

FIG. 5.—MIROGRAPH PROJECTOR.

senting a half-minute scene, there are sure to be several which portray a characteristic gesture or familiar expression in a particularly happy manner. Such selected single views are manifestly destined to enlargement, an operation easily effected. By-the-way, the perforation of the films used in "La Petite" is one square hole, centrally placed between the pictures.

These two machines are the only pin-motion machines of small gauge. Turning to the dog-motion or striker variety, the most notable is the Gaumont "Pocket Chrono," which is fitted with the well-known Demeny motion. There are several interesting points about this machine, and I have ventured to reproduce an illustration of it from 'La Nature,' which shows its chief features better than the usual catalogue cut. As will be seen from fig. 3, the working arrangements are those of the larger Demeny machines, but on a reduced scale. The film passes from spool A to spool B, the intermittent motion being given by the revolving eccentric blade C. The film takes 500 pictures $\frac{3}{4}$ inch high on a length of 16 feet, and the apparatus is available, not only as a camera, but also as printer and projector. The machine is actuated by a handle M, but a supplementary piece of apparatus may be procured which is somewhat of a novelty. This is a clockwork motor, shown in fig. 4, which may be coupled to the "Pocket

Chrono," the handle being removed. This arrangement not only renders the speed of the film less liable to interruption or variation, but also makes it possible for the operator to leave the machine and introduce himself into the view which is being taken. When projected the view may be shown 18 ins. or even 2 ft. in diameter with an incandescent gas light; the pictures will stand enlargement even to 9 ft. with more powerful illumination.

Another machine of the "striker" type, which, unfortunately, I am unable to illustrate, is Mr. Birt Acre's "Birtac." This also is very compact and serves the triple purpose of camera, projector, and printer. The films used are just half the width of ordinary ones, and have one row of standard perforations down one side only. But these perforations only serve to drive the film, the intermittent motion, as already stated, is given by a rotating eccentric rod.

So far, the machines described have been very similar to those already familiar on a larger scale. There has, however, been recently introduced in France an apparatus which has some distinctly novel points. As it has not yet, to my knowledge, made its appearance in England, I am obliged to illustrate it from 'La Nature.' It is named the "Mirograph," and is an invention of MM. Reulos and Goudeau. Its chief peculiarity, which affects the whole make of the machine, is that the film is not perforated, but is, instead, provided with dog-tooth serrations or notches along its margin. Referring to fig. 5, it will be seen that the machine is provided with a large cam-disc B, the point C of which may be supposed to catch one of the notches on the edge of the film. For one

FIG. 6.—MIROGRAPH CAMERA.

quarter of a revolution the edge of the disc approaches the centre and consequently draws the film down. During the other three-quarters the edge is truly circular, and so imparts no motion to the film, which, therefore, remains stationary for exposure. When used as a camera the machine is placed in an appropriate case, as in fig. 6, and spool boxes are attached in the usual manner. The views are ⅖ths of an inch high, or more exactly, one hundred to the meter, and it is claimed that a 4-wick oil-lamp will give a picture 3 ft. in diameter.

FIG. 7.—THE "KAMMATOGRAPH."

The only other machine which remains to be described is of an entirely special nature. Indeed, while all others may be said to be miniatures of standard machines, this is, almost of necessity, a type confined to obtaining small views. The "Kammatograph," fig. 7, is a filmless machine, the sensitive surface being a glass plate upon which the views are arranged in spiral. This disposition of the images is obtained by rotating the circular plate and at the same time traversing it behind a fixed lens. In this way 500 views are obtained on one plate. The actual mechanical arrangements are, however, of less importance than the resulting advantages of the system employed. In the first place, the machine is well adapted to satisfy the purchaser who, from one cause or another, objects to films. The man who, however unreasonably, regards films either as delicate or dangerous, at once finds his objections met. Further, development is exactly similar to ordinary work with plates ; and making positives differs in no way from the process of making lantern-slides. Added to which, the cost is entirely reasonable; the inexperienced worker having the advantage of a liberal allowance for spoiled plates, which being circular in form possess a value for re-coating. This arrangement is not of advantage to the inexperienced only ; we all know how old negatives accumulate, and there is some consolation in the thought that every five may be exchanged for a new plate.

The foregoing six machines are, I believe, the only small gauge ones on the market, at home or abroad. That there is room for tens of thousands of them can hardly be gainsaid, and the coming season should see large progress made towards their general introduction.

And now, as a means of completing my argument, I think I cannot do better than again draw attention to the minor forms of apparatus, all of which may serve a useful purpose in stimulating interest in the living picture.

Firstly, there is Short's Filoscope. I do not see it shown for sale to anything like the extent it deserves. I suppose everyone has seen these articles : if not, they should. The instrument consists of a little book of views, photographically obtained, the series being long enough to run for some twenty seconds. The action is very regular, the leaves being turned over by pressure on a metal lever and escaping from under the edge of a metal casing. They are cheap enough ; they retail at sixpence now I believe and a good choice of views is afforded; in fact with a large demand most of the standard subjects could be supplied. I noticed one in Paul's window done from one of his films, showing King Edward and the Queen—that, for instance, should be very popular. As for their effectiveness, the younger generation of my own household never tire of seeing Chirgwin divest himself of his coat and truly marvellous hat—and I presume that equal amusement would be afforded to others.

Then there is the Praxinoscope. I remember having one of these when they first appeared. Then they died out ; but during the last twelvemonth they have revived, and a good many may be seen for sale—in other windows than Opticians'. The instrument retails, in varying sizes and styles, from 2s. 6d. upwards—but I think that an energetic manufacturer might do much to improve and popularise it. As at present sold, the Praxinoscope (I believe they are all of French make) is accompanied by coloured lithographic subjects—very well printed, but after all not ideal, at anyrate in my opinion. There is no reason why the owner of a Praxinoscope should not be afforded a considerable choice of photographic subjects. The optical principle of the Praxinoscope is unique ; in that while giving appearance of motion, persistence of vision is not called into play. We can, therefore, take any cycle of motion, such as a dance, jump, etc., and from an ordinary cinematographic slip of say sixteen views per second, select the most effective single views to cover the cycle. These, mounted as a Praxinoscope band, will reproduce the motion ; but being fewer in number than in the cinematograph, the spaces of time between the pictures will be greater, and the motion somewhat more jerky. Nevertheless, as one picture

FIG. 8.—" THE KINORA."

is always on view there is no flickering effect. It seems to me that such photographic slips could easily be made, and if printed in half-tone could be retailed at a low figure. Strangely enough, I have never yet seen a Praxinoscope at work in a shop window. Yet it seems as though it should prove an attraction; it could easily be driven, regular speed is not important, and the picture can be seen from all points of the compass—there is nothing of the peep-show about it.

Lastly, there should be some sale for a good inspection apparatus, suitable for those who wish to have a selection of popular views without projection, a sort of living drawing-room album. Such an instrument is the "Kinora," fig. 8, which has not yet, so far as I know, made its appearance in England, though it has been on sale for some time in France. I am not sure, but I believe the English rights are held by the Biograph Company, who perhaps are so busy, with bigger things, that they have not time to bring it out. If so, it is a great pity; for I think the Kinora would be popular. A reel of views, just as in the ordinary mutoscope, but on a reduced scale, is inspected through a magnifier. Each reel contains about 600 views and is practically equivalent to a fifty-foot film as usually shown. The reel is placed in the machine and turned backwards so as to carry all the cards behind the escapement stop. This action winds up a spring, which then drives the views forward at a regular speed for inspection. There must be many who would never take up animated photography and who would not even purchase a projection apparatus, who would, nevertheless, welcome such an instrument as the "Kinora" if they could procure reel-views of notable events, such as the Queen's funeral or war pictures. Indeed, if an Optician could place a fair number of these machines in his locality, he might do very well by running a circulating library of views—it is only an expansion of the lantern-slide hire idea. Anyway, I hope to see the "Kinora" come out this summer. If it goes well in France, why should it not do the same here?

It may be that, after all that I have said, someone may think that I am attaching too much importance to my subject, and will be disposed to remind me that the living picture is "not the only pebble on the beach." That view is correct, of course; but I still think that more attention might well be devoted to the subject—and I am sure that the retail optical Trade has it in its power, not only to popularise a pursuit which I have found deeply engrossing, but also to establish more firmly a new and fairly lucrative source of business.

ROUND THE WORLD FOR THE BIOGRAPH

Mr. Dickson, with tent and apparatus, at Chieveley Camp in Natal.

By H. L. ADAM.

Illustrated with Photographs by the Biograph Company.

IT is doubtful if there is a more confirmed cosmopolitan than Mr. W. K. Laurie-Dickson, one of the four gentlemen who were the initiators of the Biograph.

From Land's End to John o' Groats, from China to Peru, on the sea and on the land, in the air above and under the earth beneath, this indefatigable photographer has travelled with his apparatus. And please do not imagine that by "apparatus" I mean the ordinary camera on a tripod, but implements weighing some hundredweights, with batteries, generators, etc., which, when set going, roar like a locomotive.

Many and varied have been the experiences encountered by

Queen Victoria driving in Windsor Park.

Mr. Dickson, in all parts of the world, in his efforts to obtain exceptional subjects for the Biograph.

At the same time he creates a realistic, permanent, and unique record of great events in the lives of great people.

I presume nobody will be prepared to deny that the "Biographing" of Leo XIII. was the greatest thing ever accomplished in photography.

It must be borne in mind that for eight years the Pope had not given a sitting to even an ordinary photographer, the exertion of so doing being considered too great. But Mr. Dickson would not be denied, and, with a liberal exercise of patience and diplomacy. performed what was deemed to be the impossible.

Let the traveller and diplomat narrate his experiences in his own words. We shall find him an excellent cicerone.

"Some time ago," says Mr. Dickson, ' an exhibition of Biograph pictures was given before President McKinley and some specially invited guests at Washington. Among the latter were the Apostolic Delegate, Mons. Martinelli, Cardinal Gibbons, and others. It occurred to these gentlemen that if the Biograph could obtain some pictures illustrative of the daily life of the Holy Father, it would be an excellent thing for the Roman Catholics of America, thousands upon thousands of whom would never otherwise be enabled to receive the Pope's benediction.

"The idea, once mooted, was not long being acted upon. I soon after set out for Rome, with the firm determination of obtaining access to the Vatican, and possessing myself of the coveted pictures. I was armed with powerful credentials in the shape of letters from influential ecclesiastical personages. Arrived there. I found that I possessed rivals in the field from England. France. and Germany.

"Although. at this period, I was conversant with several foreign languages. I knew nothing of Italian. It was almost essential that I should remedy this defect. I set myself to learn the language. and practically mastered it by the time I needed it.

"The Pope spoke French, but very little English—just a few words.

"I was four months in Rome before I succeeded in obtaining the Pope's consent. During that period I carried on constant negotiations with Count Sodarini. the chief officer of the Papal Court. But I owe my eventual success to the friendly offices of Count Pecci, the Pope's nephew, and an officer in the Pope's household.

"Well, altogether I took 17,000 pictures, the first series being while the Pope was on his way to the Sistine Chapel. On this occasion, for the purposes of the picture, the top of the Pope's carriage was let down, the

A unique photograph of one of the most famous scenes in the Transvaal war : The hoisting of the Union Jack on the Town Hall at Pretoria.

first time for twenty years. Two other scenes were taken in the upper Loggia of the Vatican.

"I found the Pope a most lovable man, and owe much to his kindness. He took a great interest in the pictures, and on one occasion, having received some prints from London, I showed them to him. He was delighted, and exclaimed 'Wonderful! wonderful! See me blessing!'—referring to the one representing him giving the Apostolic blessing—and turning to Mons. della Volpa, he added. 'How splendid you look!' All the time he held my hand, which he pressed affectionately.

"To my application for the last picture the Pope demurred. 'What, another!' said he. I pressed my request, explaining that it would bring joy to the hearts of many of my countrymen if he would graciously condescend. And he did.

Queen Victoria visiting Eton College.

"After I had taken the first picture I was asked to give a guarantee that I would not photograph any of the Royal family in Rome. I offered my earnest assurance that I would carry out their wishes, and this materially assisted me in the remainder of my task.

"A visit to the Vatican gives one a vivid idea of Papal state, with the Swiss, Noble, and Palatine guards. In taking the views I had to don a black robe. None of the views may be shown in a place of secular amusement, nor without the authority of the Church.

"Altogether my visit lasted six months, and cost £1000."

Mr. Dickson will now tell us how he photographed Queen Margharita of Italy.

"While in Rome," continues Mr. Dickson, "I met at a small reception the Marchesa, Lady-in-waiting to Queen Margharita. Naturally the subject of the Bio-

Lord Roberts and his Indian orderly. The Commander-in-Chief has just received a dispatch.

The late President Faure was "biographed" just before setting out on a shooting expedition.

graph came up for discussion, and I ventured to suggest that I should take some pictures of the Queen.

"The Marchesa, a charming lady, was delighted with the idea, and at once offered me her assistance. In view of my promise to the authorities of the Vatican, I could not carry out the idea in Rome, so it was eventually arranged to take place at the Queen's country residence, Villa Marina, Gressany, a mountainous district.

"In matters of this kind one must be patient and wait. So some little time elapsed before I ventured to wire to the Marchesa, reminding her of the

Doctor Jim: a hitherto unpublished photograph.

arrangement, and asking if I should come. Her reply was cordial: 'Yes, come by all means —come at once.' Accordingly I started out with my assistants and apparatus for Gressany. I travelled thus for hours, and at night arrived at a small village at the foot of the mountains. Here I halted, and sought out the Post Office, only to encounter an 'unmitigated staggerer.' A telegram was awaiting me from the Marchesa. 'Don't come— Queen away on a mountaineering expedition.' Here was a dilemma! I had to catch a train at one the next day, en route for London.

"It was a case of

To enable Mr. Dickson to take this photograph, the top of the Pope's carriage was let down—the first time in twenty years.

transit, to take off his hat and pass his hand across his brow. In order to make my meaning clear, I went through the performance with two of my assistants. In the middle of it the President called out, 'But, who am I?' I indicated with a finger that I myself was supposed to be impersonating him.

" It was on this occasion that a curious mishap occurred. Just as the President was about to appear a wire snapped in my apparatus, rendering it useless. Luckily I thought of a silver penknife I had in my pocket, and, whipping it out, made the connection with it, and so saved the situation."

Mr. Dickson relates how he photographed

do or die, now or never. So I decided to push on up the mountains to the Villa Marina, and chance what fell out. After a few hours' rest I sent on the apparatus and followed.

" Finally we reached our destination, and soon after the royal party returned, tired out. I was fortunate enough to encounter the Marchesa, and learned that it was Her Majesty's intention to sleep through the day. I explained my predicament, and the Marchesa, affable and willing as of yore, volunteered to mediate on my behalf. She explained the situation to the Queen, who, accordingly, most graciously agreed to alter her arrangements, and gave instructions to be called at eleven.

" I filled in the interim by getting everything in readiness. It was going to be close work. Prompt to the minute Queen Margharita appeared, and we soon arranged a picture. At the finish I had to go helter-skelter down the mountain, in order to catch my train.

" It was not a very difficult matter to photograph President McKinley, as his brother is a great friend of ours. It was, of course, through him that the matter was arranged.

" The pictures were taken in the garden of the Presidency, at Washington. We had a kind of rehearsal first. I just asked the President, in company with two officials, to walk from one spot to another, and, *en*

General Buller *en route* for South Africa.

Queen Wilhelmina of Holland on the way to her coronation.

consulting him. So for four and a half hours Mr. Dickson possessed his soul in patience tramping up and down the deck. At the end of that period the "Hard Nut" arose and gave the word. The baggage was "shipped," sorted. erected, and covered with a tarpaulin. Exit Mr. Dickson till the following morning.

So far, so good. Mr. Dickson duly boarded the *Olympia* next morning, and encountering the Admiral, informed him he was quite ready. Said Dewey: "Oh! don't bother me." Then ensued the following dialogue: "Come now, Admiral," persisted Mr. Dickson, "I want you to walk from there, along there, seat yourself in that chair and—" "I will do nothing of the sort!" "I'm sure you will, Admiral. That chair is quite as comfortable as the one you are sitting in." "Oh! don't bother me." And, protesting, did it.

Mr. Dickson was, of course, "on the spot" at the crowning of the young Queen of Holland. His efforts to secure a favourable

Admiral Dewey—a performance that presented many difficulties. The popular naval commander is what is frequently referred to as a "hard nut." But Mr. Dickson has quite a healthy and vigorous taste for this class of fruit, possessing some very serviceable "crackers." He set out from London with the avowed and determined intention of "capturing" the Admiral. He had for travelling companions Robert Barr and S. S. McClure. Arrived at Nice he put up at the Hotel Termini, taking an early train next morning for Villefranche Harbour, and finally a boat to the flagship *Olympia*.

Having boarded the vessel, he obtained an audience of Admiral Dewey, who refused point-blank to be confronted with the camera, adding he was tired of photographers. This did not disturb Mr. Dickson, who expected not only one but many refusals, and duly received them.

But perseverance was at length rewarded, and a reluctant consent was obtained. Back went the gratified photographer for his baggage, which was taken to the *Olympia* in small boats. Arrived at the vessel's side, another obstacle presented itself; the Admiral was indulging in his afternoon nap, and the apparatus could not be taken on board without first

The difficulties Mr. Dickson had to contend with before "capturing" Admiral Dewey, are graphically described in the text.

Queen Margharita of Italy was " biographed " at her country residence, Villa Marina, in Gressany.

coign of vantage, throw considerable light on the insatiable cupidity of the Hollander.

" The spot I selected, was a corner house, which commanded a good view of the approach to and entry into the church. The price charged was fabulous, and rose every day on a kind of sliding scale. On the day of the ceremony there were fourteen of us to be passed into the house, and at the last moment the authorities tried to exclude me in order to extort another 50 guldens. I threatened to retire elsewhere with the *whole of the money*, when they promptly conceded the extra. Arrived upstairs I found the window I was to work from covered with a flag. To take this down would have been an indignity, so I tied up one corner and so made a space for the camera."

While in Paris on one occasion, Mr. Dickson obtained an introduction to the late President Faure, who very kindly consented to be " Biographed." It was arranged to take place on a day when the President was out with a shooting party. Every facility was placed in the operator's way, as in the case of the U. S. President.

Another interesting ceremony, at which Mr. Dickson

The Duke and Duchess of Cornwall and York at Oxford.

was present, was the laying of a corner stone of a new barracks at Buda Pesth, by the Emperor Franz Josef. The occasion was made a kind of "meeting of the Emperors," of Russia, Germany, and Austria.

For ten months Mr. Dickson was in South Africa, nearly the whole of which time he boarded, lodged, and trekked with 4.7. He had a very good opportunity of studying the Boer character. In reply to my query as to what he thought of the race, he rather neatly put it thus :—

"I always had a feeling of looking behind me."

Mr. Dickson's account of how he came to sail in the same vessel with Sir Redvers Buller, and of some incidents on the voyage out is interesting.

"It was not till the last moment, that I learned that General Buller was to sail by the *Dunottar Castle*. Immediately I telephoned through for a berth, and the reply came back ' not an inch of room.' I implored them for the love of heaven to squeeze me in somehow, and went forward with my luggage. Fortunately, the Company, with a little manipulation, were able to find a corner for me, and I landed on deck with a sigh of relief.

"The General was very good to me in

Lord Dunraven taking the bearings.

giving me every opportunity to take pictures on the voyage out. On one occasion while I was photographing him, he jokingly threatened that if I did not leave him in peace he would ' throw me over the side.' And on another similar occasion he tried to push the captain in front of him, but I was too quick for him.

" Arrived at Cape Town I had some difficulty in photographing the Boer prisoners on board the *Penelope*, on account of instructions having been given that prisoners were not in any way to be treated with indignities.

"I did not attach myself to any of the War correspondents, as they were subject to such restrictions as would have considerably hampered my movements. So I pushed forward with my own contingent, and was present at many of the principal engagements. I was one of the first to enter Ladysmith with Buller, being just behind the General."

On the return journey in the *Carisbrook Castle*, Mr. Dickson had for fellow passengers Mr. Hofmeyer and Lord Dunraven, the latter of whom always "took the bearings," regularly every morning.

Some time ago at an Aldershot review, which was specially arranged for the Biograph, and at which the Duke of Connaught was present, Mr. Dickson was vividly reminded of the uncertainty of life. This occurred during a charge of some Lancers, who with lances down were coming dead straight at the apparatus.

Instinctively Mr. Dickson realised that "someone had blundered," and was on the point of making a bolt while still he might, when an officer gave the order "Divide !"

Mr. Dickson nearly lost his life while biographing this steam-tug.

Instantly the soldiers split in twain and sped past right and left of him. "It was the most wonderful manœuvre I had ever witnessed," said Mr. Dickson.

At another military display, in France, the photographer confesses that he himself was nearly answerable for the premature quietus of a fellow creature.

It was a charge of Cuirassiers, and as they were approaching, Mr. Dickson waved his hand as a signal for them to take a slightly different direction. They answered to the signal, swerved, collided, and down went one of their number, biting the dust in curious confusion. Up he rose with countenance crimson, and swore only as a trooper can swear. Oil, however, soon fell upon the troubled waters—*palm-oil*. And there was peace.

If Mr. Dickson was born to be drowned, the event should have transpired on the occasion when he "took" Portcoon Cave, Giant's Causeway, where his retreat at a critical moment was nearly cut off by a seventy-feet wave.

Failing this, his drowning should have occurred when he chartered two tugs and two skippers at £5 apiece, and put out into a boiling sea for an "effect."

Apparatus and operator were both lashed down, the latter horizontally. The whole thing was so "lively," that the hardy skippers agreed that there "wasn't no fun in it," and hinted that the £5 each hardly "met the case." But £10 each did.

Mr. Dickson has been favoured by several members of our own Royal Household, the Dukes of Cambridge and Connaught having been particularly kind to him. In addition to being cosmopolitan, he is also protean, and always adapts himself to his surroundings.

When he is taking military pictures he is a soldier; when he is on the sea he is a sailor; when he is in ecclesiastical company he is a theologian; when in royal spheres he is a courtier; when in the world of music he is a musician (he has an amateur orchestra of forty-two instrumentalists in America); and when with Legislators he is a politician. At all times he is a student. He is conversant with the technicalities and customs of all communities.

When he finds himself in a strange place, he first addresses himself to the Mayor, and invariably succeeds in obtaining what he wants.

"Finally let me tell you," he said to me, "that I never quake at a task, I go right at it. The man who apprehends a failure will probably meet with one."

Lord Roberts with his staff at Bloemfontein.

THE

SHOWMAN

An Illustrated Journal for Showmen and all Entertainers.

VOL. I.—No. 1.   **SEPTEMBER, 1900.**   ONE PENNY.

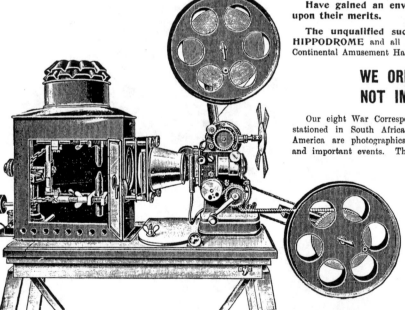

How War Films are Made.

DURING the last few months many of our readers have, doubtless, been engaged in showing war pictures of some kind, and they have probably come to the conclusion that the public most appreciates the cinematograph views. Even those who have not been directly connected with the cinematograph will be interested to hear some details of its doings in South Africa, as films having reference to the war in that country, have recently taken a large part in the programme at popular entertainments.

Messrs. Rosenthal & Hyman of the Warwick Trading Co., Ltd., 4 and 5 Warwick Court, High Holborn, were the only cinematographers who succeeded in getting to the front and remaining there. They were recognised by the War Office, so probably met with but little opposition from zealous officials, though they were occasionally reminded with tender but firm accents, of the home-made red tape, we know so well. In spite of all we have heard and read on the subject, it must not be imagined that these films are " faked," there is very much of the real thing about them, and the difficulties encountered by the cinematographer in warfare are by no means imaginary.

The method adopted by Mr. Rosenthal for conveying his luggage was a great factor in his success as it enabled him to keep ahead of the troops and come in for all the best scenes and most interesting events. All the apparatus was strapped on

Mr. Rosenthal.

the back of one mule, while another was used for personal luggage. When long marches were expected, both mules were used with a waggon, but as soon as more rapid progress was necessary, the waggon was out-spanned and left behind.

Concerning instruments, we hear that Mr. Rosenthal has one for 165 feet of film, and another carrying 650 feet, besides the tent, portable dark room, and a few chemicals for testing the film before sending it home. Our first illustration gives an excellent portrait of Mr. Rosenthal in his South African *get up*.

The work is not lacking in disappointments, and some of the best sets of films mailed to London were destroyed on the way. One series comprising an interview with Sir Alfred Milner and Lord Roberts, at Bloemfontein, was despatched by the *Mexican*, and the fate of that ship, which went down shortly after leaving Cape Town, was of course shared by the films so that a very interesting set of pictorial records lies concealed by the briny waves. Another set taken at Bloemfontein included " Hoisting the Union Jack," " The Balloon Contingent," " Entering Bloemfontein," &c., but unluckily this consignment was sent down by the convoy which the Boers captured, so this also was lost.

As far as comfort is concerned our friend seems to have fared better than the ordinary Tommy, though tinned meat and hard biscuits does not sound an appetising menu. Morning toilet on the Veldt, of which we give a picture, is rather a Bohemian performance, and does not turn out the

Troops Crossing a River.

finished man in immaculate Piccadilly attire. Such trifles are, however, insignificant beside the real dangers which the operator must encounter, and Mr. Rosenthal had some narrow shaves. When crossing the Vet river a shell exploded just in front of him, and while outside Pretoria watching a gun at work, a shell burst in the midst of the group, scattering it with all speed. On one occasion when a new field gun was being tested, someone had forgotten to take out the loaded cartridges, and the gun was to come down the hill to be fired in front of Mr. Rosenthal's camera. However, the gun capsized and the charge did no more than tear up the ground for some distance. If the programme had been carried out accurately, both camera and operator would have been sent to "kingdom come" sooner than they either expected or desired. Soon after crossing the

Rhenoster river, the nigger youth who attended to the mules, caused a disturbance. Mr. Rosenthal was aroused from his siesta by the news that the boy had found a Boer legacy in the shape of dynamite, and was dancing about with his arms full of it, regardless of the fact that it would explode if he dropped it. Slumber was no more for our friend, who observed the nigger making for him, needless to say his retreat was speedy, and at a safe distance he induced the boy, with convincing tones, to dispose of his treasure elsewhere. Later on when Mr. Rosenthal and Mr. Bennett Burleigh of the *Daily Telegraph* had outmarched Lord Roberts' column by some distance, they obtained some Kaffir corn for the mules. The boy after feeding the animals, gave them some water, an almost fatal proceeding, as the corn swells so much. The same day, they trekked on till four o'clock in the afternoon, when a homestead was reached. This was occupied by British scouts, who told the

Morning Toilet on the Veldt.

correspondents they must retire about five miles, as the Boers were numerous about there. By this time the mules were in a bad way, and one of them wanted to lie down. With great difficulty, and many blows, they were got back to the British lines and much to the relief of their owner managed to survive, as it would have been impossible to get a substitute at this time.

Among the numerous films sent home one of particular note is " The surrender of Kroonstadt to Lord Roberts," it is an excellent record as well as one of the finest films we have seen. Apart from historic value, it is a very interesting picture and is certain to be in demand for some time to come.

Britishers are always ready to applaud the doings of their heroes, and while sitting in comfortable chairs they will feel a virtuous sensation of patriotism, which makes them thoroughly appreciative of the show.

After the occupation of Pretoria there was little of importance for the cinematograph to do, so Mr. Rosenthal returned home, only to receive instructions to depart for China. Fully equipped, this enterprising cinematographer is now well on his way to the Far East.

The difficulties of obtaining animated photographs at the front are undoubtedly great, but the reward is found in the reception which the British public gives to the picture history of warfare.

THE WORLD'S HEADQUARTERS FOR.

Animated Photography.

EVERYTHING OF THE LATEST AND BEST IN

Bioscope Projectors and Cameras, Lanterns, Electric and Limelight Accessories, etc.

WARWICK FILM SUBJECTS & FILM STOCK

Are famous the World over.

When you buy an outfit you naturally expect to meet with success in your exhibits. Success is only assured by using "Warwick" product.

SEND FOR CATALOGUE (300 PAGES).

The Warwick Trading Co., Ltd.,

4 & 5 Warwick Court, High Holborn, London, W.C

Telegrams: COUSINHOOD," LONDON.

Printed and Published by the Proprietors, MARSHALL & BROOKES, Harp Alley, Farringdon Street, London E.C

William Clark.

OUR illustration is a group belonging to the show of that go-ahead and enterprising amusement caterer, Mr. William Clark, of cinematograph fame. It is an old saying—and no doubt a true one—that showmen are born and not made; and the subject of our remarks is one of the born school, for what is not known to him in the show business is not worth knowing. The group shown is a typical parading group of his, and their "Khaki" turn out (the first on the road, we believe) created not a little sensation when first produced.

From the ghost show, formerly owned by his father—who, we believe, is still hale and hearty, though about eighty-five years of age—Mr. Clark, who succeeded the father in his business, soon saw the vista of success open before him in the then almost unknown, and at the time marvellous cinematograph, and seizing the opportunity, he has never looked behind him.

Clean and bright both inside and out, his show is not only a credit to himself and family, but to the whole of the travelling world, and has on many occasions when patro-

CLARK'S CINEMATOGRAPH Co.

Referring to "M. W's" remarks in "Cinematograph Notes" two week's ago respecting a descriptive lecture and incidental business during the run of a film, we may mention that from the first production of the cinematograph, this has been adopted by Mr. Clark, he having the good fortune to possess, besides a qualified lecturer, an orchestral piano, which is well manipulated by a skilled musician; in addition to which, an efficient staff is always on hand who can attend to the incidental items which make such a feature of this show. "Up to Date" is his motto, and he never spares any expense to bring his renowned exhibition to a standard of perfection which has been the envy of numerous cinematograph exhibitors who have been from time to time engaged at the various theatres and halls in his track.

nised by the mayor and councillors in various towns he has visited, done more by its eloquent silence than columns of paper matter in elevating the occupation or calling of a travelling showman in the eyes of the powers that be.

Mr. Clark has not forgotten in his successful moments that one word "charity," and many a fund and institution has received substantial pecuniary help from benefit performances given in his booth. May his success continue as he deserves.

We may mention as showing the healthy life they must lead, that there are four generations of the family who have been brought up on the road, and are still in the best of health.

THE SHOWMAN, July 26, 1901.

SHOW-LIFE SECRETS

THE ~

SHOWMAN

An Illustrated Journal for Showmen and all Entertainers.

VOL. II.—No. 34. [All Rights Reserved] JULY 26, 1901. [Registered at the G.P.O. as a Newspaper.] TWOPENCE.

Music and "Effects" in Cinematography.

By T. C. Hepworth.

IN no class of entertainment is the help of good music and well-executed "effects" more valuable than in conjunction with "animated pictures." First, with regard to music. It has the initial advantage of covering the chattering of the machine, which fact may remind one of the old picture in *Punch*, in which a society hostess begs a pianist to strike up so that her silent guests may begin to talk. Most persons are shy in the matter of conversation, if they anticipate that their remarks, intended for one ear, are to be heard by a number, and they are grateful to the piano for drowning their voices. Such chatterers are of course not musicians, or they would not treat a musician in such a cavalier manner; but that is another story. The accompanist who does the music for the cinematograph must not be too thin-skinned, but must take the position as he finds it; he has to cover the chatter of the machine, just as the unfortunate drawing-room performer must cover the chatter of the assembled guests.

Next, as to the character of the music. Has not Mark Twain written of a pianist who played only too appropriately for a diorama of a sacred nature? We confess that we would rather meet with one of the Mark Twain stamp than with some of the wish-washy key thumpers that it has been our misfortune to come across. His music was certainly "appropriate," but it showed at the same time that he had given a little thought to the work in hand. We have met with players of a different stamp, whose little bits of waltzes, polkas, and popular airs were only less trying than "the little thing of his own," which was only his own because it was too bad to be anybody else's. But the fact is that the good accompanist, like the poet, is born, not made, and such persons are so seldom born that we very seldom meet them. We speak of a piano in connection with this matter, for a piano is usually the instrument adopted for the purpose. It can generally be found in the hall where the entertainment is given, or can be easily hired from the nearest music shop. Sometimes its strains can be augmented by a harp and a cornet, but let us beware of both these instruments, for unless the performers are really competent, they have the power to upset the equilibrium of the most evenly-balanced mind, and to arouse murderous tendencies in the most peaceful among us.

Musicians are notoriously "touchy" people. They take a pride in being touchy, because they flatter themselves that touchiness is evidence of a highly-strung nature. We have often met with such persons, and be hanged to them! —a pious wish which would see them more highly strung than ever they were before. But it is better to have one such person to deal with than three or four; so this is another argument in favour of a single pianist, rather than one augmented by a cornet and harp. But he should be a good one, who can suit the action to the sound and the sound to the action. Moreover, he should know what to do should a film break and an awkward pause ensue. The music should not break as well, but should go on gaily, as if the interruption was a thing intended.

There are plenty of pianists who can go ahead furiously so long as they keep to the beaten track. If they are directed to play so many bars of this and so many bars of that, they are all right, but directly the unexpected occurs, and the thirty bars arranged for must be stretched to sixty, they are utterly done. They cannot extemporise or "vamp" to save their lives. It is just the same with talkers—you meet with hundreds who can speak with fluency about the weather or the chief pictures in the Royal Academy, but as to an original remark, they are quite unequal to it. It is a grand treat to meet with a genius who can sit down to a piano, and as he watches the pictures on the screen, can weave out of the keys a melody exactly suited to each. We have met with such, but all too rarely.

"This may be all very true," says the practical-minded showman; "but what is the use of such perfection? Not one in a hundred among the audience will care twopence about it, or will know whether the music is good or bad!" The practical showman is unfortunately right. At almost any time one may notice in the streets a German band of of five or six performers emitting the most diabolical discords, while all around stand an apparently appreciative audience. It is sad; but if we do our best to teach people to appreciate something better we shall be doing a good work.

Having settled the musical part of the programme to the best of our ability, let us consider what "effects" can be judiciously introduced into a cinematographic entertainment.

Recent distractions in South Africa having called forth a

wave of patriotism which has surged from one corner of our mighty Empire! etc., etc. (for further particulars refer to leading articles in the dailies). This wave of patriotism, instead of damping the ardour of sightseers, as waves will sometimes do, has whetted their appetites for everything in the shape of military and naval life. Hence no cinematograph shows are considered complete without a plentiful sprinkling of the doings of Jack Tar and Tommy Atkins. Look down a list of the films which dealers offer for sale, and you will note that they form an index of the times. " Chinese Mission Houses attacked by Boxers," " Boers blowing up a Railway," " The Siege of Ladysmith," etc., are sanguinary and thunderous subjects, and you must not run them through the machine to the strains of " Where the bee sucks " or " Auld Robin Gray." You must have music of a horribly expectant nature, with plenty of bass in it, and you must have the bang of heavy guns, the pop of the rifle, and rattle of the Maxim. One showman we wot of, who was so conscientious about gun effects, that he had a dozen revolvers all loaded beforehand with blank cartridge, which he and his helpers let off behind the sheet when a cinematograph battle scene was in progress. The cartridges cost half a crown a hundred, but he argued that the smell of the powder, and the natural haze which it raised in the hall, was worth all the money. We venture to think that this is carrying realism to an absurd pitch. A deal table, with a flat lath to smack it with, gives a capital imitation of the rifle report. The performer can see through the sheet where the puffs of smoke come in, and can, with a lath in each hand, be ready for a bang with each puff. The same two laths used alternately, with sufficient quickness, will do admirably for the firing of a Maxim gun.

For cannon shots, nothing is better than a big drum—one of the " kettle " variety perhaps giving a better effect than the ordinary military drum. And it adds to the effect if the bang be lightly repeated, so as to imitate an echo. For anything in the shape of an explosion, such as that in the popular " Explosion of a Motor Car," a splendid effect is secured by banging a big drum with a drumstick held in one hand, while the other hand at the same moment uses the lath on the table as already explained. This procedure

results in a crash as well as a boom, and gives a good idea of the rending sound of an explosion and consequent breakage, as opposed to the simple boom of a cannon. We may note here that we heard once the boom of distant minute guns introduced, with marvellous effect, during the showing of the Queen's funeral films, the sounds punctuating the solemn strains of Mendelssohn's funeral dirge.

Another useful appliance which the cinematographer should have at hand is a good bell. A bell of the railway-station pattern is useful for railway scenes, but a church bell is often required. A steel tube hung on a string is all that is wanted, and gives a wonderful note if properly struck with a wooden mallet.

The swish of water, as caused by the dip of oars in a racing scene is well imitated with glass-paper. This should be of medium coarseness, and should be glued on to flat boards with rough handles at the back. A splash in water, like that caused by a diver, is well reproduced by clapping a pair of paper-covered boards, while other hands work the glass-paper board at the same moment. Whistles, of the ordinary sort, as well as bird-whistles are occasionally useful, and sometimes castinets are of assistance.

The clever and resourceful showman will doubtless add many notions to the list of " effects " which we have compiled. One we might hint at. We have always noted the want of some appliance for imitating the tread of marching men, and think that this end might be achieved in the following manner. Take a piece of wood, say 5 ft. long and 2 in. in breadth, and bore $\frac{3}{4}$-in. centre-bit holes at intervals of 2 in. along its entire length. Into these holes put turned rods of a length varying from 3 in. to 1 ft.. and let them fit so loosely that they will readily run in and out when the piece of wood is turned over. To prevent them falling out, these turned rods should have a button glued on at each end. Now, if this long piece of wood be held horizontally, and turned over and over in time to marching music, the little rods will slip backwards and forwards, and as they are not quite of the same length, they will imitate very nearly the footfalls of marching men. Even among the best-drilled regiments the footfalls are not quite simultaneous, for the notes of the band cannot reach each ear at exactly the same moment.

Cinematograph Show under the new L.C.C. Rules.

Oh! have the audience all assembled?
Have you put the barriers round?
Have you got the hydrant ready?
Laid asbestos on the ground?

Are the firemen standing steady?
Bring the blankets right up here!
Have you got the pails handy?
Is the special exit clear?

Is the fellow there who has to
Watch the films come out and in?
Have you put the fire-proof box on—
Right?—Then let the show begin!

                                    ALPHONSE COUTRLANDER.

London to Johannesburg with the Bioscope.

By J. Johnson Wood.

SINCE my return from South Africa in September last, I have had so many enquiries as to the future of South African show touring, that I write this account of my own experience during the Boer war, which may prove interesting and perhaps beneficial to those contemplating a visit to South Africa.

I need hardly describe the voyage by the Union liner, R.M.S. *Norman*, which was a most happy time. We called at beautiful Madeira, and had eight hours' stay there. Leaving Madeira behind us, our next sight of land was Cape Verde. On the sixteenth day land was again seen, this time my destination—Cape Town was in sight. It was not what I expected, but I found business was going apace, as in England, and theatrical enterprise doing a fair trade.

My opinion of South Africa for the up-to-date showman is that it forms a perfect " gold mine," providing he takes notice of the various items I mention.

First: Theatrical companies going with the intention of touring from hall to hall. I strongly advise them to stay here. It is no good unless you engage with Mr. Frank de Jong to give you a tour, as undoubtedly he appears to be the Theatrical King in South Africa. I write this more for an enterprising showman, who will take his own pavilion, and machine and films, and above all, a first-class electric-light waggon plant. Now for the showman who will do this, charging admission of 2/-, 1/- and 6d., there is a mint awaiting him. (I will give the tour to any showman who contemplates going.)

I went with bioscope, films, etc., but I was depending on getting electric light at every place, but this was not possible, and more, you cannot get cylinders of gas out there, as in England; you must either carry your own generators or electric plant—the latter I advise. I myself did very well, being the first to exhibit the bioscope in South Africa, and opened in Cape Town, showing the following pictures, viz., "The late Queen's Visit to Dublin," "Diamond Jubilee Procession in London." My great hit was colour animated photography, exhibiting the pantomime of "Cinderella" in colours, and La Loue Fuller dance in colours.

I also showed in Cape Town on July 20th, "Diamond Jubilee winning the 1900 Derby Race," and other up-to-date pictures. I made a tour of the following places, but I had to miss hundreds, as I could not obtain electric current. The show was successful at Grahamstown, Port Elizabeth, East London, Durban, Marizburg, Natal, Charlestown, Aberdeen, and Barberton. Eventually I arrived at De Air Junction, which is an important point, which cuts the journey. From Cape Town you can go on to Kimberley and Bulawayo, or travel wide to Pretoria and Johannesburg. On arriving here I was informed I would not be able to reach the Gold City for at least six months, so I at once decided to visit the Diamond Village —Kimberley. Here I met with a most enthusiastic reception, for I discovered I was the first entertainer to show in Kimberley since the relief. I did a successful three weeks here.

I then thought of a trip up to Bulawayo, but while I was arranging it I discovered that the military authorities had stopped further passenger traffic north of Kimberley; so I was done again.

Being a bit tired—or shall I say homesick—I returned; but if I had had a pavilion and electric plant, and an agreeable partner, I would be there yet. I often wondered if I would see Pat Collins unloading a gondola set at Cape Town Docks, but I didn't, although I saw Bominica's Imperial Circus arrive per the SS. *Goth*. Then I came down to Cape Town, where for two or three weeks I indulged in a slack time at the International Hotel, The Gardens, Cape Town. The proprietor, Mr. W. T. O'Callagan, made me very comfortable; and I may mention this hotel is equal to any of our English ones — beautiful gardens, etc., and band during the open-air tea, etc.

Eventually I booked my passage home per the Royal Mail *Dunvegan Castle*, and with the permission of Captain Rendle, gave exhibits on board. In conjunction with Mr. Franks Piper, the celebrated trick banjoist, I gave a very laughable sketch, entitled "The Breach of Promise," in which I enacted the part of Julia Brown, the plaintiff, causing much merriment. And I had, with some brother and sister artistes, a very happy voyage home, arriving in Southampton waters on Monday morning, September 3rd, 1900.

So though my trip to Johannesburg did not quite come off, I very nearly got there.

---->o<----

Animated Pictures and Elocution.

IN these days of go-a-head enterprise, when the ever increasing forces of competition to be first and foremost in the market with new and attractive ideas, calculated to take on with the public, the keenest forethought and study is necessary to ensure success. Amongst showmen, as amongst other professions and callings, the necessity for efficiency is apparent. The interest of the public must be aroused to enthusiasm ; from time to time this has been done with more or less success, but never in the annals of shows was there ever anything to surpass the cinematograph, but even this lacks the powers of maintaining the enthusiasm once gained.

By the introduction of the cinematograph, which is the outcome of scientific processes of photography, all kinds of life and the activity of everything material, from all quarters of the world can be brought within the sight of everybody. Thus far it is interesting ; people like pictures, and especially animative ; but pictures of the same subjects must not be introduced too often or they become stale and out-of-date ; so long as there is a continuous flow of new subjects being imparted into an exhibition, the interest is unbounding and the show will be patronised, but to keep up a continuous stock of films of the latest subjects is no small item.

As a well known owner and exhibitor of cinematograph and lime-light illustrations, I speak with knowledge from practical experience, and I affirm that the present system of exhibiting animated pictures (to be up-to-date and appreciative) is a most expensive one, and to a small showman these heavy expenses, in many instances, make the whole concern unprofitable.

The real question at issue, and one that is agitating many minds, is how to attain that high standard of efficiency that will produce the maximum of public interest and enthusiasm at a minimum cost. There is nothing calculated to delight the public more so than the cinematograph, but how is it that a film after a few times shown before the public will so soon lose its prestige, the film may still be a good one, but in the public eye it has become stale and out-of-date. The reasons are obvious. The public are not so much interested in the history of the subject, for there is no story attached and no ability displayed.

They are interested in the picture only, and, when having once seen they lose interest and demand fresh pictures. I have on many occasions when giving a cinematograph entertainment of films which in the eyes of the public have become out of date and failed to give satisfaction, selected a set of lantern slides and give a recitation from G. R. Sims's or some other famous author's works, illustrated by lime-light views, and I have always found it an admirable means to stir up enthusiasm.

A friend of mine—an elocutionist and actor of no mean ability—recites Shakespeare's plays with the aid of limelight views, and never fails to interest his audience. A good reading by an able elocutionist, illustrated by good pictures, not only pleases the audience as far as the pictures are concerned, but it tells a good story and displays ability. It not only pleases the sight of the individual, but it pleases the brain as it makes him think of what he has seen and heard ; the impression and interest gained is based on more lasting feeling.

Then why not animated pictures to illustrate plays, readings, and songs. Everybody must admit that the cinematograph as an interesting illustration is far ahead of lantern slides ; then if films were produced to fit in with some of our best plays, readings, and songs, in my opinion it would arouse greater interest in the minds of the public and be more profitable to entertainers.

Amongst the stocks of the various catalogues published by film makers, there is not the least doubt that films could be selected to answer the purpose of this suggestion. It may be that two or more films may be required, and a few slides to run in now and again to fill up and make the turn complete. In every case that necessitates the placing of films in the machine one after another, I would suggest that there be an additional lantern and operator to work a set of slides to fill up the time required. On several occasions I have noticed the audience have to face a blank sheet, which tends to dampen their interest in the entertainment.

The greatest difficulty which might present itself to the reader's mind lies in the regularity and exactness between the animated pictures and the reading—the operator and the elocutionist ; but this difficulty can, in my opinion, soon be overcome by a little practice and rehearsal.

window? said Walker. Yus! gasped our trembling penny-a-liner. Then flee for your life or out you go. We don't believe in giving ourselves away, so don't tempt us to shed " blud " by asking. But I come from THE SHOWMAN, our individual explained, and then it seemed to dawn on the interviewed that he was not dealing with a rival business house but with the press—the mighty press. Apologies ensued, and all was calm and bright once more, and the two settled down to ferret out some interesting matter to serve up in the columns of THE SHOWMAN. It seems that some seven years ago, animated pictures made their first appearance in London at the Alhambra. Within three months after that date, Mr. Walker, seeing the immense possibilities of making a remunerative business out of the sale of cinematograph films, joined partnership with his present colleagues, and they started trading with a capital of £500. So quickly did their business increase that they were not very long before their money invested in films amounted to the substantial sum of £10,000. Their method of doing business is very simple. They buy a quantity of each film that is any good from almost every maker in the trade. On their books they have a number of customers who each week require an entire change of films, so that they can give a different entertainment every seven days. There is no compulsion to have what films Messrs. Walker & Co. choose to send you, for the showman can select his own. Most of the customers, however, prefer to leave the selection to the firm, just instructing them to send comical, trick, war, or other pictures, just as may be wanted. For this, their charge is very moderate. In fact, Mr. Walker assured our representative that for one guinea a week a splendid show of films could be hired.

Walker, Turner & Dawson are well known as first-class operators, and their services are requisitioned by almost every entertainment agent in London, doubtless on account of the excellence of the show they give and the constant variety of the films they project. Roughly speaking, the apparatus and films they take for an ordinary one hour's show, is valued at no less than £450, and when such an exhibition can be procured for a few guineas, it is no wonder that their time is very much taken up. " We do not care how far we go to give a show," said Mr. Walker. " In fact, last Easter Monday I gave a display at the Devonshire Park Theatre, on the Tuesday at the Pier Pavilion, Aberystwith, on Wednesday at Hyde Park Corner, on Thursday at Liverpool, and back again in London showing on the Friday and Saturday." It will thus be seen that the firm is composed of energetic men who will work as hard as ever they can without grumbling, and it is a policy of the firm never to leave off until all the work of the day is finished.

" Do you think that the cinematograph is only a momentary craze that will wear off in a few years when something more startling comes along ? " enquired our man.

" Oh, no ! there is no such possibility. The cinematograph will certainly get much more common, in fact, it will take the place of the magic lantern, but it will never die out. All it wants now to bring it even more to the front is better facilities for the hire of films, for some of them are much too dear for any ordinary showman to purchase right out on account of their so soon getting stale. We intend doing all we can to popularise this branch of the business, and everything seems to point to success."

" You do a lot of business with the people who attend fairs, do you not, Mr. Walker ? "

" Yes. The cinematograph seems to have been a veritable saviour to showmen. It has done much to build up the reputation and the fortunes of hundreds and hundreds of those who might otherwise have had unprofitable seasons."

" Yes, Mr. SHOWMAN, I can testify to that !" and our man looked round and discovered the genial Irish showman, Mr. Mullen, who went on to say : " After I returned from South Africa I toured the fairs with my swing boats,

The House for Films.

WHERE shall I seek a welcome next, soliloquised our " special," as he stood chewing a toothpick outside the Journalists' Arms in Fleet Street. Ha, ha ! a thought, quoth he, and as quickly as his inspiration came he was in a 'bus and on his way to Holborn. Johnny Walker, please ! No, beg pardon, didn't mean that at all, you see, Johnny Walker's our editor's favourite medicine—I really wanted to see the boss, Mr. Walker, if you please. The clerk in the office of Messrs. Walker, Turner & Dawson bowed, and assured our man that the senior partner of the firm was in, and that if he would step this way, etc., etc. At last the two were face to face—Mr. Walker and that eminent personage who condescends to collect a little copy for the readers of this paper. They bowed. Mr. Walker enquired what our representative wanted, and that mere worm replied that he was a man who wanted but little here below, adding that he generally managed to get it, especially at his boarding house. On the present occasion he had come for information explanatory of Messrs. Walker, Turner & Dawson's marvellous success, and for a detailed account of how they raised their business to its present pinnacle of prosperity. See that and just lately decided that I would " chuck " that business and go in for a cinematograph. Not knowing anything about the business, I didn't know how to set about the buying of the machine until I got the " Birthday " copy of THE SHOWMAN. I immediately went and bought a £50 machine from Wrench, and have just spent a large amount on films with our friends here. It might be of interest if you just mentioned that I am off to Australia to-morrow, and am now regularly taking in THE SHOWMAN with the intention of purchasing some more novelties as soon as I see what the country is like there. That's what your paper has done for me."

Beaming with pride at hearing such praise bestowed upon the journal he represented, our man suggested wishing Mr. Mullen " Good bye and good luck " in a—but that's a story to be told some other time.

----->o<-----

MECHANICAL EFFECTS AND MOVING PICTURES

A PROFITABLE INNOVATION.

BY THE EDITOR.

ALTHOUGH moving pictures are a feature of the entertainments in the U.S.A., the latest departure has doubly popularised them. Mechanical surroundings have been introduced, which in themselves are marvels of originality and appeal to the craving for "something fresh," which is essentially a trait in the character of the American people. The idea has been to surround each subject with the characteristics peculiar to it, and these, combined with the pictures, make a wonderful impression on the minds of the spectators, the realism being so great that it is almost impossible to define where the actual illusion starts and where the reality finishes.

In many towns a store has been gutted and the stranger is surprised to find what looks like the rear of an American train. Piles of luggage, signals, the inevitable bell, the ticket collector, collector's hopper, men in railway uniform, the Pulman conductor, and other etceteras that make up a railway depôt are there, and the stentorian tones of the conductor "All aboard for San Francisco" or whatever other place is to be visited, add a realism that makes one ask how it is that cars are allowed to start from the ordinary roadway. By paying 10 cents for a ticket and mounting a rear-door, one finds himself in an ordinary long travelling car capable of seating 60 to 70 people, two abreast, all facing the engine, with a corridor running down the centre. Gauze blinds cover the windows, lamps are protected with the usual globes, adver-tisements appear on the upper sides of the car, racks for sticks and umbrellas, precaution cords and every conceivable attachment that a car has, make one feel they are starting on a lengthy journey. Suddenly the whistle sounds, the clanging bell, which every American engine carries, the sh sh of escaping steam, the rattle of wheels and the jolting of the car make one still more convinced. Suddenly, as though a window is opened in the front of the car, a panorama is presented, beautiful scenery is passed, and the conductor of the tour shouts out through a megaphone the various points of interest that are passing. As each turn in the rail comes to view the car rocks with an effect that makes one hold his breath, the whistle is sounded in entering tunnels, in fact, the whole show, were it not for the frequent bad films that one meets, makes it impossible to bring the mind back to the fact that we had not gone farther than Broadway.

But this ingenuity is not confined to the imitation of a railway journey. One sees, in another vacant spot, apparently the rear or front of an auto car. There is the horn, the lamps, the steering gear, the body on wheels, in fact, practically one of the huge auto cars that are utilised in the States for taking forty or fifty people on a tour of sight-seeing. Here, again, the heighth of realism is reached. Tours of all the chief towns, such as London, Paris, Berlin, Rome, New York, Washington, Boston, are met on the screen, and are accompanied by mechanical effects that add a realistic charm to the tour, in fact, the idea is carried so far that, by means of electrical fans, the impression of being carried through air is so extreme that we hold our hats and breath and wonder what is to happen next.

Matters, however, do not stop on the earth, for just before leaving the States we were enabled by the moving picture to travel in a balloon over New York. At a huge structure on Coney Island can be found what looks to be the entrance to a balloon shed. Inside is the car containing the various instruments for recording heat, height, etc., anchors, drag ropes, sandbags, provision bags, and many other items add to the effect. After mounting the car, which has two galleries, the people sitting round, look over and apparently down on to Mother Earth, and see stretched under them the city with its river and floating and moving population. Points of interest, such as the Flatiron Building, the Thirty-two Storey Building, the churches, etc., can be located, and the effect of the balloon swaying every now and then, thus causing the car to go quickly over a certain piece of ground and then return to its upright position (caused by a sudden movement of an individual in the car), is so realistic as to be almost painful.

This idea has been developed after much thought, and required the bravery of two individuals, who nearly lost their lives in obtaining the views. Leo Stevens and Tracy Tisdell proposed to take moving pictures for this show, and ascended at half-past two from the Union Gas Works, at 138th Street, in a balloon of 25,000 cubic feet capacity. They took with them one of the finest cameras that it was possible to obtain, and, driven by a brisk south-easterly wind, the balloon was borne towards the Hudson. All went well until it passed by Yonkers, when suddenly, through the cooling of the gas

in the bag, in an eclipse of the sun by a huge bank of clouds, the balloon dropped from 1,400 feet to 650 feet, and the throwing of ballast availed but little, and the contrivance whirled round the cliffs of Bombay Hook Point. It became uncontrollable, and shot downwards into the midst of the jutting rocks of the Hudson. Caught by a strong current all went into the water, Stevens and Tisdell, clinging to the basket, were dragged through the river across dozens of dangerous projecting rocks for about 2,000 feet. Scores of people rushed to the scene, and fortunately among these was Samuel Quinn, who put off in a launch, and guided his craft through the rocks and rescued the men from the basket. Tisdell turned the crank of his picture machine up to the very moment when, in trying to throw it on a ledge of the cliff, he only succeeded in dashing it to pieces on the rocks below. Of course, their original hopes seemed swept away, but a strip of 700 pictures was developed, and, in spite of its soaking, were found to be fairly good.

Notwithstanding the sudden succession of events, when the balloon fell Tisdell found time to close the watertight bag of films. He had been on the point of lowering it to the ground with a rope when the anchor fastening gave way. The bag was dragged over the rocks and torn open, so that it was no longer watertight and the films were soaked, but fortunately some parts made excellent pictures, and these were duly exhibited on the apparatus specially made. Nothing daunted by this experience, another attempt was to be made to obtain suitable views just before we sailed, and doubtless by the time these lines are written the pleasure seekers on Coney Island will have experienced all the sensations and dangers of travelling in the air without any attendant evil results.

LONDON

TRADE MARK.

PARIS

**Managing
Director.**

Revised List of .
High=class Original

COPYRIGHTED . .

Bioscope Films.

URBAN FILMS,

.. depicting Scenes from all Countries.

URBAN Educational Series.
GEO. MELIES' STAR FILMS.

And the best productions of . . .

Messrs. LUMIERE, G. A. SMITH, WEST'S 'Our Navy,'
WILLIAMSON, NORDON, and other Makers.

The CHARLES URBAN TRADING CO., Ltd.

48, RUPERT STREET, LONDON, W.

Telegrams:
"BIOSCOPE," LONDON.

Telephone:
3118 CENTRAL.

CONTINENTAL AGENCY:
Charles Urban Trading Co.,
33, PASSAGE DE L'OPERA, PARIS.

AMERICAN AGENCY:
204, East 38th Street, NEW YORK.

NOTICE . . .

The Film Subjects included in this Catalogue have been copyrighted and are fully protected by law. They are made from Original Negatives secured by us at large expenditure, and we will prosecute anyone who duplicates, deals in pirated copies or uses spurious copies of these Films.

IMPORTANT.

All genuine Urban Films bear a fac-simile of this Trade Mark with counter signature of C. Urban embossed on the beginning of each Film.

All Films of our Subjects not so marked are either pirated duplicated copies or rejected misprints.

You accept all so-called Urban Films without this Trade Mark at your own risk.

TERMS . . .

Our Terms are Net Cash (full Amount) with Order.

Remittances should be made either by P.O. Money Order, Certified Crossed Cheques or Drafts on London Banks.

Remittances should cover Cost of Postage or Forwarding Charges

All films are carefully inspected and packed. We do not hold ourselves responsible for damage or loss in transit.

All claims should be made within 24 hours after receipt of goods, otherwise they will not be considered.

Under no circumstances will we accept the return of Films which **have been marked or damaged by passing through a machine or otherwise,** nor Films from which the Trade Mark has been removed or ends clipped,

URBAN FILMS.

We sell blank Film at a specified price per foot, and guarantee the lengths—but we do not sell Urban, Star or Lumiére Film Subjects in this manner. We supply you with the Subject at a stated price, mentioning the approximate length (for your guidance), and we *guarantee* that for *quality, interest and novelty*, the Urban Films have no equal.

As all "padding" is eliminated, the Film may measure one or two feet *under or over* the listed length.

Urban Films are of absolute Standard American Gauge Perforations and give the steadiest reproductions, furthermore, the subjects are printed on the best film stock obtainable, and do not shrink or become brittle.

The Ideas embodied in Urban Films are original, our Staff of Photographic Operators are Experts, and we do not hesitate to incur any expense in order to produce novel, high class, and interesting results from all parts of the world. Our aim is to maintain a high standard of excellence, accuracy, and quality in production, the subjects being of an elevating or educational character. We do not cater to degenerate tastes. All films herein catalogued preclude senseless frivolity, suggestive or immoral tendencies, the depicting of criminal or depraved subjects.

You can buy Film Subjects at a cheaper price than ours—but you cannot buy high-class Film Subjects at a cheaper price than we quote.

PRICE: URBAN FILMS, Per 50 FEET LENGTH (approximately) 25s. (or 6d. per foot), LONGER LENGTHS IN PROPORTION.

(COPYRIGHT.)

The **" Unseen World "** is one of the most interesting
and instructive series of Pictures of the . . . .
" URBANORA " Entertainments. . . . . .

The Urban Educational Film and Slide Series. . . . .

WE beg to draw the attention of Principals of Colleges, Schools, and Educational Institutions ; the Secretaries and Committees of Natural History, Scientifc, Literary and Photographic Societies, and all who are engaged in Lecturing, Teaching, etc., to the remarkable and unique series of Films and Lantern Slides listed in this Catalogue.

These Films and Slides have been specially prepared to meet the requirements of Educational and Scientific Establishments, Lecturers, etc., and are throughout of the highest standard of perfection. We were the first to apply Animated Photography to the recording of living Microscopic organisms, to Zöology, Botany, Physics, Electricity, Entomology, Anthropology, etc., and the **URBAN=DUNCAN MICRO=BIOSCOPE FILMS** are in demand all over the world. Modern educational methods all prove the importance of teaching through the agency of the eye as well as the ear. A lecture or lesson demonstrated by a graphic series of pictures remains vividly impressed on the mind.

F. MARTIN-DUNCAN, F.R.H.S.,
Director Scientific and Educational Department.

" The Sensation of London."

REPRINTS of Extracts from a few Press Notices
upon the

" UNSEEN WORLD "

SERIES OF PICTURES at the ALHAMBRA, LONDON
by the

URBAN = DUNCAN   MICRO = BIOSCOPE

By kind permission of the Editors.

Unanimous Opinion of the Press and Public:

" SIMPLY MARVELLOUS."

◆

" DAILY TELEGRAPH."

Science has just added a new marvel to the marvellous powers of the Bioscope. A few years ago it was thought sufficiently wonderful to show the picture of a frog jumping. Go to the Alhambra and you may see upon the screen the blood circulating in that same frog's foot. This sounds a trifle incredible, but it is an exact statement of the truth. The new miracle has been performed by the adaptation of the microscope to the camera which takes the Bioscope films. Last night The Charles Urban Trading Co., Ltd , who has taken the photographs, had many other miracles to show and explain to a fascinated audience. Twenty-five minutes, the length of the exhibition, is a long time to give to a Bioscope turn, but **the rapt attention of the audience and the thunders of applause at the conclusion testified to the way in which popularity had been at once secured by these unique pictures.**

" MORNING POST."

There was introduced into the programme at the Alhambra last night **one of the most interesting and certainly one of the most striking turns that has been seen at a variety theatre for a long time.** By means of a new machine called the Micro-bioscope, a very marked development in " animated photography," there was thrown on to a screen a number of pictures showing life at its most minute stage. , ... The series of fifteen pictures dealing with the life of the bee **which were sufficiently charming to have engaged the admiration of Mr. Maeterlinck, sufficiently instructive to have pleased Dr. Watts, and sufficiently wonderful to excite the marvel of a world.**

. . . . .

As a music hall turn **last night's production was an unequalled success. People like to be interested, and they don't in the least mind being nterested by something worth knowing, if only someone will provide it for them.** And surely the performance must also show that the usefulness of animated pictures is not limited to amusement, but that developed on considered lines it must be of value to science, not only as an automatic and unerring record of experiments, but as a potant aid in the dissemination of knowledge,

" THE ERA."

One of the most curious, attractive, and extraordinary exhibitions which have been presented to the public by the aid of that ingenious invention the Cinematograph was introduced to a delighted audience at the Alhambra on Monday evening. . . . . . .

"The unseen World " is marvellous and intricate ; interesting and amusing. It commends itself to every class of audience, and is as beautiful as it is novel and curious. Technically the films are extremely fine, the effective items have been arranged with great skill, and the whole series forms an achievement of which the proprietors may well feel proud.

"THE STANDARD."

Most shows may be described as novel, but none are more entitled to the adjective than that presented for the first time last night at the Alhambra, &c.

"MORNING ADVERTISER."

The "Unseen World" is a scientific novelty, calculated to create a sensation for many weeks, &c.,&c.

The success of the departure was undoubted.

"DAILY NEWS."

Since the introduction of the Bioscope into England there has been no limit to the wonderful moving pictures produced for the edification and amusement of the public, **but those produced for the first time at the Alhambra last night, will probably rank as unique.** The Urban-Duncan Micro-Bioscope series as they are called, consist for the most part of microscopic studies of animal and vegetable life, and are chiefly remarkable for the fact that they include the first set of photographs of living bacteria that have ever been taken, &c., &c,, &c.

"DAILY CHRONICLE."

The Micro-Bioscope Series is undeniably interesting and should draw crowds to the Alhambra for some time to come.

The show is of real educational value, &c., &c.

"THE REFEREE."

Considering the time of year, the enormous business done at the Alhambra last week was truly remarkable. This happy state of affairs **was due in great part to the addition to an already very strong programme of a series of Remarkable Pictures, consisting of microscopic studies of insect and animal life and some particularly interesting illustrations of the incidents in the every-day existence of the ever busy bee.** By means of these pictures the management has contrived to "combine instruction with amusement" for the grown-up Sandfords and Mertons who have patronised the Alhambra, and to administer, as it were, several sugar-coated science pills.

"THE MUSIC HALL."

Yet another triumph for the Bioscope, and the inventor, Mr. Charles Urban, is to be recorded at the Alhambra, where a remarkable series of films, entitled. very appropriately. "The Unseen World," are exhibited to an astonished audience. The "Unseen World" in question is the "land of the microbe," before a combination of the microscope and Bioscope, and its immense possibilities, suggested itself to Mr. Urban some time ago. He immediately set to work upon it, with the triumphant result seen on Monday evening.

"MORNING ADVERTISER."

The "new Science" pictures have caught on in unmistakable fashion, and are drawing all London to Leicester Square.

"FREE LANCE."

The Alhambra has scored immensely over its new and sensational set of microscopic pictures of insect life. All last week the house has been crowded nightly, and this I should think is largely due to the novelty. What a sensation it would have been for the Polytechnic in the old days if it could have had something of the kind ; but perhaps it is as well that it has been reserved for a day when instruction and amusement may be combined in such a pleasant fashion as it is at the Alhambra. **These pictures are really marvellous, and should prove sensationally successful.**

"THE CITIZEN."

Really everybody ought to go and see the latest marvel of science which has been brought to the aid of the Bioscope at the Alhambra. Such enormous strides have been made in the development of this instrument that while a few years ago it was thought wonderful because it showed the picture of a frog jumping, we are now able to see upon a screen the blood circulating in that very frog's foot. The rapt attention of the audience shows that **these unique pictures have at once jumped into popularity.**

" MANCHESTER EVENING CHRONICLE."

From Shepherd's Bush I journeyed to the Alhambra in time to see the first appearance of the Micro-bioscope. **the most recent development of animated photography. To say that it is a wonderful advance is to put it very weakly. The reception. of the pictures last evening proved that this " turn " had come to stay.**

" WEEKLY DISPATCH."

I wonder who remembers that the original Alhambra was a competitor of the old Polytechnic, called the Panopticon, opened with prayer, operated under a Royal charter, and filled with scientific toys ? It does not matter much ; but the thought occurred to me when I inspected Mr. Douglas Cox's collection of scientific toys in the shape of animated photographs the other evening. Science, to be sure, has progressed a little since 1854. The microscopic and bioscopic studies of blood in circulation, vegetation in growth, cheese in animation, and so forth, **that nightly enthral the Alhambra audience are weird and fascinating.**

" NEWS OF THE WORLD."

An important step in the educational development of the music-hall has been added to the Alhambra programme. The limitations of the Bioscope appear endless judging by the **extraordinary pictures of animate natural phenomena** shown by the Urban Bioscope Company. By the aid of the microscope the Bioscope enables the minutest insect life to be reflected on the curtain with a realism quite wonderful. The series dealing with the " busy bee " are quite the most attractive, **though the whole display excites keen attention.**

" THE PEOPLE."

There seems no limit to the possibilities of the " Micro-bioscope," which is now numbered among the most interesting features of the really excellent programme at the Alhambra. The way in which the Alhambra audiences watch the screen during the presentation of the pictures of insect life is significant. Here there is something new to so many that if the educational pill is gilded, as it is at the Alhambra, that is so much gained from the entertainment point of view.

" MANCHESTER GUARDIAN."

One notes with pleasure the new ways of the Bioscope. A series of pictures exhibited at the Alhambra for the first time on Monday marks an epoch in its sensational and often frivolous career. These pictures deal with some plain facts of animal and vegetable life. The delicacy of Mr. Charles Urban's work may be gathered from the fact that the subjects have been magnified anything from 8,000,000 to 36,000,000 degrees. **The pictures had a great reception.**

" EXETER WESTERN TIMES."

It is interesting to find that Science has taken hold of the Music Hall, though Science it is, in a most attractive form. The Bioscope pictures have been received with the greatest favour, and little wonder for it. **They are marvellous.** A series representing the blood circulation of a plant is marvellously **fascinating.** We are all, of course, acquainted with the beautiful pictures of the Rev. Dr. Dallinger, but those shown at the Alhambra **are simply marvellous. It only shows how interesting Science can be made to the masses, if properly applied.**

" DAILY EXPRESS."

The possibilities of the invention are immense. In my belief there will, hardly be a school without a Micro-Bioscope in charge of its science master.

" NATURE."

A correspondent directs our attention to the fact that one feature of the programme at present in force at the Alhambra is an exhibition of the Micro-bioscope. We are glad, like our correspondent that science has being introduced—even in the form of amusement —to those, who in ordinary circumstances, take no interest in scientific matters and think with him that more might be done even with existing resources to bring a knowledge of the advances of science under the notice of the people. " The music halls are," says our correspondent, " being increasingly used for good music ; why not for good science ? The managers will put money into it if the public respond, and no objection will be made to raising the tone of their programme if the houses fill. Those interested in science need not spend the evening there ; they could go to see just what concerned them."

"Court Circular."

Popular Science at the Alhambra."

The yearning for instruction of a popular order which characterises the British race is extraordinary. By playing delicately on this peculiarity, astute speculators have disposed 'of hundreds of sets of curiously-antiquated encyclopædias, and increased by thousands the circulations of unspeakably dull weekly papers of the cheaper kinds. Instruction blended with entertainment and administered in homœpathic doses, will draw money from the major class of Englishmen. Mr. Douglas Cox, the experieneed general manager of the Alhambra, understands his public, **and he is filling that hall nightly by an appeal to this national trait.** We have had remarkable pictures, beautiful pictures, and on the Continent unseemly pictures, through the medium of one or other of the many varieties of Bioscope machines, but it remained for Mr. Cox, to grasp the educational aspect of the invention, and give us a series of pictures which combine diversion with the digestive systems of the insect creation. . . . . . . But more extraordinary than are the publications of these secrets of nature is **the absorbing interest with which they are examined by the audience. During this "turn" the bars are deserted, the promenaders are all facing one way, and every eye in the house is rivetted on the screen.**

"The Tatler."

Science in a Music Hall.

I feel sure that people want to be interested as well as made to laugh, the whole purpose of entertaining being a withdrawal from the worry of the day's work. Now the Alhambra has got **one of the most fascinating turns I have seen** in the shape of a series of bioscoped microphotographs showing all sorts of things that we have seen under a microscope. . . . . . . **The house simply sits breathless as wonder follows wonder.**

One of our greatest scientific authorities in a private letter to the Editor describes this exhibition as "epoch-making" and perfectly splendid.

"Daily Telegraph."

NATURE ON THE STAGE.

(The Article is based on an interview with the late Mr. Douglas Cox, Manager of the Alhambra, London, relative to the interest in Natural History Pictures shown by present day audiences).

This week Mr. Douglas Cox, the Manager of the Alhambra has introduced a new series of what may be called natural history lessons or, as he prefers to term them, scientific pictures. The first experiment in this direction was made last August, with a number of views entitled "The Unseen World." "I was a little in doubt," says Mr. Cox, as to whether they would appeal to the public at large. But from the very first night they were a huge success. They ran for two months, and we have now replaced them by a series entitled 'Denizens of the Deep.' When the first series was running, I received quite a nnmber of letters of appreciation. We described the pictures as 'Nature's closet secrets.' Possibly the average music-hall habitue is apt to regard the microscope as an instrument certain to bore people. But when he sees himself introduced into a new world by its aid, and makes the acquaintance of a lot of "funny little beggars" whose existence he never suspected, he finds himself imbibing knowledge, and doing it under seductive conditions. The "popular lecture," with his accompanying slides, would be regarded as intolerable. At the Alhambra the living picture of animal life, with its brief description given in a resonant voice, is quite another story. And it will still be more so when the colours come to do the subject even fuller justice. Mr. Douglas Cox thinks that natural history has a future at the halls.

"Daily Telegraph."

Encouraged by the success of the first series of natural history pictures presented by the Urban-Duncan Micro-Bioscope, the management produced last night a most interesting collection, entitled **"Denizens of the Deep and the Unseen World." More is to be learned in ten minutes of the mysteries of the unseen world below the surface of the waters than half a year's study of text-books, however well illustrated, could teach you.**

"THE GLOBE."

It is obvious that possibilities of the Urban-Duncan Micro-Bioscope are many and varied, for by its means all forms of animal life can be thrown on to the informing screen. Last night a new series of pictures was presented, dealing with various kinds of fish, from the bream and pollock to the dog-fish. conger eel, and the octopus, which are depicted feeding, fighting, and at rest. The views thrown on ths screen are of such a size that every detail can be seen from any part of the theatre. In addition, a number of pictures enlarged from the microscope were shown last night, much to the delight of a large audience. The Zermatt spider, the spider and the fly, and mounting specimens of the volvox glovator **were particularly good.**

"MORNING POST."

The series of Bioscope pictures of spiders, frogs, chameleon and other fearful wild fowl which has **proved so great a success at the Alhambra,** was last night preceded by a set of views of "The Denizens of the Deep." . . . . . **The new views are clever and interesting,** but they tend to confirm the lay view that when strange animals are neither eating or breeding they are fighting.

"DAILY MAIL."

Two novelties were introduced last evening in the London music halls. At the Alhambra the audience studied the habits of fishes and the home life of the spider, the frog. the chameleon, a new Bioscope series—**excellent.**

"THE STANDARD."

During his management, Mr. Douglas Cox has produced a number of good things at the Alhambra, **but nothing that can quite compare with the Urban-Duncan Micro-Bioscope.** By means of this invention the insects, reptiles and fishes are shown with the greatest clearness, and the pictures are such as to interest not only lovers of natural history but the public generally. . . . . . .

"THE COURT CIRCULAR."

The very latest selection of natural history wonders, which appear to be what music hall audiences are most interested in at the moment, are to be seen at the Alhambra, where, on Monday last, Mr. Douglas Cox, presented a new set of views of "The Denizens of the Deep," The views are wonderfully sharp and clear, and the orator, who discourses on the pictures as they are thrown upon the screen, is brief in his remarks and to the point. The popularity of these "turns," though well-deserved, is, when one comes to reflect upon it, **one of the most remarkable developments of the variety entertainment that the age has seen.**

"THE SUNDAY TIMES."

For some little time past the Bioscope pictures at the Alhambra have been particularly strong features in the evening's attractions. To those already popularised are added some illustrating extraordinary phases of deep sea life, giving a wonderful idea of the natural habits of the fish and crustaceans which "Little Mary" would treat with scant consideration. The spider crab, the conger eel, the dog-fish, the lobster, and the octopus are among the monsters of the deep with which we prefer an indifferently intimate acquaintance. Yet the fascination of watching these strange creatures in their own particular element is undeniable. Some clever microscopic pictures illustrate the habits of the minor beasts of prey, and altogether **the management may be heartily congratulated on their additions to their Programme.**

◆

Lack of space forbids reproducing thousands of further Press notices and articles dealing with the wonderful

URBAN NATURAL HISTORY AND MICROSCOPIC SERIES.

NOTE—The Natural History Aquarium and Microscope Series of Urban Films are supplied on condition that they are not resold or exhibited in Great Britain and America, where exclusive exhibition rights have been acquired.

NATURAL HISTORY.

Photographed by F. MARTIN-DUNCAN, F.R.H.S.

ANIMAL, BIRD, REPTILE, AND INSECT LIFE.

*We are much indebted to the **Zoological Society** for their kindness in placing at our disposal every facility for photographing the various Specimens of their wonderful Collection at the **Society's Gardens, Regent's Park, London.***

2000 ... OUR FARMYARD FRIENDS

This Film represents a striking Series of Animated Pictures of Farm Life. First we see beautiful breeds of pigeons gathering on the roof of the pigeon loft, strutting up and down, and eagerly pecking up grain. The scene changes to the poultry run where thirsty chicks are drinking, and others are at their toilet. The ducklings with fussy mother hen are being fed by the children. After meat a long drink say the Indian ducks. The geese gobbling dainty morsels in haste, then march homeward. In the meadows we visit in turn, the cow, her lord the bull, faithful Neddy the donkey, and the mare and foal. Then away to the pig pens where we see a promising litter of sucking pigs and fat mother sow. Lastly " Papa Boar," a hog of gigantic proportions. **300 feet**

2001 ... POULTRY PORTRAITURE

An amusing and popular subject, introducing a number of animated portrait heads of popular breeds of poultry, such as the Wyandotte, Buff Orpington, Minorca, etc. **100 feet**

2002 ... THE WHITE RAT AT HIS TOILET

Showing a pair of white Rats at play, daintily nibbling cheese, and cleaning up after their repast in a very laughable manner. Exceedingly good.   **60 feet**

2003 ... FEEDING PELICANS

This is a splendid and most humorous subject, full of laughable incident and animation. The pelicans rush from their pen and plunge into the well-stocked fish pond, tossing their heads, jostling each other, fighting over the fish, etc.
60 feet

2005 ... THE STORKS' TUG OF WAR

The spindle-legged long billed storks are being fed, when suddenly two of them pounce upon the same fish; round and round they go, tugging and pulling with all their might and main. A very novel and laughable subject.   **50 feet**

2008 ... THE GIANT TORTOISE FEEDING

A striking subject. This huge reptile, probably more than 100 years old, is seen devouring his food, taking great mouthfuls of cabbage. An apple for dessert is a great treat, and he rises up on tip-toe to reach it.   **60 feet**

2010 ... THE GREEDY TOAD

The greedy toad devouring garden worms, in his haste mis-calculates his swallowing powers. He seizes a giant worm and struggles wildly to swallow it. He gulps and gasps and rolls from side to side, trying to cram the monster worm into his mouth with his thumbs, and going through the most laughable contortions in his efforts.   **75 feet**

2012 ... THE MEAL OF THE AMERICAN TOAD

One of the most laughable and novel films ever produced. A great toad sits waiting for his luncheon, a complacent smile upon his face. The meal-worms arrive, and the toad at once sets to work. with marvellous rapidity he catches them, turning his head from side to side and gulping down the unfortunate meal-worms, one, two, and three at a time, his fat sides heaving with pleasure and excitement   **75 feet**

2014 ... THE BOA CONSTRICTOR

An animated head of a young boa showing the play of the tongue, followed by a view of the wonderful muscular powers of the boa when hanging by its tail. The boa is then seen coiling round a white rat, which shows not the least sign of fear, but plays about closely examining the snakes body, and quite oblivious of the danger. **75 feet**

2015 ... THE DRAGONFLY LARVÆ AND WATER SCORPION

The Dragonfly is seen in an early stage of its life ere the beautiful gauzy wings have grown. Several of these young dragonfly larvæ are seen disporting themselves in the water, darting rapidly about, while joining in their gambles comes the curious water scorpion waving his sharp pointed front legs with which he catches his prey. The last portion of this subject shows the winged and perfect insect alighting on a group of leaves. We were most fortunate in securing this picture as the dragonfly is as restless as it is beautiful. A remarkable film.

100 feet

2016 ... THE FROG

Showing the wonderful life history of the frog in all its stages. First, the tiny tadpole just escaped from the egg then the gradual increase in size of the tadpole and the appearance of the front and hind legs, until Master Taddy drops his tail and appears as a full-grown frog. **150 feet**

2017 ... THE NEWT

This series tells in striking pictures the story of the newt. The young newts are seen in various stages disporting themselves in the water, and presenting a very curious sight, for their lungs are worn outside the body and look like beautiful plumes of feathers. Then the full-grown newt that has lost these external gills and breathes with internal lungs is seen actively swimming about. **150 feet**

2018 ... "POND LIFE"

A splendid series full of life and surprises. Young wingless dragonfly larvæ dart hither and thither through the water. Great water beetles rush backwards and forwards jostling and knocking each other about. Water scorpions wave their sharp pointed arms, and the merry water spiders who build themselves beautiful diving-bell homes at the bottom of the ponds, dance a merry jig, and fight each other. Tadpoles of the frog swing swiftly about, and the strange tadpoles of the newt with external breathing gills or lungs, which look like plumes waving round their necks, gaily disport themselves, concluding with a group of full-grown newts at play **300 feet**

2019 ... MAKING FOUNDATION OF THE HONEYCOMB AND EXAMINING THE COMBS IN THE HIVE

A living picture of the preparation of the honeycomb for the reception of the luscious syrup, and the bee expert is seen examining the honeycombs in the hive, with hundreds of bees at work on the comb and flying round. **150 feet**

2020—

THE LIFE OF THE BUSY BEE.

A series of 15 Pictures showing every phase of Bee Culture.

This is the most perfect and complete series of pictures showing every phase of Bee Life and Bee Culture that has ever been produced. These remarkable pictures, 15 in number, show how the bee farmer tends his hives, and how the busy bee builds its comb, stores its honey, and feeds the young. They were procured through the courtesy of Mr. C. T. Overton, Bee Expert, Crawley.

The model Bee Farm of Mr. Overton at Crawley . . .

ORDER OF PICTURES.

1. **Capturing a Swarm of Bees.**—A large swarm of bees, numbering several thousands, has settled on a branch, from which they hang down in a solid mass. The bee farmer places a basket under the swarm, and by jarring the boughs knocks the bees into the basket.

2. **The old-fashioned Straw Skep.**—With the bees flying in front, busy collecting honey and pollen.

3. **The Platform in Front of the Hive after a Spell of Wet Weather.**—The bees come out of the hive delighted at the prospect of once more visiting the flowers. The kindly bee farmer has placed some honey on the platform, and this the bees greedily suck up before starting off to work.

4. **Bees Carrying away Flowers which have dropped in Front of Hive.**—The bees will not permit any foreign body to remain near the entrance of the hive. A flower falling at the entrance, the bees rush out, wrestle and hustle with it, and finally drag it off.

5. **Skep showing Comb and Bees.**—The skep turned upside down gives a full view of the combs filled with honey. The bees rush up in countless numbers to see why their palace has been inverted.

B

6. **Smoking out the Bees from Skep into Basket.**—The beekeeper smokes the bees to soothe them. He then attaches to the skep a basket, into which he drives the bees.

7. **Inside View of Basket containing Bees.**—The bees, numbering many thousands, have been successfully driven from the skep into the basket, and are now ready for transference to the modern frame hive.

8. **Placing Bees in Front of Hive.**—The bee farmer shakes the contents of the basket on to the platform of the hive and scoops up the bees with his hands to show them the way into the hive. Directly the bees see the way there is a general rush for the new home.

9.—**General View of a Modern Bee Farm.**—The bee farmers are at work amongst the hives. Even the bee farmer is not secure from stings, and we see one of the farmers hastily replacing the lid of the hive and picking a sting off his nose.

Section of Honeycomb with Working Bees . . .

10.—**Bee Farmer Examining Hive.**—The bee farmer is going through a hive examining each section in turn to see how the bees are doing their work.

11.—**Foundation Ready to be Placed into Hive.**—This shows the frame of foundation ready to be placed in the hive for the bees to work up into combs.

12.—**Foundation Worked by Bees.**—Here the foundation has been worked up into comb by the bees.

13.—**Brood Comb with Queen and Workers.**—The Queen, in the midst of a great mass of worker bees, is dropping her eggs into the cells, while the attendants, who crowd round her, feed her with dainties to keep up her strength. She needs constant feeding, for she lays from 1,000 to 2,000 eggs per day.

14. **Comb with Cells Capped.**—Most of the baby bees, or larvæ, have hatched out and been fed, and are now sleeping at the bottom of cells as pupæ. That their rest shall not be disturbed, little waxen doors have been fastened on their bed chambers, or, as the bee farmer says, "the cells have been capped."

15. **Magnified View of Comb.**—The eggs are seen at the bottom of the cells, and the larvæ or young, which look like fat little maggots. The worker bees rush hither and thither poking their heads in at the nursery cells and finding the young. Some of the bees are seen with half their bodies down the cells in the act of disgorging the honey on which the young larvæ are fed.

Supplied only in its complete length of 450 feet.

2023 ... THE HEDGEHOG

This is a very difficult subject to obtain, as the hedgehog spends the hours of daylight asleep, only quitting his nest with the approach of night. The hedgehog is seen curled up in a ball, he then stretches himself, and after a preliminary ramble settles down to a hearty meal. **75 feet**

2025 .. PRIMROSE AND THE BEE

This is a remarkable and interesting picture, showing a bee actually at work collecting honey and pollen, and a large view of a beautiful evening primrose. The bees alight on the petal of the flower and disappear down its trumpet in search of honey, as they emerge from the flower they are seen to come to the surface in a spiry manner, by which means they dust themselves with the pollen of the flower. This subject added to No. 2020 enhances the interest of both. **60 feet.**

An inverted skep of Bees.

2026 ... BEE CULTURE
(Four views)

We first see a modern bee farm, with experts at work examining their hives. A large swarm of bees depending from a bough. A bee farmer is then seen driving the bees out of a skep, preparatory to placing in a modern hive. A fine climax full of movement and interest is gained by a picture of the brood comb and bees at work. **50 feet**

2027 .. BEE LIFE OUT AND IN THE OLD SKEP

The bees fly in front of the old skep, they carry away the dead bodies of their fellow workers and also a flower which has fallen at the entrance of the skep. The inverted skep shows the honey comb and the bees rushing up on to the comb. **75 feet**

2028 ... BEES PREPARING TO SWARM

This is an interesting and instructive picture of bee life showing the agitation of the bees and how they rush in and out of the hive before they quit in swarms, to assure themselves that all is right. **50 feet**

2029 ... PREPARING THE COMB FOR HONEY

The Honeycomb in various stages, with the bees at work, filling the cells with honey and pollen, and capping the full cells. The honey is always stored in the topmost portion of the hive, farthest from the entrance. **50 feet**

2030 ... ENLARGED VIEWS OF HONEYCOMB AND BEES

This presents a scene of great animation. The bees are seen running over the comb, filling the cells with honey, and feeding the young. **50 feet**

B 2

2031 ... THE BROOD COMB IN VARIOUS STAGES
The frame, or foundation, ready for the bees to work into comb. The foundation worked by the bees into brood comb. Later stage of the brood comb when the cells containing the pupæ have been capped and the young bees are emerging from the cells. Workers swarming in a great mass round the queen on the brood comb. **100 feet**

2032 ... DRONE, QUEEN AND WORKER BEE CELLS ON THE COMB
In the spring the bees form on certain parts of the brood comb somewhat large cells in which the drone eggs are deposited by the queen. These drone cells, when the larvæ drones have changed to pupæ within them, are covered over with dome-shaped caps. The queen cells are always the largest that the bees construct, and are generally built upon the edge of the comb; in shape they somewhat resemble a mulberry. Two views of queen cells are shown; in the first the young queen is within the cell, passing through the pupæ stage of her life, she changes from a tiny maggot-like creature to the perfect winged insect. In the second view of the royal cells the young queens have just emerged, and we see the cells with the caps, or doors, removed. The worker bees are seen busy attending to the larvæ or bee comb. The queen bee, who is somewhat larger than her subjects and has a longer body, is seen going over the brood combs depositing her eggs. This last subject is quite unique. **150 feet**

2034 ... THE BABYHOOD OF THE WHITE RAT
Mother rat on the edge of the nest, mounting guard on her new-born babies. A closer view shows the nest so neatly and cleverly constructed from soft sweet-scented hay, and the little naked pink-skinned baby rat only an hour old. The baby rats at a week after their birth, with mother rat at her toilet. The babies, only a fortnight old, have got their beautiful white clothing. At three weeks old they are full of fun and scamper about. **50 feet**

2035 ... THE TOADS' FROLIC
This is a subject full of most laughable, grotesque, and sensational effects. The toads ride along on a tortoise, thoroughly enjoying themselves. Then a chameleon mounts on to the flagstaff carried on the back of the tortoise, and shouts his orders as he rides along to the toad escorting him. Once again the toad, riding along on the trusty steed, and having gone far enough, dismounts. The scene changes, and we see the toad resting after his frolic on top of a skull; while a viper coils its body in and out of the jaws and round the base of the skull. **50 feet**

2037 ... ZERMATT SPIDER, HER NEST AND YOUNG
The Zermatt Spider is one of the largest and boldest of the species, and builds a beautiful and remarkable nest of silk covered with the leaves of the Barberry. The spider deposits her eggs and hatches her young within the nest, only leaving it to seek for food. The spider is seen emerging from her nest; she walks about on the look out for the insects which form her food. Then the interior of the nest is shown with hundreds of baby spiders, just hatched from the eggs, creeping about in all directions. Mama Spider enraged at the opening of her nest rushes up to it and starts to work to repair the damage that has been done. **100 feet**

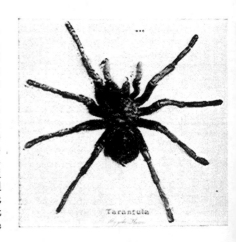

The deadly Tarantula . . .

2038 ... THE SPIDER AND THE FLY

A beautiful picture of the web of the large garden spider, with the spider awaiting the prey. The victims fall into the meshes or the wonderfully constructed web, and are at once attacked by the spider, overcome, and swathed in silk. So rich is the harvest, that a great spider from a neighbouring web is attracted upon the scenes, rushes on to the web, and fights and drives off the rightful owner, who beats a hasty and ignominous retreat. During the scuffle for the booty, the web is badly damaged and torn asunder. **125 feet.**

2039 ... MAN'S BEST FRIEND—THE DOG

Photographed by courtesy Messrs. Russell & Sons, Crystal Palace, and Mr. E. W. Jaquet, Secretary of the Kennel Club.

A grand series of pictures including the prize winners of the following classes :

Mastiffs.	Griffons.	St. Bernards.
Newfoundlands.	Great Danes.	Chow Chows.
Dalmatians.	Borzois.	Whippets.
Pointers.	Greyhounds.	Beagles.
Bloodhounds.	English, Irish and	Foxhounds.
Harriers.	Gordon Setters.	Collies.
Old English Sheep	Otterhounds.	Basset Hounds
Dogs.	Retrievers.	Skye Terriers.
Dachshunds.	Irish Woolhounds.	Airedales.
Clydesdale Terriers.	Poodles.	Welsh Terriers.
Irish Terriers.	Scotch Terriers.	Pomeranians.
Black and Tan Ter-	Deerhounds.	Italian Greyhounds.
riers.	Fox Terriers.	Pugs.
Yorkshire Terriers.	Toy Spaniels.	
Japanese.	Pekinese.	

This series is a general favourite—Fine photographic quality and of exceptional interest.

Supplied only in Complete Length 500 feet.

2040 ... AMERICAN BIG GAME

A fine series of pictures showing the Moose and herd of Buffalo among their natural surroundings. The Buffalo (numbering about 30) are being driven over the plains at base of the Sierras, Canada. Excellent quality—full of interest, expecially as these species are now seldom met with and may soon become extinct.

50 feet

2041 ... SCHWYTZ CATTLE

A herd of Alpine cattle, after being driven up the mountain, are seen grazing on its slopes. Fine cattle picture. **50 feet**

2042 ... PRIZE DOGS AT THE CRYSTAL PALACE

This includes a selection of some of the Champion Prize Winners of the Kennel Club not included in No. 2039. **200 feet**

2043 ... PRIZE CATS OF THE NATIONAL CAT SHOW, CRYSTAL PALACE, 1903

Beautiful long-haired Persians and other favourite breeds of cats are shown, presenting a very charming series of pictures. A novelty. **150 feet**

2044 ... THE COWBOY'S PET BLACK BEAR

A fine young bear, the pet of the cowboys, is seen thoroughly enjoying himself, and being fed with lumps of sugar and other dainties, he thinks nothing of climbing a pole to be rewarded with a tit-bit. **75 feet**

2045 ... THE MONKEYS OF BORNEO

Here we have a young and lazy orang-outang, the great monkey of Borneo. They are very valuable in Europe, although common in the jungle of the wild interior. The natives declare them to be the strongest of all wild animals. They have long and very strong arms, and can pull a man to pieces.

The pig-tailed monkey is a comic fellow, and gets very excited at the sight of an enemy, showing his teeth and rapidly moving from side to side.

2078 The Thirsty Monkey

The "Kra" is another Borneo monkey, small, with a very long tail and gentle ways. He is seen peacefully enjoying himself in the boughs of trees.

100 feet

2046 ... THE KARBAN OR BUFFALO OF BORNEO

The water buffalo is the most useful of animals to the natives of Borneo. Where there is any level road and a cart can be used, the buffalo is put in the shafts; its milk is good and rich. Up country they are used for ploughing and tramping the ground ready for Paddy, and the family will ride home on the beasts back at the end of the day. They are at home in and out of water, and are happiest of all when buried in a "wallow" of rich soft mud. **75 feet**

2047 ... ELEPHANTS BATHING IN A CEYLON RIVER

These elephants, kept by the descendants of some of the Old Chiefs, near Kandy, have been taught to work and earn their own living. They are here seen being "cleaned up" after their day's work, and one will be especially noticeable by the fine tusks he has. These fine fellows and the beautiful rivers with its banks covered with luxuriant foliage makes a delightful picture.

75 feet

2048 ... THE MISCHIEVOUS CAT

This is a very laughable and jolly subject. A lady is seated at her lunch, and on the table is a magnificent Persian cat, evidently a spoilt darling; as fast as the lady raises her fork with a morsel upon it, the cat reaches out its paw and lifts the food off the fork. The lady protests and slaps the cat on the head, but he is not to be driven away, and sits up and fights back. The cat is finally seen playing round a bowl containing gold-fish, which deeply interested him.

50 feet

2049 ... A SCRATCHING MATCH IN TOAD-LAND

The tortoise referee is seen solemnly marching along to the scene of the contest, closely followed by the combatants. The two gigantic toads having shaken hands in orthodox fashion, set to work in the most businesslike manner, a fine scratching match ensues; while old brer tortoise vigorously nods and waves approval. At the close of the contest, victor and vanquished mount on tortoise steeds and ride away from the battle field; the vanquished toad falling off his faithful mount, just as he passes from view. One of the most laughable and remarkable Natural History films ever produced. **125 feet**

2051 ... THE BOA CONSTRICTOR AND THE RAT

A magnificent boa constrictor is seen writhing along through the grass; suddenly a white rat appears on the scene, and a most exciting chase takes place, ending fatally for the rat. The great boa-constrictor holds its victim in his coils, and proceeds slowly and deliberately to swallow the rat, which disappears inch by inch down the throat of the boa, until only the tip of the tail is left to view. This is one of the most remarkable films ever bioscoped.　**150 feet**

2052 ... THE PILFERING RODENT

A work basket having been incautiously left near the Rodent's cage, the little creature with every sign of pleasure at once proceeds to pilfer the contents, draging into its nest the pieces of cloth, reels of cotton, &c. **75 feet**

2054 ... THE GREAT HORNBILL

The Great Hornbill is a most remarkable looking bird, its gigantic bill giving the bird a very comical topheavy appearance. With wonderful agility the great bird catches and gleefully devours quantities of grapes thrown to it by its keeper. **50 feet**

2055 .. WITHIN THE MONKEY'S CAGE

This presents an extraordinary scene of animation. Many different species of apes following are seen disporting in their cage. The novelty of having their gambols bioscoped has evidently given new zest to their frolics, and they jump and swing about with marvellous agility.

100 feet

The Baboon.

2056 ... HIGHLAND CATTLE ON THE BANKS OF THE THAMES

A charming picture of the handsome rough-coated Highland cattle coming down to the river to drink. **50 feet**

2057 ... HERDING THE THAMES SWANS AT HENLEY

The old "Swanherd," crook in hand, is seen marshalling the royal swans which are annually assembled at Henley. With the aid of his crook, the swanherd deftly guides the unruly members of his flock. The swans march along in quaint and solemn procession, and this novel and attractive film terminates in a portrait group of swan's heads. **50 feet**

2058 ... QUAINT PETS

Curious friendships amongst animals to birds are frequently mentioned in books, but not to be often seen. There we have quite a collection. A bantam cock and dog. Fox terrier and cat. Goat and horses, &c. Very quaint and laughable. **175 feet**

2059 ... THE MONKEY AND THE STRAWBERRIES

A quaint little monkey is seen thoroughly enjoying the contents of the strawberry basket. Growing tired of the luscious fruit the monkey turns his attention to the basket itself, and proceeds to pull it to pieces. **100 feet**

2060 ... THE POLAR BEAR

This is of particular interest, as it shows the late lamented Sammy at the Zoo thoroughly enjoying himself. Sammy was a particularly fine specimen of a polar bear, and was famous for his artful tricks. **60 feet**

2061 ... SWANS AND DUCKS ON ST. JAMES' PARK LAKE

A very charming picture, full of animation, showing the feeding of a large flock of ducks and swans on the beautiful lake in St. James' Park. **50 feet**

2062 ... PERFORMING DOGS AND PONIES

A marvellously clever troup of dogs and ponies go through an unique series of fresh and novel tricks showing great agility and precision. **75 feet**

No. 2084. Porcupines at the Zoo.

2063 ... THE TERRIER IN THE RAT PIT

A most exciting picture, in which a famous terrier makes very short work of upwards of thirty rats. **150 feet**

2064 ... FEEDING THE SEA-LIONS

The Sea-lions go through a very fine performance diving from a height, mounting a chair, running, etc.; and as a grand finale a gigantic sea-lion's head is seen swaying from side to side with the mouth opening to its widest capacity in expectation of another fish. **75 feet**

2065 ... THE HEDGEHOG FEEDING

As the hedgehog is a nocturnal animal to a great degree, it is a very rare sight to see one feeding, and, on account of the animal being very shy, a most difficult subject to bioscope. **50 feet**

2066 ... THE MONKEY AND THE DATES

With the greatest glee, and most astonishing rapidity, the monkey devours dates, stuffing its cheek pouches as full as they will hold. **100 feet**

2070 ... SWANS AND INDIAN DUCKS

A practically unique collection of different species of Swans, Ducks and Geese are seen swimming about in most picturesque surroudings. **50 feet**

2071 ... THE GIANT WATERBEETLE

The rare Giant Waterbeetle which is twice the size of the more generally known Dytiscus, is swimming about amongst the water weeds, and evidently having a good time. **50 feet**

2072 ... THE GREAT TRITON NEWT

Several of these most handsome creatures are seen gracefully swimming about. It is the mating season, and the males are seen with their wonderful crests which are only seen at their best in the spring time. The female has no crest down her back like the male, but makes up for it with her handsome spotted waistcoat.   **50 feet**

2073 ... EDUCATED MONKEYS IN COSTUME

A wonderful collection of different specimens of apes and monkeys dressed in quaint costumes.   The varying play of expression on the faces is most laughable.   **60 feet**

2074 ... FEEDING THE KING PENGUIN

There is something most laughably human in the solemn way in which the Penguin marches about on land, reminding one of an old gentleman who is rather unsteady on his legs.

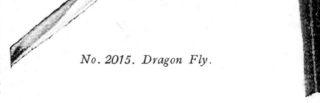

No. 2015. Dragon Fly.

But this bird when in the sea swims beneath its surface with the most astonishing rapidity.   **50 feet**

2075   SPARROWS AND PIGEONS IN HYDE PARK

A great crowd of sparrows are enjoying a hearty meal, when a number of pigeons arrive and marching up and down drive the sparrows away.   **50 feet**

2076 ... A FLOCK OF FLAMINGOES

A flock of these quaint looking yet beautifully plumaged birds wander about over marshy ground, and are seen thoroughly enjoying themselves.   **50 feet**

2077 ... AN OLD PHILOSOPHER (Monkey Portrait)

A large "head and shoulders" animated portrait of an ancient monkey. He has evidently seen much of life, and has a most expressive face that tells quite a story.   **50 feet.**

2078 ... THE THIRSTY MONKEY AND THE TEA-CUP

Master Monkey is very thirsty indeed, and standing up, extends his arms eagerly towards the cup into which he thrusts his face. When all the milk has gone, he turns the cup upside down and vainly seeks for more on the under side.   **50 feet**

2080 ... FEEDING THE HIPPOPOTAMUS (Grand Opening)

An Old Philosopher

The head of a gigantic Hippopotamus at feeding time. The great jaws slowly opening disclose the huge tongue and terrible teeth of the monster. A most sensational and remarkable picture. **50 feet**

2081 ... FEEDING THE GIRAFFES

A film full of interest and amusement, showing that a very long neck and equally lengthy legs are by no means an advantage if food has to be picked up off the ground. The giraffes are built for feeding off the upper branches of trees and tall bushes, and when they have to pick up anything from the ground they are placed at a great disadvantage. The sight of the extraordinary way in which they straddle out their legs to accomplish this is most laughable. **75 feet**

2083 ... WITHIN THE LION'S DEN

This picture, taken within the lion's den, shows to full advantage a magnificent lion and lioness. They growl and snarl, showing their terrible teeth, and are evidently angered at the intrusion of the bioscope. **75 feet**

2084 ... AMONGST THE PORCUPINES

A number of fine Porcupines are running about in all directions. They erect their quills and shake them, all ready for an encounter with any intruder. Altogether unpleasant customers to come too closely in contact with. **50 feet**

2085 ... RIDING THE ZOO ELEPHANTS

A very charming and popular picture, full of life and animation, showing crowds of happy children mounting and riding on the elephants. **75 feet**

2087 ... THE STAGHOUND KENNELS AT EXMOOR

Showing the house to some members of the famous Exmoor Kennels with its lively tenants. **60 feet**

2088 ... AMONGST THE PACK OF STAGHOUND PUPPIES

The somewhat ungainly staghound puppies are having a high old romp together, and makes a very laughable and animated picture. **60 feet**

2089 ... BULL DOG SHOW AT CRYSTAL PALACE

The very finest specimens of prize Bull Dogs are sent to the Crystal Palace Show, and all the prize winners are seen with their owners. **150 feet**

2090 ... FOXHOUND PUPPIES IN THE KENNEL RUN

The Foxhound pups are full of fun and game, running about in all directions **75 feet**

2091 ... THE LAUGHING HYENA

The hyena is never a beauty to look upon at the best of times, and this one laughing and snarling alternately, presents a weird and most uncanny appearance. **50 feet**

2092 ... IN THE DEN WITH THE STRIPED HYENAS

A fine picture showing all the savage yet cowardly nature of these fearsome animals who in their native state haunt the burial grounds, and track down lonely unarmed travellers. **60 feet**

2093 ... TWO SPORTIVE POLAR BEARS

Two young Polar Bears are having a jolly romp together, and send the water flying in all directions. The fun waxes fast and furious, the bears hugging each other, standing up and boxing, and plunging with great splashing into the water. **50 feet**

The Hyena.

2096 ... LEMUR AND MONKEYS WITH KEEPER

A charming picture of the pretty Ringtail Lemur and some of its companions, on the best of terms with their Keeper. **50 feet**

2097 ... SWANS AT THEIR TOILET

The Swans are very busy at their toilet, carefully arranging their feathers, and generally having a grand clean up. **75 feet**

2098 ... FEEDING THE CHAMELEONS

Two fine specimens of these remarkable creatures are enjoying the sunshine and a repast of mealworms, again and again the wonderful tongue, which is as long as the animal itself, is shot forth with unerring aim to the captured worm and devoured with evident relish **60 feet**

2099 ... BRAZILIAN TOADS CATCHING COCKROACHES AND MEALWORMS

These gigantic toads, are very handsome fellows, sit apparently indifferent to their surroundings, but really keeping a very sharp look out, seizing and swallowing with lightning rapidity the cockroaches and worms. **75 feet**

American Toad catching Worms.

2100 ... SCALING THE TEETH OF THE PYTHON

This is a very novel picture, showing the difficult and somewhat dangerous task of scaling the teeth of the Python.   **50 feet**

2101 ... MOCCASIN SNAKE SWALLOWING A FROG

Poor Froggy is seized by the snake, and slowly and surely swallowed head first, despite his struggles. This is a unique picture.
75 feet

ONE OF THE SENSATIONS OF THE
"URBANORA" ENTERTAINMENTS.

2015

Wild Beasts, Birds and Reptiles.

By courtesy of LORD STRATHCONA *and the* LONDON ZOOLOGICAL SOCIETY.
Photographed by F. MARTIN DUNCAN, F.R.H.S., JOSEPH ROSENTHAL,
H. M. LOMAS, J. G. AVERY *and others.*

King of Beasts.

For the first since its invention the Bioscope has been seriously and scientifically applied to obtaining a record of the ways and habits of Wild Animals, and the present series of Animated Pictures represents some of the finest results that have ever been obtained.   The work of taking Bioscope Pictures of Wild Animal Life, is one fraught with endless difficulties, and in some cases, not a little danger to the Photographer.

The greatest patience, care, thought and resource has to be employed, so as to successfully show the creatures in their natural and characteristic movements, for they are very easily disturbed and alarmed, and when frightened their whole aspect becomes changed to unnatural. In obtaining this unique series of Natural History Films, many long hours and even days have had to be spent in patient waiting, ere the characteristic picture could be procured.

For much of the works, special costly apparatus had to be designed and constructed, and many elaborate and delicate experiments carried out, but the results have yielded the highest standard of perfection that has ever been gained, and these wonderfully realistic and life-like pictures of Wild Animal Life are the admiration of all who have the good fortune to behold them.

Order of Pictures.

General View of an Avenue in the Zoo—Refreshment Pavilion—Visitors at the Bear and Hyena Dens—The Bear Pits—General View of the Lake—Geese and Ducks—Indian Ducks—Duck Cleaning its Plumage—Geese sunning—Wild Goose at Toilet—The King Penguin Feeding—Giant Hornbill and Young—The Macaw—Eagles and Hawks—Pelicans Feeding—Cygnets protected by their Parents—Herding a Flock of Swans—Flamingoes—Storks' Tug-of-War—Ostrich—Feeding Rabbits—White Rat and Young—Hedgehog—Indian Otter Feeding—Porcupines—Brazilian Toads catching Mealworms—The Chameleon Climbing and Catching Insects—Keeper with Boa Constrictors, close view of the head—A future Meal—Snake and Rat—Boa Constrictor sliding over a Tree—The Giant Tortoise Feeding—Young Alligators—Seals Feeding and Diving—Children riding Camels—Monkey looking for date and fleas—Egyptian playing with an Ourang Outang—Keeper with Chimpanzee—Playing, Feeding and sitting for Portrait—Kangaroo with Keeper—Cheetah Playing—Striped Hyenas—Black Bear Russian Béar up the Pole—Polar Bear Feeding—"Old Jim," the Indian Rhinoceros (recently died at the Zoo, of old age)—The Hippopotamus Feeding and entering Pool—A Grand Opening—Elephants with their Native Surroundings—Elephants doing Punishment—Children Riding Elephants at the Zoo—Feeding the Giraffes Herd of Buffaloes on Lord Strathcona's Range in Manitoba, Canada—Moose—Staging Resting—Stags and Does in Enclosure—A Herd of Elk on Lord Strathcona's estates in Canada—Flushing the Bears' Den—Three Playful Polar Bears — The Lion King of Beasts.

Total Length. 1950 feet—Price £50.

Duration of Exhibition Forty Minutes.

NOTE—This series is supplied only on condition that it is not to be exhibited or sold in England and America, where exclusive Exhition rights have been acquired.

Magnificent photographic quality.—A series of pictures which took over two years to collect. Unique in every respect.

OUR AQUARIUM MARINE STUDIES.

An unique series of Animated Pictures of Marine Life, photographed by F. MARTIN=DUNCAN, F.R.H.S.

These studies of Marine Life form one of the most remarkable and interesting series of Animated Pictures ever produced. Great care and attention has been devoted to the minutest details, so as to render these pictures as perfect as possible and to show the various creations in their most characteristic attitudes and occupations. The disheartening and multitudinous difficulties that have to be contended against in photographing the sly and nervous Denizens of the Deep must be personally encountered to be fully appreciated, for their name is legion, and no sooner is one difficulty overcome than another arises to take its place. It is only by the exertion of that great patience and quiet determination to conquer all difficulties, which has enabled us to so successfully take this unique series of pictures of Marine Life.

The Octopus

2200 ... DENIZENS OF THE DEEP

A striking series of thirteen Pictures of Marine Life.

1.—Sea Bream.—These beautiful fish change their colour with their emotions; thus, if frightened they change to a very bright grey, while if enraged, the colour darkens all over the body, and the fin on top of back is raised. They assemble together for courtship, and play in schools numbering 20,000 to 60,000.

2.—The Pollack.—The Pollack, cousin of the Whiting, is a very graceful, active fish. It stalks its prey in the most sportsmanlike manner, and frequently hunts in companies of considerable numbers.

3.—Sur Mullet and Weever.—Sur Mullet are very quaint looking, gaily coloured fish. They are very restless in their habits, and have on the lower lip a number of curious white tentacles which are used as organs of touch.

The Weever is a great fighter, and will hold its own in a battle with a fish considerably its superior in size. The Weever is armed with a very long, sharply-pointed fin on top of its back, which is used as a weapon of defence, and can produce a very painful and poisonous wound.

4.—The Dog-Fish.—The Dog-fish are the most common of our native sharks, frequently attaining a length exceeding five or six feet. Sometimes the Dog-fish appear in great numbers, following the pilchards and herrings.

5.—Conger Eel.—The Conger Eel has an unsatiable hunger; he is always on the look out for food, and nothing is too hard for him— nails, glass, fish hooks—once successfully swallowed are digested with ease.

6.—Skate.—Skate are very remarkable looking fish, and considering the great size and weight they attain are very rapid in their movements. The undersurface of these fish presents a very curious appearance, closely resembling the human face.

7.—Edible Crab.—The edible Crab is a merry fellow when at home under the sea. He is fond of a fight, and sometimes comes off minus a claw, but that does not trouble him for he has the power of soon growing a new one in place of the lost or damaged limb.

8.—King or Horseshoe Crab.—Probably one of the quaintest of the many strange creatures that dwell in the sea is the King or Horseshoe Crab These uncanny-looking creatures are of great interest to scientific folk, for they form an interesting connecting link with the monsters of past geological ages.

9.—The Lobster.—The battle of life is pretty keen in the Lobster world, so keen indeed that they eat each other. Whenever a couple of Lobsters meet a duel ensues, and the victor devours the vanquished.

10.—The Cray-Fish.—The Cray-fish, though belonging to the same family as the Lobster, are, except when courting, much more peaceably inclined creatures. They grow to a great size, and present a very fierce appearance with their numerous spiney legs and long feelers, or antennæ.

11.—Spider Crab.—Spider Crabs have gained their popular name from their long slender legs and fat oval bodies. These creatures hide up amongst the rocks and seaweeds, pouncing out upon their unsuspecting victims.

12.—Hermit Crabs and Ship Barnacles.—Here we see the comical old Hermit Crabs, dragging their houses about and having a friendly difference of opinion, while above a group of Ship Barnacles are waving their long feathery legs as if wishing to join in the fray.

13.—The Octopus.—The Octopus is the veritable dragon of the deep. All day long he hides up in the dark caves and crannies in the rocks, and at night he comes out in search of victims. He has the power of blushing all the colours of the rainbow. Each of his long arms is clothed with a hundred powerful suckers, and his strong jaws are like the beak of a parrot. Should he get the worst of it in the fight, he suddenly ejects a quantity of black inky fluid in the face of his astonished foe, and under cover of the dark turbid water, beats a hasty retreat.

Supplied only in its total Length of 500 feet.

2201 ... STALKED SHIP BARNACLE.

A number of these remarkable animals are shown attached to the bottom of a bottle. From the curious triangular shells which protect the bodies of the Barnacles, countless graceful feathery legs are thrust out and waved about in all directions, the creatures being busily engaged in collecting and devouring food. Barnacles are particularly remarkable and interesting animals as they pass the early stages of their lives swimming about in the warm surface water of the sea, and it is not until they have passed through several changes of form that they eventually having, so to speak, sown their wild oats, settle down to a comparatively sedentary life, becoming attached to any floating timbers, or the under sides of ships, when they form the beautiful opalescent shell which protects their bodies and for the remainder of their life they remain attached to the timber, kicking with their graceful legs, the food they require into their mouths.

75 feet

2202 ... SHORE CRABS

Here we see a mass of shore crabs, evidently enjoying themselves. The large company disperse, moving rapidly with most laughable and quaint gestures in all directions. They start to run races, wave their arms, and give evidence that some of them are spoiling for a fight. Shore crabs are great cannibals, and when one of their brethren cast off an old shell, and is still in a soft state, the new coating not having had time to harden, he is often set upon and devoured.

50 feet

The Shore Crab. . . .

2203 .. SAND HOPPERS AND SHRIMPS

Sand hoppers and shrimps suddenly make their appearance in vast numbers, descending through the water like a shower, and at once begin to swim and jump through the water in all directions. The vast numbers of sand hoppers and shrimps which appear from time to time off the coast, form the staple food of the sea anæmonies, sur mullet, and a large majority of the flat fish. **50 feet**

2204 .. THE SKATE

Some huge specimens are seen starting and swimming about in their own peculiar and characteristic way. This is a very remarkable and striking film, as it shows not only the curious movements of the skate, but very fine views of the upper and under surfaces of this fish. The under surface presents a most weird appearance, the head of the fish looking like the face of a comic old man who is looking at the audience roaring with laughter, his merriment making him gasp for breath. The skate frequently reaches very great size, specimens $5\frac{1}{2}$ by 6ft. long, and weighing as much as 200lbs., having not unfrequently been caught. **50 feet**

c

2205 ... THE ELEDON

The Eledon is a rare species of Octopus, occasionally met with off our Western and Northern coasts. It is a singularly active and curious creature, and like its cousin the large Octopus, it has the power of blushing any colour to order, so that it can change to the colour of its surroundings, no matter what tint they may take. Its arms are clothed with hundreds of suckers, by means of which it captures its prey. Its mouth, which is in the centre of the waving arms, has a most formidable beak, closely resembling that of a parrot. So powerful is this beak that the Eledon can crack the hard shell of crabs and lobsters. **50 feet**

2206 ... THE BRIGHTON AQUARIUM

A series of marine studies of 14 various subjects. This film will be found to meet the requirements of those who do not desire so detailed and varied a series as No. 2200. **225 feet**

2207 ... THE GIANT LOBSTER

A lobster of gigantic proportions arrives on the scene brandishing his arms and waving his long antennæ. He swims and marches about in a very comical and defiant manner. The inquisitive and much smaller kind of lobster appears upon the scene, and the giant, evidently displeased, attacks him, driving him hither and thither. **75 feet**

2208 ... THE OCTOPUS

The Octopus is one of the dragons of the deep. We see him at home amongst his natural surroundings of rocks and sunken wreckage. During the hours of daylight he remains quietly tucked away in a cave, looking out for stray victims that may pass near his haunts, but as night draws on he comes forth and swims backwards with powerful strokes through the water looking for his evening meal. Armed with a great circle of waving sucker-pad limbs, and cruel, powerful jaws, shaped like a gigantic parrot's beak, he is indeed a formidable and evil-looking creature. **75 feet**

2209 ... THE WHITEBAIT

These graceful and pretty little fish are seen swimming about, playing at hide and seek, capturing their food, &c., &c., the whole subject presenting a very attractive and animated scene. **50 feet**

2210 ... THE AXOLOTLE

One of the most remarkable fresh water animals is the Axolotle. This creature resembles in appearance a gigantic Newt, but has at the back of the neck a wonderful set of glands, the external gills or lungs of the animals, by means of which it draws the air from the water. **50 feet**

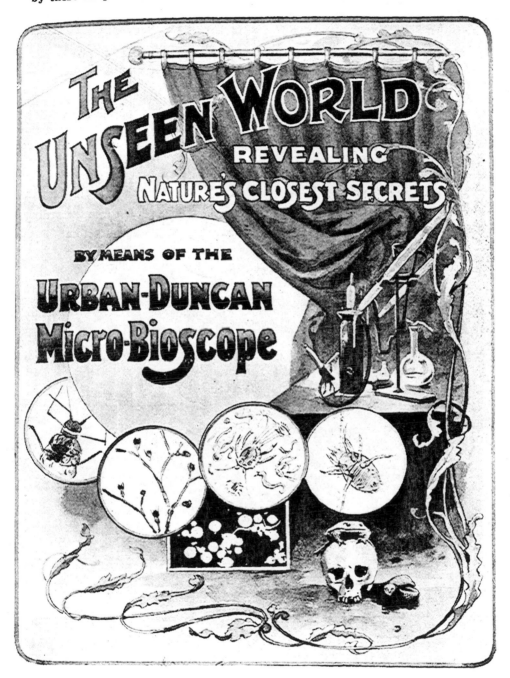

THE UNSEEN WORLD REVEALING NATURE'S CLOSEST SECRETS BY MEANS OF THE URBAN-DUNCAN Micro-Bioscope

c 2

"THE UNSEEN WORLD"

(Copyright Title.)

A Series of Microscopic Studies, Photographed by
means of

The Urban-Duncan Micro-Bioscope

The "UNSEEN WORLD" Series of Films are made to fit all
Standard American Gauge Projecting Machines.

The magnification of these Subjects as viewed from a Screen, with
picture 20 by 25 feet in size, is 2,200,000 to 28,000,000 times, according
to the extent of magnification on the Film which varies from 25 to
850 diameters.

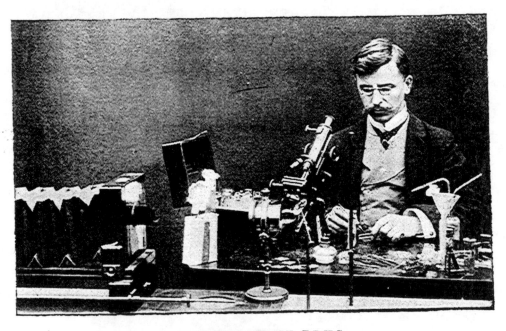

F. MARTIN-DUNCAN, F.R.H.S.

PHYSICAL PHENOMENA.

2300 ... ELECTRICAL DISCHARGES

A wonderful series of Electrical phenomena, showing how
lightning is formed and the beautiful and varied shapes taken by
the various electrical discharges   **60 feet**

2301 ... BIRTH OF A CRYSTAL

Very remarkable is the sight revealed by the microscope of the formation of a crystal from a limpid liquid. Gradually, and yet with wonderful rapidity, the crystals grow out of the liquid into the most beautiful and varied forms. Graceful fronds, minute delicate needles, spear heads, fans, exquisite palm branches, all find shape in the marvellous growth of the crystals.

50 feet

2302 ... SMOKE AND ITS MOLE-CULE

At last the molecule stands revealed. First wonderful vortices are seen, which die away in all sorts of graceful shapes. Then, by great magnification the molecules are seen rushing along in a great stream. **125 feet**

Formation of Crystals.

MICROSCOPIC SUBJECTS.

2500 ... AMERICAN BLIGHT AND GREEN-FLY

The American Blight which has invaded so many English orchards, and the Green-fly, the greatest pest of the rose garden, are shown greatly magnified, crawling about in search of food. The American Blight or Woolly Aphis presenting a very curious, untidy appearance, with bits of the woolly matter, which it has formed itself, stuck about its legs and body. *Magnified 25 diameters on film.*

75 feet

2501 ... CHEESE MITES

A gentleman reading the paper and seated at lunch suddenly detects something the matter with his cheese. He examines it with his magnifying glass, starts up and flings the cheese away, frightened at the sight of the creeping mites which his magnifying glass reveals. A ripe piece of Stilton, the size of a shilling, will contain several hundred cheese mites. In this remarkable film, the mites are seen crawling and creeping about in all directions, looking like great uncanny crabs, bristling with long spiny hairs and legs. *Magnified 50 diameters on film.* **150 feet**

2502 ... THE MAY-FLY LARVA

The May-fly larva looks like some great monster of past Geological ages as it dashes about, chasing water-fleas and other creatures; and it is difficult to realize that this great hungry-jawed creature will eventually turn into a fly with delicate gauzy wings. *Magnified 25 diameters on film.* **75 feet**

2503 ... RED SLUDGE-WORM

This is a very striking film. First a single microscopic worm is seen, and then a writhing struggling mass of the worms, looking like gigantic snakes with barbed necks. These worms are found in great masses in all rivers and ponds, and thousands are devoured by fish, this being their staple food. *Magnified 30 diameters.* **50 feet**

2504 ... RED SNOW GERMS

This is a wonderful Living Picture of the germs which cause Red Snow. This is frequently met with in the Arctic Regions, and occasionally on the Alps. Amongst them is seen a worm, similar to that which caused great sickness amongst the workmen excavating the Simplon tunnel. *Magnified 650 diameters.*　　**50 feet**

2506 ... THE BRICKMAKING ROTIFER

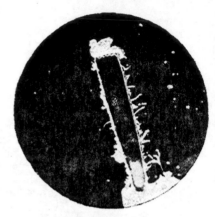

This is a very striking, remarkable and beautiful subject. The brickmaking rotifer is like a beautiful silver pansy, with the stalk incased in a tube of gauze. The tube is made by the rotifer from the undigestable portions of its food, which it forms into tiny round bricks and places one on top of the other. The beautiful flower-like head of the animal expands and contracts, is withdrawn entirely within the tube, and expands once again. *Magnified 30 diameters.*　　**100 feet**.

2507 ... THE CIRCULATION OF PROTO-PLASM IN THE WATERWEED

The waterweed is seen growing in its natural environment, then a sprig of it is shown held in the hand, and a single leaf held in a pair of microscopic forceps. This is followed by a greatly magnified picture of a portion of the leaf, showing the circulation and rotation of the protoplasm. This is one of the most wonderful sights that the microscope has ever revealed. The protoplasm is for ever moving through the cells of plants, just as the blood flows through the veins of animals. Caught in the restless stream of protoplasm are myriads of chlorophyll corpuscles, the minute oval bodies which give the beautiful green tints to the foliage and stems. Wherever the light shines strongest, as on the upper surface of the leaves, there the restless protoplasm drags the chlorophyll corpuscles, and masses them in vast numbers together. *Magnified 700 diameters*　　**75 feet**

2508 ... CIRCULATION OF THE BLOOD IN THE FROG'S FOOT

The first section of this Film portrays a frog swimming in a tank. The next view is that of the frog's webbed foot, followed by a wonderful living picture of the veins in the web of a frog's foot. The blood is seen rushing through the veins in a constant never ceasing stream, like a mountain torrent. *Magnified 500 diameters.*　　**75 feet**

2509 ... THE VOLVOX GLO-BATOR (2 Sections)

This tiny microscopic plant, which lives in ponds and lakes, and looks like a beautiful little sphere, is seen actively rolling about in all directions. It grows and is seen to burst and give birth by its death to numerous offspring which roll away in like manner, these in course of a few hours give birth again to another generation. *Magnified 20 and 45 diameters.*　　**75 feet**

2510 ... TYPHOID BACTERIA

This remarkable film shows hundreds of typhoid and other disease germs found in sewage contaminated water, in all stages of growth, and in restless unceasing movement.   **50 feet**

NOTE.—*This is the first time these germs have been photographed ALIVE, the usual method employed in examining and studying the germs is to kill, dry and stain same. Magnified 850 diameters.*

2511 ... THE FRESHWATER INFUSORIAN

This wonderful microscopic creature is seen in constant and varied motion in a drop of impure water. It is called an infusorian because it is never found in pure water, but only in water containing an infusion of vegetable and animal matter. Very curious. *Magnified 500 diameters.*
     75 feet

2512 ... THE "BACTERIA GLUTTON"

One of the most extraordinary sights ever seen. This infusorian delights to feast upon bacteria that would in most cases kill a man. The creature is seen in the midst of countless germs which it devours as long as it lives. When this infusorian dies, however, the tables are turned, and the bacteria devours it. In the hunt for bacteria the infusorian extends a beak like the bill of a snipe with which it scoops up the germs by hundreds. *Magnified 500 diameters.*   **60 feet**

2513 ... CHEESE MITES

This shows cheese mites from a minute portion of Stilton cheese The mites creep and crawl in all directions, presenting a weird and uncanny spectacle with their white fat bodies covered with long hair
     50 feet.

2514 ... THE NATURALIST AT WORK WITH THE MICROSCOPE

This shows the Naturalist surrounded with his bottles containing all sorts of microscopic treasures, and with his trusty microscope beside him, He takes an object from the bottles, places it on a glass slip and then places the slip beneath the microscope to examine it. This film forms an admirable introduction at No. 2505 or any other of he Microscopic series.   **50 feet**

2515 .. WATER FLEA AND ROTIFERS

Water flea has gained its popular name from its curious jerky motion when swimming through the water. Occasionally vast swarms of these minute microscopic creatures appear in our ponds and lakes. They do not belong to the insect world at all, but are cousins of the shrimps. We also see a number of free swimming rotifers, cousins of the brickmaker, enjoying themselves in company with the water fleas.   **50 feet**

2517 ... ANATOMY OF THE WATER FLEA

This shows the delicate arms and the wonderful internal anatomy of the water flea. An admirable companion to No. 2515.   **50 feet**

2518 ... CILIARY MOVEMENT OF THE GILLS OF A MUSSEL

One of the most wonderful sights which the microscope reveals is that of the ciliary movement of the gills of a mussel; the extremely minute and delicate cilia on the edge of the gills lash the water and produce a rapid current which carry the minute organisms down into the mouth. **75 feet**

2519 ... THE NATURALIST FISHING FOR SPECIMENS

The Naturalist, armed with his pond hunting apparatus, arrives at the scene of action. With his glass jar attached to the end of his dipping stick, he collects a sample of water, teeming with microscopic forms of life. Then with the cutting hook attached to the rod, he cuts away at the roots of the Aquatic plants, and with the aid of the grappling irons attached to a line, drags the plants to shore. **75 feet**

2520 ... THE WATER FLEA

Nearly every pond contains some of these interesting little microscopic creatures called water fleas, which are not insects at all, but cousins to the shrimps and crabs. The quaint little animals have numerous delicate legs for swimming, and it is their curious jerky motion that gives the water flea its name. **50 feet**

2521 ... DIATOMS

Diatoms are plants so minute in size as to require the strong magnification of the microscope to reveal their beauty. It would require several hundreds of them to cover a sixpence, yet in such vast numbers do they sometimes appear, that their skeletons, which are composed of silica, form great banks in lakes and rivers. Diatoms are most varied in form, and are of very great interest, for they have the unplantlike power of comparatively rapid motion. **50 feet**

2522 ... HEAD OF A HOUSE FLY

This is probably the first time that a fly has ever sat for its portrait to the bioscope, and a most strange looking face and head it has. To keep him in a good temper a needle point coated with honey is placed within reach of his tongue. The tongue of the fly is a most extraordinary piece of apparatus. Although it can tuck away into a small space when expanded, it appears to be as large as the insect's head. It is expanded in a fan-like manner, and consists of hollow tubes through which the sustenance is sucked into the mouth.
75 feet

2523 ... THE BIRTH OF A CRYSTAL

The birth of a crystal from the fluid state is a very wonderful and beautiful sight. Gradually the fluid thickens, and the delicate little crystal begins to form, growing out in beautiful needle-pointed fans. **50 feet**

2524 ... CIRCULATION OF THE BLOOD IN THE TAIL OF THE GOLDFISH

The goldfish are seen swimming about, evidently enjoying themselves. The scene changes, and reveals the wonders of the circulation of the blood. **50 feet**

2525 ... THE FISH AND ITS BLOOD CIRCULATION

The fish are at play in a tank; they are then taken out of the water, and we see an enlarged view of the tail; and finally, a wonderful picture of the circulation of the blood, as revealed by the high magnification of the microscope. The blood is seen flowing rapidly through a perfect network of veins in all directions. **75 feet**

2526 ... THE FIG MITES AND MAGGOT

This is a very interesting and novel film. A box of dried figs is opened, and a boy is seen thoroughly enjoying the contents of the box. His friend appears on the scene, and the two boys are making very short work of the figs, when one lad pulls out a magnifying glass to examine the dainties. Both boys evince surprise and alarm at the sight revealed by their magnifying glass ; but their consternation gives place to broad smiles at the curious antics of the inhabitants of the figs. Hundreds of queer, uncanny fig mites, clothed with long silvery hair, run about in all directions, fighting, chasing each other, &c. Then the portrait of the fig-maggot is seen, presenting a wonderful animated picture of how the creature forms in its mouth the silk with which it spins its cocoon, and how it uses its great jaws to remove the silk. Altogether a most striking and remarkable film. **100 feet**

2527 ... RED MITES

The Red Mite is one of the greatest pests the farmer and gardener has to fight. Although so small as to be only just visible to the naked eye as a tiny red speck, yet this insect is capable of doing frightful harm to the crops, and many thousands of pounds are spent in combating its ravages. We see in this film swarms of these little pests greatly magnified. **50 feet**

2528 ... MOSS ANIMALS, OR BRYOZOA

The Moss Animals, or Bryozoa, are very beautiful and interesting animals microscopic in size. There are many hundred species living in the sea, and these animals present a very beautiful appearance, each individual having long, graceful tenticles, which it continuously waves about in search of food. **75 feet**

2529 ... THE VORTICELLÆ, OR BELL-ANIMALCULAE

These wonderful little animals are amongst the most beautiful and interesting microscopic forms of life to be met with in ponds-lakes and rivers. In shape they resemble gracefully designed wine-glasses, the rims of which are fringed with extremely fine delicate hairs ; the bell or cup being supported on long slender stems attached at the base to a water weed. The rim of the cup-bell is fringed with extremely fine delicate hairs, which are kept in constant and circular motion, producing by their actions a vortex, into which the bacteria and other vegetable organisms on which the Bell-Animalculae feed are drawn and carried down into the mouth of the creatures. From time to time, the slender stalk is suddenly contracted into a spiral spring, and then with as great rapidity re-expanded. **100 feet**

2530 ... THE SLIPPER ANIMALCULAE (Paramecium)

A drop of water taken from a pond or lake nearly always contains countless numbers of the beautiful Slipper Animalculre (Paramecium), which are only visible when examined with the high magnifying glasses of a powerful microscope. These wonderful transparent, silvery creatures are seen to be in constant rapid movement, swimming hither and thither, devouring the bacteria and minute plants which form their food. **50 feet**

2531 ... THE WATER BEAR

One of the strangest creatures revealed by the microscope is the Water Bear, a quaint transparent bodied creature, which pushes and crawls about amongst the water weeds and moss. **75 feet**

2532 ... DUEL OF THE WATER BEARS

This is a very remarkable film, showing a battle royal between two microscopical Water Bears. **75 feet**

2533 ... THE WATER BEAR, MIDGE LARVA, AND VORTI-CELLA

This is a very striking and clear film, showing a microscopical Water Bear climbing about amongst the water weeds. An uncanny-looking creature, bristling with hairs and legs (the midge larva), then appears, and finally a beautiful group of vorticella, which expand and contract and move their cups about in all directions. **50 feet**

2534 MIDGE LARVA (enlarged view)

The tiny midge larva, greatly magnified under the microscope, presents a very wonderful appearance, showing its external gill-tufts, jaws, &c. **50 feet**

2535 ... THE HARVEST MITES

Who has not suffered from the bites of the tiny Harvest Mites ? Though almost invisible to the naked eye, the little creatures can torment one almost to madness. A gentleman sitting on the grass enjoying a quiet pipe and read, begins to feel a tickling sensation. At last he takes out his magnifying glass, and discovers an army of harvest mites are attacking him. The mites, as seen under the microscope, alive and creeping about, are then shown. **75 feet**

2536 ... THE POLYCHAETE MARINE WORM

The worms that live in the sea are by no means the least remarkable creatures that inhabit old Neptune's kingdom. Very few resemble the ordinary land worm in shape or colour, and the majority are most wonderful and unworm-like creatures. The Polychaete worm has a wonderful writhing tuft of gills on top of its head, that look like tiny snakes in constant motion, while down each side of its body it has extraordinary leg-like outgrowths, by means of which it moves rapidly over the sand and through the water. **50 feet**

2537 ... THE TUBULARIAN MARINE WORM

Many worms that inhabit the sea build themselves beautiful castles or tubes in which to live, and from this habit they have been called the Tubularian or tube-building worms. On rare occasions

they quit their towers, and then we are able to see what the body of the animal is like. One of these very rare chances was taken advantage of in photographing the tubularian, and a beautiful picture showing the transparent body and head crowned with curious tufts, was obtained. **50 feet**

2538 ... THE BLACK CURRANT BUD MITE

This minute microscopic insect, although practically invisible to the naked eye, is one of the most terrible pests the farmer and market gardener has to combat. Every year it spreads to new parts of the country, devastating the black currant bushes, and unless some new method of fighting this tiny insect and killing the thousands which swarm inside the buds is discovered, this delightful fruit will soon be unobtainable. The Mite is seen at work in the heart of a bud. **50 feet**

539 ... LIVING BACTERIA IN   DROP OF POND WATER

A wonderful sight is presented to our view when a single drop of water from a pond is placed inside the powerful magnification of a microscope. The clear limpid drop is then seen to swarm with thousands of tiny dancing forms of bacterial life, which are in constant movement. Suddenly a wonderful Slipper Animalcule, which feeds on these lower forms of life, appears.   **50 feet**

2540 ... BACTERIA FROM A WATER-BUTT

Rain water is delightfully soft to wash in, but is hardly an ideal or particularly safe drink when drawn from the rain-water butt, unless well boiled. The rain-water butt forms the happy home of countless swarms of germs, fortunately mostly harmless to mankind, but not less uncanny things to look at.   **50 feet**

2541 ... POLYCISTINA OR CONTINENT BUILDERS

The white cliffs of Old England and her beautiful chalk downs are very largely composed of millions and millions of microscopic skeletons of tiny creatures called Polycistina and Foraminifera, which lived far back in past geological ages. To-day, far out to sea, the descendants of these tiny creatures that gave their skeletons to the building of England's chalk cliffs are following the example of their pre-historic ancestors, and are forming new continents at the bottom of the sea, which will gradually rise to form new land in the dim future.   **50 feet**

2542 ... YOUNG OYSTERS

Like all young things, baby oysters are active, restless little creatures, and it is not until they have sown their wild oats, so to speak, that they settle down to a stationary dull life.   **50 feet**

2543 ... OSTRAPOD

The Ostrapod is a very remarkable denizen of the deep. Although rarely exceeding the size of a "full stop" in ordinary printing type, it appears in vast swarms at times off the coast of Scotland and Devon, and brings with it shoals of different kinds of fish, which hunt and live upon these minute cousins of the shrimp.   **50 feet**

2544 ... THE CETOCHILUS OR WHALE-FOOD SHRIMP

A most extraordinary creature is the Cetochilus, or Whale-food Shrimp. This wonderful little animal, rarely exceeding one fiftieth to one-thirtieth of an inch in length, forms the chief food of various species of Whales. It has a pair of remarkably big antennæ, which are not only employed as organs of touch, but also as a means of locomotion, the little creature rowing its way through the waters with them. The Cetochilus appears in vast numbers swimming near the surface of the sea.   **75 feet**

2545 ... THE HAIR-FOOTED CRUSTACEAN OR TOPHYROPODA

This remarkable little marine creature forms the favourite food of the herring, and appears off our coasts at certain periods of the year in countless legions, eagerly followed by a devouring shoal of herrings. It has gained its name from the curious appearance of its legs, which terminate not in a foot but in a bunch of hairs. The legs are very beautiful objects, and the curious tuft of hairs is used by the little creatures in swimming. **50 feet**

2546 ... THE COPYPOD OR JUMPING SHRIMP

The Copypod is a very quaint little creature, reminding us in its active jumping mode of locomotion of the fresh-water flea, of which it is a distant relation. The remarkable little Copypod is extremely minute in size, but appears in such vast numbers at certain times of the year as to give a curious greyish brown colour to the sea often for a couple of miles or more. **50 feet**

2547 ... THE YOUNG PRAWN

The young prawn is by no means like its full grown parent in appearance. It is a quaint looking, restless little creature, with great eyes always on the look out for food. The head presents a very remarkable appearance with its large and curious eyes, while the tail shows how the little creature is able to swim backwards so rapidly. **50 feet**

2548 ... THE BABY (Zoea) CRAB

Probably one of the most wonderful series of transformation. from the egg to the perfect fully grown creature is that of the crab It is difficult to believe that the ungainly crab which is such a familiar object on the sea shore, is during the early period of its life an active free-swimming little creature with a longish body and numerous delicate legs. From time to time as the little creature grows it casts its skin, and after each casting is seen to have altered to a greater or lesser degree in shape until at last it appears in the familiar form of the shore crab. **50 feet**

2549 ... THE BABY SPIDER CRAB

The baby spider crab, unlike its parent, leads a very active life, swimming hither and thither in the sea. From time to time it casts its skin as it grows, and with the putting on of its new clothes it changes very consderably in shape until at last it tucks its short tail up under its body to form a sort of pocket and appears like its parent. **50 feet**

2550 ... "THE FRESH-WATER HYDRA."

The Microscopist is seen seated at his well appointed laboratory table preparing his specimens. He takes a drop of pond water from a collecting tube, and, placing it on a glass slide, examines it under the microscope. The sight revealed by the magnifying powers of the microscope is truly wonderful. A number of strange creatures, shining like burnished silver, are seen in constant restless motion. Their delicate, transparent bodies are ever lengthening and contracting in telescopic fashion, while the crowning circlet of arms, which surround the hungry mouth, wave about in all directions. These uncanny looking creatures are the Freshwater Hydras, the inhabitants of nearly every pond and lake. A still more highly magnified view shows us that the arms, or tentacles, of these creatures are clothed with curious knobs, the stinging cells, by means of which the Hydra captures its prey. The tiny "Slipper" Animacules, which swim about in all directions, become entangled in the long arms of the Hydra, and held fast by the barbs of the stinging cells.   **175 feet**

2551 ... "THE ACTIVE WATER FLEA."

At certain periods of the year, ponds and lakes frequently present a curious pearly white appearance, due to the presence in the surface water of countless swarms of restless active water fleas. These active, interesting little microscopic creatures have gained their popular name from the peculiar jerky motion with which they swim through the water. They are not insects at all, but cousins to the shrimps and crabs. The quaint little creatures have a wonderful array of delicate legs, which they employ in their jerky locomotion through the water. A number of these remarkable little creatures are seen actively swimming about, until a couple coming to close quarters have a most exciting stand-up fight, using their numerous arms with the greatest vigour. So transparent are these creatures that we can watch their hearts beating, and the other internal organs expanding and contracting while they fight. This is an absolutely unique subject, and of a most novel, striking, and remarkable character.   **150 feet**

2552 ... THE FRESH-WATER MOSS ANIMALS OR POLYZOA

These remarkable creatures grow in colonies attached to water-weed. A living colony presents a wonderfully animated appearance, each member being crowned with a waving circle of long, graceful tentacles, which are kept in constant movement, and by means of which the creatures capture their food. In past Geological Ages, these animals probably were far more numerous in lakes, rivers and pools, than they are to-day. Now they are comparatively rare, though their Cousins, the Marine Moss-Animals (Polyzoa) are as numerous as ever. They are creatures that love the green shade of the deep waters of a lake, and are, therefore, particularly hard to obtain good pictures of; indeed this is certainly the first time that an animated picture of their wonderful movements has ever been taken.
50 feet

2553 ... THE WHITE CYPRIS

This strange little oval creature is found at certain seasons of the year in ponds and ditches, swimming about in vast companies. It is one of the most active, restless inhabitants of the pond, darting hither and thither with the most startling rapidity. The body of this quaint little creature is enclosed in a bivalve shell, and swims by the united action of its foot-like antennæ and legs. When alarmed, the Cypris tucks up its legs and antennæ (of which it has two pairs) inside the shell, which is then tightly closed.   **50 feet**

2554 ... AN UNWORMLIKE WORM (Nevis)

Strange, fearful, uncanny are many of the microscopic denizens of the deep, particularly is this the case with many of the worms, which do not in the least resemble their terrestrial brothers, and lead a bloodthirsty gadabout life. **60 feet**

2555 ... THE AMŒBA (the beginning of life)

From Amœba to Man, the scientist has worked, showing us that this tiny speck of jellylike substance, practically invisible to the naked eye, yet seen under the powerful magnifning glasses of the microscope to be ever changing its form, and ever on the move, a thing all stomach, multiply by splitting in half, is the very beginning of life, the first and simplest, organism in existence. Never before has its marvellous changes of shape been revealed by animated photography. **100 feet**

2556 ... THE GNAT LARVA

When the baby gnat emerges from the egg it in no way resembles its gay, dancing, tormenting parent. It lives under the water, only coming up at intervals to the surface to thrust its curious tail out of water to obtain a fresh supply of air; for this strange looking creature breathes through its tail. Later in life a great mask is formed over the head and shoulders of the larva, and it enters into the active nymph or pupa stage of its existence, coming up head first to the surface of the water, and breathing through two tubes at the back of the head. When the wings and graceful slender legs have been formed inside the mask, the pupa rises to the surface of the water; the mask splits down the back, and the perfect winged insect escapes and flies away to dance in the sunshine. In tropical cuontries the gnats, or mosquitoes, are the cause of malarial fever in man, introducing the malaria parasite when sucking the blood. Scientific investigation, having revealed the life history of the gnat, has made it possible to successfully battle with this pest, for by pouring oil on the surface of the stagnant pools in which the gnats spend the first stages of their life, the insects are smothered, for they have not strength to push their way through the oil film, and are thus killed ere they reach the winged stage of their existence, in which they are dangerous to man- kind. **50 feet**

2557 ... THE CORETHEA LARVA

This uncanny creature is one of the microscopic wonders and terrors of the pond. It passes through a wonderful series of changes or transformations, and is a most bloodthirsty creature. **50 feet**

All Picture Series reproduced during the "URBANORA" (two hours) Entertainments are absolutely exclusive.

Lantern Slide Department.

✺ ✺ ✺

WE beg to draw special attention to our Lantern Slides, which are of the finest quality and remarkably low priced. The photographs and photo-micrographs from which our lantern slides are made have all been taken specially to meet the requirements of Lecturers and Teachers. Our Botanical Series is probably the most complete and perfect set ever published; all the photo-micrographs having been taken from specially prepared and typical sections.

We are constantly adding new slides to our stock, therefore customers not finding what they require in this list, will do well to write us stating their wants.

ANIMAL HISTOLOGY.

An important series of lantern slides under this division is in active preparation and will include Protozoa, Hydrozoa, Anthrozoa, Porifera, Bryozoa, Echinoderma Holothuriodea, Vermis, Tunicata, Crustacea, Mollusca, Pisces, etc., etc. Also special type sets illustrating the Histology of Anodonta cygnea (Fresh Water Mussel); Astacus fluviatilis (Fresh Water Crayfish); the Rabbit; Human, etc., etc.

We can supply most requirements in Animal Histology, Botany, etc., etc. If you do not see what you need listed, kindly send us an enquiry and list of subjects, and we will do our best to supply.

SLIDES OF SCIENTIFIC SERIES.

Price, EIGHTEEN PENCE each net.

NOTE.—*In ordering please mention Number and Series thus*—**No. 1 B**
(meaning " Section Cotyledon of Pea).

Series B.   # BOTANICAL.

Special Contents of the Cell.

1 ... **SECTION COTYLEDON OF PEA,** showing intercellular Spaces, Starch Grains, etc.
2 ... **CROSS SECTION THROUGH GRAIN of WHEAT,** showing Pericarp Endosperm
3 ... **WHEAT STARCH GRAINS**
4 ... **POTATO STARCH GRAINS**
5 ... **OAT STARCH COMPOUND GRAINS**
6 ... **ENDOSPERM RICINUS** showing Aleurone Grains and Globoid
7 ... **SPHERIO-CRYSTALS OF INULINE**
8 ... **CYSTOLITH**
9 ... **RAPHIDES**
10 ... **LEUCOPLASTS**
11 ... **CHLOROPLASTS**
12 ... **CHROMATOPHORES**

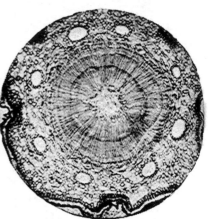

Cross Section of Pine Stem

Cell=Division and Nuclear Division.

13 ... **NUCLEAR DIVISION (KARYOKINESIS) IN VARIOUS STAGES**
14 ... **DITTO   DITTO   DITTO**
15 ... **CELLULAR DIVISION, PROTOCOCCUS VIRIDIS**

Epidermis and Structure of Leaf.

16 ... **CUTICLE OF ARAUCARIA IMBRICATA,** showing Stomata
17 ... **VERTICAL SECTION OF LEAF,** showing Palisade Cells, Spongy Parenchyma
18 ... **TRANSVERSE SECTION, OF LEAF PINUS SYLVESTRIS,** showing Stomata, Stomata Pit, Air Chamber
19 ... **GLANDULAR HAIR, SUNDEW**
20 ... **STINGING HAIR, NETTLE**
21 ... **SCALES, HIPPOPHAE RHAMNOIDES**
22 — **DEFOLIATION, FALL OF THE LEAF AND FORMATION OF NEXT YEAR'S BUD.** Longitudinal Median. Section Acer Pseudo-Platanus

Structure of Stems.

Structure of Root.

Structure of Coniferous Stem.

Algæ.

D

55 ... FUCUS VESICULOSUS ANTHERIDIA

56 ... FUCUS VESICULOSIS, ANTHERIDIUM AND OOGONIUM

Fungi.

58 ... B. ANTHRAX

59 ... B. ANTHRAX, SPORING

60 ... B. DIPHTHERIA, 48 HOURS CULTURE

61 ... B. TETANUS, SPORING

62 ... B. TYHPOID WITH FLAGELLA

63 ... MUCOR MUCEDO

64 ... BOTRYTIS CINEREA (VINE, SCLEROTINA), CONIDIO-PHORE AND CONIDIA

65 ... PUCCINIA GRAMINIS UREDO SPORES

66 ... PUCCINIA GRAMINIS TELEUTO SPORES

67 ... PUCCINIA GRAMINIS, ÆCIDIO SPORES, AND SPER-MATIA

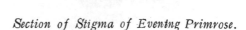

Section of Stigma of Evening Primrose.

Muscineæ.

68 ... MARCHANTIA POLYMORPHA, GEMMAE

69 ... MARCHANTIA POLYMORPHA, ANTHERIDIA

70 ... MARCHANTIA POLYMORPHA, ARCHEGONIA

71 ... MARCHANTIA POLYMORPHA, SPOROGONIA

72 ... TETRAPHIS PELLUCIDA, CUPULE AND GEMMÆ

73 ... SPHAGNUM, ARCHEGONIA

74 ... TRANSVERSE SECTION FERTILE HEAD POLYTRICHUM FORMOSUM

Vascular Cryptogams.

76 ... PROTHALLIUM OF FERN

77 ... SCOLOPENDRIUM VULGARE, SPORANGIA

78 ... TRANSVERSE SECTION RHIZOME PTERIS

Equisetinæ.

79 ... LONGITUDINAL SECTION VEGETATIVE BUD. EQUI-SETUM

80 ... TRANSVERSE SECTION VEGETATIVE BUD. EQUI-SETUM

81 ... TRANSVERSE SECTION FERTILE HEAD EQUISETUM

Lycopodinæ.

82 ... **TRANSVERSE SECTION STEM LYCOPODIUM CLA-VATUM**

83 ... **TRANSVERSE SECTION STEM SELAGINELA**

84 ... **MICRO AND MACROSPORANGIA, SELAGINELLA**

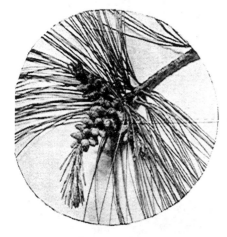

Male Pine Cones.

Reproductive Organs of Gymonopserms.

85 ... **LONGITUDINAL SECTION FEMALE FLOWER OF YEW** (Taxus Baccata)

86 ... **LONGITUDINAL SECTION MALE FLOWER OF YEW**

87 ... **TRANSVERSE SECTION MALE FLOWER OF YEW**

88 ... **LONGITUDINAL SECTION MALE CONE, PINUS SYL-VESTRIS**

89 ... **MOTILE SPERMATOZOID OF CYCAD**

Reproductive Organs of Phanerograms.

90 ... **SECTION OF POLLEN GRAIN,** showing Extine and Intine

91 ... **STIGMA WITH POLLEN GRAINS AND DEVELOPING POLLEN TUBES**

92 ... **TRANSVERSE SECTION BUD OF LILY,** showing Anthers, Stigma, Pollen, Grains, etc.

93 ... **TRANSVERSE SECTION OVARY OF POPPY**

94 ... **TRANSVERSE SECTION OVARY OF TULIP**

95 ... **TRANSVERSE SECTION OVARY OF POTATO**

96 ... **TRANSVERSE SECTION OVARY OF ORCHID**

97 to 100 ... **PROGRESSIVE DEVELOPMENT OF OVARY**

101 ... **TRANSVERSE SECTION CAPITULUM DANDELION**

102 ... **LONGITUDINAL SECTION SUNFLOWER**

103 ... **CAPSULE OF SHEPHERD'S PURSE,** showing Embryos

104 ... **LONGITUDINAL SECTION EMBRYOS OF WHEAT**

MISCELLANEOUS.

105 ... **GROWING POINT OF STEM OF PINE**

106 ... **GROWING POINT OF ROOT OF PEA**

107 ... **SECTION OF COAL,** showing Transverse and Longitudinal Section Roots and Stems

108 ... **TRANSVERSE SECTION STEM OF RUSH**

109 ... **TRANSVERSE SECTION** and Rib-leaf of Fig

110 ... **TRANSVERSE SECTION STEM OF WHITE WATER LILY**

D 2

Algæ.

111 ... PTILOTA ELEGANS

112 ... CERAMIUM ECHIONOTIUM

113 ... BONNEMAISONIA ASPARAGOIDES

114 ... SPACHALARI CIRRHOSA

115 ... CERAMIUM GRACILLIMUM

116 ... WRANGELIA MULTIFIDA

117 ... TRANSVERSE SECTION CREMOCARP OF SMYRNIUM OLUSATRUM, ALEXANDERS

118 ... OVARY OF LILY. Transverse Section

BOTANICAL—Miscellaneous.

119 ... SECTION TRANSVERSE SPRUCE FIR. P.M.

120 ... PROSENCHIMATOUS TISSUE CANADIAN PINE—P.M.

121 ... SECTION OF CLOVER STEM ATTACKED BY DODDER, SHOWING BOTH PARASITE AND HOST very fine —P.M.

122 ... CHARA FRAGILIS, fertile branch showing antheridium and oogonium—P.M.

123 ... PUCCINIA GRAMINIS, AECIDIA—P.M.

124 ... BRANCH OF RETINOSPORA SKUARROSN WITH CONES

125 ... FEMALE CONES SCOTCH PINE GROWING ON BRANCH

126 ... MALE CONES SCOTCH PINE GROWING ON BRANCH

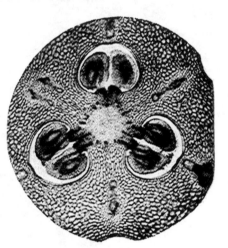

Plant Ovary.

127 ... GROUPE OF SCOTCH PINES (Pine sylvistis)

128 ... PINUS SABINIANA

129 ... FEMALE CONE P. SABINIANA, weight 8lbs.

130 ... WELLINGTONIA PINE TREE

131 ... SILVER FIR TREE (Abies)

132 ... DOUGLAS PINE (Pine douglasii) TREE

133 ... IRISH YEW TREE (Taxus baccata fastigiata)

134 ... DEODAR OR INDIAN CEDAR TREE

135 ... ARUM MACULATUM (lords and ladies,) FLOWERS

136 ... WHITE LILAC

137 ... FLOWERS OF HORSE-CHESTNUT

138 ... DAFFODIL GROWING IN NATURAL ENVIRONMENT

139 ... WILD HYACINTHS (scilla)

140 ... FOXGLOVES GROWING IN NATURAL ENVIRONMENT

141 ... CONE-FRUITED LIVERWORT (Fegatella conica) growing in natural environment, fruiting

142 ... PRIMROSES IN NATURAL ENVIRONMENT

143 ... BABY OAK WITH COTYLIDINOUS AND FOLIAGE LEAVES

144 ... FLOWERING BRANCH, SYCAMORE

145 ... POISONOUS PRIMULA GROWING

146 .. GROUP OF PURPLE IRIS

147 ... TRANSVERSE SECTION ROOT RANUNCULUS ACRIS--P.M.

148 ... BORDERED PITS PINUS—P.M.

149 ... POLLEN GRAINS PINUS—P.M.

150 ... ARCHIGONIA LIVERWORT—P.M.

151 ... SPORES LIVERWORT—P.M.

152 ... VERTICAL SECTION LICHEN- P.M.

153 ... LEAF OF ALOE.-P.M.

154 ... PLASMOLYSIS IN CELL SPIROGYRA—P.M.

155 ... VERTICAL SECTION EMBRYO WHEAT—P.M.

POND LIFE.

Series P.   P.M.—Photo-Micrograph.

1 ... WATER BEETLE MALE). (Dystiscus Marginalis).

2 ... FEMALE WATER BEETLE

3 ... LARVA OF WATER BEETLE

4 ... FRONT LEG OF MALE WATER BEETLE, SHOWING CLASPING ORGAN—P.M.

5 ... MIDDLE LEG OF MALE WATER BEETLE.—P.M.

6 ... PADDLE, OR HIND LEG OF MALE WATER BEETLE—P.M.

7 ... SPIRACLE, OR BREATHING ORGAN OF MALE WATER BEETLE

8 ... LONGITUDINAL SECTION OF EYE OF WATER BEETLE

9 .. DRAGON FLY

10 ... LARVA OF DRAGON FLY

11 ... LONGITUDINAL SECTION OF EYE OF DRAGON FLY—P.M.

12 ... NYMPH OF DRAGONFLY

13 ... FOOT OF WATER SPIDER—P.M.

14 ... SPINERETTES OF WATER SPIDER—P.M.

15 ... JAWS OF SPIDER—P.M.

16 ... ROTIFER, NOTOPS, BRACHIONUS—P.M.

17 ... ROTIFER, ASPLANCHNA BRIGHTWELLI—P.M.

18 ... BRICK-MAKING ROTIFER (Melicerta Ringens)—P.M.

19 .. HEAD OF BRICKMAKING ROTIFER—P.M.

20 ... INFUSORIAN CERATIUM TRIPAS—P.M.

21 ... WATER FLEA (Daphnia Pulex)—P.M.

22 ... FRESH WATER HYDRA—P.M.

23 ... HEAD OF MALE GNAT—P.M.

24 ... HEAD OF FEMALE GNAT—P.M.

25 ... GREAT WATER BEETLE—Male and Female

26 ... FEMALE CYCLOPS WITH EGGS—P.M.

27 ... WATER "STICK" INSECT (Ranatra Linearis)

28 ... WATER SCORPION

29 ... LARVÆ OF DRAGONFLY ATTACKING WATER BOAT-MAN

30 ... POND LIFE (Desmids and Diatoms)—P.M.

31 ... DESMID (Penium Digitus.—P.M.

32 ... DESMID (Euastrum Didelta).—P.M.

33 ... DESMID (Micrasterias Rotata).—P,M.

34 ... DESMID (Closterium).—P.M.

35 ... DIATOM NAVICULA VIRIDIS.—P.M.

36 ... SPIROGYRA NITIDA.—P.M.

For Conjugation Series see BOTANICAL.

MARINE LIFE.

Series M.   P.M.—Photo-Micrograph.

Star Fish. . .

1 ... THE SHORE CRAB IN NATURAL ENVIRONMENT

2 ... LARVAL FREE-SWIMMING STAGE OF CRAB—P.M.

3 ... THE BLENNY IN NATURAL ENVIRONMENT

4 ... THE "SEA MOUSE" WORM (Aphrodita Aculeata)

5 ... THE NORWAY LOBSTER IN NATURAL ENVIRONMENT

6 ... THE ATLANTIC SQUID (S. Atlantic) IN NATURAL ENVIRONMENT

7 ... OCTOPUS (Eledone Cirrhosus) ATTACKING A CRAB

8 ... CUTTLE-FISH ATTACKING A BLENNY

9 ... THE ROSEY FEATHER STAR-FISH IN NATURAL ENVIRONMENT

10 ... STARFISH GROWING A NEW ARM TO REPLACE ONE THAT HAS BEEN LOST

11 ... PLUTEUS LARVA OF ORPHIURID (Starfish)—P.M.

12 ... FREE-SWIMMING LARVAL STAGE OF STARFISH—P.M.

13 ... FREE-SWIMMING LARVAL STAGE (Early) BARNACLE—P.M.

14 ... LATER STAGE OF FREE-SWIM-MINGLARVA OF BARNACLE—P.M.

15 ... ACORN BARNACLES OF LIMPET SHELLS

16 .. LEGS OF BARNACLES–P.M. Very fine

17 ... STALKED BARNACLES

18 ... GROUP OF BRITISH SPONGES

19 ... SEA URCHIN (Echinus)

20 ... LONGITUDINAL SECTION SPINE OF ECHINUS—P.M.

21 ... SPINES OF SPATANGUS (a Sea URCHIN)—P.M.

22 ... GROUP OF SPONGE SPICULES —P.M.

23 ... GROUP OF SPINES OF GORGONIA. HOLOTHUNIA, etc.—P.M.

Spine of Sea Urchin·

24 ... WHEEL PLATES FROM SKIN OF CHIRODOTA VIO-LACEA (a Sea Cucumber.)

25 ... THE SEA-SIDE NATURALIST'S OUTFIT

26 ... SKIN SYNAPTA WITH PLATES AND ANCHORS IN SITU

27 ... PENTNERINOID LARVA FEATHER STAR

28 ... TRANSVERSE SECTION ECHINUS SPINE

29 ... PLUTEUS LARVA ECHINOSLIRNA

30 ... ANCHORS AND PLATES FROM SKIN SYNAPTA

31 ... STALKED SHIP BARNACLES

32 ... SEA BREAM

33 ... SHORE CRABS FIGHTING

34 ... OCTOPUS

35 ... ELIDON

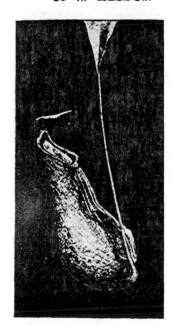

The Pitcher Plant . .

INSECTIVOROUS PLANTS.

Series I. P.   P.M.--Photo-Micrograph.

1 ... GROUP OF NEPENTHES AND SARRACENIA

2 ... SARRANCENIA (The Side - Saddle Plant)

3 ... ATTRACTIVE SURFACE OF LID OF SARRACENIA—P.M.

4 ... CONDUCTING SURFACE OF SARRACENIA—P.M.

5 ... GLANDULAR SURFACE of SARRA-CENIA—P.M.

6 ... HONEY GLANDS FROM LURE OF NEPENTHES

7 ... TWO PITCHERS OF NEPENTHES

8 ... PITCHER OF NEPENTHES

9 ... PITCHER OF NEPENTHES

10 ... HONEY GLAND FROM ATTRACT-IVE SURFACE OF LID OF NEP-ENTHES—P.M.

11 ... DIGESTING AND SECRETING GLANDS FROM INTERIOR OF ITCHER OF NEPENTHES—P.M.

12 ... LONGITUDINAL SECTION OF DIGESTING AND SE-
CRETING GLANDS FROM INTERIOR OF PITCHER
OF NEPENTHES—P.M.

13 ... BLADDER OF BLADDER-WORT (Utricularia).—P.M.

14 ... SUN-DEW (Drosera) IN NATURAL ENVIRONMENT

15 ... SUN-DEW

16 ... SUN-DEW IN FLOWER. Growing in Pot

17 ... FLOWERING SUN-DEW

18 ... LEAVES OF SUN-DEW (Drosera Rotundifolia)

19 ... LEAF OF SUN-DEW WITH CAPTURED INSECT—P.M.

Series I.   INSECTS.

1 ... TARANTULA SPIDER

2 ... FOOT OF GARDEN SPIDER—P.M.

3 ... FACE AND EYES OF GARDEN SPIDER—P.M.

4 ... THORAX GARDEN SPIDER—P.M.

5 ... AIR-SAC, GARDEN SPIDER—P.M.

6 ... SPINIRETTES GARDEN SPIDER—P.M.

7 ... EXTERIOR SAND WASPS NEST

8 ... INTERIOR SAND WASPS NEST SHOWING CELLS
LARVA

9 ... PUPÆ SPURGE HAWK MOTH (C. Euphorbiæ)

10 ... SPURGE HAWK MOTH (D. Euphorbiæ)

11 ... ELEPHANT HAWK MOTH (C. Elpenor)

12 ... SCARCE SWALLOW-TAIL BUTTERFLY (P. Podalirius)

13 ... SWALLOW-TAIL BUTTERFLY (P. Machaone)

14 ... SMALL TORTOISESHELL BUTTERFLY (V Urticæ)

15 ... SAWS OF SAW-FLY—P.M.

16 ... JAWS OF SOLDIER BEETLE—P.M.

17 ... FOOT OF HOUSE-FLY—P.M.

18 ... TONGUE OF BLOW-FLY—P.M.

19 ... PORTION OF TONGUE BLOW-FLY,
magnified.

20 ... HARVEST MITE—P.M.

21 ... HARVEST MITE, portion greatly magnified—P.M.

22 ... WING OF BUTTERFLY, showing how
scales are attached—P.M.

23 ... SPIRACLE OF FLOWER FLY—P.M.

24 ... TRACHEA OF FLOWER FLY—P.M.

Tongue of Fly. . .

FARM AND GARDEN INSECT PESTS.

Series F.I.   P.M.—Photo-Micrograph.

1 ... ANTLER OR GRASS MOTH, MALE and FEMALE

2 ... MARCH MOTH, MALE and FEMALE and LARVA

3 ... GOAT MOTH AND LARVA

4 ... SMALL OR GARDEN SWIFT MOTH

5 ... MOTTLED UMBER MOTH, MALE, FEMALE and LARVA

6 ... CABBAGE MOTH and LARVA

7 ... DOT MOTH and LARVA

8 ... LACKY MOTH and LARVA

9 ... EGGS OF LACKY MOTH

10 ... COMMON VAPOURER MOTH, MALE and FEMALE

11 ... COCOON OF COMMON VAPOURER MOTH, covered with Eggs

12 ... FIGURE-OF-8 MOTH and LARVA

13 ... WINTER MOTH, MALE and FEMALE

14 ... OTTER OR GHOST SWIFT MOTH, MALE and FEMALE

Cabbage Butterfly.

15 ... LARVA-DEATH'S HEAD MOTH

16 ... APPLE-PITH MOTH

17 ... WOOD LEPPARD MOTH

18 ... LARGE WHITE CABBAGE BUTTERFLY

19 ... HEART-AND-DART MOTH

20 ... GOOSEBERRY AND CURRANT, OR MAGPIE MOTH & LARVA

21 ... YELLOW UNDER WING MOTH

22 ... CURRANT CLEAR WING MOTH

23 ... LAPPET MOTH

24 ... SUCKER-LEGS OF CATERPILLAR—P.M.

25 ... FRONT LEGS OF CATERPILLAR.—P.M.

26 ... GROUND BEETLES

27 ... COCKCHAFER BEETLE

28 ... GOLDEN ROSE CHAFER BEETLES

29 ... CLICK BEETLES (as Larvæ Wire-Worm)

30 ... NUT WEEVIL

31 ... VINE WEEVIL

32 ... HOP VINE SNOUT MOTH

BEES AND BEE FARMING.

Series B.F.   P.M.—Photo-micrograph.

1 ... OLD FASHIONED BASKET SKEP

2 ... MODERN FRAME HIVE

3 ... GENERAL VIEW OF MODERN BEE FARM

4 ... BEE VAN OF SURREY BEE KEEPERS' ASSOCIATION

5 ... DRIVING BEES FROM SKEP INTO BASKET, preparatory to placing in Modern Hive

6 ... INVERTED SKEP SHOWING BEES ON COMB

7 ... EXAMINING BASKET (in driving) FOR QUEEN

8 ... FRAME OF FOUNDATION

9 ... FRAME OF FOUNDATION WORKED BY BEES

10 ... BROOD COMB WITH BEES AT WORK

11 ... LIFE-SIZE VIEW OF SAME

12 ... COMB WITH QUEEN

13 ... HONEY COMB

14 ... THE MOUTH OF THE HIVE, BEES ENTERING and LEAVING THE HIVE

15 }
16 } BEES CARRYING OFF A FLOWER WHICH HAS FALLEN IN FRONT OF THE HIVE.
17 }

18 ... SMALL OBSERVATION HIVE USED IN BEE VAN DEMONSTRATIONS

19 ... SWARM OF BEES

20 ... SWARM OF BEES (closer view)

21 ... TAKING A SWARM

22 ... SWARM IN FRONT OF HIVE AND ENTERING HIVE

23 ... WINGS OF BEES, showing how back and front wings are joined together in flight—P.M.

24 ... MOUTH PARTS OF BEE—P.M.

25 ... STING OF BEE—P.M.

26 ... TONGUE OF WASP—P.M.

27 ... JAW OF WASP—P.M.

ZOOLOGY AND HISTOLOGY.

Series H.Z. ## Anthozoa.

1 ... BODY WALL, Pennatula Phosphorea L

2 ... POLYPES, Pennatula Phosphorea L

3 ... POLYPES, Alyconium Palmatum Pall

4 ... T.S. BODY OF CERIANTHUS SOLITARIUS RAPP

5 ... SURFACE S. BODY OF ALYCONIUM PALMATUM

6 ... FRAGMENT WITH POLYPS Corallium rubrum Lam

7 ... FRAGMENT WITH POLYPS Gorgonia cavolinii Kock

Bryoza.

1 ... ANIMALS EXTENDED ZOOBOTRYON PELLUCIDUM EHRBG

2 ... ANIMALS EXTENDED BUGULA CALATHUS

3 ... ANIMALS EXTENDED BUGULA TURBINATA, ALDER

4 ... ANIMALS EXTENDED ESCHARA. FOLIACEA, ELLIS

5 ... ANIMALS EXTENDED LYPHOPUS CRYSTALINA

6 ... ANIMALS EXTENDED PLUMATELLA REPENS

Crustacea.

1 ... NAUPLIUS AND CYPRIS, BALANUS. perforatus Brug
2 ... ZOÆ OF HIPPOLYTE VARIANS
3 ... ERICHTRILINA OF SQUILLA EUSEBIA, RISO
4 ... ZOÆ OF PALAEMON SQUILLA, FABR
5 ... ZOÆ OF BROMIA VULGARIS EDW
6 ... ZOÆ OF CARCINUS MOENAS, LEACH
7 ... ZOÆ OF PAGURAS STRIATUS, LATR
8 ... ZOÆ OF MAJA SQUINADO, BOSE
9 ... ZOÆ OF PORCELLANA PLATYCHELES, LAM
10 ... PHYLLOSOMA LARVÆ OF SCYLLARUS ARCTUS
11 ... ENTIRE CHELURA TEREBRANS, PHIL
12 ... YOUNG ENTIRE MYSIS
13 ... ENTIRE CAPRELLA ACUTIFRONS. LATR
14 ... FRESH WATER DAPHNIA SP
15 ... FRESH WATER PHOLYPHEMA

Echinoderma.

1 ... RIPE OVUM OF ECHINUS ESCULENTUS
2 ... LARVA ASTERINA GIBBOSA
3 ... PENTACRINUS OF ANTEDON ROSACEA
4 ... AURICULARIA LARVA
5 ... BIPINNARIA LARVA
6 ... PINNÆ OF ANTEDON ROSACEA
7 TO 11...STAGES IN THE LARVAL DEVELOPMENT OF
      ASTERINA GIBBOSA
12 ... YOUNG ASTERINA GIBBOSA
13 ... AMPHIURA SQUAMATA SARS
14 ... VERT AND HORZL S. ASTERINA GIBBOSA
15 ... T.S. BODY PEACHIA HASTATA, GOSS
16 ... ENTIRE SPHAERECHINUS GRANULARIS AG.

Holothurioidea.

1 ... SKIN OF SYNAPTA INHAERENS, (for spicules)
2 ... T.S. BODY, CUCUMARIA PLANCII, Brdt.
3 ... VARIOUS STAGES IN THE DEVELOPMENT OF PHYL
      LOPHORUS URNA. GRUB
4 ... ENTIRE HOLOTHURIA POLI, D. ch

Hydrozoa.

1 ... T. AND L.S. BODY HYDRA FUSCA
2 ... GONOTHYREA LOVENII ALLM
3 ... BOUGAINVILLIA FRUCTICOSA ALLM

4 ... CORYDENDRIUM PARASITICUM COV

5 ... PENNARIA QAVOLINI GOLDF

6 ... EUDENDRIUM RACEMOSUM CAV

7 ... CORYNE FRUTICOSA

8 ... PLUMULARIA PINNATE HINCKS

9 ... CAMPANULARIA CALYCULATA HINCKS

10 ... CLYTIA JOHNSTONII ALDER

11 ... FRAGMENT OF COL ATTACHED TO SHELL Hydracti-
nia cchinata Hincks

12 ... FRAGMENT OF COL ATTACHED TO SHELL Hydracti-
nia Podocoryne carnea Hincks

13 ... OBELIA GENICULATA OR SP

14 ... OBELIA GENICULATA MEDUSA

15 ... OCEANIA CONICA MEDUSA

Mollusca

1 ... EGGS OF APLYSIA LIMACINA, L

2 ... ENTIRE APLYSIA LIMACINA

3 ... EGGS, WITH EMBROYOS OF CASSIDARIA ECHINOP
HORA

4 ... ENTIRE CRESEIS ACICULA, RANG

5 ... ENTIRE PHYLLIRRHOE BUCEPHALUM

6 ... YOUNG, just hatched, LOLIGO VULGARIS

7 ... YOUNG, just hatched, OCTOPUS VULGARIS CAM

8 ... EMBRYOS SEPIA OFFICINALIS

9 ... T.S. ARM AND SUCKER SEPIA OFFICINALIS

10 ... T.S. HEAD

11 ... T.S. OF BODY, COMMON GARDEN SLUG

12 ... L.S. EYE OF PECTEN OPERCULARIS, L

Porifera.

1 ... ENTIRE LEUCOSOLINIA NOTRYOIDES

2 ... T.S. (for collars and flagella) SYCON CILIATUM

3 ... T.S. (for collars and flagella) GRANTIA COMPRESSA

4 ... T.S. GEODIA GIGAS O.S.

5 ... T.S. STELLETTA CARBONARIA O.S.

6 ... T.S. SUSPONGIA OFFICINALIS L

7 ... T.S. CHONDROSIA RENIFORMIS NDS.

8 ... T.S. AXINELLA VERRUCOSA ESP

Protozoa.

1 ... THALASSICOLLA NUCLEATA, HUXL

2 ... FRAGMENT OF COLONY, COLLOZOUM INERME E.H.

3 ... POLYTREMA MINIACEUM PALL

4 ... FRAGMENT OF COLONY, SPHÆ ROZOUM PUNCTATUM, J. MALL

5 ... ENTIRE AULACANTHA SCOLYMANTHE, E.H

6 ... FRAGMENT OF COLONY, MYXOSPHAERA COERULEA, E.H.

7 ... NOCTILUCA MILIARIS

8 ... VARIOUS FORMS OF FORAMINIFERA

Pisces.

1 ... T.S. OF ADULT AMPHIOXUS LANCEOLATUS, YARR

2 ... T.S. YOUNG ENTIRE AMPHIOXUS LANCEOLATUS YARR

3 ... EGGS WITH EMBRYOS OF LABRAX LUMPUS, CUV

4 ... EMBRYONIC STAGE, LABRAX LUMPUS, CUV

5 ... MIGRATION OF EYE, PLATESSA VULGARIS GOSSE

6 ... EMBRYONIC STAGES, LOPHIUS PISCATORIUS, L

7 ... YOUNG, WITH HEAD APPENDAGES, LOPHIUS PISCA-TORIUS L

8 ... EGGS WITH EMBRYOS, EXECOETUS VOLITANS, L

9 TO 14 ... DEVELOPEMENT OF HIPPOCAMPUS BREVIRO-STRIS

        1st and 2nd Stage

        3rd and 4th Stage

        5th and 6th Stage

15 ... YOUNG ENTIRE HIPPOCAMPUS BREVIROSTRIS, CUV.

16 ... EGGS AND EMBYROS, OF GOBIUS SP

17 ... T.S. HEAD AND GILL-ARCHES OF COMMON STICK-LEBACK

18 ... YOUNG ENTIRE STICKLEBACK

19 ... PARASITE OF THE FISH, ARGULUS FOLIACEUS

Tunicata

1 ... LARVÆ OF DISTAPLIA MANILARVA, DELLA

2 ... LARVÆ OIKOPLEURA COPHOCERCA, GGB.

3 .. ENTIRE PEROPHORA LISTERI, WEIGM

4 ... ENTIRE CLAVELLINA LEPADIFORME, M. EDW

5 ... ENTIRE CIONA INTESTINALIS

6 ... ENTIRE SALPA DEMOCRATICA AGGREGATA

Vermes.

1 ... ENTIRE TOMOPTERIS SCOLOPENDRA

2 ... ENTIRE AMPHIGLENA MEDITERRANEA, CLAP

3 ... ENTIRE OPHRYOTROCHA PUERILIS, CLAP

4 ... ENTIRE HETERONEREIS BUMERILLII, AUD

5 ... LARVA SPIONIDÆ

6 ... MYZOSTOMA CIRRIFERUM, LEUK

7 ... T.S. ARENICOLA GRABII, CLAP

8 ... ENTIRE SAGITTA SPEC

9 ... ENTIRE LEPTOPLANA TREMELLARIS, O.F.M.

10 AND 11 ... T AND R . S. CARINELLA ANNULATA, M. INT

12 ... PLUMES

13 ... ENTIRE DASYCHONE LUCULLANA, D. CH

14 ... T.S. BODY MYXICOLA INFUNDIBULUM REN

15 AND 16 ... SECTIONS, L. AND T. MYXICOLA INFUNDIB- ULUM

17 ... T.S. LUMBRICONEREIS COCCINEA, REN

18 ... T.S. SYLLIS SPONICGOLA GRUBE

19 ... T.S. DASYCHONE LUCULLANA D. CH

20 TO 21 ... T. AND L.S. LANICE CONCHILEGA, PALL

22 ... ENTIRE SAGITTA SPEC

23 ... TYPE SLIDE, SECTION, PONTOBDELLA MURICATA, SAV

24 ... TYPE SLIDE, SECTION, HORSE BEECH

25 ... L.S. REPRODUCTIVE SEGMENTS, EARTH WORM

26 ... T.S. REPRODUCTIVE SEGMENTS, EARTH WORM

HUMAN ANATOMY.

Series H.A.

1 ... L.S. OF HEAD, frontal Showing mouth and tongue

2 ... DEVELOPING TEETH, Etc..

3 ... L. TANGL S. OF HEAD THROUGH EYE

4 ... SCALP, BRAIN, MED- ULLA OBLONGATA

5 ... LARYNX

6 ... L.S. HEART

7 ... BODY WALL OF THO- RAX

8 ... SPINAL COLUMN

9 ... LIVER, LUNG, KID ENY, STOMACH, LYM- PHATIC GLAND

10 ... V.S. OF EAR

11 ... T.S. UMBILICAL CORD, INTESTINE, PENIS, SKIN

12 ... T.S. THIGH

13 ... L.S. KNEE JOINT

14 ... T.S. LEG

15 ... T.S. ARM

16 ... T.S. HAND

17 ... L.S. FINGER

18 ... L.S. FOOT

HISTOLOGY OF FRESH WATER CRAYFISH.

Series A.F. "Aslacus Fluviatilis."

1 ... T.S. CARAPACE

2 ... L.S. NERVE CORD

3 ... L.S. BRAIN

4 ... T.S. LIVER

5 ... T.S. PYLORIC CHAM- BER OF STOMACH

6 ... L.S FLEXOR MUSCLE

7 ... T.S. HIND GUT

8 ... T.S. ŒSOPHAGUS

9 ... L.S. EYE

10 ... T.S. GREEN GLAND AND BLADDER

11 ... T.S. TESTIS AND VAS DEFERENS

12 ... MID GUT

HISTOLOGY OF FRESH WATER MUSSEL.

Series A.C. "Anodonta Cygnea."

1 ... T.S. LIVER
2 ... T.S. FOOT
3 ... T.S. HEART
4 ... T.S. OUTER GILL
5 ... T.S. INNER GILL
6 ... L.S. PEDAL GANGLIA
7 ... L.S. CEREBRAL GAN-
8 ... T.S GHA RECTUM
9 ... T.S, WALL OF STOM-
ACH AND LIVER
10 ... T.S. KIDNEY

11 ... T.S. VISCERAL MASS
AND REPRODUCTIVE
ORGAN
13 ... T.S. KEBER'S ORGAN
12 ... T.S. LABIAL PALP
14 ... T.S. INHALENT EDGE
OF MANTLE
15 ... T.S. EXHALENT EDGE
OF MANTLE
16 ... T.S. MIDDLE EDGE
OF MANTLE
17 ... T.S. INTESTINE

ZOOLOGICAL.

Series Z.

1 ... AUSTRALIAN BLACK
SWAN
2 ... ROYAL VULTURE
3 ... VOCIFEROUS SEA
EAGLE
4 ... VULTURINE EAGLE
5 ... TAWNY EAGLE
6 ... PELICAN
7 ... FLAMIGOES
8 ... GREAT EARED OWL
9 ... MACAW
10 ... EGYPTIAN GOOSE
11 ... GOLDEN PHEASANT
12 ... AMERICAN BISON
13 ... BABY INDIAN ELE-
PHANT
14 ... BABOONS AT TOILET
15 ... SACRED BABOON
16 ... HYENA

17 ... MOUNTAIN GOAT
MALE
18 ... MOUNTAIN GOAT
FEMALE
19 ... RUSSIAN BROWN
BEAR
20 ... HEAD OF HIPPOPO-
TAMUS
21 ... ZEBRA
22 ... LION
23 ... HEAD OF CAMEL
24 ... OLD ENGLISH WILD
WHITE BULL
25 ... PORCUPINE
26 ... CHAMAELEON
27 ... LEOPARD
28 ... EMU
29 ... TIGER
30 ... POLAR BEAR
31 ... SEA-LION

HISTOLOGY OF THE RABBIT.

Series R.

1 ... T. AND L.S. BONE
2 ... T. AND L.S. MUSCLE
Straited
3 ... L.S. MUSCLE Plain
4 ... BLOOD
5 ... CRYSTALS HÆMOG-
LOBIN
6 ... T. AND L.S. TOOTH

7 ... T.S. ŒSOPHAGUS
8 ... T.S. STOMACH Car-
diac and Pyloric
9 ... T. AND L.S. BUODE-
NUM
10 ... T.S. JEJUNUM
11 ... T.S. LLEUM
12 ... T.S. VERMIFORM AP-
PENDIX

HISTOLOGY OF THE RABBIT—*continued.*

13 ... T.S. CÆCUM
14 ... L.S. COLON
15 ... T.S. RECTUM
16 ... PAROTID GLAND
17 ... SUBMAXILLARY GLAND
18 ... SUBLINGUAL GLAND
19 ... T.S. PANCREAS
20 ... T.S. LIVER
21 ... T.S. KIDNEY
22 ... SUPRARENAL CAP-SULE
23 ... T.S. URETER
24 ... LUNG
25 ... T.S. BLADDER
26 ... T.S. TRACHEA
27 ... V.S. SKIN
28 ... T.S. NAIL
29 ... L.S. NERVE
30 ... T.S. SPINAL CORD, CERVICAL, BORSAL AND LUMBAR RE-GIONS

31 ... L.S. MEDULLA OBLON-GATA
32 ... T.S. CEREBELLUM
33 ... T.S. CEREBRUM
34 ... L.S. ENTIRE EYE
35 ... T.S. COATS OF EYE
36 ... T.S. TONGUE
37 ... L.S. LARYNX
38 ... T.S. TESTIS
39 ... T.S. OVARY
40 ... T.S. FALLOPIAN TUBE
41 ... T.S. UTERUS
42 ... T.S. VAGINA
43 ... T.S. THYROID GLAND
44 ... T.S. THYMUS GLAND
45 ... SPLEEN
46 ... LYMPHATIC GLAND
47 ... T.S. YELLOW ELAS-TIC CARTILAGE
48 ... T.S LACHRYMAL GLAND

The "NATURE" SERIES of Permanent Photographic Enlargement.

To meet a large and increasing demand for truthful representations of "Nature" we are offering at a very low price exquisite Photographic Enlargements framed and unframed, suitable for hanging in Class and Lecture Rooms, School Rooms, Play Rooms, etc., etc. The advantage and superiority of a first-class Photograph direct from Nature over the ordinary hideous, badly-drawn and coloured lithograph is obvious. Our "Nature" Series of Photographs, shows the Animals, Insects and Plants in their natural environment. With every Photograph we send out a short description of the subject. Size of Photographs range from 10in. by 8in. to 20in by 16in. Prices on application.

To meet the demands from the Agricultural Districts, Photographic Enlargements of our entire "Insect Pest" Series can now be supplied.

SCENES AND INCIDENTS

From All Parts of the World.

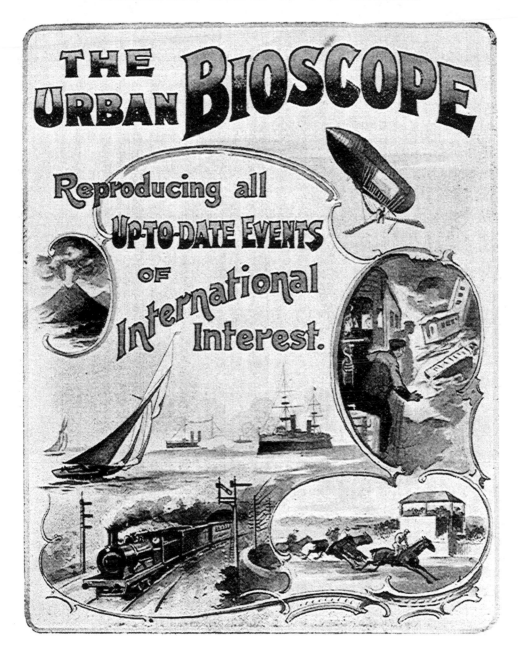

URBAN FILMS

PERFORATED to the STANDARD GAUGE, will
fit any ACCURATE Standard Gauge Machine.

E

BIOSCOPIC SERIES.
RACES, SPORTS AND CONTESTS.

A bob-sleighiug party at Grindelwald.

1004 ... ON LONGCHAMPS RACE COURSE, PARIS
A series of interesting scenes at these races especially arranged for the King including views of the Paddock, the parade of horses, the arrival of the King, the King in the Royal box, the fashionable crowds, the winner, &c., &c. Excellent views of his Majesty. **200 feet**

1006 ... THE TUG OF WAR, "FRASCATI v. TROCADERO"
Full of Life, Fun and Bottles.   **150 feet**

1007 ... THE SPORTS OF THE GENEVA UNION (Hurdle, Sack and Costume Races)
Full of animation and humor.   **125 feet**

1036 ... FENCING TOURNAMENT BETWEEN FRENCH, ITALIAN AND BRITISH SWORDSMEN AT THE ROYAL BOTANICAL GARDENS
A series of spirited contests with the foil, sword, and rapier.
                                                       150 feet

1039 ... ICE YACHTING ON THE ST. LAWRENCE   **50 feet**

1040 ... SKATING AT MONTREAL   **100 feet**

1041 ... CHAMPIONSHIP SKATING CONTEST AT MONTREAL, CANADA
                                                       150 feet

1042 ... THE SNOW SHOE CLUB OUTING   **150 feet**

1045 ... HOCKEY ON SKATES   **50 feet**

1046 ... SKI JUMPING   **75 feet**

1048 ... BOB SLEIGHING   **50 feet**

1050 ... TOBOGGANING ON THE CRESTA   **60 feet**

1052 ... **THE WAITRESSES OF THE B.T.T. AND P.P. (British Tea Table and Pearce and Plenty) WALK FROM THE MANSION HOUSE TO HYDE PARK**   **125 feet**

1060 ... **" LOOPING THE LOOP "**
The cars are shown in this film laden with venturesome spirits of both sexes who loop the loop in absolute safety, thanks to the benign influence of centrifugal force.   **50 feet**

1061 ... **" SHOOTING THE CHUTES "**
Shooting the Chutes possesses a perennial attraction. The swift rush down, the repeated dips into the lake, and the exhilirating rapidity of it all keeps this amusement a prime favourite.   **75 feet**

1069 ... **CANOE TILTING CONTEST ON THE ST. LAWRENCE**
    100 feet

1071 ... **SWISS WRESTLING ON THE TURF OF THE KURSAAL, INTERLAKEN**
This is a typical wrestling match of the catch-as-catch-can variety. Several bouts are shown in this picture, and as the contestants frequently lift each other into mid-air, and then throw, the effect is exciting and realistic. A splendid film.   **125 feet**

1089 ... **FISHERGIRLS' RACE AND DANCE**
A spirited-foot-race engaged in by a number of fishergirls in their characteristic attire, and with their fishcreels or baskets on their backs. They afterwards engage in their native " Reel " dance which they go through in very lively fashion.   **50 feet**

1105 ... **INDIAN CANOE RACES ON THE ST. LAWRENCE**
    50 feet

1136 ... **LACROSSE — CANADA'S NATIONAL GAME. Between the Westminster and Vancouver Teams**
The commencement of film shows the members of the two teams filing by the camera. The game watched by 5,000 spectators, begins in the most lively fashion and continues throughout the length, while near the end a panorama of the grounds with visitors is reproduced while the game is in progress, thus giving the spectator a fine idea of how Canada's National game is played.   **125 feet**

1165 ... **A BUN-EATING COMPETITION**
If you have ever witnessed a bun-eating competition you have had a full three minutes of huge enjoyment in watching the endeavours of the participants to grasp a bun (of which there are about a score strung along in a row, each bun separately suspended and dangling about by the least movement against it). He must capture the bun with his teeth and is disqualified if he uses his hands or arms. There are about fifteen competitors in this picture, and the antics resulting from their endeavonrs to prove the winner would make a goat laugh.   **100 feet**

1239 ... **COCK FIGHTING ON THE ICE RINK**
An exciting sport in which two contestants, seated on the ice with their arms pinioned over their knees, are endeavouring to upset one another by pushing with their feet.   **75 feet**

1241 ... **SKI RUNNING FOR AMATEURS**
An exhilarating sport, far more difficult in practice than in appearance. Frequent upsets in the snow lend much humour to the subject.   **100 feet**

1243-4 ... **MOTOR CLIMBING CONTEST AT THE CRYSTAL PALACE**
Between the 12-h.p. " Lanchester " Car, weight 22 cwt., driven by Mr. Archibald J. W. Miliership, and the 25-h.p. " Gobron-Brillie" Car, weight 28 cwt., driven by Mons. Duray up the steep flight of steps leading from the lower terrace to the Palace (gradient 1 in $2\frac{1}{2}$)
    125 feet

E 2

1240—

INTERNATIONAL WINTER SPORTS.

A grand series of exciting and unique pictures, photographed in the **United States of America, Canada, Norway, Sweden, and Switzerland,** by our Bioscopists, **Messrs. Rosenthal, Ormiston=Smith, Lansdorff,** and others.

25 Interesting Views :

1 ... STORMING THE FORT—Battle of Snowballs

2 ... ICE YACHTING ON THE HUDSON RIVER, NEW YORK

3 ... CLEARING THE RINK AFTER A HEAVY SNOW FALL

4 ... COCK FIGHTING ON THE ICE RINK

5 ... A "TIPPING" CONTEST ON THE ICE

6 ... SKATING EN MASSE AT MONTREAL

7 ... SKATE RACING ON ONE FOOT

8 ... LADIES' AND MEN'S SKATE AND SLED RACES

9 ... A GAME OF ICE HOCKEY IN SWITZERLAND

10 ... HURDLE JUMPING DURING THE WORLD'S CHAMPION-SHIP SKATING RACES AT MONTREAL

11 ... OBSTACLE SLIDE RACES IN SWEDEN

12 ... SACK RACING ON SKATES AT GRINDELWALD

13 ... "TOSSING IN THE BLANKET" IN CANADA

14 ... THE OUTING OF THE CANADIAN SNOW SHOE CLU —Crossing the frozen St. Lawrence River

15 ... A RUN OF THE BOYS' SKI CLUB IN NORWAY

16 ... AMATEURS AT SKI-RUNNING OVER SOFT SNOW

17 ... LADIES LEARNING SKI-ING ON THE ALPS

18 ... BOB SLED COASTING PARTIES AT GRINDELWALD

19 ... JUMPING FROM PLATFORM WITH AMERICAN TOBOG-GANS—a most dangerous game

20 ... THE START FROM TOP OF THE TOBOGGAN COURSE

21 ... ROUNDING THE CRESTA AT 40 MILES AN HOUR

22 ... THE SLEIGHING PARTY WITH TRAILERS

23 ... THE EXHILARATING SPORT OF TRAILING—photographed from the sleigh

24 ... SWISS SCHOOL KIDDIES OFF TO THE SLEDGING RACES

25 ... SWEEPING DOWN "DEVIL'S LEAP" – a general upset and melée of fifty boys and girls—making an exciting and humorous finish to an exceedingly fine series of unique pictures

1240 ... Total length 750 feet

PRESS NOTICES re WINTER SPORTS.

"SPORTING TIMES,"

One of the most interesting features in this week's programme at the Alhambra is a series of animated pictures of International winter sports shown by the Urban Bisocope Co. These views, which were taken in the United States, Canada, Norway, Sweden, and Switzerland. reproduce scenes in which the following pastimes are in full swing :—Ski-ing, hurdle, skate, and sled jumping, ice yachting hockey, obstacle and sack races on skates, racing on toboggans at forty miles an hour at St. Moritz, and sleighing and trailing in the Alps.

"DAILY NEWS."

One of the most interesting features in this week's programme at the Alhambra has been the series of animated pictures of international winter sports shown by the Urban Bioscope Company.

"THE SUN."

Another notable item of the Alhambra programme is a series of pictures shown by the Charles Urban Trading Company, dealing with different scenes in the present Russia-Japanese War. One picture shows the departure of the Cossacks for the seat of war from St. Petersburg. The most interesting pictures, however, are those showing the Japanese battleship "Yashima," firing off her big guns. The snow scenes dealing with Canadian life in the winter are also amongst the most brilliant dealt with by the bioscope.

A word should also be given for the pictures showing what the motor car can surmount under the most difficult circumstances. These show cars of different manufacturers climbing the steps leading from the football ground to the upper terraces of the Crystal Palace with the most ridiculous ease. The cars which accomplished this task are the Lanchester and Gobron-Brillie cars, the former of 12-h.p., and the latter of 20-h.p.

"THE ECHO."

One of the most interesting features in the week's programme at the Alhambra is the splendid series of animated pictures of international winter sports shown by the Urban Bioscope Company. These views, which were taken in the United States, Canada, Norway, Sweden, and Switzerland, reproduce scenes in which the following pastimes are in full swing : Ski-ing, hurdle, skate, and sled jumping, ice yachting, hockey, obstacle and sack races on skates, racing on toboggans at forty miles an hour at St. Moritz, and sleighing and tailing in the Alps.

"PALL MALL GAZETTE."

One of the most interesting features of this week's programme at the Alhambra is the series of animated pictures of International winter sports shown by the Urban Bioscope Company. These views, which were taken in the United States, Canada, Norway, Sweden and Switzerland, reproduce scences in which the following pastimes are in full swing :— Ski-ing, hurdle, skate, and sled jumping, ice yachting, hockey, obstacle and sack races ou skates, racing on toboggans at forty an hour at St. Moritz, and sleighing and trailing in the Alps.

"THE ERA."

A strong attraction is the series of views shown by the Urban Bioscope, Very laughable are the depictions of the merry winter sports of ice-sailing, skating, tobogganing, and "ski" racing, the tumbles in the snow of the competitors being keenly enjoyed by the spectators of the splendid exhibition given by the wonderful Bioscope. The films supplied by the Urban Trading Company are excellent in technical qualities and most effectively chosen and taken.

"PHOTOGRAPHIC NEWS."

A very fine series of cinematograph pictures is now being shown at the Alhambra Theatre, by the Chas. Urban Trading Company, Ltd. Some films showing international winter sports, such as ski-ing, ice-yachting, toboggan racing, snowballing, &c., are particularly good, the Canadian snow being beautifully rendered, and not chalky, as we have been accustomed to see it.

"MORNING ADVERTISER."

No more successful series of pictures has ever been shown at the Alhambra than The International Winter Sports given by the Urban Bioscope. These pictures will, in consequence, be retained in the programme until further notice.

1250 ... **YACHTING AT WESTCLIFF-ON-SEA**

Fine photographic quality, depicting scores of yachts with sails trimmed, scudding past the view and dodging one another in their hurry to take up good positions for a race. **75 feet**

1251 ... **THE KIDDIES' FISHING COMPETITION**

The children are tied by ropes to stakes driven into the ground to prevent their falling into the stream. **75 feet**

1252 ... **A FISHING COMPETITION ON THE RIVER WITHAM**

The gathering at the mill. Sorting hampers. Ferrying fishermen across stream. Distribution of tickets. Passing out bait. Fishing along the banks of the Tweed. **100 feet**

1262 ... **SKI JUMPING IN NORWAY**

A fine picture of this national sport of Norway which is becoming popular in other countries favoured with snow during the winter season. **100 feet**

1268 ... BOAT RACING ON THE THAMES

The most comprehensive Boat Race Series ever bioscoped—of exceptional photographic quality, showing fine portraits of the Competing Crews.

1 **The Oxford Crew getting into their Boat and pulling for the Starting Point**

2 **The Cambridge Crew manning their Racing Shell**

3 **The Race**

No. 1268 Boat Racing on the Thames.

Taken from the bow of the "Sportsman's" fast steamer which followed closely in the wake of the crews. Through their kindness we were successful in procuring one of the best pictures of the Race ever taken). Showing both crews pulling over the course.

4 **After the Race—The Oxford Crew carrying their Boat up the River Bank**

5 **The Cambridge Crew bringing their Shell ashore**

Excellent view of the interior arrangement of their craft, this they turn over and display the highly polished bottom and general outline.

A splendid subject of interest at all times. **225 feet**

1269 ... **THE OXFORD AND CAMBRIDGE BOAT RACE, 1904**

"MUSIC HALL."

Two boxes at the Alhambra on Saturday night were occupied by the Oxford and Cambridge crews at the invitation of the management of that hall, A special feature in the programme—and one of great interest to the University men—was a reproduction on the Urban Biosope, of the race rowed that very morning. The picture is an excellent reproduction of the race, and was hugely enjoyed by the visitors.

75 feet

1271 ... TUG OF WAR FOR CHALLENGE CUP

Two stalwart crews are seen exerting their combined strength in opposite directions. Three "pulls" are shown, after which the winning crew, in their exuberance over the victory, makes a splendid finish to the series. **125 feet**

1281 ... THE WRESTLING MATCH FOR £200 BETWEEN SIEGFRIED AND LURICH

An excellent example of Interior Photography. This event is **the first successfully bioscoped** in the interior of a theatre by means of the ordinary illumination—no open-air or pre-arranged studio affair. The event is an important one in the wrestling world. The match was brought off on the Alhambra stage, April 14th— Siegfried **winner**—*so is the picture.* **200 feet**

1282 ... WRESTLING MATCH IN INDIA

An Indian Regiment in " undress uniform " forms a circle, in the centre of which a spirited wrestling match wages between some of its members. These Indians are adepts at the " Hackenschmidt " game. The exhibition of the picture in contrast with the English wrestling pictures forms an interesting contrast. **125 feet**

1283 ... POLO MATCH ON ROLLER SKATES

Played on the Crystal Palace Terrace between two Polo teams. Full of action and interest. **125 feet**

1284 ... THE FINAL CUP TIE FOOTBALL MATCH

The great annual event which takes place at the Crystal Palace to decide the winning team at the close of each football season. These games have

Bioscoping Football Matches at Crystal Palace

been attended by 70,000 spectators. Exciting sport. **250 feet**

Re CRICKET AND PUSH=BALL.

" THE ERA.

The animated picture records that are the work of the Urban Bioscope Company limn even the fleeting fame of the cricketer, whom the British public loves to honour ; and we can now see nightly at the Alhambra the genial countenance of Mr. " Plum " Warner, who was specially honoured on Monday by the Authors' Club as one of the gayest and gallantest captains that ever led an eleven across the seas. Mr. Warner has splendidly sustained the high reputation for honesty, manliness, fair play, and courtesy which British sportsmen hold in all parts of the world ; and audiences in Leicester Square show conclusively what a popular celebrity he really is. He is accompanied by only one of the team—J. T. Tyldesley, of Lancashire—that went with him to Australia, but members of former elevens who have played in the land of the kangaroo include W. G. Grace, G. L. Jessop, Prince Ranjitsinghi, Richardson, and C. M'Gahey. Another interesting film is that delineating the new sport of push-ball, which was photographed at Windsor Cavalry Barracks during the rehearsals for the Military Tournament. The game is played with a huge specially made leather ball, which, when fully distended, is about 5ft. 4in. in diameter, and weighs about 1 cwt. Eight horsemen take part in a game, four on each side. The ball is propelled by the horses' knees, and an expert rider often makes his animal punt it the whole length of the field.

"THE MORNING POST."

The bioscope now gives some new pictures. We see the game of pushball on horseback played to the perturbation of several cows. We see, too, several of the first-class cricket teams emerging from their respective pavilions. In their shady hats it is not always possible to recognise the players, but Dr. Grace, "Rauji," and Mr. P. F. Warner were quickly identified and greatly cheered. There are also some pictures of a match in progress taken apparently from deep mid-off. The effect is curious, for the wickets do not look more than ten yards apart. Yet when "Ranji" glances a ball to leg he takes the usual number of steps between crease and crease.

1288 ... THE PRELIMINARY RACES FOR THE GORDON-BEN-NETT RACES IN THE ISLE OF MAN

Showing the most difficult curves and inclines over which the various competing cars raced pevious to the great Gordon Bennett Cup Races, held at Homburg, Germany. **150 feet**

1291 ... MILITARY PUSH BALL BY HORSES

A canvas covered wicker ball about 7 feet in diameter is pushed and kicked over the field by horses mounted by the players. It is the first game of this nature played in England which subsequently formed the main spectacle of the Military Tournament at the Agricultural Hall. **100 feet**

1292 ... STARS OF THE CRICKET WORLD

A grand series of excellent views of the most famous Cricket Players. Photographs by JASPER REDFERN. Fine Portrait Pictures of the Australian and English Teams, including Messrs. P. F. Warner, C. B. Fry, G. L. Jessop, A. E. Lawton, C. McGahey, F. H. Bacon, C. H. B. Marsham, J. T. Tyldesley, T. F. S. Crawford, G. W. Beldam, A. O. Jones. R. Abel, F. S. Fishwick, H. K. Foster, J. Tunnicliffe, W. G. Grace, Prince Ranjitsinhji, J. T. Hearne, G. Braun, Richardson, Trott, Lord Dalmeny, R. A. Sheppard, &c., &c., &c. The Picture of the season. **Total Length 350 feet**

1295 ... THE RACE FOR THE DERBY, 1904

Showing the Derby runners at the start, in two views rounding Tattenham Corner, with the finish of the race opposite the Grand Stand. The race was run during a terrific thunderstorm, in consequence of which hundreds of open umbrella with rain streaming from all points form a unique aspect to the picture. **150 feet**

Re 1904 DERBY.

"THE REFEREE."

Where for a long time past the Urban Biscope has, by dint of frequent changes in the series of pictures shown, provided the most constant of patrons with something fresh and up to date week by week, and sometimes several times in the same week. On Thursday evening some remarkably fine views of the race for the Derby, together with incidents on the road to and around about the course, were presented. These pictures were the more remarkable seeing that they were taken amid the Epsom Down-pours of Wednesday last. Another series showed the manner in which the *Evening News* conveys the result of a big race to the public. One sees the arrival of the news in the sub-editor's room, the intricacies of the "stop-press" are revealed, the printing of the "extra specials," their distribution by carts, motors, and newsboys graphically realised. The possibilities of the cinematograph have never before been so capitally demonstrated. In addition to these interesting "films" some views of a real Spanish bull-fight will be shown to-morrow evening, Dancrey, a Parisienne star of the first water, appears at the Alhambra tomorrow for the first time.

"THE DAILY MIRROR."

In spite of the thunderstorm which happened while the Derby was being run, the Urban Bioscope Company got three excellent pictures of the great race—the start, rounding Tattenham Corner, and the finish at the post.

When the films were shown at the Alhambra yesterday evening the arrival of St. Amant at the finish was the signal for a great outburst of cheers and applause.

The Great Motor Derby,

For the GORDON-BENNET CUP—Homburg, Germany.

1297 ... THE COMPETING RACING CARS AND THEIR DRIVERS

*Photographed during the weighing-in of the Motors at Homburg, Germany,
June 16th, 1904.*

Pictures in following Order :

1—Scene at Ritter's Park Hotel, Homburg, the principal resort of auto-
mobilists congregating for the races
2—Weighing Mors Car, No. 12, with excellent portrait of M. Salleron, the
Driver
3—Jenatzy, an interested spectator of the proceedings
4—The Wolseley Car, No. 2, with Mr. Sidney Girling, Driver
5—The Fiat Car, No. 11, in the testing yard, driven by Signor Storero
6—The Pipe Motor No. 6, with M. de Crawhez at the lever
7—The Pipe Motor No. 13, driven by M. Augieres
8—The Mercedes Car No. 10, with Herr Braun at the wheel, passing through
the testing yard
9—Replacing tyres to cars in the testing yard
10—The Turcat-Mery Car, No. 18, with M. Rougier passing through the
testing yard
11—Baron de Caters, with Mercedes Car No. 8, starting the motor
12—Excellent view of Mercedes Car No. 16, with Mr. Warden, the American
Driver
13—Herr Fritz Opel driving Opel Darracq car, No. 14
14—Mr. Chas. Jarrott piloting his Wolseley Car, No. 15, into the testing court
15—Weighing in of Napier Car, No. 2, Mr. S. F. Edge, driver
16—The explosion of petrol tank, saving Edge's car
17—Edge "Caged" after the accident
18—Mercedes Car, No. 3, driven by Herr Weiner
19—Reweighing of Mr. Edge's Napier Car, No. 2
20—A chat with Jenatzy, while inspecting Car No. 1, on the eve of the race
21—Three views of the Richard-Brasier Car, No. 5, driven by Mon. L. Théry,
the winner of the race

Excellent Views of each Car.

Magnificent Portraits—Full of Action.

Not a Dull Picture in the Series.

Perfect Photographic Quality throughout.

Total length 400 feet

1298 *Special* ... **" THE GREAT INTERNATIONAL June
17th, 1904, MOTOR RACE," Germany**

ORDER OF PICTURES.

No.
1—Panorama of Imperial Tribune, Saalburg. (The Grand Stand)
2—Starting Motors for race, Saalburg
3—Cars sweeping curve at Saalburg
4—Down the " Straight " at Wehrheim
5—The long Straight and curve from Homburg.
6—Receding view of cars up grade towards Saalburg Tribune
7—Car No. 11 rounding Curve at Kirdorf

No 1298. The Gordon Bennett Motor Car Race, 1904.

8—Motors slowing down while passing through neutral town of Neuhof, each Car preceded by Cyclists

9—Motors going at top speed down "Straight" at Weilburg

10—Cars Nos. 1, 2, 3, and 4, speeding through Saalburg Tribune

11—Cars Nos 12, 1, and 9, arriving and departing from Control of Idstein

12—Three Motors receding up the ascent towards Tribune

13—Théry with Car No. 5, coming down the Straight from Homburg, followed by Nos. 3 and 1

14—The most dangerous and picturesque spot on entire course showing Cars manipulating the acute "S" curve

15—Skidding around sharpe curve after passing Limburg Control

16—Another view of same curve showing Cars Nos 1, and 8

17—General Panorama of East end of Tribune, showing Cars rushing through the Arch

18—View of Tribune showing enormous crowds cheering Théry, Jenatzy, and de Caters, on passing the winning post

19—Two different aspects of crowds before the entrance to Tribune, during the finish

20—Arrival of H.I.M. Automobile

21—His Imperial Majesty, the Emperor of Germany leaving after the race, (we were fortunate in securing his Majesty's consent to being photographed.) After his approach with suite he is seen conversing with various notabilities directly before the camera, thus enabling us to procure a magnificent life-size portrait of the Emperor. He steps into his Motor after bidding farewell to his friends.

Total length 350 feet

Re MOTOR RACE FOR GORDON= BENNETT CUP.

"AMERICAN REGISTER,"

There is no question but that the Alhambra Theatre is the most beautiful music-hall in the world, and is reckoned as one of the sights of London for Americans to visit. This week's programme is especially fine. The Urban Bioscope **is the best seen in London,** giving life-like pictures of the Gordon-Bennett Cup Race.

" THE ERA."

There is an excellent variety entertainment at the Alhambra at present, a great attraction being the Urban Bioscope, with an entirely new set of pictures. The most sensational series is that which depicts the motor race for the Gordon Bennet Cup run in Germany on June 17 last. Marvellous, indeed, is the impression of resistless power and terrific speed which is given by the spectacle of these machines hurrying along roads, turning corners with reckless proximity to danger, and passing between lines of cheering, excited spectators, Judiciously assisted by imitative sounds in the orchestra, this " Motor Derby " film is one of the most thrilling and interesting that has been produced under " Urban " auspices.

" EVENING NEWS."

The Bioscope is a standing dish nowadays at most of our music-halls, but to see the latest combination of the photographic and mechanical arts at its very best one must go to the Alhambra, where the Urban Company's Bioscope is on view.

The Urban pictures are remarkable for their beautiful clearness and steadiness. The pictures taken during the course of the Gordon-Bennett race call forth wild bursts of enthusiasm nightly, more especially among the ladies and those in the cheaper parts of the house who have never seen a modern motor-car turning on two wheels round a corner at the rate of seventy miles an hour.

This part of the show is really very exciting, and last night it was so vigorously applauded that one would not have been surprised had an encore been given.

THE " CHRONICLE."

The Bioscope pictures in the second interval continue a great attraction. A new series were introduced last night of the recent motor race for the Gordon-Bennett Cup. They are without question the finest that have yet been produced, and may be said to represent. "the last word" in animated photography. It would seemingly be impossible to excel them.

" TOPICAL TIMES."

A very fine picture of " The Motor Derby " was shown by the Urban Bioscope at the Alhambra last Saturday night. Nine operators were at different points, and the film was taken, developed and shown within twenty-four hours. Sharp work this.

THE " REFEREE."

" The Motor Derby," as it is called, was pictorially represented last night both at the Alhambra and the Palace by the Urban Bioscope. Both succeeded in showing excellent pictures, all taken on the spot, developed, and shown within twenty-four hours."

" DAILY MIRROR."

" Snapped " the Kaiser.

A particularly fine series of pictures of the Gordon-Bennett cup race, taken by the Charles Urban Trading Company, through the courtesy of Baron Schrenk of the German Automobile Club, are shown this week on the Bioscope at the Alhambra. These pictures include a very fine view of the Kaiser, who was snapped as he was crossing the Automobile Club enclosure.

" THE ERA."

Mr. Charles Urban may be congratulated on the production at the Alhambra of his exceptionally fine bioscope views depicting the great internation motor race for the Gordon-Bennett cup held in Germany on June 17. Mr. Urban, who took over with him to Homburg eight skilful operators, stationed his men at the most interesting sections of the course, and as he had eighty-seven and a-half miles from which to select positions his task was no easy one. He received, however, every courtesy and considerable help from the French and German automobile clubs, and with the further assistance afforded by the kindly offices of Baron von Brudenburg, the chairman of the Race Committee, he was able the night before the event to distribnte his men all over the course, special care being taken to have photographers at the dangerous points.

The opening film shows the competing racing ears and their drivers as they were photographed during the weighing-in process on the day prior to the race. An excellent view is given of each machine, and the likenesses of the daring motorists are equally plain and distinct, Following these we are introduced to the Emperor and Empress of Germany on the arrival of their Majesties at Homburg, and a first-rate view is that of the Imperial Tribune at Saalsburg, where the grand stand is erected. Then the race starts, and we see the motors sweeping round curves at Saalsburg and dashing down the straight at Wehrheim with lightning-flash like speed. In one place the cars are preceded by military cyclists, and the motorists have to drive their machines at slow pace, the reason being that the privileges of high speed are not permitted in certain neutral towns, notably that of Neuhof. However, they make up for it a few seconds later in the rush down the Welburg "straight" and through Saalsburg.

It is sufficient to make one hold one's breath while watching the different motors manipulating at a terrific pace an acute "S" curve in what is considered the most dangerous part of the entire course, and hardly less exciting is the skidding round of the cars of another sharp curve after passing Limburg control. Very picturesque is the panoramic scene of the east end of the Tribune, showing cars rushing through the arch, and an exceptionally fine view is that which presents the enormous crowds cheering Théry, Jenatzy and De Caters clearing the winning post. Mr. Urban was exceedingly fortunate in securing, through the German War Minister. the Kaiser's consent to being photographed, and the portrait one gets of his Imperial Majesty leaving after the race is very life-like, as are also those where he is seen conversing with various state officials and stepping into his motor after bidding farewell to his friends.

1341 ... CAPTIVE FLYING MACHINE AT EARL'S COURT

This atraction was invented by Sir Hiram J. Maxim, and forms one of the principal attractions at Earl's Court. **75 feet**

1352 ... THE 2000 MILE NON-STOP MOTOR RACE

This is the first of the many "non-stop" Automobile races, and was promoted by the London "Daily Mirror" to determine the serviceable nature of the touring car without break-down or accident. A Talbot car was used, and driven by Mr. D. M. Weigel. The first picture shows the start from Carmelite Street; the second view, the arrival and departure at Sir Thomas Dewar's offices, Perth, Scotland; while the final scene depicts the finish of the 2,000 miles' run on the Embankment after the run from Plymouth. Mr. Weigel is cheered by the crowds assembled to witness his triumph. **150 feet**

"EVENING NEWS·"

The "Daily Mirror's" great record non-stop motor run is also treated on the Bioscope. To-night the finish in Carmelite Street will be added to the picture, thus rendering additionally intereseing a feat which is without parallel in the history of motoring.

1354 ... FRANCE v. ENGLAND SPRINTING RACES

An Exciting Series of Races.—South London Harriers v. Racing Club de France, consisting of the following events:— 100 yards, 440 yards, 880 yards, 1 mile and 3 miles, 120 yards (Hurdles) and 1,000 yards (Steeplechase), at Stamford Bridge Grounds.

The series show the start and finish of these most important matches, and all views are full of action and of best photographic quality. **200 feet**

1355 ... THE ATHLETE'S FROLIC

After the finish of the races about twenty of the athletes are seen indulging in "horse-play" and antics of a boyish nature. The picture is full of action and beautifully clear. **50 feet**

1380 ... INTERNATIONAL ATHLETIC SPORTS AND CONTESTS

1—Costume Race
2—Professional Walking Match
3—Waitress's Walking Match
4—Hurdle Jumping
5—Pick-up Contest
6—Girls' Skipping Rope Dance
7—Tug-of-War
8—Club Swinging Match
9—The Water Jump
10—" Catch as Catch Can " Wrestling.
11—Putting the Shot
12—Tossing the Caber

13—Indian Foot Ball
14—Ship Cricket
15—Goal Tennis
16—Canadian Lacrosse
17—Polo
18—Championship Walking Match
19—Running Races
20—Cricket at Lords
21—Football at Crystal Palace
22—Eights Rowing Boat Race on Thames

675 feet

Excellent quality.

Total length 675 feet. One of the best athletic series ever bioscoped.

1382 ... INTERNATIONAL COLLEGE SPORTS — Yale, Harvard Cambridge, Oxford

1—100 yards Dash—(Finish and Retiring) W. A. Schick (Harvard), 9 4-5th secs

2—1 mile Race—(2 laps and Finish) H. W. Gregson (Camb), 4 m 21 1-5th secs

3—½ mile Race (Spurt and Finish) H. E. Holding (Oxford), 1 m 56 1-5th secs

4—2 mile Race—Finish) M. H. Godby (Oxford), 9 m 50 secs

5—¼ mile Race—(2 laps, ret. aft. Finish) E. J. Dives (Harvard), 49 4 5th secs

6—Long Jump, L. T. Sheffield (Yale), 21 feet 10¾ inches **225 feet**

1388 ... ETON COLLEGE OARSMEN ON THE THAMES

Showing half-dozen boats rowed by Eton boys in various races, on the Upper Thames, opposite Windsor. An interesting boating picture. **50 feet**

1412 ... CROSS CHANNEL MOTOR BOAT RACES

The credit for the inception of the great Cross-Channel Race is due to Count Récopé, a distinguished French sportsman and ex-naval officer, who is always to be seen at the big motoring contests. He has been one of the greatest advocates for the promotion of the " entente cordiale" between France and England, and he has the idea that he will be furthering that end, and, at the same time, promoting sport by the organisation of a high-speed motor-boat race between the shores of the two countries. The contest was organised by the Automobile Club of France, and some notable trophies have been presented, as well as a number of other prizes.

The commencement of the series shows motor-boats leaving the river at Calais, previous to the start ; these are followed by three torpedo boats which acted as escort and guarded the course across the Channel. Next is shown the start of seven Motor boats practically leaping over the waters. They appear like a school of porpoises, and as they approach the camera, distinctly show the great spray thrown over their prows in their swift progress. The winner is then shown nearing the cliffs of Dover, while an excellent close view picture of Mr. Edge's Napier boats (which finish second in the race), gives a most exciting finish to the series. As we had the exclusive photographic rights on the fast Turbine Channel steamer s.s. "Queen," exceptional facilities for doing justice to this interesting event were had by us and made the most of.

250 feet

1413 ... MOTOR BOATS IN THE BRITISH CHANNEL

A similar, but shorter series to the preceding event. The scenes are not duplicates, and therefore could be added to 1412 if long series is desired, **125 feet**

1418 ... HOLBEIN AND HIS FRIENDS IN A SPORTIVE MOOD

Taken during a trial swim in the Channel previous to Holbein's attempt to swim from Dover to Calais, showing the various strokes and style of floating, feeding, &c. To conclude the view, is shown a swimming match by seven companions of Holbein, who then give an exhibition of diving from each others shoulders, &c., &c. Full of life and of fine quality. **125 feet**

1419 ... GREASLEY PREPARING TO SWIM THE ENGLISH CHANNEL

Another long distance swimmer who attempted to cross the Channel.

This picture shows Greasley being greased down previous to entering the water, the dive from a boat for trial swim, swimming by overhand strokes, floating, feeding, and return to boat.

A good picture to be used in comparison with Holbein's methods of swimming. **175 feet**

1420 ... MOTOR CAR RACING IN GERMANY

A supplementary series of Racing pictures of same event described under 1298. **200 feet**

1426 ... EDGE'S MOTOR BOAT, THE "NAPIER MINOR," UNDER FULL SPEED

While photographing the Cross-Channel Motor Races we had the unique opportunity of securing a close view of Mr. Edge's boat while the s.s. "Queen" was running parallel with the "Napier Minor," and at same high speed. The result is exciting.

60 feet

1488 ... CHUTE BOAT RACES AT EARL'S COURT

Described under "Living London." **75 feet**

1489 ... CHAMPIONSHIP GONDOLA RACES AT EARL'S COURT

This and the preceding subject are an unique series of excellent photographic quality. **100 feet**

PRESS COMMENTS.

" BLACK & WHITE."

The gondola races at Earl's Court, which have attracted so much attention, have hitherto been rowed in " Venice by Night," but last Saturday saw a gondola race in the open for the first time, Nino Salin (champion) and Giovani Moschietto (ex-champion) racing in their gondolas on the great lake in the Queen's Court. Mr Charles Urban, a well-known sporting gentleman, offered a handsome goblet for the victor. Moschietto is twenty-eight years of age, and owning to his muscular development, has hitherto been considered the strongest of the young gondolieri of Venice, Three years ago he succeeded in defeating Antonio Vianello, who up ¦to then had borne the reputation of being invincible. On the other hand, Salin represents agility and skill, more than weight and muscle. He is two years younger than his opponent, and for the past nine years has always competed in the Venetian regattas with marked success. The boats were started by Mr. H. Hewitt Griffin, who also officiated as timekeeper. As Moscheietta took a wrong course in the second round, Salin, who paddled over, won easily.

" EVENING STANDARD."

Gondola Racing at Earl's Court.

Gondola racing at Earl's Court is still very attractive. The fine weather on Saturday brought a large number of spectators together to witness a contest between Nino Salin, the champion, and Giovanni Moschietto, the ex-champion, in a race in their gondolas on the great lake in the Queen's Court. Up to the present these competitions have taken place in " Venice by Night." This is the first time they have been held ;in the open air, where all visitors could view them. Mr. Charles Urban offered a handsome silver goblet as a prize. At three o'clock the two gondoliers took up their positions at that portion of the lake close to the " Blue Grotto of Capri." Mr. H. Hewitt Griffin (official timekeeper to the National Cyclist Union) acted as timekeeper and starter. The course was five times round the lake and the two men started well together. At the close of the first round, however, Moschietto, instead of going round the buoy which marked the course, came inside it, and seeing that his chance was hopeless, gave up. Salin continued for two laps, which he did in 3min 7 2-5sec. He then paddled round, completing the five laps, and was awarded the silver goblet. There was another race between Pianese and Pizzele, which was of an exciting character. The two men kept well together for some time, until Pizzelle slipped, and Pianese gained an advantage, which he kept up to the finish and won. His time was 9min. 3 2-5sec. for the five rounds, while Pizzele's was 9min. 23 1-5sec. In addition, there was a race of chute boats. They went twice round the lake. A man named Cash did the journey in 5min. 9 1-5sec., while Dobson came in second in 6min. 18 3-5sec. Cash, the winner, was presented with a fine little model of a chute boat built to scale.

3040-1 ... TIGER AND BULL FIGHT AT SAN SEBAS-TIEN

We acquired the sole Bioscopic rights and procured an excellent series of pictures of the event as described by the *Temps* correspondent at San Sebastien. A fight between a royal Bengal tiger, aged ten years, bought at Marseilles for £280, and brought specially by steamer, and a magnificent five years old Andalusian bull was announced, and hd attracted aan enormous crowd. A cinematograph had been set up to take pictures of the scene, but the bull, before his opponents' appearance, made a dash at the operator, and the latter, though protected by a barrier, decamped like lightning, upsetting his apparatus in his haste. A cage fifty feet in diameter had been placed in the centre of the arena. In this the tiger and bull were to be let loose. Some spectators thought the enclosure hardly looked strong enough, and the correspondent says that, notwithstanding reassuring statements, he proceeded to ascend to the gallery.

After several corridas came the chief spectacle of the afternoon. Guards armed with Mausers were stationed in the arena. The two animals were brought on separately, and the bull eyed his opponent savagely, but the tiger at first refused to get out of the cart. Eventually a squib was fired which dislodged him. Instantly the bull dashed at him with horns down. The tiger was gored, but caught his opponent in the neck. The bull, shaking him off, remained stamping the ground, while the tiger retired, crouching for a leap. The self-same attacks were repeated over and over again for half an hour, when the spectators, impatient because they had expected something more exciting, began to hoot. A photographer got into the arena and prodded the tiger with a pole over the barrier. The two beasts attacked each other again, but soon fell apart, and stood looking at one another, apparently having not the least inclination to fight.

Spectators, in a fury, thereupon jumped into the arena, and shouted all the names they could think of at the animals, hissed, lit squibs, and danced like mad creatures round the cage. The bull, excited by the noise, gored the tiger once more, and got him against the bars of the enclosure. At that moment the latter barrier was seen to yield. In a few seconds it fell, and the cage was open.

No. 3041 Tiger and Bull Fight at San Sebastien

There were yells of terror, and the crowd fled in a wild panic. Simultaneously reports of firearms were heard, and several men fell wounded. The guards and everyone possessing a gun had blazed away indiscriminately. Fifty persons were hit by bullets; twelve by Mauser bullets. Fourteen are severely hurt, three are in a critical condition, and one man is dead. An American, Mr. Livingstone, of New York, was injured, and will bring an action for damages. The fusillade eventually killed the tiger, which, for that matter, had made no attempt to attack anyone, being too badly mauled.

The bull all the while stood calmly in the middle of the arena, as peaceful as his dead adversary had been. He was eventually led off, when the spectators fell like savages on the tiger's carcass, actually hacking off the head, the tail, the paws, and pieces of the skin, to take away as mementos.

"THE ERA."

The Urban Bioscope have, with praiseworthy promptitude, put on films depicting the combat between the bull and the tiger, which took place quite recently at San Sebastiene. It was splendidly done, and was watched with breathless interest.

Total Length 275 feet

3042 ... SPANISH BULL FIGHT

This series was recently photographed by us at San Sebastien Spain, the great cage in which the Tiger and Bull Fight subsequently took place, occupying the centre of the arena. In consequence, the intervening space was limited and necessitated the animals and bull fighters coming very much closer towards the spectators than is usually the case. We therefore were enabled to get the figures life size at all times, and show the fight in every detail, from the entree procession of the Bull Fighters, entrance of the bull, charging the Picadors, goring horses, unseating their riders, placing of banderillos, fierce charges on and escape of the Toreador, to the death of the bull by three sword thrusts from the Matador. *Absolutely the most exciting and best quality picture of a Spanish Bull Fight ever photographed.*

300 feet

3043 ... ROLLER SKATING IN PARIS

Showing hundreds of participants in figure and fancy skating, &c., during which many tumbles are recorded. Very lively subject. Good contrast with our Montreal Ice Rink picture—1040. **100 feet**

3044 ... CHILDREN'S CYCLE RACE

A humorous picture taken during a recent outing in Paris, where so many unique and eccentric contests are arranged, showing the the children astride the old type of "bone-shaker" cycle, the only means of propulsion being the touching of the ground by the toes, and pushing the machine along. **110 feet**

3042 Spanish Bull Fight at San Sebastien

F

MUSIC HALL SERIES.

Dances, Acrobatic, &c.

1062 ... THE HARTLEY WONDERS MARVELLOUS WATER HORSE AND CHAIR JUMP

The marvellous Hartley—the world's champion jumper—in his noted water jump, over-horse jump, and 16 chairs series jump. This film, depicting the three, all wonderful effects produced as Hartley, blindfolded, vaults lightly over the chairs from the far distance, is exceedingly fine. **100 feet**

1063 ... THE MARVELLOUS HARTLEY BARREL JUMPERS

No. 1313. The Geisha Minstrels.

Hartley and his agile lady colleague in their wonderful barrel-jumping act over and into innumerable barrels placed in all conceivable positions. Both artistes are blindfold and ankle manacled, making these wonderful feats exhibitions of great judgment and dexterity. **75 feet**

1064 ... SENORITA FILLIS QUEEN OF THE REVOLVING GLOBE

This accomplished lady, while treading the globe does a variety of conjuring acts, and her ascent and descent of the inclined plane, lends pleasing variety to her other less during exploits on the globe, of which she is Queen. **100 feet**

1065 ... LATELLES, AERIAL HIGE ROPE CYCLISTS

The aerial cycle act is a clever one, as suspended beneath the cyclist, who runs forth and back on the rope at a very high altitude, is a trapeze bearing two expert performers who during their perilous journey perform some clever evolutions in mid-air. **100 feet**

1066 ... TAMMAROTS CHIYOCHKIS—JAPANESE AERIAL ACT (2 views)

A facile slack wire and rope climbing expert, illustrate, how very closely the genus homo can emulate the monkeys ascending a single rope, toes and fingers, with lightning rapidity, while his dexterous feats in high-up space are clever and entertaining. His drop for life —both head and feet foremost—is intensely thrilling. **100 feet**

1090 ... THE "JAPS" CAKE WALK

The Cake Walk "a-la-Jap" is executed with that graceful "high step" only acquired by thorough artists. Three ladies in Japanese costume with the leader of the "Japs," dance to the music produced by another fair member of the troupe from a piano. **100 feet**

1111 ... THE WANIA TROUPE OF SLAVISH DANCERS

The acrobatic nimbleness displayed during the dance of this remarkable troupe is really wonderful to behold, the entire length of films shows a succession of various phases of the Russian style of dancing, and can not be equalled for action and quality. **125 feet**

1169 ... A TROUPE OF RUSSIAN DANCERS

These artists have without doubt reached the acme of perfection in the execution of the dance depicted in this film. The members of this troupe of acrobats, contortionists and nimble-footed dancers combined. There is a dash and grace to their performance, which pleases **100 feet**

1299 .. FAMOUS CONJURING TRICKS BY MR. CHARLES BERTRAM

Showing the dexterity with which Mr. Bertram, the Court Conjuror manipulates the five black balls and cups, also the wine glass and bottle trick. Must be seen to be appreciated. These sleight of hand tricks are performing for the first time before the Bioscope, and even the close proximity of the performance leaves one more puzzled than ever as to how the tricks are performed. **250 feet**

1401 ... COSTERS' CAKE WALK

75 feet

1402 ... DANCING ON THE TERRACE AT THE CRYSTAL PALACE

50 feet

1232 ... THE NATIONAL DANCE OF MACEDONIA

50 feet

1361 ... BULGARIAN WEDDING DANCE

50 feet

1362 ... BULGARIAN VILLAGE FESTAL DANCE

75 feet

1441 ... BULGARIAN SOLDIERS DANCE AFTER MESS

75 feet

1450 ... DANCE DU VENTRE—BULGARIA

50 feet

1451 ... TURK-ISH GIPSIES "DANCE DU VENTRE"
100 feet

1185 ... FESTAL DANCE OF THE TOMOG-ON MURUTS —BORNEO
100 feet

1186 ... THE DYAK WAR DANCE
75 feet

No. 1186. Borneo Natives preparing for a Dance.

1212 ... INDIAN DEVIL DANCERS IN CEYLON

75 feet

1313 ... THE DANCE OF THE GEISHA

75 feet

F 2

HISTORIC PERSONALITIES AND EVENTS.

KING EDWARD AND PRESIDENT LOUBET.

His Majesty's Visit to Paris.

1000 a ... **THE KING'S ARRIVAL AT THE BOIS DU BOLOUGNE STATION, PARIS**

Showing the decorated engine and Royal train entering the station, the greeting of the King by M. Loubet, the President of the French Republic. His Majesty, with M. Loubet, and the Ministers and officials, leaving the station, passing close to the camera, excellent life-size portraits resulting. The King greets the Bioscope with a broad smile. **75 feet**

1000 b ... **KING EDWARD ON HIS WAY TO THE BRITISH EMBASSY, PARIS**

Where he is received by Sir Edmond Monson, Lady Monson, and the Consular staff. M. Loubet then takes his departure. **100 feet**

1001 ... **ARRIVAL OF KING AND PRESIDENT LOUBET AT THE VINCENNES REVIEW GROUNDS, 2nd May, 1903**

Including three excellent portrait views of His Majesty and the President. I. The drive past with escort. II. The King and President stepping from their carriage. III. Panorama of the Reviewing Pavilion, with King Edward in the Royal Box. **100 feet**

1003 ... **KING EDWARD VII. AND PRESIDENT LOUBET ENTERING THEIR CARRIAGE AND LEAVING VINCENNES AFTER THE REVIEW**

Historic Picture; Life-size Figures; Magnificent Portraits. Without doubt the best animated photograph yet secured of his Majesty. **100 feet**

1044 ... **ARRIVAL OF THE EARL AND COUNTESS MINTO AT THE SKATING RINK, MONTREAL**

The opening of the Montreal Rink by the Earl and Countess Minto was a gala occasion, taken advantage of by thousands who lined the snow-bedecked roads, cheering the distinguished guests as they arrive and step from their sleighs. A fine picture. **150 feet**

1054 ... **M. LOUBET'S ARRIVAL IN LONDON AND RECEPTION BY KING EDWARD VII.**

This film depicts a most interesting military reception. The Foot Guards in their bearskins lining the streets, and the several squadrons of Life Guards that invariably accompany the Sovereign make up a scene of much animation. The portrait of King Edward as he passes in his carriage accompanied by the French President is an excellent one. **100 feet**

1055 ... **M. LOUBET LEAVING THE GUILDHALL**

The ceremonial attendant on M. Loubet's visit to the City was a record one. This film shows the President and his entourage leaving the Guildhall. **60 feet**

1144 ... T.R.M. KING AND QUEEN OF ITALY—VISIT TO PARIS

A splendid series of portrait views of the Royal couple and M. Loubet, President of the French Republic—arriving and departing from the Hotel de Ville, Paris—with Cuirassier escort.　**150 feet**

1164 ... OPENING OF THE BULGARIAN PARLIAMENT BY PRINCE FERDINAND AT SOFIA

125 feet

1267 ... THE FUNERAL OF THE LATE DUKE OF CAMBRIDGE

The coffin, draped with Union Jack, mounted on gun carriage drawn by bluejackets. An imposing picture.　**150 feet**

1373 ... KING EDWARD RECEIVING THE CITY SWORD AT HOLBORN BARS

When King Edward visited the Guildhall the cortege drew up at Holborn Bars, where the ceremony of investing the King with the City Sword and Keys was enacted.　**50 feet**

1379 ... "L'ENTENTE CORDIALE"—Opening Ceremony of the Folkestone Pier

No. 1379. "L'Entente Cordiale."

Arrival of the S.S. "Lord Warden" with M. Cambon and French Delegates. Panorama of Folkestone Pier. Disembarkation of French Visitors. Arrival of special train from London bearing British representatives and Press. Firing the salute from pier battery. Laying the Corner Stone by M. Cambon assisted by distinguished French and English personages. The invited guests promenading the pier, with Mayor of Folkestone, Military and other Officials.

300 feet

1411 ... LORD DUNDONALD LEAVING CANADA

Lord Dundonald (after his recall) receiving the address of welcome and bidding goodbye to the Imperial Army and Navy veterans at the Queen's Hotel, Toronto, July 15th, 1904, previous to his departure for England.　**100 feet**

FIRE SERIES.

1086 ... THE FOLKESTONE FIRE DRILL

A fireman is here seen in the opening section manipulating the hose-pipe and apparatus in a very brisk manner. **150 feet.**

1256 ... THE GREAT WHISKEY FIRE AT GREENOCK

The alarm. The turn out of the brigade. The run through the streets. Firemen playing on the burning building and whiskey casks. Panorama of the smouldering ruins. The crashing walls, &c. An excellent fire series. **200 feet.**

THE GREAT TORONTO FIRE.

The great fire on the night of April 19th swept fourteen acres, with the loss of $13,000,000. The area destroyed was in the wholesale and retail business district and included all the principal warehouses. Starting in a factory in the early evening, it was beyond control in less than one hour. One hundred and fourteen buildings were destroyed in eight hours.

Bioscoped by Mr. GEORGE SCOTT, *Toronto.*

1375 *Special* ... THE GREATEST CONFLAGRATION IN THE HISTORY OF TORONTO

1—**Call out of the Fire Brigade.**—Firemen dressing as they come out.

2—**One of the Largest Warehouses on Fire.**—Owing to the position of the wind and the dense volumes of smoke, this picture is a record in the annals of cinematography, being photographed exactly at midnight and under exceptional difficulties and danger. Owing to the extremely rapid advance of the fire, the engines were not permitted to approach within hundreds of yards of the fire—the fighting taking place by means of long lengths of hose, which again and again had to be abandoned, in spite of superhuman efforts, to be destroyed by the fire, which would burst out instantaneously from all sides, and sweeping across the whole street, ignite the opposite buildings as if they were so much timber. In spite of the heat of the fire being so great as to convert the jets of water from the hose into steam and buckle the stone pavement in the middle of the street, owing to expansion of the electric car rails, the weather was so cold that the water froze on the buildings not attacked, and accidentally getting the hose on our operator, his overcoat froze solid. The picture shows the destruction of the India-rubber and Gutta-percha Co.'s Building on the corner of Bay and Front Street. The firemen can be seen trying to save the adjoining building across the street, when the building behind them bursts into flame. In the middle of the picture our operator had to shift his position owing to change of wind and dense volumes of smoke from buildings to rear.

3—**Dynamiting Dangerous Walls.**—Showing the dynamiting of the Gordon McKay building by means of time fuse. The people are driven back by the police, and one fuse is seen to go off without effect. The man dynamiting then approaches, and finding the other fuse still burning, runs off, and the building collapses in the most curious way, a crack appearing from top to bottom, and the walls settling perpendicularly down with every brick loose from mortar. The mound of bricks formed piled themselves within three feet of the base of the wall.

4—**Panorama showing a Ruined City.** Not a single whole building in the entire picture. One could almost imagine oneself among the ruins of Pompeii. The view starts from where the fire ended, and shows one west, south, east, and finishes up north, where the tall building to the left in the distance, behind the safe, a firm of dry goods and notions, was where the fire originated, and all the damage ensued. The iron safe standing up in the foreground was situate in the big establishment of Messrs. W. Brock & Co., a building of massive stone and granite, which succumbed to the flames. This safe was the only one in which the papers were undamaged. The picture then shows a nearer view of poor people rooting among the salvage.

5—**Dynamiting the Premises of the Robert Darling Co., by seven charges of Dynamite exploded simultaneously by electric current.** A most unique picture, photographed at enormous risk. Both Mr. Scott and camera were struck by flying fragments of brick, and one man in the crowd, several hundred feet further back, was seriously injured. You will note the electricians lowering the electric light wires, prior to dynamiting, and finally two holes to the left, in all that was standing of the walls, made by two charges which blew their way clean through. The man who is conducting the dynamiting was killed shortly after in approaching a time fuse which failed to go off.

The most Exciting Fire Series ever Bioscoped.

Total Length 275 feet

PRESS COMMENTS.

" MORNING ADVERTISER."

A remarkable series of pictures to be shown exclusively at the Alhambra on the Urban Bioscope will establish a record in cinematography. Mr. Urban's representative, who happened to be in Toronto when the great fire broke out, on April 19th, succeeded in getting a wonderful set of photographs at midnight, the necessary light being supplied by the blazing buildings. Some extraordinary scenes of dynamiting walls are included in this notable series.

" THE OBSERVER."

It must be rather difficult just now, even for variety theatres, to rival successfully the attractions of outdoor amusement. But the Alhambra is doing wonders in the matter, with the striking Urban pictures of the War and the Great Fire in Toronto.

" THE WORLD."

A specially potent attraction is provided just now at the Alhambra in the form of **a** series of remarkably vivid "living pictures" of scenes from the Russo-Japanese war, shown by the " Urban Bioscope." The photographs thus reproduced have been quite recently taken, and depict incidents in the movements of both armies with a realism which brings home to the spectator, far more forciby than the most graphic of word-pictures, the actualities of the present great struggle in the Far East. By the " Urban Bioscope " **are also being shown some thrilling incidents of the great Toronto Fire, which cause intense excitement to the spectators.**

" THE WESTERN MAIL."

Toronto Fire Represented.

Perhaps the most sensational picture on the Bioscope just now is that displayed at the Alhambra. It is a lifelike rspresentation of the fire at Toronto. Mr. George Scott, who was fortunate enough to be present at this terrific conflagration, utilized his opportunity to the full. The newspaper accounts did not half describe this terrible disaster. Acre after acre of fine rows of buildings are seen to be in flames, huge blocks of massive structures are shown in the very act of being dynamited in order to prevent the fire from spreading, and as they fell it is almost possible to hear the crash of the walls as one witnesses the mountains duof st they raise, The passing of the picture leaves a sad feeling behind, but of the excellence of it there is no doubt,

" THE REFEREE."

The great Toronto Fire picture at the Alhambra is a triumph of the Cinematograph art.

" MORNING LEADER."

A distinct departure in Bioscope possibilites is also shown at the Alhambra in representation of the great Toronto fire of April last. The Urban Bioscope representative, who is at present engaged on a cinematograph tour of the Pacific line was at Toronto when the fire broke out, and he took his machine along to see if anything could be obtained at midnight by the light of the blazing city. Curiously enough, the films came out with an excellent representation of the flames, and they are shown amidst quaint Rembrandtesque effects,

" THE ERA."

A valuable addition to these Far East films is a series of Toronto Fire views. We see the engines hurrying to the scene of conflagration, and afterwards watch them playing upon the fire. A specially effective spectacle is that in which the orange coloured flames are seen raging amidst ruins of high houses. The necessity of dynamiting dangerous walls and buildings creates sensational subjects for the photographer. After the explosive has been fixed, comes the thundering descent of the débris, followed by the rising of immense clouds of dust and smoke. Very desolate and strange is the spectacle of the ruined streets, with miles of ghastly walls and " gutted " houses to tell of the ravage wrought by the " devouring element." Altogether, the last series of films supplied by the Charles Urban Trading Company is quite up to the high standard of that enterprising and celebrated firm, and copies are certain to be eagerly applied for in all directions.

" MORNING ADVERTISER."

The pictures of both the Japs and Russians were cordially applauded, but scarce a sound was heard from the large audience when the next series was shown. The subject was the terrible fire in Toronto, and the awful scene was brought home to those present with fearful realism. Fire engines and escapes dashing through the crowded streets was the first shown, and then the terrible sight of the burning mass, the fierce flames and dense smoke being wonderfully depicted, as seen at night. The final scenes were those of ruins, and the wide extent of the damage wrought in the fine city of Toronto was fully brought home to the audience. Whole areas of the town had been destroyed, and all that seemed left were the skeletons of what were once huge commercial offices and palatial private dwellings. There the men were at work destroying with dynamite the dangerous walls, and the actual explosions were shown in magnificent style.

At the fall of the curtain, however, applause was heartily accorded for the realistic manner in which these appalling scenes were reproduced, and they will no doubt form an important item in the Alhambra programme for some little while.

" PATENTS."

The Urban Bioscope has beaten its own records in a wonderful series of pictures shown at the Alhambra recently. The long expected views of the Toronto fire disclosed a new feature of a bioscope enterprise—photography by firelight. A weird Rembrandt-like effect accompanies the illustrations of the burning buildings, taken at midnight ; and a comprehensive survey of the devastated city gives a complete idea of the extent of the disaster.

1390 ... THE PROTECTIVE SPRAY OF THE FIRE LADDIE

Exhibition of a test before the Fire Commissioners, of a new nozzle, which allows the water to spread like an umbrella in front of the fireman as he approaches closely to a burning building, thus protecting him from the terrible heat. **60 feet**.

All Pictures included in the . . . .

"URBANORA "

Entertainments are absolutely Exclusive.

WAR CORRESPONDENTS' QUARTERS, PORT ARTHUR.

Showing Mr. **J. ROSENTHAL** our War Correspondent (catching the mail parcels) in the donga before Port Arthur. Here the English Correspondents attached to General Nogi's Japanese Army have their Headquarters.

The **URBAN** Bioscope Camera is being tended by Mr. Rosenthal's Japanese Assistant.

Foreign War Correspondents in Japan.

The following letter has been received by the Tokyo Press :—

We, the undersigned Foreign War Correspondents having learned of the spontaneous and generous action of our Japanese colleagues of the Metropolitan Press of Tokyo, in appointing a deputation on our behalf to represent to the Military General Staff the hardship of our position and the time we have spent here in waiting; and further your having in so magnanimous a spirit offered to forego your own prior rights in our favour, if it were thought disadvantageous to send so many correspondents into the field, beg most sincerely to thank you for your chivalrous and fraternal kindness to us, your journalistic brethren.

And we desire to convey not only to the Metropolitan newspapers but to the whole press of Japan our deep sense of indebtedness and to the deputation, Messrs. Shimada, Minoura and Zumoto, for their broad-mindedness and good comradeship — qualities which ever exhalt our profession and the people whom we serve.

Yours sincerely,

(Signed)

BENNETT BURLEIGH,
Daily Telegraph, London.

GEORGE LYNCH,
Daily Chronicle, London.

GUY H. SENK,
New York Globe.

PERCY FISHER,
Times, London.

FRANKLIN CLARKIN,
New York Evening Post.

Y. WHITING,
London Graphic.

W. H. BRILL,
Reuter's Telegram Co.

J. GORDON SMITH,
The Morning Post, London.

Capt. LIONEL JAMES,
The Times, Special Correspondent

RICHARD HARDING DAVIS,
Collier's Weekly.

SYDNEY SMITH,
London Daily Mail.

MELTON PRIOR,
Illustrated London News.

JOSEPH ROSENTHAL.
Urban Bioscope, London.

MARTIN EGAN,
Associated Press.

JOHN FOX, Jnr.,
Scribner's Magazine

The Great Russo=Japan War

Photographs by Mr. JOSEPH ROSENTHAL (with Japanese Forces) and Mr. GEORGE ROGERS (with the Russian Army in Manchuria).

General Kuropatkin receiving the Viceroy of Mukden.

1245 ... THE JAPANESE FLAGSHIP "MIKASA" UNDER FULL HEADWAY. (Photo by West's "Our Navy," Ltd.

Admiral Togo's flagship before it entered Eastern waters, was photographed by Mr. West in the English Channel, while under full headway. It is one of the few battleships taken under like favourable conditions, and owing to the prominent part this ship and its Commander has played in the Bombardments of Port Arthur this picture is of great interest. **50 feet**

1265 ... THE BOMBARDMENT OF PORT ARTHUR. (See "Naval and Marine")
530 feet

1300 ... THE REGIMENT OF IMPERIAL GUARDS LEAVING TOKIO FOR THE FRONT

Showing a Regiment of Japanese Troops hurrying through the streets of Tokio on their way to the front. Thousands of these valiant troopers march through the crowds, and finally break into a double quick run, which is most effective as the column winds its way like a huge figure S between shrubbery and gaily bedecked natives, who encourage and bid farewell to these gallant defenders, many of whom have already found a last resting place in Manchuria. **200 feet**

1304 ... JAPANESE TROOPS LEAVING YOKOHAMA

This is a similar picture to the preceding, although not so picturesque or complete. **100 feet**

1306 ... THE "JAP STANDARD BEARER" (Arranged Scene)

To supply the want of a picture which would faithfully reproduce the single-handed combat of the famous Standard Bearer of the Yalu, against four attacking Cossacks, in defence of the Flag, we have pre-arranged this scene of the fight amidst appropriate scenery. The contestants are expert swordsmen, and display much tact and precision in their onslaught on the lonely Jap, who is seen

No, 1306.

The Japanese Standard Bearer.

emerging from a wood with the regimental colours. He stops to rest, but instinctively anticipates pursuit. In this he is not disappointed, for presently we see a Cossack rushing forward to attack with drawn sword. Before the latter is despatched another, and another arrive to join in the fray, until finally all four Cossacks are stretched to the ground, with the Jap, mortally wounded, falling amongst them, kissing his flag before he succumbs.   **150 feet**

1310 ... MILITARY FUNERAL OF A JAPANESE NAVAL OFFICER KILLED DURING THE BOMBARDMENT OF PORT ARTHUR

One of the most impressive subjects ever photographed, although of a highly picturesque character.

The head of the funeral procession consists of hundreds of Japanese in native garb carrying huge banners and flags. These are followed by priests carrying four pine trees planted in boxes. Then we see a military band, and the comrades of the officer whose remains are carried in a casket at end of the procession. The deceased officer's sword and cap, prayer wheels, &c., are displayed resting on cushions borne by comrades and priests. Finally there pass before our view about forty white-robed priests who escort the casket, while both sides of the street are crowded with sympathetic spectators, both Japanese and foreign. Excellent photographic quality   **150 feet**

1238 ... THE JAPANESE CRUISER "YASHIMA" AS ON THE YELLOW SEA. (Photographed by Messrs. Downey and Son.)

The "Yashima" has likewise distinguished itself in Eastern waters, and in this picture the battleship is shown to good advantage, having been photographed just previous to leaving England for the East.   **60 feet**

1383 ... **NAILING THE FLAG TO THE MAST OF THE "MALACCA"**

50 feet

1435 ... **RUSSIAN CAVALRY DESCENDING STEEP MOUNTAIN PASS AND FORDING STREAM**

Shewing the negotiations of some of the mountain accesses to Motien-ing Pass by a number of Russian Officers in order to accustom their mounts to the rough and steep ascents. The horses are seemingly surefooted, and easily reach the base of the mountains where they next ford their steeds across a rapid stream. An interesting subject. **100 feet**

No. 3021. Siberian Cossacks on the March.

1436 ... **MANŒUVRES OF RUSSIAN ARTILLERY AT HARBIN**

Manœuvres of Artillery before leaving for the front, showing the placing of guns in position, unlimbering, firing, limber-up and departure. Most effective picture. **75 feet**

1437 ... **RUSSIAN GUNS IN MOTIEN-LING PASS**

A squad of Mountain Artillery arriving on the summit of a prominent height of the range. The guns, carried in sections by ponies are unstrapped, assembled, aimed and fired. The officers then proceed down a narrow mountain path in single file, the footing being too limited to allow of more than one rider and mount to pass at one time **125 feet**

1438 ... **RUSSIAN MOUNTED PATROL LEAVING HARBIN FOR SENTINEL DUTY**

A splendid body of mounted troops, starting on their round of sentry patrol surrounding districts in which the Russian army is encamped **75 feet**

1439 ... **ARRIVAL OF REINFORCEMENTS AT LIAOYANG KUROPATKIN'S INFANTRY AND ARTILLERY**

One of the best pictures of the series showing a large body of infantry (in summer uniform) proceeding in a free and easy manner along the road leading to Liaoyang where the first great encounter of the Russian-Jap War took place. Then follow Red Cross Ambulance and a score of field guns, many of which have long since "changed hands."

The gun crews mounted on the caisson and limber as well as drivers appear to be in good trim and spirits after their long march. They evidently appreciate a decent "road" over which to transport these engines of war.

200 feet

No. 3018. Cossacks starting on March across Lake Baikal.

"With the Russian Army in Siberia."

A wonderful series of pictures showing the various phases of transport of the Czar's vast army across the Siberian desert from St. Petersburg to Manchuria

NOTE.—This and the preceding are the only series of actual Pictures from the Far East connected with the Russo-Japanese War.

Photographed by Mr. George Rogers.

They were secured at great expense, besides entailing hardship and endurance under most difficult conditions on behalf of Mr. Rogers —who braved a 19,000 miles journey through Russia, Siberia and over the frozen Baikal Lake in the midst of winter (with thermometer at 10 to 30 degrees below zero) into Manchuria, in order to depict scenes in connection with the vast task of transporting the Russian Troops across this bleak territory to meet their foes in the Far East.

3007. ... CHARGES OF THE RUSSIAN HUSSARS AND MOUNTED INFANTRY

The Cavalrymen the Japanese are facing during the struggle (Fine picture). **100 feet.**

Mr. Rogers and " Gil Blas " Correspondent at Baikal Station.

3016 ... SCENES ALONG THE TRANS - SIBERIAN RAILWAY CROSSING THE URAL MOUNTAINS

Some of the most interesting bits of scenery viewed by the troops from the transport trains while crossing the Siberian desert, a journey of 3,300 miles. **100 feet**

3017 ... GENERAL KUROPATKIN ON HIS WAY TO MANCHURIA.

The Market Place of Tshita, a town situated about 800 versts from Irkutsk) crowded with Buriats (the inhabitants) discussing the Declaration of War. Tshita is one of the largest towns in the Trans-Baikalian Provinces, where exist huge Russian railway works and hospitals are now building for the reception of the wounded. The Japanese have their eye on this place, as in case of the defeat of General Kuropatkin's army in Manchuria, Tshita will be the town where the retreating army will make a strong stand, the place being a natural fortress, encircled by huge hills. The distance to Manchuria Station, the frontier, is 600 versts, while Harbin lies 1200 versts to the south-east.

Scene 2 shows the arrival of General Kuropatkin by special traain at Petrowsky Savod, being received by Generals Rennenkampf, Grekoff, and Nadaroff (now promoted to Governor of Trans-Baikal Province). General Kuropatkin and staff are seen inspecting the troops drawn up along the platform. He is next seen inspecting the 1st Brigade Sa-Baikalsky Cossacks.

Scene 3, Station at Irkutsk, showing reservists and infantry hurrying to the trains which carry them to the seat of war. The majority of these men will never see their homes again. **200 feet**

No. 3017. General Rennenkampf reeciving General Kuropatkin
at Petrowsky Savod.   .   .   .

3018 ... TROOPS OF COSSACKS STARTING THE MARCH ACROSS LAKE BAIKAL

From Baikal Station they proceed in long files and columns, winding their way continuously amongst the ice hummocks which abound along the shore end of Lake Baikal in winter.

100 feet

3019 ... RUSSIAN INFANTRY CROSSING THE FROZEN LAKE BAIKAL ON FOOT

The background in the picture shows the Canteen in the middle of the Lake, fifteen miles from either shore, stationed there as a place of refreshment for the troops who are compelled to march across the 30 miles of frozen surface of the lake.

125 feet

3020 ... TRANSPORT OF ARMY PROVISIONS ACROSS LAKE BAIKAL

On Troikas drawn by the sturdy Manchurian ponies; also showing the Red Cross and Ammunition Sledges crossing the frozen lake, which at this point is over half-mile deep.   Excellent picture.

100 feet

3021 ... BAIKAL COSSACKS ON THE MARCH ACROSS MANCHURIA

A fine troop of hardy fighters on their March to the Yalu after having crossed Baikal Lake. These are the fighters of whom much is expected in the battles of the Russians with the sturdy Japs. General Rennenkampf is seen galloping forward to meet the men and cheer them on their march to Manchuria.

150 feet

No. 3021. Siberian Cossacks ready for the March into Manchuria.

3023 ... ARRIVAL OF GENERAL KUROPATKIN AT MUKDEN, MANCHURIA, AND INSPECTION OF THE 1st REGIMENT SIBERIAN SHARP-SHOOTERS

Fine quality, full of action, and greatest interest. The only animated picture of the Russian General in existence. The interest of the world is centred on the Commanding General of the Russian Forces in the Far East. He is seen mounting his famous White Charger at the Railway Station of Mukden. The next view shows him and his Escort making their way to the City, where the General reviews the Regiment of Sharpshooters. He and his entire Staff ride to the fields outside the city (where at the time he thought of camping a large number of reserves who were not required at the front). Very few of the men he is reviewing here are now left. as the majority have fallen in the recent great battle with the Japs ; they have covered the retreat of the Main Army. Here, probably, the next great battle will be fought in the expulsion of the Russians from Manchuria. *A splendid picture.* **150 feet**

No. 3026. Reservists Arrival at Harbin.

G

3024 ... THE RUSSIAN SURVIVORS OF THE NAVAL BATTLE OF CHEMULPO

Arriving at Baikal, on their way to St. Petersburg, of about 800 Marines of the two battleships, "Variag" and "Korietz," blown up by the Japanese, this remnant of 62 men are the sole survivors. These sailors, not having been placed under parole, are again on their way to Vladivostock to join the Russian Squadron stationed there.

125 feet

No. 3025. Gen. Rennenkampf and the Cossacks.

3025 ... EXTRAORDINARY FEATS OF HORSEMANSHIP BY A SQUAD OF SIBERIAN COSSACKS at Mukden, Manchuria

This series comprises an exhibition of marvellous riding feats of Cossacks while in full gallop. First we see the squad in review, then single riders racing towards the camera, laying over their saddles, picking articles off the ground, laying over the horses croups, standing on saddles with sword play. Three men on two horses, five men on three horses, showing method of helping wounded comrades, &c. A most exciting series.

275 feet

Barracks and Fortifications at Harbin.

3026 ... THE ARRIVAL OF THE 1st SIBERIAN SHARP-SHOOTERS AT HARBIN

Showing panorama view of the Station with this Russian Regiment disembarking. This is the best station yard on the entire Trans Siberian or Manchurian section of the railway and depicts thousands of Reserves, just disembarked, marching towards the camp. It is here that the line branches off to Vladivostock, and will probably be the scene of the next great battle.

75 feet

3027 ... STREET SCENE IN MUKDEN NATIVE QUARTERS

Mukden's streets should by now be almost deserted by Russians. The first two figures on horseback seen in the picture are Mr. Douglas Story, *Daily Express*, and Mr. Middleton, *Associated Press*, correspondents, on their way to the R. R. Station. The last view shows a crowd of Chinese beggars scrambling for " cash " thrown them for purposes of leading further animation to the picture **75 feet**

3028 ... EXECUTION OF "LI-TANG" THE CHUNCHUS CHIEF OF MANCHURIAN BANDITS

The only animated picture of a Chinese execution ever taken. Gruesome, but faithfully depicting the actual scene. **75 feet**

No 3028. Execution of a Chinese Bandit.

G 2

Reprint from " DAILY TELEGRAPH," *July 4th,* 1904. (*By kind permission of the Editor.*)

An Execution at Mukden.

Writing from Mukden, Mr. A. G. Simpson, our Special Correspondent with the Russian Army, says :—

It is hot and the town busy, for the Manchurian grows fat on the war. His prices rise like the thermometer in the sun, and he receives his exorbitant selling price if not the one he first demands. Fields are tilled, smiths hammer, carpenters plane, saddlers and tailors stitch, and everyone toils for the gain to be got from the great grabbing game. And all the while Chinese justice pursues its steady course. Daily the Board of Punishment sits to assist in the good government of the province—fifteen hundred heads a year chopped off in public to " impress the people."

At a desolate patch outside the mudwall is a small expectant crowd. They chatter and laugh near suggestive mounds or examine the space where the sand is stained and dogs sniff hungrily. Within the walls the sound of rancous instruments. From the gates armed horsemen come galloping. A mass of humanity dirty but picturesque, streams along after them, over their heads waving a huge banner with a black ground and white Chinese lettering. As the pedestrians spread to right and left appears the head of a small procession. There are more native soldiers on rough ponies—some ten men in all. Behind is a heavy springless cart, drawn by two mules, and in it a bound man with a dazed expression, the object of enthusiastic attention. Two others sit beside him—the executioner and his assistant, gaily exchanging compliments with those near by. Following close comes a detachment of Russian infantry, then mounted Mandarins, a few native police and more of the surging multitude. Kept back by the soldiers they circle the baneful spot, while into the ring the jolting cart is dragged. Thrice the huge horns sound, the victim is helped to the ground, and a muscular man, with a brutal face and a curved, sweeping blade, bids him kneel. More tightly still the arms are drawn behind, the head placed in position, while the dealer of Death stands waiting by. One moment to aim, and a flash ——.

When you look the bugles are sending forth a long drawn note, the horsemen trotting away, and the crowd dispersing, excepting for a small group gathered critically around the motionless, mutilated object that lies at their feet. Only a criminal, without friends, he shall lie where he fell, for the pariahs and the crows. From the moment of arrival to that when the spectators turn to resume their everyday toil scarcely two minutes has elapsed, and as with a feeling of sickness, you move from the ghastly spot, the spectacle still vivid before you, into your face a grinning urchin peers, and asks, " All right, was it not?"

This is Manchuria—China in contrasts.

3029 ... ARRIVAL AND DEPARTURE OF THE ICE-CRUSHING STEAMER " BAIKAL " AT BAIKAL. SIBERIA

By this steamer the majority of Russian Troops are ferried across Lake Baikal on their way to the front, it being the only means (until the completion of the railway around the lake) of transporting reinforcements to General Kuropatkin, the capacity of the "Baikal" being 5,000 troops per day. This ice-crushing steamer was built on the Clyde and transported to the lake by rail in pieces, and was re-constructed under the supervision of the Scotch shipbuilders. **125 feet**

No. 3027. Principal Street in Mukden.

3030 ... PANORAMA OF THE MOUNTAINOUS URAL DISTRICT OF SIBERIA, INCLUDING VIEW OF CONVICT SETTLEMENT

Photographed from the Trans-Siberian Railway during the summer of 1904.   **200 feet**

3031 ... RAILWAY PANORAMA ALONG THE BANKS OF A SIBERIAN RIVER

Showing the character of the vast expanse of country across which Russia must transport her troops and army provisions for the front.   **75 feet**

Bioscope Troika crossing Frozen Lake Baikal, Siberia.

3032 ... NOBLES LEAVING THE KREMLIN, MOSCOW, AFTER RECEPTION OF THE CZAR

An exceedingly interesting series of views of the Kremlin, the Moscow residence of the Czar, where all public functions are held. The " droshkies " driving past the Camera, drawn by one, two or three horses, seat many Russian nobles and titled personages who are returning after a reception at the Palace. Splendid quality. **100 feet**

3033 ... THE WAR CORRESPONDENT AND THE CUBS

When Baron Binder von Kreigelstein (correspondent of the " Kreuz Zeitung ") with the Russian forces in Manchuria had time hanging heavy, he went bear-hunting, and had not long to wait for the excitement he sought. He shot a male bear, and was attacked by its mate, which he also dispatched after a struggle. The bear's lair he discovered close by, and took therefrom two cubs hardly three weeks old. To these cubs the war correspondent has been a " foster mother " ever since, the picture showing them both climbing up his legs and body after a couple of feeding bottles, the contents of which they evidently relish. Many humorous antics are performed by these cubs during the entire duration of the picture. **150 feet**

Re RUSSO=JAPANESE WAR.

" DAILY TELEGRAPH."

To the altogether excellent programme now being given at the Alhambra, there was added last night a very interesting series of pictures, which have been taken chiefly in Siberia by the Urban Bioscope Company. Though not depicting scenes of actual fighting, they convey none the less a very clear and vivid impression of what must be the real conditions of the Russian advance towards Manchuria, and especially well caught in the regular and orderly movement of a long succession of Cossack troops across the rough and frozen surface of Lake Baikal. Russian infantry on the march, too, are shown, and their brisk steps are well suggested. A transport train of sledges, conveying provisions, the arrival of General Kuropatkin at Irkutsk, scenery in the Ural Mountains, and other subjects are depicted, concluding with a presentment of the Japanese warship "Asama" under full steam.

" DAILY CHRONICLE."

Last night the Urban Bioscope provided the first Exhibition of pictures actually taken at the front. They aroused much interest.

" DAILY MAIL."

The Russian views, which were obviously taken under very severe difficulties, are admirable and give a remarkably good idea of the rough, hardy war material at the disposal of the Czar.

And the sympathy of the house? With the Japanese, but the reception of the Russian views was nevertheless friendly.

" DAILY NEWS."

The war pictures which may now be seen in the "Urban" Bioscope at the Alhambra form a thoroughly interesting addition to the entertainment. Mr. George Rogers, who took the photographs, has succeeded in getting some excellent negatives, and the pictures thrown on the screen give some really life-like representations of St. Petersburg, the Trans-Siberian Railway, troops marching across Lake Baikal. the entraining and disentraining of troops, and finally a battleship in action. The two pictures which gave the most characteristic representation of Russian movements were that of the closely muffled infantry as they marched across the ice of Lake Baikal, and that of mounted Cossacks riding with erect figures and free movement, in every way bearing out the popular conception of these hardy and soldierly troops. This Bioscope is well managed at the Alhambra, and was as heartily cheered as the ballets and the acrobats and the comediennes. We understand that further consignments of photographs are now on their way, and will be added as soon as they arrive in England.

" MORNING POST."

The Series is very effective, and was enthusiastically applauded.

" DAILY ILLUSTRATED MIRROR."

The *Mirror*, through an arrangement with the Charles Urban Trading Company, will publish the latest photographs of the war in the Far East, taken from the Russian side.

Mr. George Rogers, the war correspondent of the Bioscope Company, is an American. Knowing that anyone from England would have but small chance of gaining a permit to go to the front as a photographer, he made his application from Paris. Here he waited three months before a permit was granted, but he had by chance met a Russian Prince, who promised to help him. After waiting three weeks in St. Petersburg he was allowed to proceed as far as Irkutsk.

At this town he was turned out of the train. on the ground that transport was needed for the military for war stores. So Mr. Rogers bought a sledge and three ponies, and fortunately falling in with a troop of Cossacks, arrived after seventeen days' travelling at Harbin, where he now is,

Mr. George Rogers in Siberia.

The photographs which we publish to-day had to be sent to St. Petersburg for censorship, and thence to the Russian Embassy at Paris, and only arrived in London yesterday morning,

" Morning Leader."

There is a very living interest about the new Bioscope pictures at the Alhambra—the first actual war pictures, Mr. Urban claims, that have been shown in London. The illustrations of the movements of Russian troops give a well-defined idea of the sort of enemy which the Japanese army has to face, and the pictures of transport across the frozen Lake Baikal show the completeness of the Russian arrangements. A view of a Japanese battleship in full fire discloses some marvellous smoke-cloud effects.

"Sunday Times."

There is no war special who with pen or pencil can present the circumstance of war so realistically as the Bioscope and therefore there was much interest in the first series of pictures of the present campaign which has reached this country, and was seen at the Alhambra on Monday night.

" Patents."

The chief feature of some new and brilliant pictures from the Far East is a representation of Kuropatkin—the first moving picture that is said to have been taken of the Russian commander. Some remarkable feats of horsemanship and life-saving while at full gallop by Siberian Cossacks are also shown.

" The Echo."

The Urban Bioscope is delighting large audiences with up-to-date pictures from the scene of the present war.

" Topical Times."

The Urban Bioscope pictures of the Far East War now at the Alhambra are well worth witnessing, great applause greeting their production.

" Daily Graphic."

A fine series of pictures.

" The Sporting and Dramatic News."

The Urban Bioscope War Pictures now at the Alhambra are a particularly interesting series.

" The Encore."

Business at the Alhambra this week has been particularly bright, which is to be accounted for by the programme being kept up to Alhambra traditions, a new series of the Urban Bioscope War Pictures now forming the main attraction. It is a triumph of film-work, for it must have been taken under exceptionally difficult circumstances.

" The Stage."

The Urban Bioscope remains one of the chief attractions of the evening; the pictures are always up to date, and excellently taken. The present series includes some remarkable views of the deadly struggle in the Far East.

" Westminster Gazette."

Apparently the new war correspondent is to be the man with the bioscope. He was very prominent during the South African War, enabling London, if not to see the actual fighting, at least to witness many of the incidents which attend the progress of a campaign. Even with the restrictions of the Censorship, he is going to be a big factor in the conflict in the Far East. At the Alhambra the first series of war pictures was shown to an interested audience. It is promised that the series will develop as the war progresses, and already it is exceedingly interesting.

" The Globe."

Patrons of The Alhambra—and they are many—cannot complain that their tastes are not studied. The programme is constantly being changed, and is never allowed to flag from want of variety. Certainly the efforts of the management to win approbation are not in vain. One of the foremost attractions is the " Urban " Bioscope, by means of which a series of pictures, illustrating many incidents in connection with the Russian-Japanese war, are shown to the audience. Such a turn cannot fail to be of the greatest interest to the public at the present moment, for they are of great assistance to those who are following the course of events.

"Sporting Life."

The programme provided for the numerous patrons of the Alhambra maintains a high standard of excellence. Mr. Scott is evidently determined to provide the most up-to-date items, and on Monday evening last the first series of actual war pictures were exhibited, and met with unstinted admiration, special arrangemements for their exclusive production have been made with the Urban Bioscope Company, and being exhibited with splendid clearness they are sure to acquire popularity.

"Pall Mall Gazette."

The programme at the great variety theatre in Leicester Square, combined with the maintained popularity of the house, are causing the theatre to be crowded nightly; and last night by ten o'clock there was not a vacant seat. The Urban Bioscope is now giving a number of admirable war-pictures showing both sides, e.g., Cossacks crossing the Baikal Lake, and a Japanese war-ship firing her guns in every direction; and the applause of the audience significantly shows to which side in the struggle popular sympathy leans, a sharp outburst of cheers hailing a picture of the Japanese flag flying bravely at a masthead.

"Free Lance."

The long-promised bioscope pictures actually taken at the seat of war are now being exhibited at the Alhambra, and are an exceptional testimony not only to the business enterprise of the Urban Bioscope Company, but also to their high administrative skill in mastering apparently insurmountable obstacles. Stories of the Russian Censorship have prepared us for a recital of difficulties in the path of anyone who would direct publicity to Russian doings, so that a proposal to exhibit actual pictures of Russian military operations might well have been expected to astound and horrify the Russian authorities. The new films have been taken by Mr. George Rogers, who is with the Russian forces at Harbin, Manchuria. The Urban Company had given a bond to the Russian Government guaranteeing that nothing objectionable would be published; but, notwithstanding this assurance, the first films were "held up" by the Censor at St. Petersburg. Indeed, as Mr. Urban somewhat naïvely confesses, it was seen from the first that it would be wise to make all arrangements for the pictures through Paris; and by this study of the *suaviter in modo* success was finally ensured. Both the Urban Company and the Alhambra are to be congratulated on a feature of exceptional value and extreme interest.

"Vanity Fair."

One of the most interesting and instructive shows now to be seen in London is the series of War Pictures taken by the Urban Bioscope Company, and exhibited every evening at the Alhambra. The opening scenes of what may well prove a very big war indeed are here reproduced with startling fidelity. The "show" is sure to be appreciated, and Mr. George Scott may be heartily congratulated upon his enterprise and acumen in hitting the public taste so adroitly.

"Financial News."

There is an especially fine programme at the Alhambra just now. Short of actual fighting, the incidents of the war between Russia and Japan are amply illustrated by the Urban Bioscope.

"Daily Graphic."

New War Pictures at the Alhambra.—The Urban Company have received from their agents in the Far East some interesting new bioscope views, which were shown at the Alhambra last night; and from the west have come some films of the great fire at Toronto. The march of the Japanese Imperial Guard through Tokio, the arrival of Kuropatkin at Harbin, and some remarkable feats of horsemanship by Cossacks, were the most popular of the pictures.

"Pall Mall Gazette."

The novelty on the programme in which the audience were most interested was a series of Russo-Japanese War Pictures on the Urban Bioscope. There has, so far, been nothing shown in London to equal them; and they were followed with the deepest interest last evening. These and other pictures enable the public to get an idea of the war and all it means, far more vivid than is to be obtained from the comparatively lifeless black and white of the printed letter.

"Globe."

However excellent the programme may be, the "Urban" Bioscope will always hold a good place in point of attractiveness. Perhaps the pictures which excite the greatest interest and evoke the loudest applause are those that were recently taken in connection with the Russo-Japanese war,

"MORNING POST."

Altogether the management is not very wide of the mark in asserting that the pictures are probably the most interesting and important bioscope pictures ever exhibited in this country.

"MORNING ADVERTISER."

They constitute the most interesting and important bioscope pictures ever exhibited in this country.

"DAILY TELEGRAPH."

Several new series of animated pictures, showing scenes from the war between Russia and Japan, are the chief attraction at present in the Alhambra programme. General Kuropatkin is seen with his staff reviewing a vast army. Although the sympathies of his audience were clearly with the Japs, the Russian general was greeted with loud and continuous applause by an audience generous enough to appreciate his pluck and that of the men, which seems superior to many defeats. In another series are depicted the wounded survivors of the battle of Chemulpo on their way to St. Petersburg. Cossack cavalry have been photographed while going through exercises in horsemanship, and in the performance of the humane duty of carrying wounded men off the field. The arrival of the Siberian Sharpshooters is a stirring demonstration. The pictures which proved most popular were those in which the Japanese Guards are seen marching through the streets of Tokio. The audience was obviously touched by a military funeral procession of a Japanese standard-bearer who had fallen in action. There are also photographs of grotesque models of Russians and Cossacks which are being sold in the Japanese towns. Altogether these pictures, which have been taken by the war correspondents of the Charles Urban Trading Company, form a particularly interesting item in a programme which is both full and varied.

Lack of space forbids the reproduction of hundreds of other Press Notices equally favourable to the Russo=Japanese War Series.

"THE SIEGE OF PORT ARTHUR."

In a recent despatch received from our Mr. Rosenthal (with the 3rd Division Japanese Troops, before Port Arthur), he assures us that General Nogi and Staff have given him permission and extended every facility for procuring a comprehensive series of bioscope pictures of the extensive operations now in progress. Mr. Rosenthal has secured some highly interesting pictures, but these cannot be forwarded to England until after the fall of Port Arthur, when they will receive their first public reproduction at the Alhambra, London.

LATER.—By the surrender of Port Arthur a vast accumulation of Bioscope films taken by Mr. Rosenthal during the siege will be released.

NAVAL AND MARINE.

1037 ... **NIAGARA—THE WORLD'S WONDER**
200 feet

1037* ... **NIAGARA GORGE BY ELECTRIC RAILWAY**
150 feet

1085 ... **STEAMER LEAVING INTERLAKEN AND PANORAMA LAKE BRIENZ, SWITZERLAND**
175 feet

A Sunset on the Black Sea.

1087 ... PROCESSION AND LAUNCH OF LIFEBOAT

This gives a very fine view of the lifeboat being borne on wheels through the streets of Folkestone to the beach, where it is launched in fine style on to the bosom of the tide, and as it dips down into the water through the thousands of spectators lining the beach the effect is very fine. **75 feet**

1096 ... HEAVY SEA ON SOUTH COAST

During the recent gales along the South Coast we were fortunate in securing this splendid view of heavy seas breaking against the pier and breakwater and rolling up the shore amidst volumes of foam and spray. One of the best. **75 feet**

1101 ... THE " EMPRESS OF CHINA " LEAVING VANCOUVER FOR THE FAR EAST

The " Pride of the Pacific Fleet " of the Canadian Pacific Railway is seen approaching the camera at full speed, the progress of this liner being followed by means of our rotary tripod, thus giving a splendid view of the steamship ploughing through the waters. **50 feet**

1147 ... RACE BETWEEN THE "CITY OF SEATTLE" AND THE C.P.R. STEAMER "PRINCESS VICTORIA"

A fine picture of an exciting race between these two crack steamers of rival navigation companies on their way to Vancouver, up the Straits of Georgia, British Columbia. **60 feet**

1166 ... TRAINING OF OUR BLUEJACKETS

An excellent series of scenes on board a training ship showing the youthful aspirant to naval service at drill and play. A picture which pleases all. Full of action and fun, especially when the officers in command remove all restraints and the boys go at it with a desire to get as much fun out of the game for themselves as they create for the onlookers. **125 feet**

1167 ... DRILL AND PLAY ON A TRAINING SHIP

This is a similar picture to the preceding, but embodies the best sections of the entire series. The first scene shows the bluejackets marching down the ship's deck, preceded by the ship's band. Then follow in rapid succession the gun drill, the cutlass drill, Indian club exercises, fencing, boxing, horizontal, and vertical bar exercises, &c., &c., succeeded by the hornpipe danced by an "Old Tar," leap frog, jumping over horse, cock fights, and other games, concluding with a grand rush of the boys towards the camera for assurance from the operator as to whether each individuals antics have been bioscoped. This subject is of exceptional photographic quality and interesting throughout. **250 feet**

1238 ... THE JAPANESE CRUISER "YASHIMA" LEAVING ENGLAND

60 feet

1245 ... THE JAPANESE BATTLESHIP "MIKASA" UNDER FULL HEADWAY

50 feet

The only picture showing a warship ploughing the waters under full steam pressure.

The Battleship "Mikasa" took part in the recent bombardment of Vladivostock, and has since held the honoured place of Flagship to Admiral Togo, of the Japanese Navy.

1246 The "Pekin Wall" Evolutions.

Photographs by West's "Our Navy."

Reproducing the demonstration OF THE "HANDY-MEN" BEFORE H.M. THE KING, as given at Whale Island, Portsmouth, February 22nd, 1904.

I.—Skirmishers leading the Attack

II.—Bluejackets scaling the wall and parbuckling a 12-pounder field gun

III.—Make way for the 4·7 Naval Gun (used at Ladysmith). Blowing breach into wall with dynamite

An exciting patriotic subject. **Length 350 feet**

1265 ... A WONDERFUL REPRESENTATION OF ..

The Bombardment of Port Arthur

And Landing of Marines and Guns . . . .

. . . . . while under Fire from Shore Batteries.

Manœuvres by British Bluejackets Afloat and Ashore during the "Attack and Defence of Whale Island."

These grand Series of Pictures were photographed for us by WEST'S "OUR NAVY," LTD., and are, without exception, the most vivid realization of Naval and Land Warfare yet reproduced by Animated Photography.

ORDER OF SCENES.

1 ... **THE BOMBARDMENT BY ATTACKING FLEET OF BATTLESHIPS, CRUISERS, GUN AND TORPEDO BOATS**—wonderful smoke effects

2 ... **THE DEFENDING CREW OPERATING A 12-POUNDER FROM THE FORT**

3 ... **PANORAMA OF THE FORTIFICATIONS DURING REPLY FIRE OF ITS BATTERIES**—as seen from a battleship

4 ... **THE DEFENDING CREW OF LAND BATTERY DESTROYED BY A BURSTING SHELL**

5 ... **LANDING OF THE ENEMY FROM SHIPS' BOATS**

6 ... **BLOWING UP THE HARBOUR DEFENCE BOOM**

7 ... **BLOWING UP A BOAT'S CREW BY SUBMARINE MINE**—an awe-inspiring scene as the boat and occupants are blown to fragments while hundreds of tons of water are hurled over 200 feet into the air, by the terrific explosion

S.Y. "Argonaut."

8 ... **LANDING OF THE HANDYMEN DURING THE THICK OF THE FIGHT**

9 ... **HAULING 12-POUNDERS ASHORE**

10 ... **THE MAXIM GUNS IN ACTION**

11 ... **ANOTHER BATTERY PUT OUT OF ACTION**

12 ... **GETTING THE 4·7 GUN ASHORE**

13 ... **SCRAMBLE UP THE CLIFFS**

14 ... **SKIRMISHING ACROSS THE ISLAND**

15 ... **CEASE FIRE**

16 ... **ASSEMBLY OF THE FORCES**

17 ... **THREE CHEERS FOR THE VICTORS**

Total length 530 feet

1247 ... **LAUNCH AND HAUL-IN OF THE FIREFLY LIFEBOAT**

Fine portraits of the Lifeboat Crew as they march by, making a splendid finish to an ever popular subject. An excellent picture.

100 feet

1248 ... **THE ISLE OF MAN STEAMERS, "QUEEN VICTORIA" AND "EMPRESS QUEEN," LEAVING DOUGLAS**
Four views. **50 feet**

1249 ... **THE TURBINE STEAMER, "QUEEN ALEXANDRA" PACKED WITH EXCURSIONISTS PASSING UP THE CLYDE**

A splendid picture. **50 feet**

1270 ... **THE SUBMARINE BOAT SKIMMING THE WATERS AT FULL SPEED**

Showing her officers standing on the top of the boat, the only sections exposed to view being the turtle-back deck, conning tower, and flag-staff.

The Second Section shows a Squad of Bluejackets assisting a Diver, who descends into the sea from the boat. **125 feet**

1280 ... **LIFE ON BOARD THE S.Y. "ARGONAUT"**

The Steamer chartered by Dr. H. S. LUNN.

Photographs by F. ORMISTON-SMITH.

1—**Inspection.** Capt. Roach and Officers at Sunday morning inspection.

2—**Fire Drill.** A lively turn-out.

3—**Cricket on Deck.** Amusing efforts of lady bowlers.

4—**Obstacle Race.** An exciting contest.

5—**Cock Fighting.** Capital picture of this familiar ship sport.

6 — **Spa Boxing.** A difficult feat in balancing. **225 feet**

No. 1280 Cricket on Board S.Y. "Argonaut."

1331 ... **THE ROYAL BARGE PARTY AT WINDSOR**
100 feet

1333 ... **SUMMER LIFE ON THE UPPER THAMES**
150 feet

1334 ... **THROUGH BOULTER'S LOCK ON ASCOT SUNDAY**
200 feet

1351 ... LONDON TO WALTON BY "BELLE" STEAMER

Showing embarkation of passengers, steamer leaving the docks under way, arrival at Walton Pier, electric tram on pier, departure of steamer, &c. **150 feet**

1372 ... HAMBLEDON WEIR ON THE UPPER THAMES
60 feet

1383 ... NAILING THE FLAG TO THE MAST

An incident during the boarding of the s.s. "Malacca" by the officers of Russian battleship, which occurrence caused much excitement in Europe at the time. When the Russian flag was hoisted, after hauling down the British ensign, a sailor of the "Malacca" climbed to the top of one of the masts and nailed thereto a small Union Jack, which is seen fluttering in the breeze in defiance. **50 feet**

1391 ... BOATS ENTERING THE BLUE GROTTO, CAPRI

During high tide or rough weather it is a difficult matter to to enter this far famed Grotto through its only opening which is shown in this picture, including many small boats dodging through between waves during which entrance the passengers must lie down in the bottom of the boat to avoid being dashed against the overhanging rocks. A fine picture full of action. **50 feet**

1427 ... SCENES ON BOARD THE CHANNEL TURBINE STEAMER "QUEEN"

Crowded with passengers viewing the great Motor Boat Races across Channel. The officers, crews and spectators are, according to this picture, making the best of this holiday occasion.
75 feet

No. 1277 The Entrance to the Black Sea

1467 ... THAMES RIVER SCENES—from the Houses of Parliament to the Tower
200 feet

1468 ... PANORAMA OF LONDON RIVER FRONT—from London Bridge to Greenwich
200 feet

1469 ... LIFE ON THE UPPER THAMES
175 feet

1471 ... S.S. "CLEOPATRA" LEAVING DOCK
50 feet

1475 ... THE S.S. "ALBERT" DISEMBARKING PASSENGERS AT QUEENSTOWN, IRELAND

Excellent photographic quality. Splendid portraits of Tourists, Clergy and Irish passengers as these pass close by the camera after leaving the boat. **75 feet**

No 1276. The Landing Stage at Piraeus, Greece.

1479 ... PANORAMA OF THE SHIPPING OF MARSEILLES THE "CITY OF STRIKES"

A veritable Forest of Masts of sailing vessels tied up to the landing stages and docks. This picture was secured from the deck of a specially chartered steamer, and faithfully shows the picturesque water front of this famous Mediterranean Port of France ; its fine buildings, warehouses, steamers and small craft. The stereoscopic effects are equal to our Canadian Train Panoramas, and in general has much resemblance to the Venetian views along the Grand Canal. **100 feet**

No. 3050. Coaling a Russian Torpedo Boat at Port Said.

3050 ... THE RUSSIAN FLEET ON ITS WAY TO THE FAR EAST *Photographed by Mr. George Rogers.*

Showing the torpedo boats and battleships of the Baltic Fleet coaling at Port Said and passing through the Suez Canal. An interesting subject at the present critical stage of the Russo-Japan War. This is the Fleet which fired on the British fishing boats at Dogger Bank, the incident almost causing an international rupture. **275 feet**

VOYAGE TO NEW YORK.

Via N.D.L. s.s. "KAISER WILHELM II." (fastest Mail Steamship afloat.)

Seventy Bioscope Pictures by Mr. Charles Urban.

By courtesy of the NORDDEUTSCHER LLOYD and the NEW YORK HARBOUR MASTER.

N.D.L. s.s. " Kaiser Wilhelm II."

The pictures taken on board the N.D.L. s.s. "KAISER WILHELM II." represent a few incidents during the passage across the North Atlantic. The scenes of the River frontage on the western side of New York City and Hoboken on the Hudson, and of the eastern side of New York City with Brooklyn Bridge on the East River, were taken partly from the Mail steamer as she approached the docks and partly from the Company's tender, which was placed at Mr. Urban's disposal for the purpose. It is desired to call attention to the fact that the pictures include three interior views, the taking of which represents a feat for the first time accomplished on board ship, viz.: 1. In the Wheel House on the navigation bridge, where the man at the wheel is receiving his instructions from the officer in commond ; 2. A Corner in the Kitchen ; 3. A View in the Engine-room, right down in the hold of the ship, some 80 feet below the navigation bridge, showing the Stone-Lloyd Watertight Bulkhead Door in operation. This last innocent-looking piece of mechanism represents one of the most important inventions of recent years for securing safety at sea. Up till now there has been a long list of terrible disasters—due to there not having been time to close the openings in the water-tight bulkheads. On the approach of danger all the 33 openings in the " Kaiser Wilhelm II." can be closed from the navigation bridge in a few seconds, thus rendering all the ship's many compartments absolutely watertight.

A few Particulars regarding the . . .

N.D.L. S.S. "KAISER WILHELM II."

20,000 tons Register.   40,000 Horse Power.
Length 706 feet all over.   7 Decks.
4 Sets of Engines.   Driving Shaft weighs 230 tons.
46½ miles of Tubes in Condensers.   Heating Surface of Boilers 2½ Acres
Coal Bunkers equal to those of the four largest Battleships afloat.
Fires consume One Ton of Coal every 2½ minutes
Engine Room Staff 237 individuals.   Crew 600, exclusive of Officers
Speed 24 Knots=28 Land Miles per hour.

1500   ORDER OF PICTURES

Section A ... OFF FOR AMERICA— Crossing the Atlantic

s.s. " Kaiser Wilhelm II." leaving Southampton Water

General View of Hurricane Deck and Turtle - back crowded with Emigrants

Two Views of the extensive Boat Deck

The Helmsman at the Wheel receiving instructions, from the Officer in Command—*Splendid view of Instruments in Pilot House*

The Ship's Photographer taking a picture of a group of passengers

ss. "Kaiser Wilhelm II." at Southampton Docks.

H

Making Good Headway—Splendid wave picture, from side of ship.
Captain Hoegeman and Officers taking Observations on the Navigation Bridge
The Sextant (close view), an Important Instrument to all Skippers
Closing the Water-tight Bulkhead Doors from the Captain's Bridge
One of the 33 Stone-Lloyd Watertight Bulkhead Doors in operation
A Corner of the Extensive Kitchens during Dinner Service
Stewards Serving Light Refreshments on the Promenade Deck
Band Concert on the Upper Deck
An Appreciative Audience on the Hurricane Deck
Emigrants Dancing and Generally Enjoying Themselves
A Scramble for Coins Thrown by First Class Passengers
Hoisting Baggage from the Hold Preparatory to Landing in New York.

475 feet

Emigrants on Upper Deck during fine weather

Section B ... ENTERING NEW YORK HARBOUR

Meeting an Outward Bound Steamer
A Welcome Sight to the Voyagers—The Statue of Liberty (3 views)
Ellis Island (2 views). Panoramic scenes of this, the emigrants' haven
First Glimpse of New York City
Passing the Battery and Old Castle Garden (Aquarium)
The Skyscrapers of Lower New York
The Great Steamship Docks along the Hudson River front of New York City
The Extensive Docks of the North German Lloyd, Hoboken   **475 feet**

Sunset off Sandy Hook, U.S A.

Section C ... A SAIL UP THE EAST RIVER TO BROOKLYN NAVY YARD

Numerous Ferryboats Plying on the Hudson and East Rivers
Four Panoramic Views of East River, from Entrance
One of the New York Harbour Fire Boats Ready for a Call
Passing Under the Brooklyn Suspension Bridge (2 views)
Three Views of the New Brooklyn Bridge (just opened for traffic)
Battleships and Torpedo Boats in the Brooklyn Navy Yard   **300 feet**

Section D ... PREPARATIONS FOR THE RETURN PASSAGE

The good Ship in Dock

Mr. Urban consulting with the Chief Engineer, Mr. Schriever

Repainting the gigantic Smoke Stacks (their enormous size is well noted in proportion to the size of the men on the scaffolding)

Sorting the soiled Linen for the Laundry (after each trip the pieces of linen used by passengers number many thousands, these are distributed in small hillocks all over the deck and tied into bundles by a small army of stewards

Coaling—A fine picture, showing myriads of navvies tying up a coal barge alongside the ship when the buckets are lowered, filled, and contents shot into coal bunkers. A busy scene

Fire Drill on Board Ship— Showing the crew manning the apparatus and throwing 36 jets of water fron the various decks and portholes

H 2

Life Boat Drill—At a signal from the officers, the crew swarm the boat deck, prepare the boats, swing same outwards on the davits, man and lower these into the sea. This picture shows the whole operation from various points of vantage, from which can also be had a good idea of the tremendous size and height of the ship. **450 feet**

Section E .. LEAVING NEW YORK FOR PLYMOUTH AND CHERBOURG

Crowds on Dock cheering their departing friends.

Dropping the Pilot off Sandy Hook.

Crowds cheering the passing ship from the docks.

Going 24 knots an hour. Beautiful view of the churned waters seen from stern of ship.

The Ship's Band playing a Fanfare.

Games of Shuffleboard and Deck Quoits on the Vienna Cafe Deck.

Life on the Promenade deck on a fine day.

Passengers enjoying a blow on the " Turtle Back."

Third Class passengers crowding the forward decks during good weather.

300 feet

Section F. ... IN MID-OCEAN AND ARRIVAL AT PLYMOUTH

Running into a gale—Magnificent view of the spray cast from the foam crested waves

The Storm increases—Showing the prow shipping enormous waves, as viewed from the navigation bridge

The heavy seas subside

A sunset after the storm. A masterpiece of photography

This and the following sections have been tinted to represent the actual glow of colour characteristic of a sunset, and the cold blue sheen of a moonlight view at sea.

N.D.L. Kaiser Wilhelm II.   Saloon—under the Dome.

Moonlight on the sea—The last night on board ship.

Excellent view of the Ship approaching the tender from which the picture is taken.

Panorama of the Ship.   Close view of decks crowded with passengers.

Transferring the mails and gold and silver bullion to the decks of tender.

The Tender leaving for Plymouth Docks.

Back to Old England once again—Union Jack.   **300 feet**

No. 1,500 - Total Length, 2,300 feet.

Duration of Exhibit, 45 minutes.

Supplied only in complete length, Price £57 10s.

———— • • • ————

NOTE.—We shall be pleased to negotiate for the exclusive exhibition rights of this Series for various countries.

Re Urbanora.

MATINEES at the ALHAMBRA THEATRE, LONDON.

PRESS OPINIONS

Re "Voyage to New York" & "Wild Beast, &c., &c."

Reprint of Extracts with kind permission of the Editors.

"MANCHESTER CHRONICLE."
Sugar-Coated Science.

The stir created by the series of cinematograph pictures dealing with the natural historyo f the busy bee and the anxious ant brought to the music-hall many folk who had never been before and who have conscientious objections to the variety performance. This set Mr. Charles Urban thinking, and the outcome of his thought was that he sent photographers to various parts of the world to secure moving pictures of life in far-off places, he won the help of naturalists in bioscoping the habits of unconsidered insects, he gained access to factories, and he crossed to America and back in order that he might obtain films to show the working of an Atlantic liner. These educational pictures are to be shown as afternoon performances in the Alhambra, beginning on the 9th of next month. It is obvious that young people, and adults too, for that matter, can be far more easily instructed through the eye than through the ear, and, to sugar-coat still more thickly these illustrated lecturettes on science, geography, and natural history, there will be music, and one specially selected performer on the stage. As another encouragement to the ladies and children, smoking will not be permitted in the auditorium, and afternoon tea will be served, while half prices are to be charged to all parts of the house save the gallery, which will not be opened. The entertainment lasts two hours, of which ninety minutes are devoted to the animated pictures. I hear that already arrangements are being made by various educational bodies to bring scholars to the Alhambra in their hundreds.

"PALL MALL GAZETTE."

It is a most attractive programme which the management of the Alhambra has organized for the series of matinees begun yesterday, and in juvenile circles the entertainment **ought to prove one of the most popular** of the season. In every aspect "Urbanora" must be pronounced **one of the best and most intelligent entertainments available at this season.**

"DAILY EXPRESS."

"Urbanora." Amusement Combined with Instruction. Novel Matinees.

One of the most remarkable experiments ever started in connection with the music-hall is to be made at the Alhambra on Monday, January 9, when the management will begin a series of daily matinees, with the object of instructing as well as entertaining their patrons.

The promenade will be converted into an afternoon tea-room, the bars will be closed, and there will be no smoking in the auditorium.

The entertainment, which will last from three till five o'clock, will consist of a display of Urban Bioscope pictures, with two sets of scientific, geographical, and historical interest.

In the ten minutes' interval between the two sets musical selections will be given.

Mr. Charles Urban, who is responsible for this latest development of the music-hall, is confident of success.

The biograph, he explained to an "Express" representative yesterday, has been debased to unworthy uses too long. It deserved a better fate than to be merely the agency for the presentment of frivolous pictures.

"There is a great future in store for this new form of matinee," he observed. "To amuse and entertain is good. To do both and instruct is better! That is our motto."

"The pictures will all deal with actualities. We shall illustrate every step in the great industries, A series on rubber, for instance, will begin with the sapping of gum 1,200 miles up the Amazon and end with the tyre of a motor-car revolving through Hyde Park. Every picture will have been taken on the spot.

"The children can take their first botany lesson at the Alhambra. Things seen by the eye stamp themselves on the memory of the child, There is, in fact, no limit to the developments of "Urbanora," as the new matinee is called."

"THE SUNDAY TIMES."

Under the title of " Urbanora " the Alhambra is giving a series of daily matinées which should obtain a large measure of public favour. The principal feature is the presentation, in a more synthetic form than is practicable in the evening programme, of some of the latest achievements of the bioscope. Thus for the first hour we are taken on a voyage by the " Kaiser Wilhelm II." to and from New York, and are given such wonderful ocean-scapes, such *apercus* of the working of a big liner and the occupations and amusements of the passengers, saloon and steerage, that it needs little exercise of the imagination to feel that one is actually *en voyage* and seeing everything at first hand. During the ship's stay at New York we are taken up the East River and given a vivid picture of the hideous sky-serapers that are the most salient feature of the Empire City, as well as of the Brooklyn Bridge, the wharves of the great transport companies, and the United States battleships in Brooklyn Navy Yard. **The pictures are remarkably clear and free from jumpiness, and their variety and range are as remarkable as their plan is excellent.** The other series deals with the inhabitants of the Zoo, and gives us a closer view of their habits and customs than is possible for the casual visitor to Regent's Park.

" MORNING ADVERTISER."

The experiment of giving daily matinées at the Alhambra, under the title of "Urbanora," **has proved to be a gratifying success.** Mr. Charles Urban has produced some remarkably realistic bioscopic pictures, which are greatly appreciated by the happy juveniles for whose delight and instruction they are presented. The first part of the programme consists of a number of pictures portraying the voyage of the " Kaiser Wilhelm II. to New York from Southampton, The second series of pictures deals with beasts, birds, and reptiles, **being remarkably comprehensive and effective.**

" WESTMINSTER GAZETTE."

Those fond of bioscope pictures—and who is not ?—could not do better than drop in at the Alhambra one afternoon just now to see the new show which has been put on here for a series of matinées, under the title of " Urbanora." Two sets of pictures are shown—the first illustrating the incidents of a voyage to New York and back on board the " Kaiser Wilhelm II.," while the second take one to the Zoo and show all the wonderful beasts, birds, and reptiles of that establishment. Both sets of pictures are splendid examples of their kind, while their continuous character—the one show lasts over an hour, and the second over thirty-five minutes—adds to their effectiveness.

" THE ERA."

"To amuse and entertain is good; to do both and instruct is better " is the motto that has been adopted ior the entertainment, specially designed for the young folk, which was presented at the Alhambra for the first time on Monday afternoon under the generic name of " Urbanora." This new title is happily appropriate, for the genius and originality of Mr. Charles Urban will, in this instance, as in others, be responsible for many pleasant hours with the Bioscope. His voyage to New York and back by the splendid Norddeutscher Lloyd liner Kaiser Wilhelm II. (the fastest mail steamship afloat) may be quoted not only as an instance of his wonderful enterprise, but as a proof of the power, in skilled hands, of vivid reproductions belonging to the " cameraic " machine which he has done so much to perfect. Mr. Urban virtually takes us with him on his trip across the Atlantic, and pictures the real jollity and knowledge to be derived from such an enjoyable form or holiday in a number of remarkable films. We see the great floating hotel leaving Southampton Water, and are borne away on the mighty main at excellent speed. We have a view of Captain Hoegeman and his officers taking observations, and watch the mode of using the sextant. We are present, as it were, at the closing of the water-tight bulkhead doors, and see one of the thirty safety Stone-Lloyd bulkhead doors in operation. Soon after assisting at a band concert on the upper deck, we enter New York Harbour and view the Statue of Liberty, and visit well-known scenes in the Empire City. On the return journey the vessel runs into a storm, which gradually subsides, and a beautiful seascape is the moon rising on a vast expanse of water. The life of the passengers on board is depicted in various ways, and the interesting voyage concludes with the arrival of the " Kaiser Wilhelm II." in Plymouth Harbour. The " Urbanora " second series of films depicts chiefly animal, bird, and reptile life in the Zoo, and is as instructive as it is amusing. The delights of a visit to the celebrated gardens in Regent's Park begin with a view of the dens of the larger carnivora, including that interesting creature, the polar bear. A general view of the lake is taken, with the foreign ducks and geese enjoying themselves. A comic picture is a tug-of-war between storks; and it is an intensely curious experience to assist at the luncheon of the Brazilian toads, whose batrachian palates relish a good fat mealworm, Another " amoozin' cuss " is the chameleon, for when at his feed his length of tongue and the way he takes his food supply a very diverting picture. The boa constrictor, we know, never exceeds the bounds of good digestion, and is taken in the company of a rat—his next meal,

A number of bison on Lord Strathcona's ranch in Manitoba and a herd of elk on the same nobleman's estate give a capital idea of these animais in their semi-wild state. The greatest patience, care, thought, and resource have had to be employed so as to show successfully the creatures in their natural and characterisitic movements, and for much of the work special costly apparatus had to be designed and constructed, and many elaborate and delicate experiments carried out. But the results of the labours of the operators have yielded the highest perfection.

"Morning Leader."

The first of the daily matinees at the Alhambra, which, under the name of "Urbanora," **promise to become one of the most popular afternoon functions,** took place yesterday, and a large audience enjoyed the entertaining programme which the Alhambra provided upon a novel variety plan. The bioscope pictures to come range over a wonderful series of educative and amusing subjects, and the **entertaining possibilities of the new scheme are incalculable.**

"Morning Advertiser."

No boy or girl will be satisfied to return to scholastic duties without having seen "Urbanora."

"Daily Telegraph."

An interesting esries of matinees, specially designed for the entertainment of young people, but well adapted also to the tastes of their elders, was started at the Alhambra yesterday under the title of "Urbanora." The programme began with a number of attractive pictures on the bioscope illustrative of a voyage on board the "Kaiser Wilhelm II," to and from New York. The steamer is first seen leaving Southampton Water, and thereafter the daily life of the passengers, from the moment of their awakening to the time of their retiring, is vividly and minutely depicted. Then follows the arrival of the huge steamer in New York Harbour, and presently its occupants are permitted to enjoy a sail up the East River, and, incidentally, to inspect the United States Battleships in Navy Yard. Soon, however, the instant comes for starting upon the return passage, and once more the passengers resume their former places on board. Of the home voyage one of the most exciting features is the fire and lifeboat drill, a scene of wonderful animation and lifelike realism. The second part of the programme is devoted to the exhibition of a number of pictures dealing with animal life at the Zoo. It is not difficult to imagine that in securing these the photographer ran a considerable risk of injury to himself, but the results are certainly of a kind to repay him for his trouble. For all those, indeed, who are unable to make their way to Regent's Park, the Alhambra series offers ample compensation, inasmuch as that popular place of amusement they can study every afternoon the ways and manners of most of the Zoo's inmates, including bears. boa-constrictors, alligators, kangaroos, giraffes, seals, tigers and lions. As a matter of fact **the entertainment is not only thoroughly interesting, but also highly instructive.**

"The Financial Times."

The first of a series of "Urbanora" daily matinees—exclusively-bioscopic entertainments under the direction of Mr. Charles Urban—took place yesterday at the Alhambra. The first part, consisting of seventy bioscopic pictures, depicted the many and varied scenes of a voyage to New York and back ; and the second, which included seventy motion pictures of wild beasts, birds and reptiles, was the result of a visit to the Regent's Park Zoo and to Lord Strathcona's ranch in Manitoba. **From the photographic point of view the pictures were a triumph of the art to which Mr. Urban has contributed so much.**

"The Sportsman."

Nearly the whole of the programme is devoted to a series of new bioscope pictures, **which are not only amusing, but possess a unique educational value.** The first part consists of seventy pictures describing the voyage of the Kaiser Wilhelm II. to New York from Southampton. We are given a penetrating insight into the daily routine and recreations of the passengers and crew, a splendid panoramic view of New York Harbour, and records of incidents of the return passage, including three very effective pictures of a storm, sunset, and moonlight at sea. **Such a unique selection of pictures is calculated to enlarge the outlook of the child-mind much more than dry geographical tomes or lectures.** In the second part of the entertainment we are given a trip to the Zoological Gardens, and spend a delightful half-hour studying the ways and habits of the wild beasts, birds and reptiles. **The pictures are most realistic,** especially those taken at feeding-time. The interpolated pictures of wild buffaloes and elk taken on Lord Strathcona's ranch and estate, under no small difficulties, **are the perfection of motion photography.**

"Morning Post."

"Urbanora" is **interesting and funny, and sent the spectators away thoroughly pleased with an afternoon's amusement and instruction.**

"The Globe."

The **"Urbanora" Pictures are excellent.**

"Referee."

The management of the Alhambra has also done its best to amuse the dear children, inasmuch as the programme at the series of

Urbanora Matinees,

which started on Monday, was not only devised to amuse and entertain the younger generation, but also to give it "Object Lessons" in **the pleasantest and most interesting manner possible.** Not that the entertainment is calculated to please children only, for I may assure grown-up Refereaders that they can while away an afternoon **very delightfully** during the run of these Alhambra matinées, **and most of them may learn a little at the same time.**

"The World."

These novel **"Urbanora Matinees" will, doubtless, be widely appreciated.**

"Amateur Photographer."

Under the title "Urbanora," there are being given daily matinées at the Alhambra Theatre, in which the entertainment consists almost entirely of the high-class Cinematograph Pictures with which the Charles Urban Trading Company have become identified. A most delightful and instructive show is provided, than which no better afternoon's occupation could be suggested. **By these high-class and really instructive Bioscope displays,** which are also nightly included in the Alhambra programme, and the keen interest shown therein by all classes of the audience, Mr. Charles Urban has been the means of satisfactorily proving, if proof is necessary, that in the reformed modern "variety" theatre it is by no means the wholly frivolous, still less the vicious, that meets with the approval of the majority.

"News of the World."

"To amuse and entertain is good. To do both and instruct is better." This is the motto of Mr. Charles Urban in giving some unique and exclusive bioscopic afternoon entertainments at the Alhambra, and he certainly acts up to it. **The pictures are the finest and most realistic ever thrown on a screen.** At present the matinées are divided into two parts, In the first a remarkably fine scene depicting a voyage to New York and back, with all its many incidents, is given, and in the second a series dealing with wild beasts, birds, and reptiles. This is the first time that the bioscope has been seriously and scienitfically applied in obtaining a record of the ways and habits of wild animals. **The results are wonderful, full of interest, but always enjoyable.**

Extracts from hundreds of other "Press Opinions" will be sent if you want further convincing that the "URBANORA" Series of Pictures are the

MOST NOVEL, INTERESTING AND INSTRUCTIVE EVER PRODUCED.

AGRICULTURAL AND INDUSTRIAL SERIES.

1070 ... **HARVESTING HAY IN SWITZERLAND**

50 feet

1072 ... **LIFE AT A SUMMERTHAL CATTLE FARM**

125 feet

1118 ... **CATTLE CROSSING A GLACIER TO HIGHER PASTURES—Swiss**
50 feet

1119 ... **GOAT HERDING AT GRIMSEL HOSPICE**
100 feet

1149 ... **THRESHING WHEAT ON A MANITOBA FARM—Canada**
75 feet

Harvesting Scene in France.

1151 ... **AFTER THE HARVEST ON A CANADIAN WHEAT FARM**

50 feet

1159 ... **A TOBACCO FARM AT CRAPITS—Bulgaria**

75 feet

1369 ... **TRANSPORTING GRAIN AT THE PORT OF BULGAS**

150 feet

1448 ... **HARVESTING BLOSSOMS IN THE VALLEY OF ROSES**

75 feet

1019 ... **PLOUGHING BY BULLOCKS IN INDIA**

60 feet

1182 ... **THE DARVEL BAY TOBACCO ESTATES—Borneo**

125 feet

1274c ... **LIFE ON A CEYLON TEA PLANTATION**

275 feet

1005 ... **THE HAZARDOUS OCCUPATION OF THE STEEPLE JACK**

125 feet

1033 ... **MOVING TIMBER BY ELEPHANTS IN INDIA**

200 feet

1077 ... **LACE MAKING BY SWISS PEASANTS**

60 feet

1092 ... **TRAPPING SALMON IN THE FRASER RIVER**

400 feet

1093 ... **HAULING IN SALMON NETS**

75 feet

1102 ... **SALMON FISHING OFF VANCOUVER**

75 feet

1106 ... **FELLING PINE TREES IN NORTH-WESTERN TERRITORY, CANADA**

60 feet

1108 ... **LUMBERING IN CANADIAN FORESTS**

300 feet

No. 1397. *Scene in Petticoat Lane.*

RELIGIOUS CEREMONIES, SCENES, PROCESSIONS, etc., etc.

1239 ... THE PROCESSION OF THE RELIC OF THE HOLY BLOOD AT BRUGES, BELGIUM

This Procession, probably of its kind the finest in Europe, takes place annually on the first Monday after the 2nd May. The Relic on this occasion is taken from its chapel, which is called after it, to the Cathedral, where Pontifical Mass is celebrated, after which the Procession starts from here, traversing the town, and finishing with the impressive sight of the Benediction with the Relic outside of its chapel on the Place du Bourg. The Relic was given to Thierry of Alsace, Count of Flanders, by his brother-in-law, Baldwin III.,

No. 1289 " Holy Blood " Procession at Bruges

King of Jerusalem, as a reward for his services as a Crusader. The Relic, which was then deposited in the Church of Jerusalem, was divided into two parts, one of which was filled into a phial and then presented to Thierry by the Patriarch of Jerusalem. Thierry, with his Flemish army, leaving the Holy Land, brought the Relic to Bruges in 1148, where later it was placed in the Chapel of the Holy Blood.

The Relic is exposed every Friday for public veneration in its chapel. Documents extant testify to the visits of Bishops, Patriarchs, Princes, Kings and Emperors to this wonderful shrine. On 25th October, 1485, a party of English sailors with their captain, made a pilgrimage to Bruges to venerate this Relic, and this year (1904) a party of British pilgrims, under the auspices of the Catholic Association, London, took a prominent part in the grand procession, the Archbishops of Calcutta and Westminster and the Bishop of Birmingham being likewise present for the occasion.

Order of the Procession :

I.—**The Nativity of Our Lord** (This is represented on the car drawn by six horses.) This is preceded by sixty young girls singing the " Gloria in excelsis," and immediately following the car a group of shepherds singing the " Adeste Fideles."

2.—**Jesus is seen discoursing** in the midst of the Doctors.

3. **Triumphal Entry of Jesus** into Jerusalem. (This is preceded by a number of persons waving branches of palm, and singing " Hosannah."

This is considered one of the most striking scenes in the whole procession, and reminds many people of the Passion Play of Oberammergau.

No. 1289 Religious Procession at Bruges

4.—**Reliquary** (containing relics of Christian Martyrs.)—The Reliquary is preceded by four English boys, each carrying a small flag — the Union Jack, English, Irish, and Scottish flags respectively.

5. — **Their Lordships the Bishops** (in the following order) : Bishop of Bruges, Archbishop of Calcutta, Archbishop of Westminster, and the Bishop of Birmingham.

6.—**Members of the Noble Confraternity.**— These are dressed in toga and cap of 16th century style. This Confraternity of Noblemen was founded centuries ago in connection with the Relic and its chapel—the Chapel of the Holy Blood

Finale—The Benediction with the Relic on the Place du Bourg, the Bishop of Bruges giving the blessing **425 feet**

1376 ... THE INTERNATIONAL CONGRESS OF THE SALVATION ARMY. General Booth reviews the "Army" at the Crystal Palace, July 5th, 1904.

No. 1310 *Funeral Procession in Tokio*

Excellent view of General Booth as he greets the various contingents from all countries passing in review before him.

NOTE.—This subject is equal in variety and interest to the Diamond Jubilee and Coronation Processions — unique throughout.

By courtesy of MESSRS. RUSSELL & SONS *and the* CRYSTAL PALACE, *we obtained the exclusive Bioscope rights to photograph this historic demonstration. We extended the privilege to the Salvation Army Photographers on condition that the pictures secured by them should be confined strictly to the advancement of their own work.*

Exhibited with great success at the London Hippodrome.

Total length 400 feet

PRESS COMMENTS.

"PICK ME UP."

Then there was an extra turn of a bioscopic kind. We saw General Booth at the Crystal Palace saluting the various home and foreign contingents of his wonderful "army" The picture must have lasted a clear ten minutes, and I believe that represents a very large number of films indeed. But the mechanism, admirable as it was, did not constitute the interest of the turn The centre of attraction was the tall, white-haired figure standing up up in a motor car, and waving his hat energetically by way of returning the salutes of his followers, who, bearing the flags of their respective nationalities, marched past him. You got a very fair idea of what the real scene of frantic enthusiasm must have been like; and then, as the lights went up you were left to reflect on the most remarkable phase of emotional religion that history can record, To the student of social phenomena the Salvation Army is an absorbing topic—and we are all students of sociology now.

"BLACK AND WHITE."

At the Hippodrome, as an off-set to the tragic sensations of this startling spectacle the management offers the longest cinematographic film ever produced—representing the Salvation Army demonstration at the Crystal Palace. This is the high-water mark in moving pictures, and not at all the least interesting feature of a very fine programme.

"LLOYD'S NEWS."

The Bioscope has become as important a feature of the miscellaneous entertainment here as it is elsewhere. Mr. H. E. Moss has certainly hit upon a popular incident in illustrating the march past General Booth of the Salvation Army contingents assembled at the Crystal Palace. The arrangement of the gigantic picture is good, and the numerous groups possess an air of reality that evoke hearty cheers from the spectators. It is both an interesting and an attractive item of the liberal programme always characterising the Hippodrome management.

"REYNOLD'S NEWSPAPER."

On Monday at the London Hippodrome, Mr. H. E. Moss showed one of the most marvellous animated pictures ever taken. It depicts every phase of the great Salvation Army Congress at the Crystal Palace. Every nationality of Salvationists in their national costumes are shown with great brilliancy throughout the picture. The veteran, General Booth, is seen addressing the myriads of followers all the way through, and the great march past is shown as being one of the liveliest occurrences that could ever have happened. This picture is shown exclusively at the Hippodrome, and constitutes a very instructive entertainment in itself. It is also the longest animated picture on a single film that has been taken, either in England or any other country.

"NEWS OF THE WORLD."

The management of the Hippodrome did a capital piece of business when they secured Urban's Bioscope of the Salvation Army Congress at the Crystal Palace. It is stated to be the longest animated picture on a single film which has ever been taken. During the nine minutes which it rapidly ran it was particularly steady and remarkably clear, whilst the interest with which it was followed by the house was only natural, and as befitted the magnitude of the event. Salvationists in their thousands filed past the Hippodrome audience, Every nationality was represented—Americans, Scandinavians, Germans, gaudily bedecked tropical Salvation soldiers—all gaily waving their handkerchiefs to the "General," a tall, white-headed, and bearded figure, who stood on a raised platform above them, where, surrounded by his staff, he joyously acknowledged his soldiers' salutations by waving his silk hat in response It was a moving spectacle, in which a friendly sympathy mingled with the spectators' cheers.

"THE PEOPLE."

The Urban Bioscope pictures of the Salvation Army Congress at the Crystal Palace justify all the promises made respecting them, They prove an interesting addition to the Hippodrome programme, which is attracting good audiences in spite of the hot weather. It was delightful to listen to the cheers which greeted on Monday night the passage of the "Jap" Salvationists across the screen.

"DAILY TELEGRAPH."

The feature at the Hippodrome is Urban's animated pictures, showing General Booth at the Crystal Palace reviewing the battalions representing the forces gathered from all nations to combat the powers of darkness. It is not so long ago that the Salvation Army could not be mentioned without merriment. The cheering of the audience in the Hippodrome testified at once to the perfection of these strikingly vivid pictures and to the sincere hold which the General has gained upon the public as well as his followers.

"DAILY EXPRESS."

Of quite a different nature is a new turn at the Hippodrome, where, on the bioscope was displayed the great Salvation Army gathering at the Crystal Palace. This series of pictures was of unusual excellence.

"MORNING POST."

The spectacle was one full of interest. and it was watched by the audience with close attention and friendly sympathy.

"STANDARD."

One of the most interesting items in the entertainment at the Hippodrome this week is the presentation on Urban's Bioscope of a splendid film depicting every phase of the Salvation Army Congress at the Crystal Palace. This is the longest animated picture on a single film which has ever been taken, and the detachments from the various nations are shown in their march past the "General" with wonderful clearness, Last night these scenes were watched by a large audience with the greatest attention, and were loudly applauded.

"DAILY GRAPHIC."

The Urban Bioscope picture of the Review of the Salvation Army before General Booth was most successful, and much applauded as a welcome novelty in a very strong programme.

"THE TIMES."

A scene of extraordinary enthusiasm, the picture being admirably clear and steady.

"THE PALL MALL GAZETTE."

Admirers of the cinematograph form of entertainment will be interested in an exhibition at the Hippodrome this week, which consists of the largest animated picture on a single film which has ever been taken in England or elsewhere. It represents the recent Salvation Army Congress at the Crystal Palace, with "General" Booth addressing his followers, and the great march past is one of the most stirring spectacles that could possibly have been preserved through the medium of the mechanism which is now so popular a source of entertainment.

1417 ...GENERAL BOOTH'S MOTOR CAR TOUR

Excellent portrait of General Booth, surrounded by his friends and Members of the Army, all wishing him well as he boards the Motor Car and proceeds on his "Army Work" Trip through England. The second Motor contains his daughter, Mary Booth-Tucker, who has also taken a prominent part in the past work of the Army.

100 feet

1155 ... THE FEAST OF ST. JOHN AT RILO MONASTERY—BULGARIA
(See description under " Macedonia ")   **150 feet**

No. 1279b The Holy Sepulchre, Jerusalem

1279 ... A PILGRIMAGE TO JERUSALEM — The Holy City
(S e e description under "Arabia and Palestine") **650 feet**

1017 ... CONVERTING THE HEATHEN—Bible Classes in India 75 feet

1025 ... THE LEPERS AT MANDALAY 150 feet

1026 MEN, WOMEN AND CHILDREN RESCUED FROM DEVIL WORSHIP IN INDIA 200 feet

1027.. PROCESSION OF 1,800 CHILD WIDOWS OF THE RAMALIAN MISSION India 300 feet

1030 ... THE 777 PAGODAS OF MANDALAY 100 feet

1031 ... SCENES IN THE MOST SACRED PAGODA IN BURMAH
(See descriptions of the above under "India, Burmah, &c.") **150 feet**

1310 ... FUNERAL PROCESSION IN TOKIO, Japan 150 feet

1311 ... THE GREAT SACRED PROCESSION OF THE NIKKO TEMPLE—Japan
(For descriptions see " Japan " Series)   **300 feet**

IRELAND.

1416 ... **SHOOTING THE KILLARNEY RAPIDS**

One of the famous show places of the Killarney Lake district. Tourists seldom fail to participate in the exhilarating sport of shooting the rapids by boats which are most skilfully guided around sharp turnings in their rapid descent down stream. Seven crowded boat loads pass the view, the passengers cheering our operator while gliding by. **60 feet**

1432 ... **THE GIANTS' CAUSEWAY—North of Ireland**

A splendid panoramic view of this wonderful work of nature, showing hundreds of tourists arriving at the station, clambering over the irregular heights of the Columnar basalt of hexagon shape, panoramic views of various sections of this famous promontory, the base of which is washed by the sea. An excellent series. **150 feet**

1475 ... **THE S.S. "ALBERT" DISCHARGING PASSENGERS AT QUEENSTOWN**

Description under "NAVAL AND MARINE." **75 feet**

PANORAMA OF RIVER LEE ... AND CORK HARBOUR

By Courtesy of the Cork, Blackrock and Passage Railway.

1476 ... **FROM GLENBROOK TO MONKSTOWN**

Tourists and visitors to Cork should not miss an opportunity of viewing its magnificent harbour, which is considered one of the finest in the world, and which practically can afford safe anchorage for nearly the entire British Navy. **175 feet**

1477 ... **MONKSTOWN BAY TO DRAKE'S POOL**

The Bioscope views show bits of this lovely little railway from Glenbrook, along the banks of the Lee to Monkstown, thence along the shores of Monkstown Bay, from which a grand view of the harbour and the islands with which it is dotted is obtained, and also Fort Carlisle commanding the eastern side of the entrance to the harbour and Fort Camden on the western. As we proceed along this lovely estuary (the Owenabuee) some charming views of pretty river scenery are obtained which are crowned by that of Drake's Pool, as the train sweeps around the curve about half-a-mile from Crosshaven Station. **200 feet**

1478 ... **DRAKE'S POOL TO CROSSHAVEN**

The historic Drake's Pool is where the celebrated Admiral Drake, in 1587, took shelter from the Spaniards who pursued him into the harbour and were unable to trace his whereabouts, owing to the winding nature of the creek, and the high formation of the hills surrounding it. Crosshaven is the popular sea-side resort for the citizens of Cork and the South of Ireland, being beautifully sheltered inside the mouth of the harbour and within a few minutes' walk of the Atlantic Ocean where splendid bathing is available on the lovely bays dotting the coast. There are few places in the United Kingdom of Great Britain and Ireland where such magnificent bits of scenery are encompassed in such a small area, and are so accessible as this pretty region is from Cork. **100 feet**

Nos. 1476 to 1478 (inclusive) "River Lee and Cork Harbour Panorama." Total Length 475 feet.

I

LIVING CANADA.

Photographs by JOSEPH ROSENTHAL.

The Tall Pines of the Rocky Mountains.

1037 ... NIAGARA, THE WORLD'S WONDER, 10 views of Niagara Falls

An awe-inspiring subject, often described and pictured, but never yet reproduced with such vivid detail and grand aspect as in this wonderful series which was procured under greatest difficulties. Herein is included the American and Horseshoe Falls with columns of shooting spray, the breaking up of the ice-bridge in early Spring, the new steel Arch Bridge with Trams and R. R. Trains crossing the chasm, etc., etc. **200 feet**

1037 ... A TRIP THROUGH THE NIAGARA GORGE ON THE ELECTRIC RAILWAY

Depicting a continuous view of the Whirlpool Rapids (where Captain Webb lost his life), and a Panorama of the Gorge, through which rush the wild waters of " Niagara Rapids." A grand subject. **150 feet**

1038 ... SNAPSHOTS OF NIAGARA

A shorter series of views of the falls and rapids. **125 feet**

1039 ... YACHTING ON THE ST. LAWRENCE

An exciting and exhilarating sport, forming one of the principal winter pastimes in Canada and the States, where extensive ice fields or wide frozen rivers are available. **50 feet**

1040 .. MONTREAL ON SKATES

Showing an extensive view of the Montreal Skating rink, over which glide thousands of men, women and children all on "blades," upon which they are apparently " at home," as not one fall is noted among the multitudes who skate past the camera. **100 feet**

1041 ... SKATING for the WORLD'S CHAMPIONSHIP AT MONTREAL

Showing crowds on the M.A.A. Grounds watching the brushes between Johnny Nilsson, McCollock, Baptie and the other fast skaters, Great rivalry and competition is displayed, the men practically flying over the track of ice. Hurdle jumping and back-skating races are also indulged in. **150 feet**

1042 ... THE OUTING OF THE "OLD TUQUE BLUE" SNOW-SHOEING CLUB OF MONTREAL

An unique series of pictures showing about thirty members of this famous club, togged out in their picturesque garb. tramping over the soft snows in single and double files, portraying the rapid progress made by aid of the Canadian snow-shoe. **150 feet**

1043 ... TOSSING IN THE BLANKET

After the preceding photographic operations were concluded the members of the Snow-shoe Club, brimming over with fun, surrounded our operator and applied to him a "ragging" by repeatedly tossing him into the air and catching him before he touched the snows in his descent. **50 feet**

1068 ... THE C.P.R, "IMPERIAL LIMITED" AT FULL SPEED

Showing this superb train in a portion of its 3,000 miles journey across Canada. There are three trains depicted on this film, but as the "Imperial Limited" rushes forward at 60 miles an hour, the spectator feels imbued with the exhilarating rush of the flyer.

50 feet

1069 ... CANOE TILTING CONTEST BETWEEN THE INDIAN SHAWNO AND M. WEST the champion of the Pan-American Exhibition

As the tilting contestants face each other, on the rapidly rushing waters, and dexterously poised on the edges of their bark canoes, engage in strenuous combat, the effect is most exciting. Three times successfully does the champion with his marvellously weilded paddle toss his opponent from his flimsy footing into the surging waters

100 feet

No 1092 Taking Salmon from the Traps on the Fraser River.

1092 ... SALMON FISHING ON FRASER RIVER

This series furnishes views of the salmon fishing and canning industry on the Fraser River, British Colombia.

By courtesy of the ANGLO BRITISH COLUMBIA PACKING COMPANY, LIMITED.

No 1092. Emptying Salmon into Barge on the Fraser River.

Scene 1,—The water-front at Steveston, which is a fishing village at the mouth of the Fraser River, aed is situated about 12 miles south of Vancouver. To this place the fishing population—a mixed lot of Indians, Japanese, Chinese and whites of all nationalities—flock during the fishing season ; the busiest time being from July 15th to August 20th, when some 2,000 to 3,000 boats are employed.

Scene 2.—Towing out of Fleet. There is a weekly close time from 6 p.m. on Saturday night till 6 p.m. on Sunday night, at which hour a gun is fired to notify fishermen that they may begin. The picture depicts boats being towed out and casting off to take up their positions ready to begin, and it is a fine sight to see hundreds of boats all casting their nets simultaneously at gun fire.

Scene 3.—Fish Traps This picture shows the lifting of salmon traps. These traps are substantial and costly structures, consisting of piles with netting attached, which extend to the bottom. The "Pot" is emptied by means of "Handbrailer" and "Steam Brailer"—(both of which are shown)—the latter being a small net worked from a boom by a steam winch on the attendant tug-boat. By means of "Steam-brailing" 15,000 fish may be lifted in half-an-hour.

Scene 4.—Towing Barges or "Fish Scows." Each trap requires two fish scows, in which the fish are loaded and towed to destination —they hold from 6,000 to 10,000 salmon, which are delivered ready for canning at the factories within a few hours of being lifted.

Scene 5.—Interior Work. This picture shows the first process after the delivery of fish at the factory, when the heads, fins and tails are taken off, and they are carefully cleaned, scraped, brushed and washed several times. The latter work of cutting up into sizes and nearly all subsequent processing is done by machinery—except the actual filling of the tins. The skilled labour inside the canneries is all Chinese, under the supervision of white men—the unskilled consist largely of Indian women. **400 feet**

1093 ... TRAPPING SALMON ON THE FRASER RIVER

Another view of a salmon trap showing the fishermen emptying the nets. The salmon are caught in thousands by this method of trapping, and the sight fairly turns the head of a fisher after salmon who traverses a stream for two hours and finally lands a sprat. **75 feet**

1102 ... HAULING IN SALMON NETS AT VANCOUVER

A lively scene among the fishing fleet on the Fraser River during the salmon season, showing hundreds of salmon struggling in the nets as these are drawn to the surface and finally emptied of their contents. **75 feet**

1103 ... THE NORTH AMERICAN INDIAN AT "PEACE" DANCE

An unique subject, depicting a tribe of North American Indians in full native costume performing a picturesque " Peace Dance." **100 feet**

1104 ... I.—INDIANS GAMBLING FOR FURS. II.—IS IT WAR OR PEACE ?

There are good as well as bad Indians. In this scene the former falls a victim to the latter, who deprives his dupe of the spoils of a fur hunting season. The second section depicts a life-size view of a warrior in his canoe, mocking and threatening his enemies, after which the expressions on his face change to that of a friendly smile and invitation to join him in smoking the Pipe of Peace. **60 feet**

134

1105 ... INDIAN CANOE RACES

An animated scene of a Canoe Racing Contest betweeu Canadian Indians on the Sault Saint Marie River, showing great activity among the warriors in paddling their birch bark canoes towards the winning post.   **50 feet**

1106 ... FELLING PINES IN NORTH WEST TERRITORY

The gigantic pines of the North West Territory are the envy of the Lumbering world. This picture shows the axemen and sawyers attacking one of these trees, who, after cutting and sawing throuhg its trunk upset its perpendicular by driving a wedge. The giant falls with a crash, carrying with it many branches of surrounding trees in its descent.   **60 feet**

1108 ... LOGGING IN CANADIAN FOREST

This series of pictures depict the methods employed in felling and transporting pine logs during the summer months in British Columbia

Scene I.—The first scene hows the Axemen supported on platforms 8 feet from the base of the tree, attacking same from the side in the direction it is intended the tree should fall. Expert sawyers now cut through the trunk. After which a wedge is driven into the "cut" from the opposite direction in which the tree falls.

Lumbering near Welcome, B.C.

Scene 2.—The logs are then hauled through the forest over gullies and irregular places by means of block and tackle to the vicinity of corduroy roads

Scene 3.—Where they are transported to the sea, being "snigged" by a team of ten horses. The corduroy road is built by placing smaller timbers across the road, as sleepers are laid for a railroad bed. At regular intervals are placed grooved timbers, which act as guides to obviate the side-rolling of the logs during their progress over this road. You will note the occupation of the man preceding the team he greases the grooves to prevent friction and facilitate the draught. These logs average 40 feet in length, weighing from one to one-and-a half tons each, and are coupled by means of chains attached to "dogs" driven into the ends.

Scene 4.—As each train of logs reaches the chute, the teams are hitched to the back of the log train, and as the "dogs" have been removed, the result is that, as each log reaches the end of the chute, it falls into the water with a splash.

Scene 5.—After being towed in rafts to the sawmills, the logs are guided into a race, where the grips of an endless chain carry them up the incline to be sawn.

Scene 6.—The last picture shows the refuse heaps outside a sawmill, where the superfluous cuttings and slabs are burnt, as in British Columbia it costs more to transport these cuttings than their value.

300 feet

1109 ... MILLING LOGS ON PACIFIC COAST (NORTH WEST TERRITORY) CANADA

Here we give an excellent panoramic view of the log rafts, having been floated down the river and caught by chained "booms," are held in tow until required to be milled into lumber, when they are drawn from the water over a log-way by means of an endless chain-gear. Arriving at the mill, they are sawed into boards and proper lengths, these again being loaded into the hold of a ship lying alongside the mill dock, while the refuse (sawdust and cuttings) is chuted into a heap in the mill yard and consumed by fire. **150 feet**

1128 ... LABOUR DAY PARADE IN VANCOUVER, BRITISH COLOMBIA

A procession of marching members of Labour Societies in uniforms characteristic of their trades, headed by bands and banners, while many floats of elaborate design, bearing machinery in motion, manufacturing processes in operation, and others representing various trades, are drawn past the camera by teams of four, six and eight horses each **250 feet**

1129 ... CHINESE MERCHANT'S FUNERAL PROCESSION THROUGH STREETS OF VANCOUVER, BRITISH COLUMBIA

The funeral of a prominent Chinese merchant *en route* from Chinatown to the cemetery. The funeral was under the auspices of the Chinese Empire Reform Association and other Celestial organisations. The procession was headed by the city band, and there was a big turnout of Chinese. An unique subject. **75 feet**

1136 ... CANADA'S NATIONAL GAME, "LACROSSE"

As exciting as cricket but more violent and active. **125 feet**

1148 ... SPEARING FISH IN BRITISH COLUMBIA

This picture shows a party of five men spearing salmon in a Canadian river. As each fish is taken from the spear, it is handed to the dog, who carries the prize ashore. A laughable incident occurs when one of the fishermen, forgetting the dog, flings the fish on to the banks. The dog, taking exception to this slight, hurries to the bank, picks up the fish in his teeth, and carries it to the party in the river who has committed the breach of faith. **100 feet**

1149 ... THRESHING WHEAT ON A MANITOBA FARM

This is an animated scene of a threshing outfit, showing the traction engine and threshers in full operation. Waggons with great loads of sheaves of wheat arrive. These are quickly unloaded by the farm hands, many of whom are engaged in feeding the thresher with great quantities of unthreshed wheat.

In the foreground will be noted the loading of other waggons with the grain tied in sacks, while from the threshers' funnel blow great masses of empty straw, which form a stack of large dimensions. **75 feet**

1150 ... AFTER THE HARVEST

Similar scene to the above, but does not include a view of the engine which is usually stationed many yards from the thresher and connected thereto by means of a great endless belt.

A scene full of animation, and one which would be viewed with much interest by the British farmer. **50 feet**

1151 ... BANFF AND ITS SURROUNDINGS

Banff is in the very heart of the Rockies—charmingly located in the centre of the most easterly of the two parks. The Valley of the Bow, in which it lies, is encircled on all sides by lofty mountains some fir-clad in their summits. This grand circular panoramic series was obtained by means of our Rotary Bioscope Camera, and includes a fine view of Bow River with its picturesque cascades and falls. Excellent photographic quality. **125 feet**

No. 1108--Logging in the Canadian Pine Forests.

1215 ... ALONG THE WATER FRONT OF STEVESTON, B.C.

Steveston is a fishing village at the mouth of the Fraser River and is situated about 12 miles south of Vancouver B.C. To this place a mixed lot of Indians, Japanese, Chinese, and Whites flock during the fishing season, when some 2,000 to 3,000 boats are employed. This shows a panoramic view of the Canneries and whole water front of the village. **75 feet**

1216 ... BRANDING COLTS AT ALBERTA, N.W.T.

In spring and the fall of the year the cowboys attached to the western ranches round-up the cattle and horses which roam at large during the intervening months, grazing on the surrounding prairie land. Arriving at the Ranch, the colts are separated from the herd for the purpose of branding in order to be easily identified. The picture portrays a scene inside a corral, showing cowboys lassoing, throwing, and branding a colt. These animals being practically in a wild state, do not submit kindly to the treatment, and many a hard tussle is experienced before the colts are thrown.

100 feet

1375 ... THE GREAT TORONTO FIRE

See description " Fire Series " **275 feet**

1411 ... LORD DUNDONALD LEAVING CANADA

See description under " Personages and Events." **100 feet**

---

*Extract from "*THE STANDARD,*" November 22nd, 1904.*

The Alhambra Theatre.—Visit of the Queen.

Probably not one-half of the large audience assembled last night at the Alhambra knew of the presence there of the Queen, who, with the Princess Victoria and Prince and Princess Louis of Battenberg, occupied a stage-box on the dress-circle tier. The Queen displayed great interest in all the items of the programme, from the opening ballet, *All the Year Round,* to the closing one, *The Entente Cordiale,* and seemed **especially pleased with the " Urban " Bioscope Pictures,** representing a trip to the sun, and entitled " Whirling the Worlds." This clever and mirth-provoking fantasy covers a film of over 1,200 feet—the longest ever presented to the public—and is a wonderful piece of ingenuity The portrait of our guest, the King of Portugal, thrown on the screen by the Bioscope, was warmly received by the audience.

Since the visit of HER MAJESTY QUEEN ALEXANDRA to the Alhambra, the Urban Bioscope Exhibitions there have been honoured with the attendance of :—

T.R.H. the DUKE and DUCHESS OF FIFE.

H.M. KING CARLOS OF PORTUGAL.

H.R.H. DUKE OF CONNAUGHT.

THE ROCKY MOUNTAINS, CANADA.

A series of Panorama Views taken from the front of the Express Train passing through the most gorgeous scenery of the Kicking Horse, Beavermouth and Fraser Canyons.

By courtesy of the CANADIAN PACIFIC RAILWAY.

1098 ... PANORAMA OF THE KICKING HORSE CANYON

A wonderful picture of majestic scenery as the train (from the front of which these photos were secured), speeds over the rails, around curves, over bridges and ledges cut into the rocky sides of the mountain, with the torrent below and the towering mountain peaks above, ever in view, and of constant changing aspect. This is the shortest Section of one of the most wonderful railway pictures ever bioscoped. **150 feet**

No. 1099. A glimpse of the Kicking Horse Canyon.

1099 ... THE KICKING HORSE CANYON AND THE GREAT LOOP AT GLACIER HOUSE

The line, which has gradually curved towards the south since crossing the summit at Stephen, runs due south from here to *Lean-choil,* where the Beaverfoot River comes in from the south and joins the Kicking Horse. At the left, the lofty peaks of the Ottertail Mts., walled, massive and castellated, rise abruptly to an immense height. The river turns abruptly against its base and plunges into the lower Kicking Horse Canyon, down which it disputes the passage with the railway. The next Section shows the great curve at Glacier House, which the train negociates by passing through tunnels, &c. The railroad forms a complete loop or circle at this point, and by a gradual ascent, passes over itself at the higher altitude. **250 feet**

1100 ... WITH THE IMPERIAL LIMITED THROUGH THE KICKING HORSE CANYON

This is *perhaps* the most varied Section of the "Kicking Horse Canyon" Series, the scenery, however, being of a more rugged character than in the preceding films. Bridges, curves, and tunnels are more numerous. The canyon at this point rapidly deepens, until beyond *Palliser*, the mountain sides become vertical, rising straight up thousands of feet, in a bronze wall crested by a long line of nameless peaks, and within an easy stone's throw from wall to wall. Down this vast chasm go the railway and the river together, the former crossing from side to side to ledges cut out of the solid rock, and twisting and turning in every direction, and every minute or two plunging through projecting angles of rock which seem to close the way. **325 feet**

No. 1100. A Tunnel on the Kicking Horse Canyon of the C.P. Railway.

1217 ... THROUGH THE BEAVERMOUTH CANYON SELKIRK MOUNTAINS, DURING A BLIZZARD

Here the Rockies and Selkirks crowding together force the river through a deep, narrow gorge, the railway clinging to the slopes high above it. Emerging from the gorge at Beavermouth, the most northerly station on the transcontinental route, the line soon turns abruptly to the left and enters the Selkirks through the Gate of the Beaver River—a passage so narrow that a felled tree serves as a footbridge over it.

NOTE.—*This picture and the following one differ from all other railway panoramas ever photographed as it does not only show the approaching and passing scenery, but shows the entire train with the puffing engine drawing the coaches constantly in view.* **A new sensation. 200 feet**

1218 ... WITH THE IMPERIAL EXPRESS ALONG THE COLUMBIA RIVER—ROCKY MOUNTAINS IN WINTER

A sublime panorama of the Rocky Mountains in winter, snow covering the roadbed, mountain slopes and pines. A raging mountain torrent runs parallel with the railway, and as at each curve another aspect of the panorama opens to view, the picture is one of the most interesting ever taken. The entire train in view each time it curves to the left as the picture was photographed from a special platform constructed, overhanging the side of the last coach of the train. The last portion shows the descent from the Glacier House, and following around the mountain-side. The Loop is soon reached, where the line makes several turns and twists, first crossing a valley over a high trestle, then doubling back to the right a mile or more upon itself, then sweeping around to the right, crossing again to the left, and at last shooting down the valley parallel with its former course. A wonderful picture—new sensation! **300 feet**

1219 ... THE GLORIOUS FRASER CAYNON, B.C.—Encountering Eight Tunnels, Forty-eight Curves, and crossing a very high Trestle

The train runs suddenly along the very brink of several remarkably deep fissures in the solid rock, whose walls rise straight up, hundreds of feet on both sides, to wooded craigs, above which sharp distant peaks cut the sky. The most striking of these canyons is the Fraser, where the river is seen nearly 300 feet below the railway, compressed into a boiling flume scarcely 20 feet wide.

NOTE.—*This film is in various sections, and comprises the cheapest portions of panorama of glorious Mountain Scenery selected from over 1,500 feet of film exposed.* **300 feet**

1220 ... CROSSING THE GOLD RANGE, B.C., ON THE C.P.R.
225 feet

1221 ... THROUGH THE GLENOGLE GULCH, ROCKY MOUNTAINS
175 feet

1222 ... CROSSING THE ROCKIES VIA C.P.R.
150 feet

1223 ... ASCENDING THE SLOPES OF THE ROCKIES
150 feet

1224 ... OVER THE COAST RANGE B.C.
100 feet

1225 ... PASSING NORTHBEND STATION (Fraser Canyon)
75 feet

No. 1220. Along the Gold Range, C.P.R. Rocky Mountains.

1226 ... THE SELKIRKS FROM FRONT OF A TRAIN
75 feet

1227 ... APPROACHING PALLISIER, UP THE ROCKIES
60 feet

NOTE.—Films No. 1220 to 1227 are of equal interest to the preceding pictures described although of shorter length. All are taken from the front of a special engine and depict the glorious scenery of the Rocky Mountains as seen from the Train of the C.P.R.

SWITZERLAND AND THE ALPS.

Generals Views and Mountain Climbing.

Photographs by F. ORMISTON-SMITH.

The Matterhorn (14,780 feet), Village of Zermatt at base.

1045 ... HOCKEY ON SKATES

A game of great skill Full of action, and of fine photographic quality.   **50 feet**

1046 ... SKI-JUMPING IN THE ALPS

This Norwegian sport is much practised by the Swiss youth as well as the visitors to the winter resorts. Many successful jumps (the unsuccessful attempts predominating), are recorded from various close positions, so that none of the detail is lost   **75 feet**

1047 ... OUTING OF THE SKI-CLUB IN THE ALPS

Showing hundreds of boys, girls and adults on " Ski " descending a steep snow-covered bank. An excellent film, full of action and accidents.   **50 feet**

1048 ... BOB SLEIGHING IN THE ALPS

The first section shows the " crew " bestriding the bob-sledge and starting same down hill. The second section includes pictures of many sledge parties, singly and in groups, sliding past the camera.
50 feet

1050 ... TOBOGANNING ON THE CRESTA AT 40 MILES AN HOUR

Much nerve is required by those who participate in this sport as some of the curves of the course are most acute and dangerous, especially at the speed which is indulged in. **60 feet**

1051 ... FUN ON THE SKATING RINK AFTER A SNOW-STORM IN THE ALPS

Clearing the rink after a snow-storm is generally accomplished with much merry making and practical joking amongst the busy workers. The exhibition of this subject has a warming effect in Winter and a cooling one in Summer. Exceedingly good in photographic quality and interest.

75 feet

1070 ... HARVESTING HAY ON THE BEAR ICE RINK, GRINDELWALD

An animated scene of harvesting hay on the great winter playground. The group of busy reapers, with hand scythes, in the foreground, the Swiss maids who accompany them and help load the hay on the two-horsed waggons awaiting, make up an interesting picture of rural Swiss interest. **50 feet**

1071 ... SWISS WRESTLING AT INTERLAKEN

125 feet

1072 ... LIFE AT A SIMMENTHAL CATTLE FARM

The world-famed Simmenthal cattle, bred by Herr Rebmann, are seen leaving the valley for the summer pastures on the Grimmalp. The herds are accompanied by the farmer and his assistants, and followed by a bevy of charmingly picturesque Swiss milkmaids carrying milk bins and other dairy impediments. Then the arrival at the farm makes up a scene of great animation, concluding with a close-up view of milking in the near foreground. **125 feet**

1074 ... PANORAMA OF KANDERSTEG AND THE BLUEMLISALP

Kandersteg, the highest mountain village on the Gemmi route, is a delightful spot and the centre of fine excursions in the mountain regions of the Bleumisalp. **50 feet**

1075 ... TOURISTS LEAVING THE HOTEL, KANDERSTEG

The Bear Hotel, Kandersteg, is the recognised starting place for the journey over the Gemmi pass. **50 feet**

No. 1276b. Mount Lycabettus, Athens.

1076 ... THE GEMMI PASS AND THE OESCHINEN LAKE

Tourists leaving the Bear Hotel, Kandersteg, to cross the Gemmi. Many ladies of the party are seen mounting the hardy ponies at the hotel front. and as some of the ponies are frisky, this portion of the picture is a brisk one. Then we have a fine portrayal of a crowd of lady climbers leaving on foot with alpenstocks, and oxen with luncheon baskets make up the rear portion of this interesting cavalcade. When arriving by the lake they dismount, and entering boats, row out on the azure waters of the Oeschinen. The return of the party and the landing brings to an appropriate conclusion an excellent picture. **100 feet**

1077 ... LACE MAKING IN A VILLAGE STREET, MURREN

The quiet industry of the Alps is well rendered. The stalls with their keepers and stores of laces are being inspected by English and American tourists, who no doubt take away with them a goodly stock of the fragile fabrics to decorate Mayfair and Long Island. **60 feet**

1078 ... SNOW BREAKING ON THE WENGERALP RAILWAY

This film gives a fine panoramic view of this wonderful railway track through immense gorges and cuttings and snow banks of from 15 to 20 feet high on either hand. Large squads of men are met at short intervals on this trip, busily and deftly clearing away the huge snow accumulations—in fact cutting the railway path through solid snow-wreaths. Then we see the Railway Hotel on the summit of the Wegner Alp and other groups of snow diggers displaying great activity, and filling car load after car load with the frozen snow until at the signal for stopping time, they rush wildly and gladly away, waving their shovels aloft in triumph at the day's work accomplished. A lively subject. **150 feet**

1080 ... PANORAMA FROM A DESCENDING CAR OF THE REICHENBACH RAILWAY, MEIRINGEN

Of mountain railway panoramas this is a good example. Taken from the front of a descending car, the track and the way in which the fertile valleys open out on either side, with the huge snow-capped mountains in the back ground, and the fine stereoscopic effect of the ever changing scene depicted in this film render it a truly telling picture. **150 feet**

A Winter Scene in the Alps

1081 ... THE REICHENBACH FALLS, MEIRINGEN

A beautiful picture of this famous waterfall—noted as the spot selected by Sir Conan Doyle as the death place of that immortal creation of his—Sherlock Holmes. The peculiarity of this waterfall, with its narrow funnel-shaped opening, from which, on to the jagged rocks the torrent dashes, is here portrayed in all its pristine grandeur and beauty. **50 feet**

1082 ... AFTER CHURCH IN A VILLAGE STREET, MEIRINGEN

A quiet village scene of pleasing restfulness, permitting us to see how the Swiss villagers maintain their reputation as regular Churchgoers. The old street and church are the only remains of the former village of Meiringen, which was destroyed by fire ten years ago, **50 feet**

1085 ... STEAMER LEAVING INTERLAKEN AND PANORAMA OF ISELTWALD, LAKE BREINZ

Departure of the steamer from Interlaken. The stereoscopic effect secured in the passing panorama of the village of Iseltwald is unusually fine. Short of an actual visit to the place this film is absolutely satisfying to those who admire the lovely places in our "little hemisphere" **175 feet**

1114 ... PANORAMA OF THE MUERREN RANGE OF ALPS

A famous view of the Eiger, Monch, Jungfrau, Silberhorn, Schwarza Monch, Ebne Fluh, Mittaghorn, Grosshorn, Breithorn, Tschingethorn, and Gspaltenhorn. **50 feet**

1117 ... LACE MAKING AT MURREN

Swiss lace is world famed, and much of the best of it is produced by the busy hands of the inhabitants of this pretty Swiss village. **50 feet**

1118 ... CATTLE CROSSING THE GRINDELWALD EISMEER ON THEIR WAY TO HIGH PASTURE

A curious incident which happened in early summer, when the cattle are taken to the high pastures for three months. **50 feet**

1119 ... THE HERD OF GOATS AT THE GRIMSEL HOSPICE

The goats of the Grimsel are almost as famous as the Hospice itself, and form a most attractive picture among the bleak and desolate surroundings. **100 feet**

1120 ... PANORAMA OF GRIMSEL HOSPICE AND LAKE. THE STAGE LEAVING FOR RHONE GLACIER

Grimsel was the scene of the Austrian-French conflict of 1799. It is now one of the most popular passes in the Alps. **75 feet**

1121 ... DEPARTURE OF THE DILIGENCE FOR MEIRINGEN

The chief event of the day at the Grimsel Hospice. An excellent picture, full of animation. **75 feet**

1122 ... STAGE COACH V. MOTOR, OVER A MOUNTAIN ROAD

A striking instance of the march of time is the the frequent appearance of a motor on mountain roads, which only a year or so ago were only crossed by the old world stage coach. **75 feet**

1125 ... STREET SCENES IN BERNE

The capital of Switzerland is an interesting town, and the national life is, perhaps, best seen in the streets. Tuesdays are days of great excitement in the quiet old town of Berne, when the whole population is bent on getting very much for very little. **125 feet**

1127 ... THE JUNGFRAU ELECTRIC RAILWAY

The most astounding enterprise of modern times. The train leaving the Schiedegg station and entering the Eiger tunnel *en route* for the station Eigerwand, at present the highest completed portion. **75 feet**

K

THE MATTERHORN.

(14,780 FEET).

CONQUERED BY THE BIOSCOPE.

Photographs by Mr. F. Ormiston-Smith.

The Bioscope Expedition with the Matterhorn in background

On September 28th, 1903, the Urban Mountaineering Expedition left Zermatt to attempt the conquest of the most famous Mountain in the World, and at mid-day, on the 29th the conquest was completed by the Bioscoping of the marvellous panorama from the actual summit of the Matterhorn, 14,780 feet above the level of the sea.

Christian Burgener, the leading guide of the Expedition, is one of the best men in the Alps, with him were the well-known Zermatt Guides, Gabriel Zumtaugwald, Joseph Taugwalder, Peter Perren, and Felix Julen.

Herr Dethleffsen of Berne, accompanied the Expedition, together with the porters who carried the apparatus and provisions, while the organizing and photographing were carried out by Mr. F. Ormiston-Smith, the eminent mountaineering photographer.

The following series of pictures which illustrate the entire ascent of the Matterhorn, are probably the most wonderful Bioscope pictures ever taken in the face of tremendous difficulty and danger.

Such renowned portions of the mountain, as the Old Cabane, (the scene of Mr. Whymper's first exploits); the Shoulder (where four of the first party who ever trod the summit, met their deaths during the descent), and the marvellous summit ridge and incomparable panorama are included; so that the result of the Bioscope ascent is likely to rival in interest the famous ascent of 1865, when all the world rang with the news of the conquest of the Matterhorn, and its terrible vengeance.

1137 ... THE ASCENT OF THE MATTERHORN

1 ... **THE VILLAGE OF ZERMATT** (5,315 feet)

2 ... **THE SEILER HOTELS AND CATTLE GRAZING ON THE BANKS OF THE MATTERIRSP.**

3 ... **THE MATTERHORN SEEN FROM ZERMATT**

4 ... **THE BIOSCOPE EXPEDITION TRYING THEIR STRENGTH**

5 ... **PREPARATIONS FOR THE DEPARTURE FROM THE HOTEL MONTE ROSA**

6 ... **THROUGH THE VILLAGE OF ZERMATT**

7 ... **LEAVING ZERMATT BEHIND**

8 ... **APPROACHING THE SCHWARZEE HOTEL** (8,494 feet)

9 ... **LEAVING THE SCHWARZEE HOTEL FOR THE HORNLI**

10 ... **THE HORNLI RIDGE** (9,492 feet)

11 ... **ARRIVAL AT THE MATTERHORN CABANE** (10,160 feet)

12 ... **PANORAMA OF THE MONTE ROSA CHAIN FROM THE CABANE**

13 ... **TRAVERSING THE LEDGES NEAR "WHYPER'S" CAMP**

14 ... **THE OLD CABANE ON THE EAST FACE** (12,526 feet)

15 ... **THE ROCKS ABOVE THE OLD HUT**

16 ... **CLIMBING BY THE FIXED ROPES**

17 ... **THE SHOULDER** (14,110)

18 ... **BELOW THE SUMMIT RIDGE**

19 ... **REACHING THE SUMMIT** (14,780)

20 ... **PANORAMA FROM THE SUMMIT** (14,780)

Total Length 500 feet.

Sold only in complete lengths.

1139 ... **THE MATTERHORN, THE VILLAGE OF ZERMATT AND GROUP OF SCHWYZ CATTLE**

The fine peak of the Matterhorn as seen from the Hotel at the Lac Noir, with a picturesque view of the valley of Zermatt and Herr Seiler's cattle grazing near the hotels. **75 feet**

1140 ... **CLIMBERS LUNCHING AT THE SCHWARZEE HOTEL**

A climbing party about to ascend the Matterhorn seen lunching at the hotel near the base of the mountain. **75 feet**

1141 ... **A ZERMATT WASHERWOMAN**

A peculiar, but eminently practical method of washing. which dispenses with soap and utilizes the river. **50 feet**

1142 ... **MULES BRINGING UP WOOD TO THE HOTEL JUNG-FRAU AT THE EGGISHORN** (7,195 feet)

Fuel is brought up by mules to many of the high Alpine resorts; the picture shows the interesting manner of unloading. **50 feet**

K 2

The Members of the Urban Alpine Expedition, with the "Jungfrau" in background.

1143 ... ASCENT OF THE JUNGFRAU (13,670 feet)

First ascended in 1881. A difficult and fatiguing snow climb, the dangers of which depend largely on the condition of the snow.

The ascent was successfully made by the Urban Alpine Expedition, headed by Mr. F. Ormiston-Smith, the well-known mountaineering photographer, on September 24th, 1903, and a fine series of pictures were secured illustrating the whole ascent, and culminating with a panorama from the summit (a most wonderful picture).

The following pictures comprise the series:—

1 ... **THE JUNGFRAU SEEN FROM INTERLAKEN**
2 ... **THE BAREGG (5,140 feet)**
3 ... **THE LADDERS FROM THE BAREGG**
4 ... **CROSSING THE MORAINE OF THE EISMEER**
5 ... **KALLI SLOPES**
6 ... **THE BREAKFAST PLACE**
7 ... **THE BERGLI HUT (10,825 feet)**
8 ... **PUTTING ON THE ROPE**
9 ... **SOFT SNOW ON THE MÖNCH-JOCH**
10 ... **THE UPPER MÖNCH-JOCH (11,870 feet)**
11 ... **THE JUNGFRAU FIRN**
12 ... **NEARING THE SATTEL**
13 ... **THE ROTHAL SATTEL (12,330 feet)**
14 ... **THE SUMMIT SLOPE AND SUMMIT (13,670 feet)**
15 ... **THE PANORAMA FROM THE SUMMIT**

Total Length 500 feet.

1248 ... THE INTERNATIONAL WATER SPORTS

(For description see Races and Sports). **750 feet**

1241 ... AMATEURS SKI COMPETITION

100 feet

1263 ... A GRAND PANORAMIC VIEW OF GRINDLEWALD AFTER A SNOWSTORM

A magnificent snow scene such as is not to be met with outside of picturesque Switzerland

60 feet

1264 ... A WINTER FAIRYLAND

One of the most pleasing and picturesque sights is had in the Swiss Alps. after a heavy fall of snow. The boughs and branchesl of trees and shrubs, the Chalets, Statuary, hedges, fences and generaf landscape of valley and mountain are covered with a blanket ot soft snow, brilliantly lighted by the sun, making a wonderful sight not often experienced **100 feet**

"THE PLAYGROUND OF EUROPE."

A Trip through picturesque Switzerland.

Photographs by Mr. F. Ormiston-Smith

1275 a (Section 1)

No.

1 ... BASKET-MAKERS OF BERNE
2 ... MARKET DAY IN BERNE
3 ... GENERAL STREET SCENE, BERNE
4 ... ARRIVAL AT INTERLAKEN BY STEAMER
5 ... STEAMER LANDING AND TOURISTS DISEMBARKING
6 .. THE BUS STAND OF INTERLAKEN
7 ... MOTORING ON THE HOHEWEG, INTERLAKEN
8 ... ON LAKE BRIENZ BY STEAMER
9 ... TWO VIEWS OF THE GEISSBACK FALLS
10 ... THE GREAT VIADUCT OVER THE GORGE OF AAR
11 ... MOUNTAIN RAILWAY, Descending and Climbing over Viaduct
12 ... THE FAMOUS REICHENBACH FALLS (Upper and Lower)

325 feet.

1275 b ... PLAYGROUND OF EUROPE (Section 2)

13 ... A TRIP OVER THE MURREN RAILWAY—views front of train
14 ... TO THE SIMMERTHAL BY STAGE COACH
15 ... DRIVING CATTLE THROUGH THE VALLEY
16 ... THE FAMOUS PRIZE CATTLE OF THE SIMMERTHAL
17 ... MILKING THE COWS ON A SWISS FARM
18 ... FEEDING THE HANDECK RABBITS
19 ... HARVESTING HAY AT GRINDELWALD
20 ... A TRAIN ON THE JUNGFRAU RAILWAY

325 feet

Method of photographing Mountain Railway Panoramas

1275 c ... PLAYGROUND OF EUROPE (Section 3)

21 ... **A TRIP UP THE GORNER GRAT RAILWAY**

22 ... **GRAND VIEW OF THE GREAT ALPINE RANGE**

23 ... **THE SNOW CAPPED PEAKS OF THE MATTERHORN BREITH, MONTA ROSA, RIMPFISHHORN, MISCHABEL, DOM WEISSHORN, AND DENT BLANCHE,** (seen from an altitude of 4000 feet)

24 ... **TO THE GRIMMALP BY DILIGENCE**

25 ... **THE GRIMSEL HOSPICE AND ITS HERD OF GOATS**

26 ... **FUN ON A GOAT FARM**

325 feet.

1275 d ... PLAYGROUND OF EUROPE (Section 4)

27 ... **TRAVERSING THE GEMMI PASS**

28 ... **ARRIVAL AT OSCHIENEN LAKE**

29 ... **EMBARKING FOR A ROW ON THE LAKE**

30 ... **TOURISTS RETURNING FROM LAKE EXCURSION**

150 feet.

1275 Complete in one continuous roll total length 1125 feet.

1403 ... SNOW AVALANCHE ON THE SHERCKHORN

A very common incident, one of the dangers of Alpine climbing frequently encountered on this most difficult mountain.   **60 feet**

1404 ... DIFFICULT ASCENT OF A ROCK PEAK

A fine picture of the scaling of a rock arete or ridge. On either side are tremendous precipices of thousands of feet. The use of the rope is particularly well portrayed.   **75 feet**

1405 .. A CLOSE CALL—DANGEROUS CLIMBING

One of the many dangers of mountain climbing lies in the over-hanging snow cornice. This feature has been responsible for many of the worst accidents. A climbing party is seen negotiating this diffi-culty.   **75 feet**

1406 ... DESCENT OF STEEP SNOW DRIFT

An excellent picture of the descent of a snow col or ridge. The long shadows of the climbers thrown across the snow fields, moving slowly downwards are weirdly attractive.   **75 feet**

1407 ... CROSSING A DANGEROUS SNOW BRIDGE

A thrilling incident on the Great Fiescherhorn. The climber falls through the breaking of the snow, and is rescued by his guides' manipulation of the rope and great exertions on his part to regain a foothold.   **75 feet**

1480 ... FUSILADE OF ROCKS ON THE ALPS

Rock falls are probably the most frequent causes of accidents to climbers. The mountaineering party move cautiously from ledge to ledge, dodging the falling stones.   **75 feet**

1481 ... DESCENDING A STEEP ROCK-FACED MOUNTAIN SIDE

Smooth rocks are always a great danger, owing to lack of foot-hold. The guides are seen helping one another and taking every precaution to avoid a slip.   **60 feet**

1493 ... CAPT. SPELTERINI'S BALLOON TRIP ACROSS THE JUNGFRAU

        75 feet

1494 ... SURMOUNTING THE SUMMIT OF THE FINSTERAAR-JOCH

No more thrilling picture of the perils and difficulties of Alpine climbing has ever been secured. The Finsteraar-joch is regarded by climbers as one of the most difficult passes, and this bioscopic repre-sentation of the conquering of this mountain is certainly a masterpiece of mountaineering photography.   **150 feet**

The Urban Bioscope at the Alhambra is beyond doubt the best and most up-to-date Motion Picture Exhibition in Europe.

—Vide Daily Telegraph.

GREECE.

By kind assistance of Dr. H. S. LUNN.

Bioscoped for the first time by Mr. F. ORMISTON-SMITH.

1276 .. PIRAEUS—THE GATEWAY OF ATHENS

No.

1—**The Corinth Canal.** Over three miles in length. First commenced by the Emperor Nero.

2—**Piræus, the Landing Stage.** The Port of Athens.

3—**The Market Place.** Typical view of modern Grecian life.

4—**The Great Harbour.** Formerly Porto Leone, full of Grecian, French Italian, Russian and Austrian shipping.

5—**Street Cafes.** A glimpse of the many street cafés of Piræus.

6—**The Market Square.** Showing the peculiar booths of a Grecian market.

7—**Arrival of a Steamer.** The Grecian boatmen swarming up the sides before the anchor is dropped. **200 feet**

No. 1276a. Hoisting Cattle on Board Ship.

1276 a ... HOISTING CATTLE ON STEAMER

1—**Mooring Cattle on Barges.** Preparatory to shipping them to Constantinople.

2—**Taking Cattle off to the Steamer.** Towing the laden barges through the Harbour.

3—**Hoisting the Cattle on Board.** The cattle being slung by legs and horns from the barges to the liner. **150 feet**

1276 b ... ATHENS AND THE ACROPOLIS

1—**Panoramic View from the Acropolis.** A fine view of modern Athens.

2—**Mar's Hill.** Probable site of St. Paul preaching to the Athenians.

3 — **A View of the Acropolis from the Hill of the Muses.** Showing the Propylæa, Parthenon, and Theatre of Dionysus.

4 — **The Arch of Adrian.** Built by Adrian on the completion of the Olympieum.

5—**The Olympieum.** A few of the original 104 columns of this Temple are seen.

No. 1276b. Temple of Victory, Athens.

6 —**Temple of Victory.** Originally built to commemorate three of the most celebrated Athenian victories.

7—**The Propylæa.** Begun in 437 B.C. The entrance to the Acropolis.

8—**The Erectheum.** With the famous caryatid Porch.

9—**The Parthenon.** Three views of this beautiful Temple, built 454 B.C.

10—**Mount Lycabettus.** Commanding a magnificent view of Athens.

275 feet

TURKEY AND EGYPT.

Special permission granted by Turkish Authorities and facilities kindly rendered by Dr. H. S. Lunn ; Photographs by Mr. F. Ormiston-Smith.

1277 a (Section 1) ... SIGHTS IN CONSTANTINOPLE

No. 2277 b. St. Sophia Mosque, Constantinople.

1—**The Galata Bridge.** Connecting Galata with Pera; £400 taken daily in ½d. tolls on this bridge.

2—**A second view of the Bridge.** Showing the Galata Tower.

3—**The old Slave Market.** The oldest part of the city; full of Oriental life

4—**Turkish Porters.** Picturesque natives of the Bulgarian quarter.

5—**Street near Seraskeriat.** The surroundings of the War Office.

6—**The Market Place.** A scene of life and bustle.

7—**The Pigeon Mosque.** Built in 1497 ; named from the sacred pigeons living around it.

250 feet.

1277 b (Section 2) ... CONSTANTINOPLE

8—**Mosque of St. Sophia.** One of the finest mosques in the world.

9—**Outside the Mosque.** Showing the life in the main streets.

10—**The Government Buildings.** Typical view of every-day life in the busiest part of Constantinople.

11—**Court of the Pigeon Mosque.** Fine picture of the sacred pigeons.

12—**Children scrambling for "Backsheesh."** A familiar weakness of the Turk

13—**Street in Stamboul.** Showing some of the latest inhabitants.

14—**Boot Cleaning.** The Turkish " Day & Martin " boys.

15—**The Bohemian Quarter.** An interesting study of native life.

16—**Outside the Prison.** The heart of the city.

17—**Bullock Carts near the Slave Market.** A picturesque street scene.

18—**The Fruit Market.** Quaint Oriental market life.

19—**The Dogs of Constantinople.** The scavengers of this Eastern city.

150 feet.

1277 c THE DARDANELLES AND THE BOSPHORUS.

1—**Chanak**: the strongly fortified entrance to the Dardenelles

2—**Summer Palaces** on the Bosphorous.   A particularly beautiful reach of the Straits.

3—**Distant View of the Roumeli Hissar.** The Tower of Europe; most imposing.

4—**The Entrance to the Black Sea.** Showing the fortifications on the European and Asiatic sides.

5—**The Golden Horn.** The entrance to the Bosphorus.

6—**Graveyard near the Great Tower of Bebek.** Fine stereoscopic panoama.

No. 1277 a The Pigeon Mosque, Constantinople.

7—**The Tower of Europe.**   Built in 1452 on the site of ancient fortresses of Greek Emperors.   **200 feet.**

1277 Complete, total length 600 feet.

1422 ... **BOATING ON THE NILE NEAR CAIRO**

Showing a splendid panorama of the Banks of the Nile above Cairo, with the Nile boats and steamers plying up and down the river.   **75 feet**

No. 1422 Panorama of the Nile Banks.

1423 ... TOURISTS RIDING DONKEYS ON NILE BANKS

Upon the arrival of the Nile excursion steamers, the tourists after disembarking generally proceed to the scene of their contem-

No. 1423 Tourists riding Donkeys on Banks of Nile.

plated visit by donkey. Much humour is added to the picture by some of the attitudes of the riders who probably never had mounted an animal before. **60 feet**

1424 ... CAMEL CARAVANS CROSSING KASR - EN - NIL BRIDGE, CAIRO

A familiar scene in the morning, when the Nile Bridge closes (after being open all night for boat traffic), showing a continuous procession of camels loaded with hay, brushwood, and all sorts of merchandise, transporting same into Cairo from the opposite bank of the Nile. **75 feet**

1424 ... CAMEL TRANSPORT ON NILE BANKS

This shows the difficulty of trying to move a camel when it had made up its mind to the contrary. A caravan is descending a steep bank to the river's edge. Splendid palm grove in background. **60 feet**

1449 ... " TURKISH DELIGHT "

A young Turkish beauty, who after a great amount of persuasion at length consented to remove her Hiak, and be photographed. We here see her smoking, evidently with great enjoyment, the ever-soothing Turkish cigarette. **50 feet**

1450 ... " DANCE DU VENTRE "

This dance became famous at the Chicago World's Fair, and has been imitated by many, but it takes the Oriental to do justice to same. Must be seen to be appreciated. **50 feet**

1451 ... TURKISH GIPSY DANCE
  The Ketcheek, or Turkish Gipsy Dance—danced by " Emine," a
celebrated Turkish dancer, a pupil of the renowned Turkish Gipsy

No. 1277a   Galata Bridge, Constantinople.

Dancer, " Urmuze," who is said to possess wonderful power in fore-
telling the future of all those who will cross her hand with a gold or
silver coin.   The dance is grace itself.   **100 feet**

BULGARIA AND MACEDONIA.

Photographs by C. Rider Noble. *These pictures were secured at great expense and risk, and are the only Animated Pictures of Macedonian and Bulgarian Scenes in existence.*

TVANTCHO QUEVGUELIISKY.

An Insurgent Band . . .

1154 ... REFUGEES AT RILO MONASTERY

These poor Christian fugitives from the Turkish villages of Macedonia have fled, in fear of massacre, across the frontier into Bulgaria, seeking the protection of the Monks of Rilo Monastery, in the Balkans. They are in a deplorable condition, with little or no money, and almost without clothing, many having crossed the rugged and snowy mountains (in the clothing they are here depicted, some being barefooted), fleeing from districts hundreds of miles from their present sanctuary. **100 feet**

1155 ... THE FEAST OF ST. JOHN AT RILO MONASTERY

Rilo Monastery was founded 400 years ago, but on various occasions was destroyed by fire. The present building was erected some 40 years ago, and its reconstruction is celebrated each year, after service in the Church, by a procession of monks, joined by Bulgarian and Macedonian peasants, who perform a pilgrimage to Rilo to be present on this occasion. The band consists of a young man beating a piece of wood and another with a bell. Excellent photographic quality. **150 feet**

1156 ... REFUGEES AT SAMOKOVE

Refugees at Samokove seeking protection in this small town, which is only about 1½ hour's march from the Frontier, having been exiled from the villages in the district of Belitza, Camen, and Obedin. These poor creatures are now being fed on bread and soup once a day. **100 feet**

1157 ... OUTSIDE THE FRONTIER TOWN OF SAMOKOVE

Thirty-five miles east of Sofia, an important post near the Turkish frontier. The first section shows the monks leaving church after prayer. This picture shows many poor refugees seeking shelter and food, having fled from Macedonia to escape the Turk, some travelling a hundred miles, always at night, in hiding during the day, and present truly a most pitiable sight. **75 feet**

1158 ... TYPICAL STREET OF DOUBNITZA, BULGARIA

The buildings skirting the streets are not of great architectural beauty, while the paving of the streets does no credit to the municipality. Over these roughly paved but picturesque streets are seen oxcarts, pack-horses, &c., carrying casks of wine of the country. **50 feet**

The Monks at Rilo Monas'ry, Bulgaria . . ,

1159 ... A TOBACCO FARM AT CRAPITS

This shows the tobacco leaf strung in long garlands being shaken during the process of drying by the farmer or grower and his sons, while the other members of the family are all occupied in spinning carding wool, &c., convincing in itself that the Bulgarian peasant makes the best use of his or her time **75 feet**

1160 ... H.E. MINISTER OF WAR, M. SAVOFF, OF BULGARIA HIS STAFF AND BODYGUARD

The first picture shows M. Savoff, the Minister of War, cheerfully chatting with his Staff Officers. The next shows a regiment of Bulgarian troops lined for inspection. while the last section shows the march past of the bodyguard, a squad of men of fine physique and training, carring the conviction of high military training. **150 feet**

1161 ... BULGARIAN MOUNTAIN INFANTRY IN THE BALKANS

A troupe of Mountain Infantry unloading guns and carriages from pack horses, assembling and firing same. These men are noted for the expeditious manner in which they perform their duties. The last section shows a squad of Frontier Patrol descending steep defile. **125 feet**

1162 ... BULGARIAN INFANTRY PATROLLING THE FRONTIER AT DOUBNITZA

Bulgarian Mounted Infantry march past. These are picked men, and do duty along the different passes. They are very fine horsemen, and keep an eye on miles of frontier.

The last section shows a squad of this mounted patrol proceeding through a steep defile, the path being too narrow to allow of other-order of procedure except in single file. **75 feet**

1163 ... THE BULGARIAN FRONTIER AT BARACOYO

This picture shows one of the most interesting posts on the Bulgarian-Turkish frontier, as over this bridge the Turks must enter the Bulgarian country from the south-east. This is really one of the most interesting pictures of the series, as it shows the Bulgarian and Turkish sentinels keeping post immediately on the frontier, only a few feet separating them. Should either cross the line, these opponents would, without hesitation, open fire upon them, which would practically mean a declaration of war. **50 feet**

1164 ... OPENING OF THE BULGARIAN PARLIAMENT BY PRINCE FERDINAND OF BULGARIA, at Sofia, Nov. 15th, 1903

Who granted us special permission and facilities to Bioscope the event.

The action in this picture shows the arrival of troops, the advance guard, the body guard of the Prince, and the carriages drawn up at the stairs leading to the entrance From these ascend Prince Ferdinand, the Minister of War, and other officials who are likely to come most prominently before the world by Spring, when it is expected that hostilities open in real earnest. Excellent portraits, unique. **125 feet**

Macedonian Insurgent Leaders . . .

1228 ... AN INSURGENT BAND IN COVER

This picture shows a portion of Quevguelliisky's Band around a camp fire in a clearing surrounded by heavy undergrowth. The men are constantly on the alert against surprises by the Turks, who are harrassing them whenever possible. **50 feet**

1229 ... A MACEDONIAN INSURGENT BAND ON THE MARCH

(*Under the leadership of Tvantcho Quevgueliisky*).

The idea of this picture was to produce a portrait likeness of each member of this famous band, and permission of the Commander was given to have his followers march towards and past the camera in single file. The brave bearing of each man, the resolute expressions of their faces as well as their peculiar uniforms lend themselves to the picturesque aspect of this subject. The last section depicts a group of the band surrounding their leader who is seen discussing the contents of a despatch with his lieutenant. **100 feet**

1230 ... A SKIRMISH WITH THE TURKS IN THE BALKANS

By one of the most important Insurgent Bands, under the direct lead of GENERAL TZONTCHEFF.

The first section gives a general view of the snow covered Balkan Mountains with the Insurgent Band wending their way through the deep snow. They rest in the middle of the day and light a fire. The man on the look-out gives an alarm to the General, who orders his men under arms ready for an attack. They take fresh cover and await the onslaught of the Turks, who fire at them from a distant knoll. The Insurgents now take matters in hand, and their mode of fighting is here shown to great advantage. **200 feet**

1321 ... MACEDONIAN INSURGENTS' FIGHT WITH THE TURKS

An every day incident with this Band under the leadership of Quevgueliisky, during their progress through Macedonia.

The opening section of this picture shows the precautions taken by the band in preventing being ambuscaded by the Turks. One of the band is sent in advance to throw a dynamite bomb into a clump of trees to make certain that there are no enemy in hiding. He is seen lighting the fuse of a bomb running towards the likely ambush into which he throws a bomb. He drops to the ground awaiting the explosion, and seeing no quarry the band moves on. This is a certain test as no Turk will face this terrible explosion of dynamite. We next see the band halting by the way, hidden in tall fir undergrowth. Some of the band are cleaning their guns while others are on sentinel duty.

The third picture shows the band making its way in single file over a mountain stream. One of the men is seen to fall, his companions taking a hurried look at him, and then pass on quickly to revenge themselves on the Turk who fired the shot.

The fourth scene shows the band making through a wood, dodging from tree to tree, and cautiously looking from right to left for any sign of danger.

The fifth view depicts a clearing which the men must cross. While so doing another of the band is shot. His comrades always ready in case of attack, quicken their pace and rush towards the cover from which the shot was fired.

We now see them advance in earnest and taking their position under the best cover in hand, open fire on the squad of Turks. Four members of the band are seen to fall, though wounded they continue to pump lead into the enemy. **An exciting picture.** **225 feet**

This and the preceding three are ABSOLUTELY the only Genuine Animated Pictures in existence of Macedonian Insurgent Bands operating in hostile territory.

L

1232 ... THE NATIONAL DANCE OF MACEDONIA AND BULGARIA

The young people are dressed in their best, and continue the same dance for hours together, on Sunday afternoons or any holiday occasions. Their attire is most picturesque.

This picture was taken in the village of Gornia Bania, about half-an-hour's drive from Sofia. **50 feet**

1233 ... INITIATING A NEW MEMBER INTO AN INSURGENT BAND

The joining member is taken blindfolded to a meeting-place of the Insurgents in the Balkan Mountains, where he is put to severe tests as to his faithfulness and loyalty to the cause, after which the oath is taken, and he then receives the salutations of his brothers-in-arms. **60 feet**

1358 ... RAILROAD PANORAMA OF THE PASS OF TIRNOVO

This photograph shows how beautifully picturesque the Tirnovo Valley really is, and the wonderful approach to the ancient and historical capital of Bulgaria, which is practically built in horseshoe form on the mountain side, with its houses, placed contour upon contour, rising to many hundreds of feet above the river bed.

200 feet

No. 1359 Bulgarian Officers' Garden Party at Stara Zagora

1359 ... MILITARY GARDEN PARTY

A Military Garden Party being held at the Officers' Club, Stara Zagora, under the presence and patronage of the garrison commanding officer, General Major Veltcheff, one of the most noted Bulgarian officers. A fine portrait of this officer, with his Staff, may be seen. **50 feet**

1360 ... TURKS SMOKING HUBBLE BUBBLE PIPES

An every afternoon custom when drinking coffee after lunch. The tobacco used is very strong, and is grown in Asia. Before it is placed in the pipe it is made damp, or one might say washed; then a large quantity is placed in the bowl of the pipe, then red hot charcoal is placed on the top, when the pipe is ready to be smoked. The smoke is drawn through water in the lower vessel, which serves the purpose of both cleansing and cooling the smoke. The Turks have a great delight in placing cherries and strawberries in this vessel, and when the smoke is drawn through they see how long they can keep them bobbing up and down in the water. **50 feet**

1361 ... BULGARIAN WEDDING DANCE

This photograph was taken in the village of Basabovo, near Roustchauk, on the Danube. It is the custom that all weddings shall take place on the Sunday. As both men and women work on their farms, this is the only day of rest. The villagers assemble from the surrounding districts, and all join in the native dance, called the " Korah." **50 feet**

No. 1363.   Bulgarian Village Dance.

1362 ... VILLAGE FESTAL SCENES

The villagers then go to the house of the bridegroom and form into procession, then make their way to the bride's house, who joins the party. They then proceed to the church, dancing and singing all the way, the bride and bridegroom holding each other in their arms. **75 feet**

1363 ... BULGARIAN VILLAGE DANCE

The newly-married young people are seen returning from the church, and they and their friends indulge in the National Dance. **60 feet**

1364 ... TYPES OF BULGARIAN PEASANT BEAUTIES

Four typical Country Girls taking a rest after the dance. They take a great delight in dancing in their best, placing flowers in their hair, &c, and are seen in lively animation after the excitement of the dance. **50 feet**

L 2

1365 ... BULGARIAN CAVALRY DESCENDING THE MOUNTAIN SIDE AND FORDING A MOUNTAIN STREAM

These are the officers of the 2nd Cavalry Regiment, and this photograph shows in the most graphic manner how well the horses are trained, and with what courage the officers handle them. After the descent they cross the stream in a most exciting manner. **100 feet**

1366 ... MANŒUVRE BY THE 5th BATTERY BULGARIAN ARTILLERY stationed in the Chomler district

The soldiers here depicted compare most favourably in execution of drill, manual at arms and stalwart bearing to some of the select regiments of the greater Powers. **75 feet**

1367 ... THE CHOMLER GARRISON RECRUIT DRILL

Showing the high standard of perfection these young soldiers have attained after only two months' training. The use of the bayonet and attack is well illustrated by means of a charge upon dummy figures representing the foe. **125 feet**

1368 THE GRAIN TRAFFIC AT THE PORT OF BULGAS

Showing a typical Black Sea trawler, the s.s. "Margaret Jones" of Cardiff. It is interesting to know that from this port large quantities of grain is continually being shipped to this country, as well as to other parts of the world.

Bulgas is one of the only two ports owned by Bulgaria, and this photograph shows what a quaint old Turkish town it is, as seen from the ship's side, and the panorama well shows the large quantity of grain waiting on the quay for shipment. **50 feet**

1369 ... THE GRAIN TRAFFIC AT THE PORT OF BULGAS

The s.s. "Margaret Jones" in full work, and is seen with the grain being carried and shot into the hold from bags, mostly by Turkish labour, and it is most interesting to see how quickly these men run the planks and deposit their load. **150 feet**

1440 ... INFANTRY MESS IN CAMP. (Stara Zagora district)

In the first portion of this picture we see the soldiers told off for mess duty, carrying large copper pots from the cook-house, placing the same on roughly constructed tables. We next see the men arriving, who all turn their faces to the East. With uncovered heads sing or chant their grace, by word of command from their officer. Grace over, they produce their spoons, which they carry tucked down in the tops of their jack boots. Each copper pot contains the food for eight men. It is amusing to see them going for the tit-bits. Dinner over, they return to their duty. **100 feet**

General Veltcheff, Commander of the Shoumla Garrison.

1441 ... GENERAL SAROFF, WAR MINISTER, Entertaining Staff and Garrison Officers at Lunch after a big mornings sham Fight.
We get a good likeness of the General making his speech, after which all the officers break into the national dance, "The Horah."
75 feet

1442 ... SOFIAS GARRISON INFANTRY ON THE MARCH
An interesting picture. Men setting out to take part in a big field day in the Sofia district. They are of splendid physique, and seem to thoroughly enjoy the hard work of a long march. **75 feet**

1443 ... BULGARIAN INFANTRY, ARTILLERY AND CAVALRY
Here we see the joint forces on the march, just before going into action on sham fight and manœuvre day, Sofia district, and can easily be seen they are made of the right sort of stuff. **100 feet**

1444 ... THE TRAINING COURSE OF CAVALRY HORSES
Under officers showing the young cavalryman how to mount and dismount under difficulties. **50 feet**

1445 ... BULGARIAN MOUNTED GENDARMERIE ON THE MARCH
The march-past of this regiment is a pleasing sight, and the men's bearing and precision speak much for the high training which the men and horses have undergone. **75 feet**

1446 ... CAVALRY ON THE MARCH
The Cavalry is one of the most proficient branches of the Bulgarian Army. This picture shows them marching past the camera in review order. Splendid military subject. **75 feet**

1447 ... 1st CAVALRY REGIMENT ON MANŒUVRE DRILL
A powerful squad well handled. An excellent military subject.
150 feet

1448 ... HARVESTING—Blossoms in the Valley of Roses
Kazaulak Valley, for purpose of distilling "Otto of Roses." A splendid series, showing the peasants starting out among the Rose Gardens equipped with huge baskets, which they fill with blossoms, carrying same to the distillery, &c. Splendid picture. **75 feet**

Bulgarian Officers of the Shoumla Garrison, the largest and most important in Bulgaria.

PRESS COMMENTS.

"THE ERA."

One of the great advantages of the Bioscope is that it " opens the minds " of the people, brings before them actualities and truths, and emphasises the importance of nations and movements which are often forgotten when other interests appeal to the public, What with the fiscal question and the threatened war in the East, the yearnings of the Bulgarians for freedom are apt to be overlooked ; but the splendid series of films which have been taken by Mr. C. Rider Noble, and were shown by the Imperial Bioscope at the Alhambra, recalls to us the fact that the Bulgarians are determined to exact reform, if necessary, at the point of the bayonet. Rarely has the strain on the relations between Turkey and Bulgaria been brought before our eyes as plainly as by the film showing the sentries of the two nations marching on either side of the boundary line on the frontier, and Turkish oppression is powerfully and properly exposed by the spactacle of the hundreds of wretched refugees at Rylo Monastery, the mothers with their babes in their arms, in rags, and all evidently half starved and exhausted. It is impossible not to sympathise with the efforts of the insurgent bands who have taken up arms to throw off the yoke of Turkish tyranny; and Mr. Rider Noble is seen in the centre of one of these guerilla gatherings. He kisses the flag, and in the ceremony of initiation into the " brotherhood" which follows, the leaders of the insurgents kiss him. As illustrating the lighter and brighter side of Bulgarian life, the film devoted to the national dance of the country is excellent. The peasant girls, in their pretty costumes, join hands in a ring, and go through some quaint movements. How much civilisation, at least upon the surface, exists in the Bulgaria, is brought home to us by the views depicting the opening of the national parliament, and the stalwart troops and their bluff, genial officers evidently constitute a force which may be destined to create a force which represent the guerillas advancing over streams and through woods, and engaging in a hot skirmish with the enemy. Very picturesque is the descent of a mounted party of inspecion down a rugged mountain path. Altogether these Bulgaria views are a most important oontribution to contemporary enlightenment, besides being vividly and intensely interesting in themselves.

"ILLUSTRATED LONDON NEWS."

Extremely interesting, in consideration of the political tension which still exists in the Balkans, is the new feature of the Alhambra Theatre's programme—to wit, a series of animated pictures illustrating the Macedonian and Bulgarian insarrection. For the most part, the Bioscope speaks for itself, and seems to suggest that its owner has been in many hot corners; but there is also a lecturer on the Alhambra stage to explain any obscurity in the views. We see Bulgarian girls performing prettily their national dance in picturesque gala attire. and we watch in grim contrast miserable Macedonian refugees seeking refuge in a monastery. Finally, after being shown a frontier outpost, we are plunged into the midst of skirmishers, and observe Turks and insurgents falling wounded or dead, and wonder how the Bioscope escaped the bullets of the combatants.

"BLACK AND WHITE."

A wonderful new set of bioscopic pictures, depicting the work of the insurgents in Macedonia, is now on view at the Alhambra. Mr. C. Rider Noble, who took these pictures, was attached to one of the insurgent bands, and has certainly used his time to excellent purpose. One of the films represents an actual fight, while others, though less bloodthirsty are full of interest.

"THE MUSIC HALL."

The new Macedonian pictures were enthusiastically received.

"WHITEHALL REVIEW."

At the Alhambra, the ever-popular Bioscope is showing views of the Bulgarian and Macedonian insurrection. The pictures are all very interesting, and a lecturer explains the various "points." One of the most striking pictures is that of the national dance of Bulgaria as danced by young glrls in their picturesque holiday clothes. The pictures of the Macedonian refugees as they seek the protection of the Monks of Rilo are provocative of many expressions of sympathy for the unfortunate people, There is a remarkable illustration, too, of a frontier bridge, with the Turkish and the Bulgarian sentinels posted within a few feet of each other. The display of these pictures is announced for a fortnight only.

"MORNING POST."

Last night the Bioscope turned its attention and ours to the Bulgarian and Macedonian insurrection. The views are stated to have been taken by Mr. Rider Noble, who must in the battle scenes have run considerable personal risk, especially as, having taken the oath of loyalty to the insurgent chief, he was fair game to Turks. The pictures vary greatly in merit, but all are interesting, and a lecturer adds to their interest by his comments. Very pretty is the national dance of Bulgaria as danced by young girls in their picturesque holiday clothes. Anything but pretty are the pictures of the Macedonian refugees as they herd to seek the protection of the Monks of Rilo. There is a strange view, too, of a frontier bridge, with the Turkish and the Bulgarian sentinels posted within a few feet of each other, And there are several scenes of actual skirmishing in which we see men fall. Some of these pictures are rather painful, and the Bioscope seems to have borne a charmed life, The whole collection is well worth seeing ; the Bioscope tells you a wonderful lot in a very few minutes, and the lecturer helps where help is wanted.

"THE STANDARD."

One of the most interesting series of pictures which has yet been seen at the Alhambra was presented last night by means of the Imperial Bioycope, The subject dealt with was the disturbancef which have occurred in Bulgaria and Macedonia, and Mr. C. Rider Noble, who took the original photographs, must have been at considerable difficulty and in some personal danger to obtain them. All facilities were refused by the Turkish Government, and Mr. Noble had to join the Bulgarians, and the incident of his taking the oath to King Ferdinand I. is thrown on the screen. First of all comes the opening of the Bulgarian Parliament at Sofia on November 15 of last year, and then follow a number of typical scenes of life in the Near East. Military pictures follow, and these are particularly interesting. A review of Bulgarian troops by M. Savoff, the Minister of War, is depicted, and the physique and bearing of the men, as far as can be judged, leave nothing to be desired. One of the best things shown is a famous Macedonian band of insurgents on the march, the features and varied attire of the men being easily distinguishable. Finally there is a skirmish between the insurgents and a detachment of Turkish troops, the irregulars advancing through bush and then in open order across exposed ground. The casualties which take place when the firing commences in earnest are almost too realistic.

"TRUTH."

The Alhambra Theatre announces for production this week a new series of bioscope pictures illustrative of the troubles in Macedonia. These pictures, it declares. have been obtained through the agency of the Urban Trading Company, but not without difficulty, owing to the refusal of the Turkish Government to permit the photographers to penetrate the Turkish lines. This difficulty, the Alhambra assures us, was overcome "by stratagem,' which is, perhaps, another name for backsheesh judiciously distributed,

"VANITY FAIR."

The serious complications in the Far East have, to a certain extent, placed the Macedonian trouble, for the moment, in the background, but in face of the war that will surely occur sooner or later between Turkey and Bulgaria, and to draw attention to the misery endured by the Macedonian Refugees, the management of the Alhambra have obtained through the Chas. Urban Trading Company, Limited, a series of most interesting pictures of Bulgaria which are shown on the Bioscope this week. Owing to the refusal of the Turkish Government to grant passports in order to render facilities to obtain these pictures, the Urban expedition had by stratagem, to get through the Turkish lines as best they could, at great personal risk, and join issue with the Bulgarians, swearing allegiance to King Ferdinand I. The management of the Alhambra have again succeeded in obtaining exclusive use of this series of unique pictures, which, following on the Micro-Bioscope pictures, and those of the Lumbering and Salmon Fishing, again exemplify the up-to-dateness of the present management.

"DAILY CHRONICLE.;'

The Bioscope has become a war correspondent. Upon the screen on the Alhambra stage are now shown experiences with the insurgents in Bulgaria explained by a lecturer who says enough, but not a word too much.

＊   ＊   ＊   ＊   ＊

Upon securing such an interesting and instructive item as this vivid illustration of incidents of the Macedonian insurrection, Mr. Moul may be congratulated.

"MORNING POST."

The whole collection is well worth seeing, the bioscope tells you a wonderful lot in a very few minutes, and the lecturer helps where help is wanted. "The man in the Inverness cape," he observed, " was a spy, and has since been shot." And truly he does not face the bioscope with the same composure as the others. The display of these pictures is announced for a fortnight only, so those who wish to see them should lose no time,

"THE PELICAN."

Realism has assuredly reached somewhere very near its apex in the new Animated Pictures now on show at the Alhambra. In the space of a few minutes the audience is whirled through a goodly portion of that most distressful country, Bulgaria, in company with a number of Bulgarian irregulars, who in the matter of appearance and varied get-up, certainly do not belie their name. These brigands are seen skirmishing through woods and across fields, and at intervals pop goes a Turkish rifle and over rolls one of the Bulgarians. The spectacle of seeing men actually killed before one's eyes on the field of battle has never before been shown, and it is at once gruesome and fascinating to a degree.

The way some of the poor wretches drop and roll over and then come to an awful stop suggests popped-at rabbits more than anything else. It is remarkable to notice, too, that when a man falls he is left severely alone by his companions. No one goes to his assistance, and of medical staff and appliances there would seem to be none. One's admiration certainly goes out to Mr. Rider Noble, who cinematographed the pictures, and who in the accomplishment of his arduous and peculiarly dangerous task. must have run a most excellent chance of getting his machine smashed and himself riddled with Turkish bullets.

"FINANCIAL NEWS."

Few more interesting pictures have been exploited by the cinematograph than those now on view at the Alhambra, illustrating the insurrection in Macedonia.

ARABIA AND PALESTINE.

By courtesy of Dr. H. S. Lunn.   Photographed by F. Ormiston-Smith.

No. 1279a   Jaffa Street Scene.

1279 a ... JAFFA AND ITS HARBOUR

1.—**Jaffa from the Sea.** The Port of Jerusalem. The worst Harbour in the world.

2.—**Through the Rocks and Surf.**—The Syrian boatmen shooting the narrows.

3.—**The Landing Stage.** Showing the many shore boats at the Quay.

4.—**A street in Jaffa.** One of the busiest towns in Palestine.

5—**Camels carrying oranges to the quays.** The details of exporting the famous Jaffa oranges.

6—**The surf.** Showing the dangerous belt of rocks.

7—**The orange boats.** Syrian boatmen waiting for the oranges.

8—**Loading the oranges.** Filling the boats at the wharf.

9—**Camels transporting oranges.** Bringing the oranges from the groves to the quayside. **225 feet**

No. 1279c, Via Dolorosa, Jerusalem.

1279 b .. JERUSALEM, the Holy City (Section 1)

1.—**The Jaffa Gate and Jaffa Road.** The principal entrance to the City of Jerusalem.

2.—**The Tower of David.** A portion of the original tower built by Herod.

3.—**The Walls of the City.** The road by which the Wise Men travelled to Bethlehem.

4.—**Jerusalem from the Convent.** Striking view of the city from the house-tops.

5.—**David Street.** Inside the walls. The market place of Jerusalem.

6.—**The Holy Sepulchre.** For 16 centuries the supposed site of Calvary.

7.—**The Temple Area.** The site of Solomon's and Herod's Temples.

8.—**The Mosque of Omar.** Built in 637, A.D., by Omar after his conquest of Jerusalem.

9—**Filling water skins at a well.** Picturesque Eastern scene. **350 feet**

1279 c ... VISIT TO JERUSALEM (Section 2)

10—**Via Dolorosa.** The road of Christ's journey to Calvary.

11—**The Garden of Gethsemane.** The site of Christ's agony and betrayal.

12—**The Mount of Olives.** Full of sacred associations.

13—**The Damascus Gate.** Authentic site of the original North Gate oi Jerusalem.

14—**Jerusalem from the Mount of Olives.** A magnificent view of the Holy City from outside the walls.

15—**The Good Samaritan Inn.** The basis of the Parable of the Good Samaritan.

16—**The escort on the Jericho Road.** Picturesque Arab horsemen.

17—**The Jordan.** The most sacred and historical river in the world.

18—**Ascending the Jordan.** Showing the swiftness of the current.

19—**General Panorama.** Fine view of the banks of the Jordan.

20—**The return of tourists.** A very modern pilgrimage. **300 feet**

1279 Complete (Jaffa and Jerusalam) Total length 875 feet.

CEYLON SERIES,

1196 ... COOLIE BOYS DIVING FOR COINS, COLOMBO

These quaint little brown boys crowd around vessels in Colombo Harbour, calling "Have a dive, have a dive!" They are marvellous divers, going after coins and securing them as they sink through the clear water. A steam launch rather "upsets" their performance. A most amusing scene. **75 feet**

1197 ... ARRIVAL AT SINGAPORE—Scenes on board the Steamer

There are always a good number of Malay and Chinese deck passengers on the boats running from Borneo and the islands around there to Singapore. On arriving at the latter place, a crowd of Chinamen in their small boats surround the steamers to secure the baggage and take it ashore, making a lively and interesting scene. On our way from Singapore to Europe we probably coal at Port Said, where Arabs

No. 1197. Chinese Boatmen at Singapore.

a contrast from the Chinese come around the boat, and are employed to carry the coal **75 feet**

1199 ... A STREET SCENE AND THE TROPICAL GARDENS OF THE GRAND ORIENTAL HOTEL, COLOMBO

A busy Street scene outside the Grand Oriental Hotel, Colombo. The Ceylon cabby drives with more valour than discretion, and people on foot crossing the road have a lively time of it among racing carriages. The tropical foliage of the "Isle of Spices" is well shown in the garden at the Grand Oriental Hotel, where magnificent palms and plants of every description flourish in rich abundance. **50 feet**

1202 ... THE MARKET, NATIVE SECTION, COLOMBO

This picture gives us a glimpse of the ways of the Eastern market woman as she sells her wares or her fruit to the bargaining purchasers. Tamils and Singalese are here hurrying to and fro, out of the cool shade into the hot tropical sunlight, carrying their various goods. Fruit is here in rich abundance —strange kinds never seen in England—as well as the familiar pineapple and banana. **75 feet**

1203 ... LIFE IN AN OLD STREET OF COLOMBO

There are some curious old-world streets hidden away behind the more modern buildings in Colombo, the inhabitants seeming to be in no hurry, and enjoying the cool of their verandahs. Then some people will come hurrying through this quiet part, or a ricksha, with perhaps a white man in it, will take this road as a short cut to the busier parts, but they are soon gone, and the sleepy old street is quiet again. A delightful picture. **50 feet**

1204 ... BUSINESS SECTION OF COLOMBO

Colombo, as a town of any size and importance, has only existed for a matter of ten or twenty years, but has made up for lost time by becoming a most important and busy centre for Eastern and Western trade, and is important in connection with the Indian shipping service. It is a beautiful town, with its fine buildings (sometimes of terra-cotta), its fine streets with the cool shade afforded by trees growing along them, and by the covered in arcades.

75 feet

1205 ... SIGHTS IN THE OLD NATIVE TOWN OF COLOMBO

This is a fascinating and ever-changing picture, as we hurry through streets of picturesque houses and shops, with shabby stone verandahs, hung sometimes with wares for sale, sometimes with beautiful creepers and tropical growth. Beautiful palms and trees, with their acceptable shade, make a contrast from the glare of the roadway. Everywhere are types of Eastern peoples hurrying to and fro, with the picturesque bullock-carts moving slowly amongst them, all is life and animation, and so utterly different from the life in England to which we are accustomed.

75 feet

1206 ... THE OUTSKIRTS OF COLOMBO, CEYLON

The pretty streets of one-storey houses, with beautiful trees and palms above them, the hurrying crowd of Tamils and Singalese, with their burdens of goods going to or from market, are indeed an interesting scene. The Indian bullocks going easily along, and the gossipers in the shade of the houses, make the crowd of people on the road seem all the more animated by the contrast they afford.

150 feet.

1208 ... SIGHTS IN PENANG

A most lively town is Penang, situated in the Malay Peninsula with the hurried traffic of 'Rickshas. These frail vehicles are drawn along at a great pace by the Chinese "'Ricksha Boys," and one expects every minute to see a collision or some bad upset, but these "Boys" like our own wily cab horses, are very 'cute in threading their way through a maze of spinning wheels, and accidents seldom occur.

1209 ... SCENES IN PERADENIYA VILLAGE, CEYLON

A characteristic Singalese Village in the tea planting district, is Peradeniya. Pretty cottages run up the shady road with children and fowls (two indispensible things in a Singalese Village) all over the place. A happy and gentle people, living amidst beautiful scenery, and noted themselves for their good looks, they indeed make a delightful picture.

1210 ... A STROLL THROUGH KANDY STREETS

Kandy is the old capital of the interior of Ceylon, where the Kings of Kandy for centuries defied even the white man. Now it is a favorite resort of the Europeans in Ceylon, and the streets and shops of the native parts are an everchanging and often amusing sight. There is a beautiful lake close to the town. Street repairing goes on in a primitive though most effectual way here, the streets being gay with coloured paper and flags, as a festival is on.

50 feet,

1212 ... INDIAN FAKIR AND DEVIL DANCE

The Madras Juggler, Ramsannay, gives an exhibition of his magic powers, and does the mango trick. The strange way he becomes visible and can also make his apparatus and cobra vanish and appear at will heightens one's interest in the performance. Next comes a Devil Dance and dance of Tamil girls, a peculiar performance, and most picturesque. **75 feet.**

No. 1279.—Jaffa Harbour.

NOTICE.– Tho following series are **supplied on condition** that they are not re-sold or exhibited in the **United Kingdom** or **U.S. of America,** where sole exhibition rights have been acquired by the **Urbanora Exhibition Co.**

THE CINGALEE.

A Tour through the Malay Peninsula and Ceylon.

Photographed by Mr. H. M. Lomas.

1274a (Section 1) ... SINGAPORE AND COLOMBO

No.

1 ... **PANORAMA OF THE HARBOUR, DOCKS AND SHIPPING OF SINGAPORE**

2 ... **TRAFFIC OVER THE DRAW BRIDGE**

3 ... **MALAYS WITH RICKSHAWS, &c., ON THE MAIN STREET**

4 ... **NATIVE MOVING PREPARATIONS**

5 ... **CHINESE PORTERS REMOVING HOUSEHOLD EFFECTS**

6 ... **BOILED RICE VENDOR AND HIS CUSTOMERS**

7 ... **CINGALESE WAITERS IN THE GARDENS OF THE GRAND ORIENTAL HOTEL, COLOMBO**

8 ... **PANORAMA OF A GROUP OF NATIVE CHILDREN**

9 ... **LIFE IN AN OLD STREET OF COLOMBO**

10 .. **THE MARKET OF THE OLD NATIVE QUARTER**

11 ... **THE COOLIES REPAIRING A STREET IN COLOMBO**

12 ... **PANORAMA OF THE NATIVE VILLAGE STREET, as seen from the front of an electric tram**

375 feet.

1274 b (Section 2) ... THE CINGALEE

13 ... ON THE CEYLON RAILWAY TO KANDY

14 ... ALONG THE PADDY FIELDS

15 ... STREET SCENE IN KANDY

16 ...CIRCULAR PANORAMA OF THE PAVILION and LAKE

17 ... THE "TEMPLE OF THE TOOTH" AT KANDY

18 ... PANORAMA OF THE TEMPLE MOAT, PALM GARDENS, AND THE GOLDEN PAGODA

No. 1277. Mosque and Minarets, Constantinople.

19 ... BATHING ELEPHANTS IN THE UPPER RIVER

20 ... NATIVE WASHING AN OLD BULL ELEPHANT

21 ... COOLIES IN THE RIVER, Washing their Carts, Bullocks, Clothes, and Themselves

22 ... THE DHOBIE MAN in the WASH-HOUSE ENCLOSURE

350 feet.

1274 c (Section 3) ... THE CINGALEE (TEA ESTATE)

23 ... PANORAMA OF A CEYLON TEA ESTATE

24 ... SCENE ON THE TEA PLANTATIONS

25 ... CINGALESE WOMEN PICKING LEAVES FROM TEA PLANT

26 ... WEIGHING THE DAY'S PICKINGS

27 ... PERFORMING THE DEVIL DANCE AFTER THE DAY'S WORK

28 ... A STREET IN THE PICKERS' VILLAGE, ON THE ESTATE

29 ... UNLOADING CHESTS OF TEA FROM BULLOCK CARTS AT THE TEA WAREHOUSE, COLOMBO

30 ... BARGES AND SAMPANS CARRYING TEA TO A LINER IN COLOMBO HARBOUR FOR EXPORT TO ENGLAND

31 ... A BRITISH TEA GARDEN

275 feet.

1274 (complete) ... Total Length 1,000 feet.

INDIA, BURMAH AND CASHMERE.

Photographed by Dr. J. GREGORY MANTLE.

1010 ... THE FROLIC OF THE WATER CARRIERS OF CAL-CUTTA DURING THE PASSING OF A WEDDING PROCESSION

The "Bhisti," or water carrier, is familiar in all the cities and villages in India. The operator persuaded a group of these men in Bombay to turn the contents of their water skins upon one another.

75 feet

1014 ... THE BURMESE GAME OF FOOTBALL

Continuation of the preceding subject including many clever and tricky catches of the ball with the feet. **100 feet**

No. 1279b The Mosque of St. Omar, Jerusalem.

1015 ... BURMESE CHILDREN PLAYING THE GAME OF "COCK FIGHTING"

One of the popular games among the children in Burmah is a very comical game called "Cock Fighting." The children crouch on the ground and endeavour to imitate the action of the Burmese poultry. **50 feet**

1016 ... BURMESE GIRLS' CHATTI RACE

Another popular game among the Burmese girls is known as the "Chatti Race." Each girl carries on her head a vessel of water, and the more completely they get drenched as they race about, the more thoroughly they enjoy the game. **40 feet**

1017 ... CONVERTING THE HEATHEN, BIBLE CLASSES CON-DUCTED IN THE OPEN AIR

This picture illustrates some of the most successful Missionary work that is being done in India. The groups of people under the trees are gathered from surrounding villages and are being taught by native Evangelists who have come under the elevating power of Christianity. **75 feet**

1018 ... THE PERSIAN WELLS OF NORTHERN INDIA.
One of the peculiarities of India is the large variety of wells, indispensable for the cultivation of the ground. The Persian wells are the most ancient and picturesque. **50 feet**

1019 ... BULLOCK'S PLOUGHING WITH ANCIENT NORTH INDIAN IMPLEMENTS
The native plough does little more than scratch the ground, an Eastern proverb relating to the fertility of the soil being, "You have only to scratch the ground and it laughs." **60 feet**

1020 ... SCENES ON THE RIVER JHELUM, THE CHIEF WATERWAY OF SRINAGAR, THE CAPITAL OF CASHMERE
The City of Srinagar is remarkable for its waterways, and some idea of the variety of craft on the Jhelum may be obtained from this picture. **100 feet**

1021 ... WOMEN MAKING "CHAPPATI. THE BREAD CAKE OF THE PEOPLE OF NORTH INDIA
The "Chappati" is a cake unleavened bread, in common use all over India. The process of making "Chappaties" is depicted in this film. **60 feet**

1022 ... BURMESE AMUSEMENT CALLED "PWAY" (Group in Masks)
The national amusement of the people of Burmah is "Pwe" (pronounced "Pway.") The performance portrays various incidents in Burmese history. It takes place in the open air, frequently lasts all night, and the majority of the audience are accustomed to stay from eight o'clock in the evening until sunrise the next morning. The performance consists of acting, singing, dancing and clowning. **100 feet**

1023 ... BURMESE HISTORY PORTRAYED BY CHARACTER ACTING (Group)
Continuation of the preceding subject, showing a different performance by an unmasked group. **100 feet**

1024 ... BURMESE CHARACTER ACTING (The Monkey and the Imp)
Another section of the preceding film. Very amusing. **100 feet**

1025 ... PROCESSION OF 140 LEPERS AT MANDALAY
This pathetic picture of lepers in Mandalay, Burma, illustrates the beneficent work that is being done among these terribly afflicted people. In the Asylum in which these lepers are gathered there are doomed creatures in various stages of tubercular and anæsthetic leprosy, ranging in age from tiny children to old men and women some of whom are quite unable to rise.
150 feet

No. 1279 Cargo of Oranges, Jaffa.

1026 ... THE OUTCASTS OF INDIA (Procession of Men, Women and Children Reclaimed from Degradation and Devil Worship)

This remarkable subject depicts the marvellous way in which India has been opened to Christian influence by the ministry of healing. The key that opened this door was held by lady doctors. No degradation could be greater than that into which these people had fallen, and the transforming influence of the Christian religion, evidenced in their dress, countenance, speech and habits of life, are wonderful indeed. In this group are several who were formerly Devil Priests and Devil Priestesses, and the Heathen Temples they have left wait in vain for their return. **200 feet**

1027 ... PROCESSION OF 1,800 WIDOWS ON THE RAMABAI COLONY, INDIA

The remarkable Brahmin Woman who heads this Procession consisting of eighteen hundred High-caste Widows and deserted Wives, is Pundita Ramabai. The clearness of her views on the subject of child marriage, and the eloquence of her expression were such that the Pundits of Calcutta conferred on her the title of "Sarasvati" (Goddess of Wisdom). There are twenty-three millions of widows in India, and of these nearly seventy-eight thousand are under nine years of age. No words can express the misery, torture and suffering of the child-widow. This cruel custom constitutes the open sore of India, for "once a widow always a widow," and the life of Ramabai the Reformer, is devoted towards rescuing child-widows and deserted wives from their unhappy surroundings and bringing them under the kindliest Christian influence. **300 feet**

1028 NATIVES CROSSING THE SNOW-FED RIVER "RAVI" NORTH OF LAHORE

Within a quarter of a mile of this ford across the Ravi River, there is a pontoon bridge, the toll of which is one rupee, or 1s. 4d. in English money. To evade this toll the economical Hindu farmer crosses the river at the point and in the fashion shown in this film.

100 feet

1029 ... GALLOPING TONGAS ON THE ROAD TO SRINAGAR

In the absence of a railway there is at present no way of reaching Srinagar, capital of Cashmere, excepting by these galloping tongas. The journey from Rawal Pindi to Srinagar occupies two days. These ponies, who do the whole journey at a gallop, are changed every three or every five miles according to the gradient. The journey is one of the wildest, most exciting and romantic in the world. **75 feet**

1030 ... THE 777 PAGODAS OF MANDALAY

These pagodas in Mandalay are very remarkable. King Thebaw's uncle, anxious that the holy books of Buddhism should be recorded in an enduring form, caused the purest version of the commandments to be engraved on large stones. Over each of these a pagoda has been erected, in the centre of these a temple stands, from the steps of which our operator obtained a panoramic view of the 777 pagodas

100 feet

1031 ... MONKS AND WORSHIPPERS ENTERING THE "SHWE DAGON" (GOLDEN SWORD) PAGODA, THE MOST SACRED IN BURMA, Panorama of the Interior and Shrines

The Shwe Dagon (pronounced "Shway Dagon") Pagoda, is the most venerable, the finest, and the most universally visited of all places of worship in Indo-China. It is the only Pagoda which is credited with containing relics, not only of Caudama, but of the three Buddhas who preceded him. It attracts countless pilgrims, not only from all parts of Burma, but from Siam, Chida, Korea and Ceylon. The panorama is taken from the platform, which is 900 feet long by 685 feet wide. Here are hundreds of images of Buddha, large and

No. 1279c The Damascus Gate, Jerusalem

small, sitting, standing and reclining, white and black, some of alabaster, others of clay, or of wood. Interspersed among these are multitudes of bells of all sizes. These the worshipper strikes as he passes with the deer's antlers that lie beside them, to call attention to his acts of piety. The platform is never deserted, night or day, and constitutes one of the most interesting sights in the world. The central Pagoda rises to a height of 375 feet, a little higher than St. Paul's Cathedral.   **150 feet**

1033 ... ELEPHANTS WORKING AT MACGREGORS TIMBER YARDS AND MILLS AT RANGOON

These elephants have been photographed thousands of times, but no cinematograph picture of them has ever been taken before. Their sagacity in pulling, pushing and stacking timber is remarkable. Within a week of being captured in the jungle, the elephants are sufficiently tame to do such light work as is indicated in a portion of the film.   **200 feet**

M

CURIOUS SIGHTS IN BURMAH AND CASHMERE.

The following pictures of which this series is comprised, includes the best portions of the various films listed and separately described under preceding numbers, and form the most comprehensive as well as unique picture or Life in the North of India.

Photographed by Dr. J. Gregory Mantle.

1273 a (Section 1) Pictures in following Order.

No.
1 ... WORSHIPPERS ENTERING THE SHWE DAGON TEMPLE
2 ... PANORAMA OF INNER PAGODA AND SHRINES
3 ... THE 777 PAGODAS OF MANDALAY
4 ... OPEN AIR SCHOOL FOR HINDUS
5 ... CHILDREN'S CHATTI RACE
6 ... A GAME OF "COCK FIGHTING"
7 ... BURMESE GAME OF FOOTBALL

8 ... THE PERSIAN WALLS OF BURMAH

9 ... FROLIC OF THE HINDU WATER CARRIERS

10 ... COOLIES TRANSPORTING CROPS ACROSS A STREAM

11 ... CARTING JUNGLE GRASS ACROSS THE RIVER RAVI
300 feet.

No. 1379c The River Jordan, Palestine

1273 b (Section 2) BURMAH AND CASHMERE

12 ... THE GALLOPING TONGA ON THE SRINAGAR ROAD
13 ... THE BULLOCK EXPRESS OF CASHMERE
14 ... ELEPHANTS REMOVING TIMBER AT THE RANGOON MILLS
15 ... AN OLD "TUSKER" CARRYING A HEAVY TEAK LOG
16 ... A FEAT OF TREMENDOUS STRENGTH BY TRAINED ELEPHANTS
17 ... STATE ELEPHANTS OF THE MAHARAJAH
18 ... SCENES BEFORE THE PALACE GATES
19 ... THE LLAMAS OF THIBET LEAVING THE WINTER PALACE
20 ... THE STATE BAND OF THE RAJAH OF CASHMERE
300 feet.

No. 1273 (complete) ... Total length 600 feet.

NORTH BORNEO.

A Grand Series of unique Pictures, photographed by Mr. H. M. LOMAS *who conducted the* **Urban Bioscope Expedition through Borneo.**

This expedition was started and equipped by us for the purpose of securing bioscopic records of native life and scenes in the interior of North Borneo. The unparalleled idea of taking the bioscope into an almost unknown district of the tropics with all the attendant risks and difficulties of travel was enthusiastically supported by the Government. We were fortunate in further securing the co-operation of the **British North Borneo Company,** and much of the success of the series of pictures is due to the facilities granted us by the **British Officers** and **Government Officials,** stationed there.

The " Wild Men of Borneo."

1173 ... HEAD-HUNTERS OF BORNEO AT THEIR PEACE AND WAR DANCES

A series of pictures taken in the interior of Borneo, showing the reclaimed savages practising their various rites and dances. **50 feet**

1174 ... BORNEO SAVAGES STALKING AN ENEMY

They cautiously wend their way in a bent position, Indian file, through tall grass, jungle, and stream, following an enemy's track, hoping thus to surprise him and add his head to their other similar trophies. **100 feet**

1175 NATIVE AND CHINESE QUARTERS AT SANDAKAN

Scenes in Sandakan, which is the present capital of British North-Borneo, showing the streets of Chinese traders' shops with their wooden roadway, built on piles over reclaimed swampy ground. "Copra," or the inside of the cocoanut, is being dried in the sun for export to Europe. Strange native and Sulu boats come here to trade and fish. **100 feet**

M 2

1176 ... LIFE AND SCENES AT SANDAKAN

Government House, the residence of His Excellency the Governor of British North Borneo, is situated on one of the hills overlooking the sea and town of Sandakan. The house is shown in this film, also the magnificent panoramic view obtained from the garden, of the European houses below, the jetty, and Chinese shops. The Chinese are excellent market gardeners; their gardens are here shown. **125 feet**

1178 ... RAILROAD PANORAMA OF JUNGLE AND MOUNTAIN DISTRICTS

There is another line of Railroad from Beaufort to Jesselton, running through tracts of primeval forests and across swamps, where the large pig-tailed monkeys live. Strange land crabs live in these swamps. We also get a glimpse of the hill country, and of a train of Chinese coolies going out with ballast to mend the line, after heavy floods have swept down the valleys. **200 feet**

1179 ... SCENES ON THE PADAS RIVER AND THE PENOTAL GORGE

The source of the River Padas is unknown, but it is supposed to rise in the adjacent kingdom of Brunei. Above the gorge it runs still strong and deep, 600 feet above sea level. Here the natives go about in "dugout" boats, near the village of Tenom The Muruts are excellent boatmen, but sometimes have an upset, when they have to beware of crocodiles. Next comes the Gates of the Gorge, where the river narrows and rushes down in fierce rapids and whirlpools, where no native dare take his boat. The backwash along the banks is very strong, running up stream. On both sides of the river rise steep mountains, which, save for the one track, are utterly unknown to the white man. An impressive piece of wild scenery. **200 feet**

The Rapids of the Padas River.

1181 ... NATIVE LIFE IN THE DUSAN VILLAGE OF PUTATAN

The village of Putatan is built along the river banks. The houses, made of bamboo and thatched with leaves, are raised up on poles, out of the reach of crocodiles and wild animals. The boys come racing out to see the white man's "picture-box," and are very interested in the camera. Fishing is the main industry of this village, and they dry the fish outside their cottage doors on raised platforms, ready for their own consumption. **75 feet**

1182 ... ON THE DARVEL BAY TOBACCO ESTATES

We are indebted to T. A. BALL, Esq., Acting Manager of the New Darvel Bay Tobacco Plantations Ltd, for kindly arranging for this picture to be taken.

Down the East Coast, 24 hours run on a Steam Launch, from the capital of Sandakan (which town we see at the commencement of this film) is the magnificent Darvel Bay. From here we drive through Lahat Datu to the Tobacco Estates, along a turf road cut through the the Jungle. Drying Sheds can be seen in the distance; carpenters busy with new sheds, and now the Managers arrive to take us round the Estates. Here are huge fermenting sheds, fine wooden buildings where the tobacco leaves are piled up to ferment, after having been dried in the open and smaller sheds we see about the Estate. In the distance is the Segma River, and in the foreground are the stumps of old forest trees, where the Jungle has been cleared the undergrowth burnt down, and tobacco planted. Malay coolies carry the leaf to the drying sheds in peculiar shaped baskets on their shoulders.

125 feet

A Mixed Train on the Borneo Railway . . .

1183 ... THR URBAN EXPEDITION PASSING THROUGH THE JUNGLE

View of the Expedition crossing the mountains between Tenom and Tambunan, on a native track through the Jungle, by the edge of of a vast precipice, with miles of dense jungle stretching away as far as the eye can reach, beds, stores, cooking utensils, and apparatus being carried by native Murut coolies, as these mountains are too steep for mules. **50 feet**

1185 — FESTAL DANCE OF TOMOGON MURUTS

These pictures illustrate the native customs around Tenon in the interior. They are here preparing the Jar of Arak for the festival by collecting the gongs, and making all ready, the audience of Muruts squat around. Then comes the dance and chant by the men and women. Note the Jar of Arak and its admirers in the distance, show they wisely add more and more water to keep it always full, and seemingly untouched. The movements of the dance are very wierd and cannot easily be described. **100 feet**

1186 . THE DYAK WAR DANCE

The audience of natives, mostly of Murut tribes, near Sapong, squat on the ground and watch the preparing of the jar and the metal gongs. The Head Hunter's War Dance is now performed by the Dyaks, who are a most warlike, but at the same time a most faithful, people. They, as well as the other tribes of Borneo, are noted as "Head Hunters." Every tribe was at war with every other tribe in the old days, and a man who had not taken a head was but an insignificant creature. **75 feet**

1187 ... LIFE AT KUDAT

This film shows the arrival of His Excellency the Governor at Kudat, also the Chinese traders' shops in the little town, and a Bajau chief with his wives and relations. Finally, the Marudu Pony Races —got up by the Officers and Planters and nick-named "Borneo Derby," in which native Princes take part—are run, the natives taking great interest in the affairs, and crowding around the paddock and enclosure to see the races. A group of these excitable but excellent little steeds is shown. **100 feet**

1190 ... NATIVE FAIR AT TARITIPAN

The ever present bad boys have a race. Here is a native "Tamu" or fair, and Bajaus and Dusuns with their Karbau (water buffalo) assembled around a Chinese trader's house. Dusun houses on stilts, cocoanut palms, and rich tropical growth, make a picturesque scene, and the costumes and ornaments of the natives are varied and of great interest **60 feet**

1191 ... THE MILITARY POLICE AT SANDAKAN

March-past and salute by the Sikhs at Sandakan with Maxim guns on the ground to the left. The Dyak police are posted round the parade ground. As will be seen from this interesting picture, the Sikh police keep up their Indian reputation for promptness and excellent time in marching. **50 feet**

1192 ... PANORAMA OF KOTABELUD

Taken from the rising ground in the Tempassuk plains, where the one English officer lives, with his force of Sikh police, right up country, away from all other white men, and among Dusun and Bajou tribes, who cultivate paddy on the vast plains round. In the distance can be seen ranges of mountains covered with dense jungle, below us a beautiful river winds through the low land. **100 feet**

Bamboo and Wire Bridge.

1193 ... FORT AND GOVERNMENT STATION AT KOTABELUD

View of the Block House Fort at Kotabelud, and panorama of the vast view from these over plains and jungle-covered mountains, with Mount Kinabalu, the highest mountain in the Malay Archipelago, 13,960 feet high, in the distance—a land of strange tribes and wild animals. View of the officers' residence, and the Urban Expedition preparing to leave, the baggage being packed on to water Buffalo.

75 feet

1194 PANORAMAS OF BORNEO UP-COUNTRY SCENES

(*a*) A Murut village, with quaint wooden houses thatched with "Attaps," or mats, made of leaves of the sago palm, and surrounded by tropical trees and a deep and strong running river beyond.

(*b*) Another type of inland scenery. Here are great plains, rising mounds and hills covered with coarse grass, seen from "Execution Hill," where three rebel chiefs were executed some years ago.

(*c*) European houses—still made of wood and thatched with "Attaps," but most comfortable and delightfully cool in that hot climate.

75 feet.

A Station on the Borneo Railway—

1195 ... PANORAMA OF JESSELTON AND HARBOUR

This enterprising but young settlement is situated on the West Coast, in Gaya Bay, which is seen in the picture, with Gaya Island in the distance. To the left can be seen the Bajau village, built over the sea. The Bajaus are excellent boatmen, and used to be noted as sea pirates not very many years ago. To the left are the new British offices, &c., and houses. the ever present Chinese shops.

50 feet.

"INTO THE WILDS OF BORNEO."

Photographed by Mr. H. M. Lomas, *who conducted the Urban Bioscope Expedition into Borneo.*

1272 a (Section No. 1) ... WILDS OF BORNEO

No.

1 ... **OUR ARAB STOKERS**

2 ... **CHINESE and MALAY PASSENGERS ON THE FORWARD DECK**

3 ... **NATIVES IN SMALL BOATS PLYING FOR A FARE**

4 ... **COOLIE BOYS DIVING FOR COINS**

5 ... **NATIVE BOATS IN SANDAKAN HARBOUR**

6 ... **NATIVE QUARTERS AND SANDAKAN DOCKS**

7 ... **THE CHINESE TRADERS OF THE EAST**

8 ... **APPROACH OF A TRAIN ON THE BORNEO RAILWAY**

Mr Lomas with the Bioscope on front of " Puffing Billy."

9 ... **COOLIE PASSENGERS ON THE BORNEO TRAIN**

10 ... **RAILROAD PANORAMA OF THE PENOTAL GORGE**

11 ... **"PUFFING BILLY" Passing Over BRIDGE IN JUNGLE**

12 ... **A "STREET" IN TARITIPAN**

13 ... **THE NATIVE MARKET IN TARITIPAN**

14 ... **COOLIE CHILDREN PLAYING ON OUTSKIRTS OF VILLAGE**

15 ... **THROUGH THE JUNGLE AND PALM FOREST BY RAIL**

400 feet.

1272 b (Section 2) ... WILDS OF BORNEO

16 ... A TRIBE OF THE INTERIOR TRADING WITH WHITE MEN
17 ... THE DUSAN VILLAGE OF PUTATAN
18 ... ASCENDING THE PADAS RIVER BY BOATS
19 ... PANORAMA OF THE PADAS RIVER
20 ... PASSING A MANGO SWAMP
21 ... GENERAL VIEW OF THE VEGETATION ON RIVER BANKS
22 ... NATIVE BOYS BATHING IN RIVER
23 ... THE RAPIDS OF THE GORGE
24 ... WORKING MANGANESE ROCKS IN THE BALAIGONG GORGE

325 feet.

A Borneo Village.

1272 c (Section 3) ... WILDS OF BORNEO

25 ... THE URBAN EXPEDITION CROSSING A STREAM
26 ... A NATIVE TRIBE RETURNING FROM A TRADING EXPEDITION
27 ... FESTAL DANCE OF THE TOMOGON MURUTS
28 ... THE DYAK WAR DANCE
29 ... BORNEO HEADHUNTERS ON THE WARPATH
30 ... A SKIRMISH IN THE JUNGLE GRASS
31 ... THE WILD MEN OF BORNEO
32 ... THE MONKEYS OF BORNEO

300 feet.

1272 (complete) ... Total length 1025 feet.

PRESS COMMENTS.

"The Citizen."

The management of the Alhambra have been successful in securing a series of most interesting pictures illustrating an expedition to North Borneo, which will be shown on Monday next, the 18th inst, This expedition, which was organised by the Charles Urban Trading Company, was conducted by H. M. Lomas with the co-operation of the Government and the British North Borneo Company, assisted by the British officers and the Government officials there, the services of guides being used for crossing the mountains, while thirty coolies were requisitioned for the transport of foodstuffs, camp equipment, apparatus, &c. One hundred and twenty-seven miles into the interior were traversed, some parts of which had never been trodden by a white man before, and the journey into the "wilds of Borneo" was consequently not fulfilled without many difficulties.

"Daily Telegraph."

Dinner and Pictures.

Everybody has heard of the "wild men" who are reputed to come from Borneo, but many people are still unacquainted with the plantations and the wonderful natural resources of that interesting country. The necessity for enlightenment having been realised, the North Borneo Company's dinner at the Hotel Cecil last night was followed by a series of Urban bioscopic pictures with lecture. In this entertaining way the beautiful scenery of the country and its commercial riches were realised without—as one of the speakers said— "the boredom attaching to long speeches." On account of the pictorial show, the toast list was cut very short.

Mr. W. C. Cowie (managing director of the North Borneo Company), in proposing "The Guests," spoke of North Borneo as a country affording profitable outlet for British capital and abundant employment for Chinese coolies. Without the help of the minerals which existed they had found an estate which paid its way and which promised in every sense to become not only a very valuable asset for shareholders, but a worthy adjunct of the British Empire. It was well to know, said Mr. Cowie, that by the expenditure of a million or two of Imperial funds Borneo could be made a naval base of the utmost importance to the China Sea Squadron; in fact, it might be made a fortress in the midst of the many foreign camps which now threatened our position in the Far East.

Sir Walter Peace responded.

Lord Brassey proposed "The State of North Borneo," to which the chairman (Sir Charles Jessel) replied.

Sir Richard Temple submitted "The North Borneo Service," a toast which was acknowledged by Mr. A. Cook.

The guests at the dinner included his Excellency Chang Ta Yen, Minister for China, several of the Agents-General for the Colonies, and many gentlemen connected with trade in No. th Borneo.

"The People."

Wonders, especially in relation to the cinematograph, will never cease. Mr, Charles Urban's latest enterprise is the supersession of the after-dinner speech. On Tuesday night the Borneo dinner took place: many persons of distinction interested in that country were present; it was indeed a vast, important function. After dinner a series of pictures were thrown upon the screen, designed, in the first instance,-to illustrate the progress of Borneo to those immediately concerned therein, but afterwards for use in the theatre. Rarely have we seen so excellent, and we will add, so valuable an exhibition of the cinematograph. The pictures are clear, vivid, and, indeed, unique.

"Morning Post."

"Worthy of an Empire."

Animated photographs as an aid to digestion are new even to the British North Borneo Company, though its annual dinners have hitherto held a position of splendid isolation, due to lantern views of the old-fashioned kind. It was, no doubt, advancing prosperity that led these merchant adventurers to insert a bioscopic exhibition between the first and second toasts at their yearly banquet last night, and the innovation was welcome to the two hundred and sixty gentlemen who dined and the fifty or more ladies who looked on in the Great Hall of the Hotel Cecil. It was not a haphazard exhibition. It was full of "actuality," as people were fond of saying a few years ago, for it reproduced scenes in North Borneo, views photographed by an expedition lately conducted by Mr. H. M. Lomas, leader of an expedition sent out by the Charles Urban Trading Company, a body subsidiary to the hosts of the evening. That the British North Borneo Company's territory is as large as Ireland is hardly surprising to men "of the blood," though it would stagger those of a less Imperial race. The fact, however, partly accounts for the strangeness of some of the scenes exhibited last night. Stay-at-home folk have not often the opportunity of seeing a railway train moving, not only through tropical forests, but past Malay houses, built on piles, or beholding the descendants of ferocious pirates walking along the iron way, turning round from time to time to see how near the steam monster was, and then mildly stepping aside to watch it pass. In the cut-throat days of not long ago they would either have run away or tried to wreck the train. Experience has taught them that the native shares the benefits of British enterprise. There was more than one scene of Malays and Chinese at work under the eyes of Europeans, and the rapidity with which the labourers moved astonished and amused last night's gathering. "They are earning dividends for the shareholders," said a humorist; but the truth is, that the natives are eager to work for the British, and, when allowed to do so, are most zealous.

"THE STAR."

The Borneo pictures, which have assumed unusual interest in view of this weeks developments in that country, have been retained in the Alhambra programme.

"MUSIC HALL."

Deeply interesting are the pictures of life in Borneo, shown at the Alhambra by the Bioscope. They were secured, as we have stated, by the special expedition which Mr. Charles Urban organised to penetrate the interior under the personal direction of Mr. H. M. Lomas. This gentleman took the interesting pictures which are now exhibited. One of the best, both as regards clearness and general interest, shows the tribes of the interior trading for the first time with white men. Their return over the mountains gives some splendid glimpses of wild and tropical scenery,

The wonderful Borneo railway, which has cut a way through the deepest portion of the jungle, yields a very good series of pictures; as does the Padas river, the source of which is unknown. There is a panoramic view of the banks of the river, which has been very cleverly taken. The exhibition, which is an undeniable triumph for the Urban Trading Company, concludes with a stirring march and mock fight of the " wild men of Borneo."

"FINANCIAL NEWS."

Few more interesting and, let it be added, instructive, pictures have been shown by the cinematograph than those of North Borneo now to be seen at the Alhambra.

"MORNING LEADER."

The First White Man.

Some interesting pictures ware introduced into the Alhambra programme this week They were taken in North Borneo, in places where the operator was the first white man to go, "Undiscovered Lands by Bioscope" are the newest development of this wonderful recording machine, H. W.

"THE KING AND HIS ARMY AND NAVY."

The management of the Alhambra have been successful in securing a series of most interesting pictures illustrating an expedition to North Borneo, The expedition, which was organised by the Charles Urban Trading Company, was conducted by H. M. Lomas with the co-operation of the Government and the British North Borneo Company, assisted by the British officers and the Government officials there, the services of guides being used for crossing the mountains.

"DAILY MAIL," *December 7th*, 1904.

Very Up-to-Date Method.

With a directorate greatly strengthened by recent additions, the North Borneo Company gave its usual annual dinner at the Hotel Cecil last evening. It is always a novel event. The guests smoke North Borneo cigars and drink North Borneo coffee, both excellent. They have annually an exhibition of bioscopic views of North Borneo, for which purpose the company specially commissions the Urban Trading Company, Ltd. to visit the country. This is an excellent investment, for, as the managing director, Mr. W. C. Cowie, last night stated, the exhibition last year thereby pro= duced half a million of extra capital.

LONDON.

Scenes and Types of Life in and about the World's Greatest City.

1059 ... THE CRYSTAL PALACE INTERIOR AND EXTERIOR PANORAMAS

150 feet

1060 ... LOOPING THE LOOP AT THE CRYSTAL PALACE
Showing five cars with passengers circling the loop.

50 feet

1061 ... SHOOTING THE CHUTES AT CRYSTAL PALACE
An exciting and excellent subject.   75 feet

1067 ... THE CRYSTAL PALACE PALM GARDENS
A splendid panoramic view of the visitors passing between statuary and Palm Gardens in the interior of the Palace.   75 feet

1243-4 ... MOTOR CLIMBING CONTEST AT CRYSTAL PALACE
Two motor cars climb the steep terrace steps leading to the Crystal Palace.   125 feet

1258 ... BOAT RACING ON THE THAMES
Showing two boat crews of eight oarsmen each at their best.   An exciting race

1283 ... ROLLER SKATE POLO MATCH AT CRYSTAL PALACE
A splendid film of an exciting game.   125 feet

1284 ... FINAL CUP TIE FOOTBALL MATCH AT CRYSTAL PALACE
The " Manchester City " Team, followed by the " Bolton Wanderers " are seen issuing from under the Grand Stand to the field. Splendid portraits of the men were here secured. The most important play of the match is shown as three cameras, one at each end and the middle of the field recorded everything of note. The spirited contests was concluded with the score: Manchester City, 1 goal; Bolton, 0. Played April 23, 1904.   250 feet

1332 ... WOMEN PHOTOGRAPHERS ON THE THAMES
Visitors to the Upper Thames, especially foreigners are easy prey to the journeyman photographer. This picture shows a middle aged woman securing a customer, posing him before her camera, getting into a portable " Darkroom," developing the plate and delivering the finished article to the evident satisfaction of the " sitter." 75 feet

1333 ... SUMMER LIFE ON THE UPPER THAMES
One of the charms of London Life is to be experienced during its summer season on the Upper Thames. The lively scenes on the river, the beautiful surrounding scenery and the general variety of incident, which this series portrays, lend much to the general interest of a most popular subject.   150 feet

1134 ... THROUGH BOULTER'S LOCK ON ASCOT SUN- DAY

Scene 1. Punts, boats and canoes waiting for the Lock gates to open.

Scene 2. The gates open and boats, so closely packed that no water is visible, crowd into the lock, when the gates are again closed and the basin filled, thus showing the hundreds of various water craft gradually rising as the water reaches the level of the river outside the further gates.

Scene 3. As these are opened, all seem bent upon getting their boats out first and everything is hustle and bustle until the lock is emptied and the operation is resumed with hundreds waiting by the lower gate. Thousands of spectators on both banks and the bridge watch this spirited scene. **200 feet**

"THE ERA."

Very pretty, indeed is the representation of " Ascot Sunday at Boulters' Lock," with its hundreds of different pleasure craft passing, in succession. between the well-known walls In addition, we have some picturesque views of riparian " bits," and a reproduction of a Thames " reach," with launches coming down it at a smart pace. Attractive, especially to dog lovers, are the illustrations of the recent Ladies' Kennel Club Show, in the Botanic Gardens, Regent's Park. The Charles Urban Trading Company, Limited, may be congratulated upon the choice of subjects for these capital films.

1340 ... A VISIT TO EARL'S COURT

Showing the open main Court crowded with visitors, enjoying the strains of music by orchestra performing from the band stands. We next show the Shooting the Chutes and the chute boats shooting under the Lagoon Bridge, also the electric launches and canoes passing along the lake, in the centre of which is noted the whirling boats attached to Sir Hiram Maxim's Captive Airship Structure. Full of life and variety. Splendid photographic quality. **150 feet**

1342 ... HOW LONDON STREETS ARE PAVED

Every phase of repaving London streets is shown in this series. Hundreds of workmen are employed laying concrete foundations, cementing top, laying cedar blocks, tarring same, spreading grave, and then going on to next section where operations are repeated. **125 feet**

1343 ... THE UMBRELLA TINKER ON THE HIGHWAYS

One meets with quaint characters in the roads leading to London. Such was our fortune when one of our operators espied a jolly old umbrella mender without a coin in his pocket who took on a job and finished same, and his reward at the nearest public house. **75 feet**

1344 ... THE CARELESS HOD CARRIER

A hod carrier ascending a ladder with a load of bricks, accidentally drops a few on the head of a man passing by who is thereby struck to earth, but assistance from next building arrives in due course. **50 feet**

1350 ... A VISIT TO THE ENGINE YARD AT PADDINGTON STATION

175 feet

1351 ... LONDON TO WALTON BY " BELLE " STEAMER

A delightful trip on the Thames can be enjoyed from the decks of these comodious steamers. First is shown the steamers taking on passengers, under way, views along the river, and, arrival and disembarking at Walton Pier. **150 feet**

1370 ... SOLDIERS OF THE BRITISH ARMY STATIONED IN LONDON

(See Military Series). **325 feet**

1374 ... LADIES' KENNEL CLUB SHOW AT THE BOTANICAL GARDENS

275 feet

1376 ... SALVATION ARMY INTERNATIONAL CONGRESS AT CRYSTAL PALACE

400 feet

1377 ... METROPOLITAN POLICE AMBULANCE DRILL
150 feet

1389 .. COACH MEET IN ROTTEN ROW, HYDE PARK

The Coach meet in the spring of the year when all the trees are bedecked with fresh foliage, and the walks and lawns of the Park, are crowded with visitors, is certainly a never-to-be-forgotten sight. Scores of four-in-hand Coaches pass amongst these lively surroundings in rapid procession. A splendid picture. **60 feet**

1396 ... THE FLOWER AND VEGETABLE MARKET AT COVENT GARDEN

This and the preceding picture were secured by the courtesy of Mr. J. Assbee, Supt. of Covent Garden Market.

Covent Garden is world-famed. Here London gets its main supply of cut flowers and pot plants, the majority of which are further distributed from this point through the Flower Girl and the Coster. Hundreds of these dealers throng the scene of activity where hard bargains are being driven and hundreds of thousands of plants and blossoms changing hands daily.

The picture starts with general views of the street approaches to and surrounding Covent Garden Market. Thousands of heavily laden wagons and carts arriving and departing, unloading or reloading. Stacks of baskets carried on heads of porters, either empty or filled. Fruit in crates, baskets, barrels, and bunches are seen everywhere. Women shelling peas, flower girls removing their purchases, vegetables being loaded on coster carts which are driven off as soon as filled, &c., &c. Whole volumes could be written in explanation of the great activity as portrayed by this series which is the first of its kind, the scenes being faithful reproductions of Covent Garden life in full swing. **275 feet**

1397 ... THE LONDON GHETTO — Sunday Morning in Petticoat Lane, Whitechapel

We are much indebted to Mr. E. Barnett, the " Kosher King," for facilities placed at our disposal, by which assistance only was it possible to procure the successful results depicted in this series.

One of the most interesting sights of London life is to be had in Middlesex Street (formerly Petticoat Lane) on Sunday morning and

Fridays, the latter being the Jewish market day. The series comprises about 50 pictures of the most interesting incidents, both vendors

No. 1397 Types of Petticoat Lane

and buyers being faithfully depicted. The first view shows a general picture of the entire length of the Lane with its thousands of stalls and surging crowds of buyers all seeking after a bargain. Here one can purchase anything from rusty nails to gold? watches, eel jelly to live geese and chickens, clothes, fish, ice creams, vegetables, carpet, old shoes, keys, saws, iron safes, meats; get your teeth drawn, your corns cured, second hand garments to fit everyone, china and crockery, eggs, butter, &c., &c.

For human types of East London and their occupations on the mornings of the specified days there are none more interesting or picturesque. This series portrays all absolutely true to nature.

250 feet

1400 ... **THE LONDON COSTER AT PLAY**

There are a few occasions when the Coster absolutely abandons all care and worry and gives up the day to pleasure of one sort or another, as on a Bank Holiday and at such popular resort as the Crystal Palace. Here he and his "Arriet" are seen at their best. Dancing on the Terrace to the tune of a mouth-organ, imitating ballet dancing—doing the cake walk "en concert" and such other diversions which only the coster can get the most enjoyment from. Excellent quality **150 feet**

1401 ... **THE COSTERS' CAKE WALK**

Showing four couples doing the Cake Walk surrounded by hundreds of spectators and friends who cheer them on in their gymnastic efforts to outdo one another. Full of fun and action.

75 feet

1402 ... **HOLIDAY MAKERS DANCING ON THE CRYSTAL PALACE TERRACE**

A group of merrymakers in which the coster and his "donah" predominates, making the best of the day's outing. Dancing, singing and general roystering seem to be the height of their amusement.

50 feet

1410 ... **BROCK'S DISPLAY OF FIREWORKS AT THE CRYSTAL PALACE**

A miscellaneous series of Set pieces, Catherine Wheels, Rockets, Mines and Roman Candles; photographed during the setting off of the display by Messrs. Brock & Son at the Crystal Palace. The first firework display ever successfully bioscoped.

125 feet

NOTE.—For more elaborate set, See 1409.

1468 ... PANORAMA OF LONDON RIVER FRONT — from London Bridge to Greenwich

SCENE.

1—Scene at London Bridge with Steamer leaving
2—Customs House and Billingsgate Fish Market
3—Warehouses and Shipping along the Pool
4—Steamers and barges plying on the Thames
5—Approaching the Tower of London
6—Panorama of the Thames front of the Tower of London
7—Panorama of Thames—Passing Tower Bridge
8—The Thames Steamers under way
9—Arrival and general view of Greenwich   **200 feet**

1469 ... LIFE ON THE UPPER THAMES

A truly animated sight amidst picturesque surroundings, as punts, Canoes, Yachts and small boats laden with holiday makers in gay attire pass by the camera and crowd around the base of the lock gate to be ultimately admitted to the higher waters above the lock. Splendid photographic quality   **175 feet**

1471 ... THE S.S. "CLEOPATRA" LEAVING DOCK FOR THAMES TRIP

Showing the boarding of the steamer by passengers, casting off the line, withdrawing the gang-plank, and the steamer leaving the dock for the trip down the river Thames.   **50 feet**

1473 ... THE BANK OF ENGLAND AND MANSION HOUSE

The "heart and pulse" of the World's Metropolis with its great volume of traffic diverging in all directions. The busiest street scene in the world.   **60 feet**

1488 ... CHUTE BOAT RACES AT EARL'S COURT

Three "Shooting the Chute" boats entered for the race, and the manner in which this unique craft is managed around sharp turnings and propelled along the course speaks much for the proficiency of the crew.   **75 feet**

1489 .. CHAMPIONSHIP GONDOLA RACES AT EARL'S COURT

See description under "Races, Sports and Contests."   **100 feet**

1491-2 Supplied in one roll.   Total Length 500 feet.

"THE DAILY MAIL, *Dec. 7th*, 1904.

Very Up-to-Date Method.

With a directorate greatly strengthened by recent additions, the North Borneo Company gave its usual Annual Dinner at the Hotel Cecil last evening. It is always a novel event. The guests smoke North Borneo cigars and drink North Borneo coffee, both excellent. They have annually an Exhibition of **Bioscope Views of North Borneo,** for which purpose the Company specially commissions the Charles Urban Trading Company, Ltd. to visit the country. This is an excellent investment, for, as the managing director, Mr. W. C. Cowie, last night stated, **the Exhibition last year thereby produced half a million of extra capital.**

Can we help you Increase your Capital?

CAUTION.—The resale or Exhibition of this Film is prohibited in the UNITED KINGDOM and the UNITED STATES OF AMERICA, where the exclusive exhibition rights have been acquired.

The Film is supplied on these conditions only, and acceptance is taken as a legal agreement to these terms.

"LIVING LONDON."

A Grand Series of Pictures showing varying phases of life, scenes, and events in the

. . World's Metropolis . .

Photographed by our staff of four Bioscopic Artists during the Summer and Autumn of 1904, in co-operation with

Mr. GEORGE R. SIMS

Editor of the "REFEREE" *and* "LIVING LONDON."

NOTE.—The 280 different views comprising this series depict sights along a route over the most important thoroughfares of London, not merely showing street scenes with the principal edifices, monuments, bridges, etc., but include "snapshots" of the various human types and their different occupations and pleasures to be found in all the districts touched upon in our "Bioscopic Ramble," from fashionable West End London to the slums of Whitechapel, etc.

Each complete series of "LIVING LONDON" *will be supplied,* **gratis,** *with a copy of the Descriptive Lecture given by* **Mr. Frank Stevens** *during the highly successful run of this series with the* "**Urbanora**" **Entertainments** *at the Alhambra Theatre, London.*

1501   Order of Pictures.

Section A.—London sleeps—London wakes—Early morning in Knightsbridge—The Nursemaid and the Policeman—Regulating the traffic—The Motor Asphalt Repair Outfit get an early start—The finish of the Tea-room Girls' Walking Match to Hyde Park—Hyde Park Corner—A Coach Meet in Hyde Park—Duke of Wellington's Monument and Arch as seen from St. George's Hospital—Constitution Hill—Buckingham Palace—The New Mall—Sparrows and Pigeons in St. James' Park—Visitors crossing the Bridge—Boys Fishing and Wading in the Lake, St. James' Park.   **300 feet**

Section B.—Guard Mount at St. James' Palace—The Horse Guard's Parade Ground, end of Mall—The traffic in Whitehall—The Colonial Offices—St. Margaret's Church and the Clock Tower from Parliament Street—Lord Beaconsfield's Statue on Primrose Day—Scenes before the Houses of Parliament—The Embankment from Westminster Bridge—Houses of Parliament from Surrey side—The Penny Steamer starting from Westminster Bridge—Panorama of the Buildings on Victoria Embankment, including view of Cleopatra's Needle—Children on steps leading to the Thames throwing their dog into the water to try its swimming capabilities.   **250 feet**

N

Section C.—Incidents at a drinking fountain and trough on the Embankment —Panorama of the Embankment from a Steamer—Passing under Waterloo Bridge—Somerset House—The Naval Reserve Training Ship, H.M.S. Buzzard—London Bridge—Billingsgate—Customs House— Thames Barges and Steamers—The Pool—Distant view of Tower Bridge—Opening of Tower Bridge for passing ship, as seen from the roadway—Closing Bridge and resumption of traffic—The Tower of London from Tower Hill—The Tower of London from the Thames— Dock Labourers unloading Lumber—Method of dumping City refuse into barges. **300 feet**

Section D.—Children of the Slums in the Minories—The Scissors Grinder— The Ghetto—Middlesex Street on Sunday morning, showing the various types of people inhabiting this and the surrounding White- chapel district—The crowded "Petticoat Lane"—The Shop of Barnett the "Kosher King"—General view of Crowds and Stalls as viewed from Messrs. Barnett's building—Miscellaneous vendors of old boots, collar buttons and everything imaginable—The Auctioneer of Hand- kerchiefs: "eight silks at a bob"—Old Clothes Merchant—Eggs, Vegetables and Fish Stalls—The old Onion Woman—Auctioneering live Chickens—The Jew Pants Pedlar—The Orange Woman and surrounding groups—Capturing live Eels **300 feet**.

Section E.—A "Tuppenny" Grab for live Eels—Temperance Procession passing through Whitechapel district—Coster Flower Vendor— Costers and their Carts driving home from Market—"'Arry" and "'Arriet" off on a Jaunt—Accident to the Moke—A Whitechapel Bird Store—Street Performance by a "Strong Man"—Baker's Man, Organ-grinder, and Flower Girls—"Take yer Portrait, Sir?" Street Photographer—Old Keys and Locks and Hardware—Street Stalls off City Road—The polite Vegetable Vendor—Shrimps, Crabs and Lobsters—Fresh Fish—News Stands on Finsbury Pavement— Scene in Newgate and Aldersgate Street. **300 feet**

Section F.—Busy Newgate Street—Holborn from Holborn Viaduct— Farringdon Street and Holborn Viaduct—Farringdon Road as viewed from the Viaduct—Long Lane and Meat Markets—Market Buildings from St. John Street—Holborn Circus—T.M. King and Queen at Holborn Bars—Receiving the City Sword on their visit to the Guild- hall—The Old Flower Woman at Regent Circus—The Bus Driver— Seeing London from top of a Bus—Regent Street—Regulating the Traffic at Piccadilly Circus—Panorama of Piccadilly Circus—The Flower Girls on Piccadilly Fountain Steps—Brigade of "Urbanora" Sandwich Men. **300 feet**

Section G.— The Sandwichman—The Haymarket—The Carlton Hotel and Haymarket Theatre—Pall Mall, East—St. Martin's Church—National Art Gallery—Trafalgar Square—The Nelson Monument—Landseer's Lions—The Playing Fountains—Feeding the Pigeons in Trafalgar Square—Charing Cross Station—Receiving Milk Supply—The Busy Strand—The usual "Streets up"—Strand Improvements in front of New Savoy Hotel Building—The Cecil Hotel Entrance—Traffic over Waterloo Bridge, seen from the Strand—Covent Garden— General Views of the Vegetable and Flower Markets—Arrival of Waggon Loads of Fruits—Sampling Berries, &c., &c. **300 feet**

Section H.—Covent Garden Market Scenes : (15 views)—Girls and Women Shelling Peas—The Central Hall—The Flower Market—Strand Gutter Merchants—The Strand, shewing St. Clement Danes' Church—The Salvation Army Temple (temporarily erected on the site of Strand Improvement during the International Salvation Army Congress)—another view of the Strand—Law Courts—Passage leading to Temple Gardens—a quite nook off the Strand—Fleet Street—St. Paul's, from Ludgate Circus—Kerbstone Merchants—Electric Light Repair Gang --The Bootblack **300 feet**

Section I.—Newgate and Cheapside—Robert Peel Monument—Cheapside and Bow Church—Princes and Queen Victoria Streets—Moorgate Street and Bank of England—" The Old Lady of Theadneedle Street —Panorama of the " Heart of London " (from the Mansion House) finishing with the Royal Exchange, and the tremendous traffic at this point. **150 feet**

SUPPLIED COMPLETE ONLY.

Total Length, 2,500 feet.   Price, £62 10s.

(Duration of Exhibit 45 minutes.)

CAUTION.—The resale or Exhibition of this Film is prohibited in the **UNITED KINGDOM** and the **UNITED STATES OF AMERICA**, where the exclusive exhibiton rights have been acquired.

The Film is supplied on these conditions only, and acceptance is taken as a legal agreement to these terms.

JUVENILE SERIES.

1088 ... THE CHILDREN IN GOAT CARTS

A familiar sight at the south coast seaside resorts. Full of action, goats and kiddies. **60 feet**

1325 ... THE KIDDIES DINNER

Showing three young children at dinner, the facial expression of the youngsters shows ve y clearly that they quite appreciate the good things of the lavishly spread table before them. **50 feet**

1326 ... THE CHILDREN'S GARDEN DINNER PARTY

We have here quite a number of young people at dinner, being assiduously looked after by the mama, they enjoy things immensely, much fun is created towards the end of the repast by their efforts, and the most juvenile member in the first place to resent and next to appreciate the humour that may be obtained by assuming papa's hat. **150 feet**

1327 ... A ROMP ON THE LAWN

This is a very good film, which every lover of children will fully appreciate the rolling about on the lawn amidst the children's wicker and other chairs makes a varied and entertaining subject. **150 feet**

N 2

1328 ... **"CHILDREN CRY FOR IT"**

This shows a charming little tot being teased tremendously regarding chocolate, and resenting the teasing immensely the tears and the sorrow of the little one is well depicted, until at the final the loving kiss of mama restores comparative calm and he is carried off in triumph, the place being taken by a demure little maiden who eats up a luscious piece of pine apple with great gusto.   **125 feet**

1329 ... **A JUVENILE COMEDIAN**

This charming little comedian in his hurry to anticipate manhood shows what he can do with pa's hat, pipe, and sporting cap, and the energy of his action and the extreme breadth of the fun is extremely pleasing.   **100 feet**

1353 ... **BOYS DRILL AT THE REEDHAM ORPHANAGE**

The boys of this orphanage at physical drill, and executing many pleasing evolutions showing designs of geometric pattern which folding and unfolding with a precision of movement that is really mar vellous, makes this a most desirable subject.   **15 0feet**

COMIC SERIES.

1010 ... **FROLICS OF THE WATER CARRIERS OF CALCUTTA**

Showing a Hindoo wedding procession passing along the streets of Calcutta, and the assembled crowd are afterwards treated to a cold douche by the water carriers of the city, who ply the crystal stream upon the assembled sightseers in a most profuse and vigorous manner.   **75 feet**

1043 ... **INITIATING A NOVICE TO THE SNOW SHOE CLUB**

This showing the initiation of a new member in the person of the Photographer, who being unceremoniously thrown into a blanket, is vigorously tossed and tossed again until he must feel that Canada is after all not such a very cold country.   **50 feet**

1051 ... **FUN ON THE RINK AFTER A SNOWSTORM**

The fun attendant on clearing the ice rink is here shown, both ladies and gentlemen briskly engage iu the operations amid the bustle and excitement of the winter sportsman's delight.   **75 feet**

1384 .. **THE BATHERS' REVENGE**

Some youths enjoying a refreshing dip in a stream, having left their wardrobe on a seat on the bank. A spooning couple coming up, toss the bathers' belongings contemptuously aside, and the bathers in revenge pull the seat, and so tumble the interrupters into the water, from which they escape after only the most determined and ludicrous exertions.   **75 feet**

1385 ... **BRUTALITY REWARDED**

A beggar woman solicits alms from a passing pedestrian, who not only refuses them, but turns on the woman and handles her roughly. Others quickly gather, and he finds himself belaboured on all sides and attempts with difficulty to escape. He is pursued to the river bank, seized, and flung ignominiously into the all-encircling waters.   **75 feet**

1386 ... **THE MEDDLING POLICEMAN**

Here we see a too oppressive police officer interrupt a pair who who are evidently diagnosing the contents of a provision basket; they return the attack, wind the guardian of the law in strings of sausages, deluge him with flour and other condiments, until his appearance is less picturesque than pitiable. **125 feet**

1414 ... **FLYNN'S BIRTHDAY CELEBRATION**

A very laughable account of how Flynn is being visited by his friend, whose greeting of Mrs. Flynn is certainly very cordial, goes for a refresher, and having partaken not wisely but too well, returns to celebrate the birthday. The series of episodes and the havoc wrought in the Flynn household by their enactment is brimful of laughter, and the final and somewhat unconventional disappearance of Mrs. Flynn, wrong end up, through the window, means thus a proper scream. **125 feet**

1415 ... **THE BITER BITTEN**

Two tramps of the fighting order lie in ambush for a seemingly unsuspecting cyclist, who, cuter than they counted dodges them into belabouring each other, and completes their discomfiture by returning with a savage dog to accelerate their flight. **50 feet**

MILITARY AND POLICE.

No. 3023. General Kuropatkin reviews 1st Siberian Sharpshooters.

1002 ... **REVIEW OF THE VARIOUS BRANCHES OF THE ARMY OF FRANCE**

An excellent marching subject, including sections of every branch of the French Army—the Infantry, Artillery, Dragoons, Hussars, Cuirassiers, &c., ending with imposing sight of a Charge of 3,000 Troops. **275 feet**

1002b ... **THE ZOUAVES OF ALGIERS AND FRENCH MILITARY ON REVIEW AT VINCENNES**

The first occasion of the French Algerian Regiment being bioscoped in France. An excellent marching subject. **150 feet**

1011 ... **CLUB EXERCISES OF THE 15th SIKHS**

These club exercises by one of the finest native regiments in India were repeated after the assault at arms at the Durbar, for the special benefit of the Bioscope operator. **125 feet**

1012 ... REVIEW AND FIRING MANŒUVRES OF THE 15th SIKHS UNDER COMMAND OF LIEUT.-COL. G. F. ROWCROFT, D.S.O.

This full dress review of a native regiment, which European officers are always proud to command, was specially granted to the Bioscope operator. **175 feet**

1130 ... SANTOS DUMONT IN HIS AIRSHIP SAILING OVER THE REVIEW GROUNDS IN PARIS, AND SALUTING PRESIDENT LOUBET FROM OVERHEAD.

During a recent Review of Troops before President Loubet, Santos Dumont navigated his Airship right over the heads of the Presidential party, and in passing fired a salute from mid-air. Splendid portrait of M. Loubet. **60 feet**

1131 ... PRESIDENT LOUBET DECORATING FRENCH OFFICERS

A close view of President Loubet pinning decorations on the breasts of deserving officers and gendarmes, concluding the ceremony in each instance by kissing the soldier on the cheek, as is the custom in France. **50 feet**

1132 ... REVIEW OF THE ALGERIAN REGIMENT BEFORE THE PRESIDENT OF FRANCE

This is a picturesque scene of the French regiment of Algerian troops, marching in company formation past the camera. **50 feet**

Bioscoping Military operations on frozen Lake Baikal.

1145 ... REVIEW OF TROOPS BY LORD DUNDONALD

This subject depicts the Review of the Flower of Canadian Soldiery — including Infantry, Cavalry, Artillery, and every branch of the Army. An inspiring sight as these stalwart troopers file past Lord Dundonald and his Staff, in column and company formation. **150 feet**

1255 KING EDWARD AND THE GORDON HIGHLANDERS

An excellent portrait of T.M. the King and Queen, escorted by a Troop of Scotch Hussars and a regiment of the picturesque Gordons. **75 feet**

1359 ... MILITARY GARDEN PARTY AT SOFIA, BULGARIA
50 feet

1365 ... CAVALRY MANŒUVRES IN THE BALKANS
100 feet

1366 ... A MOUNTAIN BATTERY OF BULGARIAN ARTILLERY
75 feet

1367 ... SCHAUMLER GARRISON DRILL FOR RECRUITS
125 feet

1370 ... THE SOLDIERS OF THE BRITISH ARMY—
Past, Present and Future

Past.—The Old Heroes of Past Battles.—Chelsea Pensioners.

Present.—The Scots Guards and Gordon Highlanders at Buckingham Palace.

Future.—The Boys of the Duke of York Military School.

The past, present and prospective material of Britain's fighting machine is here excellently depicted. The Chelsea Pensioners, the heroes of a hundred fights march past, giving fine portraits. They are next viewed in panorama during recreation time. Then we see the present—the Guards and Highlanders at Buckingham Palace. The Boys of the Duke of York's School make a picturesque and fitting finish, as they march past in different formations, to the best and most typical British military picture ever secured.

No. 3019. Russian Infantry on the March.

Reprint from "THE ERA."

The splendid series of views shown at the Alhambra by means of the Urban Bioscope forms an important part of the attractive programme at this popular place of amusement. The films depicting three stages of the careers of the soldiers of the British Army appeal strongly to patriotic feeling. We are first shown the veterans at Chelsea Hospital; then the Scots Guards passing along the Mall; and lastly, the Boys of the Duke of York's Royal Military School marching with "eyes left" in the most approved fashion of respectful acknowledgment of the presence of a superior.

An excellent Series of Military Subjects. Total length, 325 feet

1377 ... AMBULANCE DRILL OF METROPOLITAN POLICE

This is an excellent picture of Police ambulance and first aid drill. The smart and business-like methods at first aid and stretcher-bearer operations are very fine, and as the men are close up to the camera large, sharp, clearly defined images make this an exceptionally good film. **150 feet**

THE "INVASION OF ENGLAND."

BY GENERAL FRENCH AND THE BLUE ARMY.

1452 ... THE MILITARY CAMP AT SOUTHAMPTON

Commander of the Bulgarian Army
(See page 165)

This picture in the form of a panoramic view of the camp, shows a varied and interesting scene of great activity, soldiers moving busily about and the piled arms in the foreground denoting readiness to strike camp at any moment. **75 feet**

1453 ... THE CAMP POST OFFICE

The Camp Post Office is usually the centre of the greatest activity, and here at the postal tent its many officials are seen busily engaged in attending to the innumerable duties of receiving and despatching service and other correspondence. **50 feet**

1454 ... TOMMY ATKINS PRE· PARING FOR INSPECTION

A close view of "Tommys" in front of their tents going through the morning shave and other congenial tastes. As the images are large and clearly defined, this is an excellent subject, the facial expressions being well brought out of the "Tommy" shaving himself while his companion holds the mirror up to Nature. **75 feet**

1455 ... GAME OF "BIFF" IN CAMP

The game of Biff is an exceedingly amusing and somewhat vigorous pastime, to which the soldiers delight to devote their spare moments. That the game here is diverting is evidenced by the keen interest displayed by both participants and spectators. **60 feet**

1456 ... FUN IN CAMP

This is a good film of work and play in camp, "Biff" and Button polishing amusingly alternating. The final melee at the interruption is unusually animated and spirited, making a first-rate finish. **75 feet**

1457 ... CAMP "KITCHENS" IN FULL BLAST

As a great general has said, "An army marches on its stomach," it is good to see in this picture that our military authorities accept the truism. Here the full activity of the camp kitchens is well portrayed, the bustle and excitement of the scene and the tranquil ascent of the smoke from the fires affording excellent contrasts.

100 feet

No. 1459. Argyle Highlanders

1458 ... GRENADIER GUARDS ON THE MARCH

A fine view of this noted regiment in full marching order carrying all equipment as in time of actual warfare. As they pass close to the camera. every detail is well seen, and the subject is certain to be well received by any audience. **75 feet**

1459 ... MARCH OF THE ARGYLE HIGHLANDERS

A magnificent picture of this regiment of Highlanders, with their characteristic swinging step, marching directly before the camera. The detail shown is unusually fine, and the completeness of the picture enhances its value. **100 feet**

1460 ... ROYAL SCOTS GUARDS LEAVING CAMP.

An excellent view of the Scots Guards, similar to the above, to which it could well be added, all being clean and crisp photography.

75 feet

1461 MILITARY TRANSPORTS ON THE HIGH ROADS

The important sections of waggon transport and Military horses are here shown, and the briskness of the whole scene, comined with the large images obtained at close quarters of the

No. 1462. Loading Army Transports

concluding section of the transport, make a fine picture. **100 feet**

1462 ... LOADING HORSES, GUNS, &c., ON BOARD TRANS-PORTS

This is one of the finest pictures of this class that could possibly be wished. The hoisting aboard of the guns and gun-carriages, and the hoisting aboard of the horses, make it an ideal Military transport picture. The unique effects secured by the direction of the lighting in this film is particularly good. **200 feet**

1463 ... EMBARKATION OF HIGHLANDERS AND GRENADIERS

Good views are here presented of the soldiers alertly ascending the ship's gangways, the regiments shown being the Grenadiers and the Highlanders. **75 feet**

1464 ... TROOPS CROWDING DECK OF TRANSPORTS

The transport leaving Southampton, showing the decks crowded with eager Tommies as they "sail away" in eager anticipation of "hard fighting" in the Essex Downs.

50 feet

No. 1464. Troops on Transports.

1465 ... TROOP TRANSPORTS AT SEA

The transports going to sea, and views of the surrounding ships as they sail outwards from Southampton Harbour. **75 feet**

1466 ... LANDING OF TROOPS, GUNS, &c., ON SHORES OF ESSEX

In this excedingly interesting film a complete series of the operations of the invaders are depicted. The arrival of the transports off the Essex coast, the landing of the troops by boats and pontoon, dragging the big guns up the sands, and the thousand and one incidents of the landing of the invading Army, give a most graphic and realistic idea of what might actually be expected in real warfare. The getting into readiness and the marching inland afford many striking pictures: the spirited horses of the Artillery briskly rushing up the guns on steep inclines, and the horse and foot troops briskly accompanying, make this film one of great interest and value. All the best points of view were selected, and the series of pictures secured leave nothing to be desired for sprightliness and quality.

SCENES—
1—**Landing of Troops** by small boats.
2—**Landing of Argyle Highlanders** by boats and floats.
3—**Highlanders ascending** the coast inland.
4—**Engineer Corps** landing sections of pontoons.

No. 1466 b.   Artillery rushing a hill.

5—**Scots Guards** proceeding inland.

6—**Troops hauling** in barges and unloading horses

7—**Troops hauling Maxims** and water carts uphill.

8—**Troops hauling pontoons** and transports uphill

9—**Artillery,** drawn by horses, dashing up the ascent.

10—**Massed Troops** marching inland.
11—**Field Artillery** negociating the hill in gallop.
12—**Cavalry** and spare Artillery horses.
13—**More troops** descending coast.
14—**Argyle Highlanders** rushing up a hill.

A spirited Military subject, always of interest. Full of action throughout.

525 feet

1499 ... OPENING OF PARLIAMENT, 1905
Showing the Royal Procession and State Carriage leaving Buckingham Palace. **150 feet**

THE GREAT RUSSO-JAPANESE WAR
For Military Subjects see " Russo-Jap War " Series.

TURKISH AND BULGARIAN MILITARY SERIES
Are described under " Macedonia and Bulgarai."

General Kuropatkin and General Mah.

JAPAN (General).

1261 ... THE JAPANESE ENSIGN FLUTTERING IN THE BREEZE

An appropriate picture to precede the Japanese Series.

Price 6d. per foot (minimum length 20 feet.)

1301 ... JAPANESE SWORD COMBAT

A scene in Tokio showing two expert swordsmen giving an exhibition of the dexterious manner of handling the keen blade in defence and attack. **125 feet**

No. 1302.   Sword and Lance Combat at Tokio.

1302   JAPANESE SWORD AND LANCE COMBAT

Another competition with the long Japanese sword and the lance. Full of action. **100 feet**

1303 ... TWO-HANDED SWORD COMBAT

This is one of the liveliest of duels, each combatant being armed with the two-handed sword. Truly a dangerous game, especially when enacted by experts who "give and take" according to the slightest opportunities offered.

100 feet.

1305 ... JAPANESE WOMEN JUGGLING WITH SPINNING TOPS

One of the sights in the street of any Japanese town are these women jugglers who in this instance perform all manners of difficult tricks with the spinning Top.

100 feet

Bioscoping Japanese Jugglers in Tokio.

1307 ... THE JAPANESE OGRE

A Group of Jap Kiddies

An automatic toy sold in the streets of Japanese towns for the low price (about the value of 2d.) shows a wood model of a hidious figure taking huge bites out of a watermelon (labelled "Cossacks") evidently intended to portray the American Negro eating Melon this being adopted to depict the Japs devouring the Russians.

50 feet

1308 ... BOYS' SPORTS AT TOKIO

Japs young and old enjoying themselves on the ladder, horizontal bar, swings and other means for gymnastic exercises. **50 feet**

1309 ... JAPANESE BALANCING ON SWINGING LOG

This source of amusement would "catch on" with the British Holiday Crowds. It consists of a very long log in its natural state, being swung between two chains suspended from trees at either end. As many as twenty boys and men jump on to this swinging log at one time and perform the most comical attitudes in their endeavor to retain their balance. **75 feet**

No. 1310. Military Funeral of the Japanese Standard Bearer.

1310 ... FUNERAL PROCESSION IN STREETS OF TOKIO

A most impressive sight, showing a funeral of a naval officer killed during the naval battle off Port Arthur. The companions of the fallen hero accompanying his remains, dressed in their modern uniform while they are preceded and followed by quaintly costumed priests, &c. An unique picture. **150 feet**

GREAT TEMPLE PROCESSION AT NIKKO.

1311 ... THE FESTIVAL OF THE TEMPLES AT NIKKO.

The great annual festival of the temples is held on the 1st and 2nd June. The sacred palanquins (Mikoski) containing the divine symbols are then borne in procession, when ancient costumes, masks and armour are donned by the villagers, old and young alike taking part in the display.

ORDER OF THE PROCESSION.

THE SACRED CHAIRS start from Futawara Temple.
THE SAKAKI (Sacred Tree), carried by 150 men.
ONE HUNDRED LANCERS.

LION AND LIONESS, each carried by three men.
EIGHT SACRED DANCING WOMEN.
TWO SHINTO PRIESTS, on horseback.
FIFTY GUN-CARRIERS.
FIFTY BOW-CARRIERS
FIFTY SPEAR MEN.
ONE HUNDRED ARMOURED MEN.
TEN MEN carrying hawks.

TWO STANDS for Sacred Chairs each carried by two men.
THE CHIEF SHINTO PRIEST, of first rank on horseback.
FIFTY MEN in uniform.

No. 1311. Procession of the Temples at Nikko

THE CHIEF SACRED CHAIR, carried by fifty white attired men and forty guards.

A GOHEI (Sacred Paper), carried by a Shinto Priest.

A SACRED CHAIR, carried by fifty white attired men and twenty guards.

A DRUM, carried by three white attired men.

A BELL, carried by one white attired man.

TWO STANDS for Sacred Chairs.

A SACRED CHAIR, carried by fifty men and forty guards.

THREE SHINTO PRIESTS on horseback.

Total length 300 feet.

1312 ... THE DANCE OF THE GEISHA

A group of charming Jap girls performing a graceful dance. Full of action and best photographic quality.
75 feet

1313 ... THE GEISHA MINSTRELS

A pretty picture of three Jap girls performing on quaint - looking instruments.
50 feet

No. 1312.   Dance of the Geisha

1314 ... JAPANESE GIRLS SMOKING

The Geisha enjoys her pipe as well as anyone.   In thi groupe is a very young girl, who is induced by the others to try her very first smoke.   The result is comical.   **75 feet**

No. 1314.   Japanese Girls Smoking

1315 ... THE GEISHA ENJOYS HER PIPE

The Japanese pipe, which only holds a pinch of tobacco, and has to be lighted for each puff of smoke, is one of the means of lending enjoyment, as well as killing time to the Geisha girl.

Between puffs — smile — a n d   g r e e t i n g.   A splendid picture.

60 feet

3006 ... IRRIGATING T H E   P A D D Y FIELDS AND HARVESTING RICE IN JAPAN

Cultivating and harvesting the main Food Supply of the Japanese Army.   **100 feet**

3008 ... **HOME LIFE OF THE JOLLY JAP**
A splendid picture of the Japanese with their domestic pastimes.
100 feet

3009 ... **THE GEISHAS OF THE FLOWERY KINGDOM**
An excellent series of four views of Japanese maidens playing, singing and dancing.
100 feet

3010 ... **JAPANESE ACTORS PERFORMING IN DRAMA**
A study of expressions and expertness of the Jap actor. Three views of exceeding interest.
150 feet

3011 ... **A JAPANESE SWORDSMAN ATTACKED BY ROBBERS**
Showing the manner in which an expert sword and lance may can hold his own against great odds.
100 feet

3012 ... **STREET LIFE IN THE MIKADO'S CAPITAL**
Seven charming pictures of principal views in Tokio and surrounding district. Full of life and interest.
225 feet

3012* ... **STREET SCENES IN TOKIO**
Shorter series of the above.
150 feet

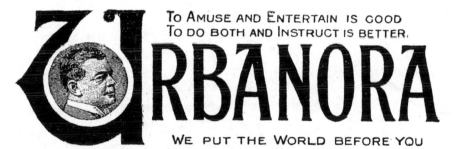

TO AMUSE AND ENTERTAIN IS GOOD
TO DO BOTH AND INSTRUCT IS BETTER.

WE PUT THE WORLD BEFORE YOU

A Superior Entertainment for the Refined Public.

THE LATEST SENSATION.

THE LIVING HISTORY OF THE ...

Russo=Japan War

In THREE SERIES, viz.:

"The Russian Army in Manchuria."
"The Siege of Port Arthur."
"The Surrender of Port Arthur."

ABSOLUTELY the ONLY GENUINE LIFE MOTION PICTURES SECURED.

O

MISCELLANEOUS.

Mr. J. Rosenthal, our War Correspondent, at Work.

1005 ... THE DEMOLITION OF THE GIGANTIC CHIMNEY
Showing every phase of the demolition of the gigantic chimney, from the operation of saturating the pile with paraffin, lighting the under-propping. The Burning Pile, the fall and breaking of the Shaft, crowds surging over the debris. A fine picture. **125 feet.**

1008 ... THE KURSAAL AND REVOLVING TOWER AT SOUTH-END ON A BANK HOLIDAY

100 feet.

1034 ... A DARING DAYLIGHT BURGLARY. Exciting Chase and Capture by the Police.

Excellent photographic quality. Natural scenery and surroundings

The opening scene shows the garden of a gentleman's country house. The burglar enters the yard by scaling the wall, and, after looking round, cautiously breaks open the window and enters the house. Meanwhile, a boy has observed the burglar at his task from the top of a wall, and the scene then changes to the village police-station, showing the boy running in and informing the police. The policemen enter the yard by the wall, one goes inside the house while the other keeps watch. The scene then changes to the house-top where a desperate struggle ensues between the policeman and burglar in which the former is *thrown from the roof* to the road below.

The scene next changes to the road where the body of the police-man is lying. His comrade summonses the Ambulance which arrives and conveys the body to the mortuary.

Meanwhile, two policeman take up the chase along the country road, where another desperate struggle takes place. The burglar throws his assailant to the ground and escapes over the wall, hotly pursued by another policeman.

The next scenes depict the exciting chase down the cliff, over the stepping stones of the river.

The scene again changes to a country railway station showing the train. Just as the train moves off, the burglar rushes across the platform and enters a compartment The policeman is seen hurrying after his quarry, but too late.

The last picture shows another railway station, some miles away to which the police have telegraphed, and just as the burglar alights from the train he is promptly captured by a policeman, but only after a terrible struggle in which the burglar is thrown to the ground, and with the assistance of porters he is eventually handcuffed and marched off, forming a splendid and rousing finish to one of the most sensational pictures ever cinematographed. *Creates unbounded applause and enthusiasm.* **275 feet.**

1056 ... THE CRYSTAL PALACE (INTERIOR AND EXTERIOR) PANORAMAS

The Crystal Palace is par excellence the sight of London, and it is well portrayed, interior and exterior, in this most excellent picture.

No. 1276b The Parthenon, Athens

The vast interior is first shown with its tropical palm gardens, through which crowds of pleasure seekers are briskly moving about. The crystal fountains, the statuary, and the other components of a beautiful scene, are well rendered; then we have panoramas of the outside gardens, with crowds of gaily dressed holiday makers, and lastly the panorama of the Fairy Archipelago and water chutes, which, with swings in background, and electric launches on lake in foreground, make up a most animated and interesting picture. **150 feet.**

1067 ... PANORAMA OF THE PALM GARDENS, CRYSTAL PALACE

75 feet

1094 ... PROF. STANLEY SPENCER STARTING HIS AIRSHIP FROM THE CRYSTAL PALACE PREPARATORY TO HIS FLIGHT AROUND ST. PAUL'S, September 17th 1903.

The first attempt made by Professor Stanley Spencer to navigate his Airship around St. Paul's. The only picture showing in detail the structure of the airship, transporting same from its shed at the Crystal Palace, the start, and sailing in mid-air. **150 feet**

o 2

"HIAWATHA."

THE MESSIAH OF THE OJIBWAY.

*A Presentation in Dramatic form of Longfellow's Poem,
"Song of Hiawatha,"*

Enacted by North American Indians of the Ojibway Tribe at
Desbarats, Ontario.

THE PASSION PLAY OF AMERICA.

Haiwatha—The Warriors Assembling for Council . . .

ORDER OF PICTURES.

1 ... **THE GREAT SPIRIT CALLS THE WARRIORS OF
MANY NATIONS TO COUNCIL**

2 ... **INDIANS MANIFESTING HOSTILITY.** The Pipe of Peace

3 ... **NOKORNIS SINGS THE PAPOOSE** (Baby Hiawatha) **TO
SLEEP**

4 ... **HIAWATHA** (the Boy) **LEARNING TO SHOOT WITH BOW
AND ARROW**

5 ... **HIAWATHA** (the Youth) **TAUGHT TO DANCE BY THE WARRIORS**

6 ... **THE TRIBAL DANCE OF THE OJIBWAYS**

7 ... **THE MYSTERIOUS DEPARTURE OF HIAWATHA TO WOO MINNEHAHA**

8 ... **SCENE IN THE WOODS.** Hiawatha Stalks and Kills a Deer

9 ... **HIAWATHA LAYS THE DEER AT THE FEET OF MINNEHAHA**

Hiawatha and his Bride depart from the Old Arrow Maker.

10 ... **THE TRIBE WELCOMING THE RETURN OF HIAWATHA AND HIS BRIDE**

11 ... **THE WARRIORS REJOICING**

The " Bridal Dance " by the tribe, led by Hiawatha and Minnehaha.

12 ... **ARRIVAL OF PAU-PUK-KEEWIS, THE MISCHIEF MAKER**

13 ... **THE CUNNING PAU-PUK-KEEWIS, GAMBLING FOR FURS**

14 ... **PAU-PUK-KEEWIS INSULTS MINNEHAHA**

He escapes the fury of Warriors by taking to his Canoe.

Minnehaha

15 ... **ESCAPE AND PURSUIT OF PAU - PUK - KEEWIS BY THE TRIBE**

16 ... **THE " BAD INDIAN " MOCKING AND DEFYING HIS PURSUERS**

17 .. **PAU-PUK-KEEWIS FLINGING HIMSELF FROM A CLIFF AND TURNING INTO A BEAVER**

18 ... **THE TRIBE INDULGES IN THE ELK DANCE IN CELEBRATION OF THEIR VICTORY**

19 ... **APPEARANCE OF THE FIRST PALE FACE** (A Canadian Missionary)

20 ... **MYSTERIOUS DEPARTURE OF HIAWATHA FOR THE WEST**

Total Length 800 feet. Duration of Exhibit, 15 minutes.

Hiawatha—Participants of the Elk Dance . . .

1095 ... MAJOR WOODS' METHOD OF CONQUERING A 3-YEAR OLD UNBROKEN COLT

Major Woods' method of breaking a colt differs vastly from the usual and cruel method in vogue. He lassoes a wild unbroken colt, wrestles with same, conquers it, and within a few hours will saddle and drive the animal in harness thoroughly SUBDUED. Once Major Woods "floors" a colt, a child can with safety sit between his hocks and a lady ride or drive it an hour after. This picture portrays a wrestling match between Major Woods and an unbroken colt (16 hands high), the Major coming off the victor, and is full of action and of great interest to all lovers of animal creation.

No. 1279b David Street—Outside Jerusalem

200 feet.

1097 ... **GAME OF LIVING WHIST**

An excellent picture of a game of Living Whist recently played at Dulwich. Each person representing one of the 52 cards of the pack is appropriately costumed to depict the different suits and face cards. The game is then played by the figures advancing or receding singly or in suit, as the case may be, and forms one continuous picture of ever-changing evolutions and groupings. A novelty.   **175 feet.**

DICK TURPIN, THE HIGHWAYMAN.

EXCITING INCIDENTS OF 100 YEARS AGO.

1110 ... **ROBBERY OF THE MAIL COACH**

Scene 1.—The film commences, showing the exterior of a roadside Inn, where the landlord and a country yokel are seated, smoking and drinking, when they catch sight of the coach The coach pulls up and passengers alight and partake of refreshments. The coach drives off and scene changes to a cross road

Scene 2.—The coach is seen approaching. Suddenly Turpin and a pal appear on the scene, and calling to the passengers "Hands up," shoot both the driver and guard. They proceed to relieve the passengers of their valuables, one of the lady passengers meanwhile having fainted, and another stubbornly resisting her persecutors. Having attained their object, they mount their steeds, raise their hats and ride away. Shortly after two Kingsmen ride up evidently seeking information as to the whereabouts of the highwaymen, and having acquired same ride away in pursuit.

Scene 3.—This scene shows the wayside Inn to which the highwaymen ride up and dismount and enter for refreshments. Whilst inside the Kingsmen arrive and having asked and obtained information of the landlord, enter the Inn.

Scene 4.—Meanwhile the highwaymen have seen their approach, and the scene changes to the back of the Inn, where the highwaymen are seen to throw a rope from an upper window and escape by this means. The Kingsmen perceiving the rope at the window, follow.

Scene 5.—A pretty river scene into which the highwaymen leap in their endeavour to escape. In the rush across the stream one of them shoots at their pursuers but without effect.

Scenes 6 and 7.—The film is now reaching an exciting stage and two changes of scene takes place, in which the pursuit is hotly continued, many pistol shots being exchanged.

Scene 8.—Next is seen a clump of trees, out of which pursuers and pursued emerge. A desperate struggle takes place, in which the Kingsmen are thrown to the ground. The highwaymen manage to escape but lose their pistols in the encounter.

Scene 9. The next and last scene showing a tree into which the highwaymen climb in a vain endeavour to elude their pursuers. They are discovered in the act by the Kingsmen who raise their pistols and shoot. Both highwaymen are seen to fall violently from the tree to the ground. Whilst the Kingsmen are attending to one, the other with difficulty endeavours to get away but is promptly shot in the attempt, making a thrilling finish to an exciting and novel subject.

A film that is full of exciting incidents and of a unique and novel character. All the dresses in this picture are the style of 100 years ago. All the scenes are well chosen, including the Inn, which was a popular calling place in the old coaching days of that period. **Total length 375 feet.**

Among the Pyramids, Egypt . . .

1153 ... "A DASH FOR LIBERTY"

Or the Convict's Escape and Capture.

A splendid Sequel to our Film No. 1034, "A Daring Daylight Burglary."

Scene 1.—Stone quarry showing convicts at work while the warder mounts guard. Two of these convicts have determined to make a desperate dash for liberty, and upon the return of the warder one of them pretends to have hurt his foot with the pick he was wielding. While the warder stoops to inspect the injury, the convict at work on an upper ledge of rock prostrates the warder with a blow from a large stone flung at him. Both convicts now make for liberty.

Scene 2.—Two warders seeing the fleeing "jail-birds," give chase. The latter, in their blind desire to get away, run into a quarry working from which there is no outlet. Cornered like rats they defend themselves against the onrush of the warders. One succeeds in wrenching the gun from his pursuer, and is about to brain him with his weapon when another warder arrives in time to stop this crime by shooting the culprit, while the other one gets away, still pursued.

Scene 3.—The escaping convict, on reaching a road leading past the quarry, espies a farmer driving along. He follows, dodging about awaiting his opportunity to mount the cart, forcing its owner into the road, and escapes by whipping up the horse, while the two warders just coming over the brow of the hill are soon joined by the farmer, who points out the direction taken by the convict. The pursuit now becomes hot, but the convict having gained distance, stops at the first place likely to offer him temporary safety.

Scene 4.—He espies a line from which hang various articles of female wearing apparel, does not stop long to consider, and proceeds to don the woman's clothes, thus disguising his appearance, so that when the officers rush up to the supposed old lady and breathlessly inquire as to the whereabouts of the convict, he puts them off on the wrong scent, and rushes away in the opposite direction.

Scene 5.—Exhausted and worn out, the convict laboriously works his way over the downs. He just reaches the crest of a hill when the warders overtake him, and he is shot down. During the struggle and hand-to-hand conflict which now ensues between the desperately wounded man and the two warders, the former is gradually overcome and re-captured. Pinioned between the two, he is seen staggering out of the picture, his face contorted with pain and hatred.

An exciting subject.　　Natural scenery.　　Enacted by men who know their business.　　Splendid quality.　　　　　　**300 feet**

The Pyramids, Egypt . . .

1168 ... CRAZY PICTURE OF AN INDIAN OPIUM DEN

Depicting the scene in an opium and gambling hell in India, as well as another showing a very narrow street with natives rushing about in such ludicrous manner decided us to list this with the results, that instead of depicting a serious subject as intended, has been created a film, which will, by reproduction, create roars of laughter.

75 feet

1259 ... TRANSPORT OF THE GIGANTIC 100 TON ARMOUR PLATE MOULD FROM SHEFFIELD BY THE GREAT CENTRAL RAILWAY

Owing to its enormous size, monopolising both up and down lines of the Railway, this Armour Plate Mould was conveyed on a Sunday when all other traffic was stopped. With splendid panoramic effect.

100 feet

Urban Bioscope Staff at the Derby—Epsom Downs

1260 ... THE GLEN CONCERT AT PAISELEY

General Panoramas from heights. The audience on the hill slope. The chorus of 1,500 with full band and conductor during rendition of song. Unique and interesting. **175 feet**

1276 a ... HOISTING CATTLE ON BOARD A STEAMER

1—**Mooring Cattle on Barge** preparatory to shipping them to Constantinople.

2—**Taking Cattle off to the Steamer.** Towing the laden barges through the Harbour.

3—**Hoisting the Cattle on Board.** The cattle being slung by legs and horns from the barges to the liner, all kicking and struggling as they are suspended in mid-air on the end of a cable which finally lands them on the deck of the steamer. **150 feet**

1287 ... FIRING TEN GALLONS OF PETROL

Test of the " Nonex " device. The process of filling a large iron drum with ten gallons of petrol—motor spirit—in an open fire. When the safety plug blew out, more petrol was poured into the heated drum. The fire was then extinguished by means of a small cloth. Excellent fire and smoke effects. **150 feet**

"THE STAGE."

The Urban Bioscope Company are showing an excellent picture of the recent test of the non-explosive tank before a representative gathering of experts at the Cadogan Garage on Thursday last. The view shows the interesting experiment of filling a large iron drum with ten gallons of petrol motor-spirit in an open fire. The safety plug having blown out, more petrol is poured in the heated drum, and the fire is then extinguished by means of a small cloth. The picture is of considerable interest as illustrative of the effects of one of the most important inventions of modern times.

1290 ... ROBBERY OF A MAIL CONVOY BY BANDITS

1.—The Mounted Escort and Mail Van.
2.—Bushrangers in Camp—Advice of approach of mail convoy
3.—The Troopers striking camp.
4.—Bushrangers attack camp and rob mail train.
5.—Detachment of Colonials to the rescue.
6.—Robbers decamp with booty.
7.—Refuge and fight at the deserted hut.
8.—Capture of Bandits.
9.—The Court Martial in camp.
10.—Comrades avenged.

A mail Convoy is seen passing a clump of woods skirting a hill. The Escort consists of a dozen mounted Colonial Troopers. This little party is watched by a bandit scout who hurries with his information to where the robber band is encamped. They hurriedly put out the camp fire, snatch their weapons and follow in wake of the scout who directs them to the troopers camp, the latter being just in the act of erecting their tents, unhitching the horses, tethering their mounts, etc. After light refreshments they retire to their tents, leaving the camp in charge of the sentry. This is the robbers opportunity. The sentry is stabbed from the back, but is able to fire his gun, awaking his comrades, who rush from the tent and grapple with the bandits, whose force had arrived. After the main body of the guard are despatched or disabled the balance are tied to the wheels of the mail van, which is rifled of its contents. The Bandits always on the alert, hear the thunder of a further attachment of troopers appoaching and run off with as much booty as they can carry.

The Cavalrymen, some 20 in number, who arrive in meantime, are surprised to find the camp despoiled, and being informed of the direction taken by the fleeing robbers, they first release the bound men and then start in hot pursuit on the trail of the robbers, which latter take refuge in a deserted hut, from which they fire a regular fusilade at the now charging troopers. Being outnumbered they surrender, but not without a struggle, in which their numbers are reduced to three men. These are securely bound and led, with ropes around their necks, to the camp which they had robbed. Here a court-martial is held, and the unanimous verdict being death, the Bandits are led forth, lined up and shot, thus avenging the death of the man they had killed.

350 feet

No. 1279b. A Street—Jerusalem.

1294 ... THE HUMOUR OF EPSOM ON DERBY DAY

A series of 25 excellent pictures showing the varied sights along the road to Epsom, including the brakes, coaches, vans, coster carts and all man-ner of vehi-cles, some of the curious individuals met with, views of the Epsom Race Course Grand Stand Paddocks, Coachstands and the enor-mous crowds gathering there, the amusements such as swings, cocoanut shying, roundabouts, gipsy vans, &c., and refreshment bars, hard

No. 1294 Scenes on Epsom Downs

boiled egg and fish stalls; the bookies, tipsters and, in fact, every noteworthy sight to be met with on Derby Day.   **400 feet.**

"DAILY MIRROR," *June 3rd.*

A Newspaper in Making.

Bioscope illustrates the Marvels of Modern Journalism.

Great interest was evinced last night at the Alhambra by a series of Bioscope pictures disclosing the secrets of a newspaper office.

The largest and most popular evening paper, the "Evening News," forms the subject of these most interesting films.

The interest centres not only in the fact of their being the first complete series illus-trating the making of the modern journal, but by reason of the conditions under which they were taken. Every kind of artificial lamp was used, including specially-prepared mercurial vapour lamps, and the result is a triumph for the Charles Urban Trading Company.

From the applause which greeted these remarkable pictures last night it was evident they will become one of the most popular items of the Alhambra's attractive programme.

"THE REFEREE," *June 5th.*

Ever since a series of animated pictures became part and parcel of the modern variety entertainment, praiseworthy efforts have been made by sundry managements to make this item in the programme a practically permanent attraction, No instance of this has been more sucessful than at the Alhambra, where for a long time past the Urban Bioscope has, by dint of frequent changes in the series of pictures shown, provided the most constant of patrons with something fresh and up to date week by week, and sometimes several times in the same week. On Thursday evening some remarkably fine views of the race for the Derby, together with incidents on the road to and round about the course, were presented. These pictures were the more remarkable seeing that they were taken amid the Epsom Down-pours of Wednesday last. Another series showed the manner in which the "Evening News" conveys the result of a big race to the public. One sees the arrival of the news in the sub-editor's room, the intricacies of the "stop-press" are revealed, the printing of the "extra specials," their distribution by carts, motors and newsboys graphi-cally realised. The possibilities of the cinematograph have never before been so capitally demonstrated.

1296 ... "A NEWSPAPER IN MAKING."

"Millions read the Papers, not one per cent. know how it is prepared."—This is an " eye-opener."

By courtesy of the LONDON EVENING NEWS.

No. 1296. View of " Plateing " a Hoe Press.

The exhibition of this series of extraordinary Pictures created a sensation among publishers and the general public as well as the Photographic Trades.

The lighting of the various interior scenes was accomplished by means of the Angola Photo Process Arc Lamp, supplied by the GENERAL ELECTRIC COMPANY, London.

ORDER OF PICTURES.

1 The Incident. (NOTE.—Any incident can be inserted here.)
2 The Editor's Table.
3 Linotyping.
4 Preparing the Forme.
5 Making the Matrix.
6 Casting the Plate.
7 Trimming the Plate.
8 Receiving "Stop" News.
9 Printing the Edition.
10 From Press Room to Office.
11 Supplying Newsboys over Counter.
12 The News Carts and Cycle Corps leaving the Newspaper Buildings.
13 Arrival of Cart—The Newsboy does the rest.

A most Remarkable Series of .. " Interior " Photographs.

A GREAT SUCCESS.

Total length 600 feet

Reprint from The London "EVENING NEWS," *June 3rd, 1904.*

"Evening News" Living Pictures.

Bioscope Shows how an Up-to-date Journal is Produced—Three Minutes' Flash—From the Finish of the Derby to Readers Scanning the Printed Page.

One of the marvels of modern times—the rapidity with which the "Evening News" is produced and distributed—is being shown nightly at the Alhambra, Leicester Square, on the Urban Bioscope.

The pictures show the publication of the result of the Derby, and illustrate how hundreds of hands and brains work in combination to place the news of the day before the public within a few moments of its happening.

First there is flashed on the screen the exciting finish of the great race with St. Amant first past the post.

Then is shown the sub-editorial room of the "Evening News," where, almost simultaneously, the details are being received by telephone from the sporting reporters in the Press box.

The chief sub-editor, surrounded by his staff, and the details of the editorial room are all depicted.

This is where the tape machines click out the world's news, and where are all the contrivances that annihilate time and distance.

Telephoning the "Derby" Result.

The telephoned Derby result is set down on paper by the flying pencil of the chief sub-editor, and a waiting boy rushes with the "copy" into an adjacent room, where the linotype operators sit before their wonderful machine.

The "linos" consist of many inventions worked into one perfect whole. There is a lettered keyboard, not unlike a typewriter; and the "copy" under the lightning fingers of the "lino" man is set up into lines faster than the act can be described.

The next picture shows the news, now in lines of type, being "made-up" into "formes"—which is the type fixed together into oblong shapes corresponding to the size of the printed newspaper pages.

Then by a swift transition the bioscope views show the stereotyping process, in which a mould is taken of the "formes" from which are cast, as by magic, the cylinder-shaped plates that fit on to the printing machines.

Giant Printing Machines at Work.

The underground hall in which stand the giant printing machines is next visited. The plates have been fixed, and, with express speed, the great rolls of paper feed the cylinders, and emerge, cut and counted, as the "Evening News."

Outside are the eager newsboys clamouring for "the winners." It is thrilling to see the motor-bicycle riders and carters seize their bundles of papers, as they come up by an ingeniously-contrived lift from below.

A second later and there comes the dash from Carmelite Street to all parts of the Metropolis—and the carts and motors go almost as quickly as did the racehorses a few moments before on the Epsom course.

The Clamouring Newsboys.

The arrival of a cart at a depot; the distribution of the paper to the clamouring newsboys; and the sale of a paper to a member of the public within three minutes of the Derby winner passing the post are clearly shown. The purchaser, judging by his delight, has clearly backed the winner.

The pictures are in themselves the more remarkable as the interior ones are taken by artificial light, as for many of the views it was impossible to get the sunlight.

These living pictures were shown last night at the Alhambra for the first time, and were received with the greatest enthusiasm.

No. 1425 *The Banks of the Nile*

1330 ... ANCIENT CEREMONY AT ETON COLLEGE

A most picturesque series taken during the visit of T. R. H. Prince and Princess of Wales to Eton College. Full of life and quaint surroundings. **125 feet**

No. 2023. Kuropatkin Reviewing Troops.

1331 ... THE ROYAL BARGE PARTY AT WINDSOR

The Royal Barge and the Ancient Institute of Royal Watermen are now but seldom brought into requisition. During a recent visit of the King and Queen to Windsor and Eton, this gorgeous Barge with their Royal Passengers form the most prominent features of a beautifully unique picture. **100 feet**

1341 ... SIR HIRAM MAXIM'S CAPTIVE FLYING MACHINES

A popular means of creating new sensations with thousand of visitors to the Crystal Palace and Earls Court who avail themselves of these "Flying Machines" which form a prominent feature at both places. **75 feet**

No 3017. General Rennenkampf at Irkutsk.

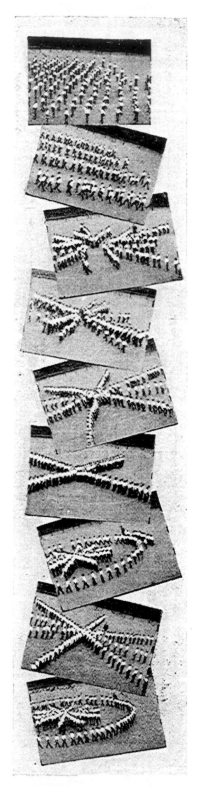

No. 1353. Reedham Orphan Drill.

1345 ... RAILWAY ACCIDENT AT THE METROPOLITAN GAS WORKS

During the photographing of a picture series of the different phases of the making of gas our operator was fortunate enough in being in position with his camera at the time of a railway smash-up which occured on the premises, many coal trucks were derailed and thrown from the line through the collision.

100 feet

1346 ... RED CROSS RESCUE OF VICTIMS OF CHIMNEY ACCIDENT

Showing a labourer having been overcome by the fumes at the top of a tall chimney being rescued and lowered from his perilous position by the Red Cross Society members who just arrived in the nick of time.

60 feet

1343 .. VICTIMS OF GAS EXPLOSION ATTENDED BY RED CROSS SOCIETY

Rescue of a family from a building which was wrecked through a gas explosion. After lowering the people from the upper stories they are carried off by ambulance and given first aid by the "Red Cross" Staff. **150 feet**

1348 ... RESCUE OF WOUNDED FROM RAILWAY WRECK

Described under "Railway Series."

275 feet

1353 ... BOYS' DRILL AT THE REEDHAM ORPHANAGE

One of the most active and unique pictures ever taken. The precision of movement by the hundreds of little orphans performing the various evolutions speaks highly for their training. The various illustrations convey a better idea of the subject than mere word description. **150 feet**

1356 ... "PIERROT'S ROMANCE."

A Tragedy Dramatic Sketch, by Signor G. V. Rosi.

Introduction.

The scene in the introduction represents a magnificent drawing room of Lisette, a Parisian milliner. It is late, and as her sweetheart, Pierrot (who is a simpleton and believes her the most honest and purest of women), does not come to make her the usual scranade, she is pacing the room impatiently. Lisette wonders if he has at last discovered who she is, and her real station in life. She hopes not, as she is sincerely and thoroughly in love with Pierrot; but the latter is poor, and cannot afford to satisfy all her costly caprices.

100 feet

1357 ... "PIERROT'S ROMANCE": A Tragedy

Scene same as No. 1356 (Introduction).

The sweet accents of a violin come to interrupt the course of her sad thoughts. It is Pierrot. Lisette runs to the balcony, and, with a kiss, she throws him the key, after which she sits at a table, giving to her features a humble and modest

express-sion.

Pierrot enters, confused and shy, with a big bouquet of flowers, with which he approaches to make her a present. Lisette, perceiving his bashfulness, encourages him with smiles, and bids him to come closer. Pierrot, falling on his knees, offers the flowers, which are warmly accepted by Lisette. Still kneeling, he begs her to listen to him, but she forces him to stand up, and gently pushes him towards a sofa, on which she sits, while Pierrot, on his knees again, tells her the tale of his ardent love.

She is happy, and listens to him as lost in a dream, till she falls upon his bosom, forgetting the dreadful past, and only enjoying the ecstasy of the moment.

P

The ringing of a bell recalls her to reality. She is frightened, and does not know how or where to conceal her friend, as the visitor is too valuable to be remanded.

Pierrot looks very surprised, and cannot account for what is happening. He is about to ask for an explanation, when a new summons of the bell decides Lisette to conceal Pierrot behind a screen. Bidding him not to stir till her return, Lisette hastens then to open the door, and a wealthy old gentleman enters. He would embrace her, but Lisette is afraid of being seen by Pierrot, and invites him to enter another room.

The room being deserted, Pierrot, who is tired of waiting. peeps forth from the screen, but looks in vain for his sweetheart. His eyes fall on Lisette's photo on the wall, and, kneeling before it, recounts his love again.

All at once he hears sighs and wailings in the other room. He runs to the door, and, looking through the key-hole, he sees Lisette in another's arms. Sorrow-stricken, he falls on a chair by the table, and cries bitterly. The idea of revenge suddenly crosses his mind, and seeing on the table a silver paper cutter, he catches hold of it, and swears revenge. The turning of a key startles him, and, not being in time to return behind the screen, he hides under the table.

Lisette enters, in dressing-gown and dishevelled. She throws furtive glances beside her. Seeing nobody, she takes courage again, and shows out her visitor, who, before going, kisses her.

Pierrot, who has seen and heard everything, loses his temper, and catches hold of Lisette, who on her knees implores forgiveness.

But Pierrot, blinded by jealousy, drags her into the next room, and, in his mad desire for revenge, he stabs her to the heart. Broken hearted and despairing on seeing the dead form of his love, he is overcome with anguish, and, using his weapon on himself, falls dead by her side. *A most thrilling episode.* **450 feet**

Complete Total Length (with No. 1356) 550 feet.

1378 ... "STRAWBERRIES"

An excellent series showing the Cultivating, Picking, Marketing, and eating this Luscious Fruit, Panorama of Extensive Strawberry Patch, Pickers at Work, close view, Loading Baskets of Berries, from Cart to R.R. truck, Arrival of Berries at Covent Garden, Sale of Cartload of Berries, Children enjoying the fruit, so does a Monkey, whose grimaces while eating the berries are exceedingly funny. **150 feet**

1387 ... "FIELD DAY AT ETON COLLEGE"

An Outing of the Eton Boys and their friends always means a lively time. The picture does justice to the event. **50 feet**

Grand Display of Brock's Fireworks

AT THE CRYSTAL PALACE.

By courtesy of Messrs. C. T. Brock & Co., *the Crystal Palace Pyrotechnists*
This is the first successful series of pictures of a Night Fireworks display
on a large scale.

1409   **ORDER OF PICTURES.**

Grand Display of Roman Candles (various colours).
Fiery Serpents } Gold, Brilliant Effect.
Golden Rain }
Grand Illumination by Coloured Fire (Red).
Bombardment of a Battleship by Torpedo Boats.
      Set piece, *Torpedo Boat*, golden ; *Waves*, green ; *Battleship*, red.
The Gigantic Catherine Wheel (variegated colours).
A Cock Fight (active design in two colours).
Firing a 20-foot Oval of Mines, various colours and with most brilliant effect.
Cottage on Fire (30ft. set piece), red.
Arrival of Fire Engine (life size, fine apparatus, and men in outlines of blue,
     gold and green).
Niagara (silver).
Grand Discharge of 100 Bombshells (various colours).
The King and Queen (starts with silver, then gold, green and red).
           Price, Coloured £10 10s. 0d. 275 feet.

No 3018.   Cossacks crossing over Ice of frozen Lake Baikal.

1410 ... FIREWORKS DISPLAY AT CRYSTAL PALACE
     A shorter length of the previous subject, from which however
the more important "displays" are eliminated.   Views as follows:—
Roman Candles—Golden Rain—Catherine Wheel—Cock Fight—Set
Piece—Niagara—Coloured Fire—Bombardment by Torpedo Boats.
           Coloured £4 10s.   125 feet

**1421 ... PHILLIPS' NEW FLYING MACHINE AT THE CRY-
STAL PALACE**
     Another form of machine for the invasion of the ariel regions.
Splendid picture showing the detail of the engine motor and general
construction with a fine portrait of the inventor.   **100 feet**

1474 Horse=Breaking Extraordinary,

By MAJOR H. B. WOODS.

The method employed by Major Woods in catching and thoroughly conquering an unbroken colt, as depicted in this series, contrasts most forcibly with the usual harsh and cruel methods employed by professional horse-breakers and trainers. The following scenes faithfully portray various phases of the training of a three year old unbroken colt, which demonstration was given by Major Woods before many witnesses, among whom were Mr. J. Reilly (stud groom for Mr. Lionel de Rothschild), Mr. J. Scutts (stud groom for the Earl of Orkney), Messrs. R. Rowland, J. Stevens, Ted Wilson (trainer), Chas. Stevens, and G. Pratt, Esq., all of Oving, Creslow, and Wing, Aylesbury. These gentlemen can testify to

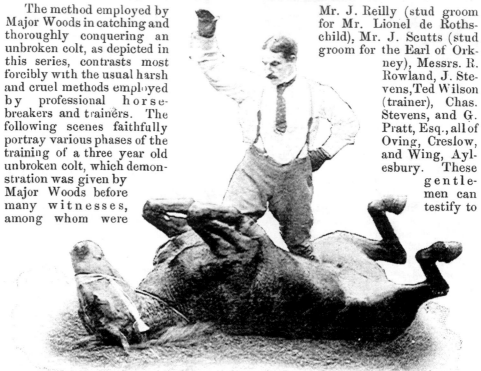

the genuineness of the performance by Major Woods, of capturing a wild colt and driving same in harness along a public road *in the limited time of two hours and forty minutes*. It usually occupies six to seven weeks with the ordinary methods employed to train a colt to this stage. During the course of training as practised by Major Woods, no tackle is used and all cruelty eliminated —he simply conquers the colt by the use of sheer strength in wrestling until the animal is thrown. When thus mastered the colt is handled in every manner in order to convince it that it will not be hurt; thus having gained its confidence, the rest is easily managed. It is certainly a most unique performance and the reproduction of this series of pictures is bound to be of the greatest interest to all admirers of the horse.

Order of Pictures.

1—**Lassoing the Unbroken Colt.** The colt dodging the rope.
2—**Getting the Head Collar on.** Five men holding lasso with plunging colt.
3—**First Stage of Subduing,** by wrestling.
4—**Conquering the Colt by Wrestling and throwing without tackle.**
5—**Process of Taming by handling.**
6—**Eating Grass while lying on the ground,** which proves that it is not distressed, in pain or frightened.
7—**Standing on Horse while lying down.**
8—**Throwing the second time.**

9--**Mounting the Colt and dismounting.** (Eating corn from sieve).

10—**Wrestling a third time.** (More difficult on account of cunning).

11—**Turned on his back in order to handle the legs,** to get him accustomed to shoeing.

12—**Lady sitting between the hocks,** horse with feet up-turned.

13—**Horse rising while mounted.**

14—**The Horse again on its back,** little boy sitting between hocks.

15—**Boy mounting Horse while latter lying on ground eating grass.**

16—**Colt Rising,** boy hanging on and standing on horse. (Falls off.)

17—**Colt so tame will follow the trainer without leading rein.**

18—**Putting a Child on the Colt's back**

19—**Saddling and handling Colt for the first time**

20—**Dismounting by sliding over the croup**

21—**First time riding with man's saddle**

22—**Putting on lady's saddle for first time**

23—**Trying the side saddle for the first time**

24—**Inexperienced lady rider** mounting and riding first time. (Falls to ground owing to colt taking step sideways, but colt not frightened)

25—**Horse being led by leading rein.** (Mouth still soft and colt answering awkwardly to it.)

26—**Lady riding without leading rein.**

27—**Lady dismounting.** Colt rapidly becoming accustomed to new surroundings

28—**Slipping saddle over croup** (to teach the colt to become accustomed to obstacles falling at its heels)

29—**Putting on collar for the first time.** Colt does not take kindly to this but gradually submits.

30—**Putting on driving bridle and blinkers,** and driving harness for first time. (Rubber stretched from collar to breeching, in order to give impression of pulling). Colt awkward.

31—**Teaching Colt to answer to the bit,** and be accustomed to the cracking of a whip.

32—**Frog put on croup,** to convince the colt that contact with other living subjects will not hurt him.

33—**Going through the process of shoeing.** (Four feet)

34—**Familiarising him with the object he has to pull.** Showing him the cart for the first time. (Head foremost between shafts, smelling the cart.)

35—**Rattling the cart to accustom him to the noise** and the touch of the shafts against his sides, thus preventing him jumping and plunging when properly hitched between the shafts.

36—**Hitting the dash-board**

37—**Hitching to Cart**

38—**Pulling Cart for the first time.** (A little inclined to kick if he were not already accustomed to noises and contacts.)

39—**Getting more accustomed to it.**

> NOTE.—This colt is now being driven and ridden daily, and its entire demeanour since being caught and tamed speaks greatly in favour of Major Woods' humane and rapid methods of training—which he claims can be applied to successfully subdue the most unmanageable horse.

Total length 850 feet

1487 ... THE BICYCLE THIEF (Comic)

Two cyclists meet on the road and after stepping from their machines are so intent on the conversation which ensues that they do not observe a tramp who steals and rides off with one of their bikes. The loss is discovered, and by the aid of a policeman and a constant addition to the crowd, which starts in pursuit of the thief, the latter after trying many tricks to evade capture, is finally secured after a struggle and led from the scene amidst great hilarity of the assembled spectators. A lively and splendid subject. **200 feet**

No. 1297. Motor Cars and their Drivers.

1490 .. **"HOPPING" IN KENT**

By Courtesy of Messrs. A. E. WHITE, LTD., *Bettering, Kent.*

Varied scenes in the famous Kent Hop Gardens, showing the picking, collecting, weighing, baleing, sampling, and transporting this essential ingredient to the Beer brewing Art. The pickers and surroundings are of a most picturesque nature.   **175 feet**

1497 ... **SAMPLING HOPS AFTER HARVEST**

After the hops are compressed into bales, a sample of the contents of each bale is withdrawn, packed and registered with the respective number of the bale. The workers are adepts at their business, and lend much active interest to the picture.   **60 feet**

1493 ... **Capt. SPELTERINI'S BALLOON TRIP ACROSS THE JUNGFRAU**

Showing the inflation of the balloon, the release of the same and the sailing of its intrepid passenger by this means over one of the highest mountains in Switzerland.   **75 feet**

No. 1279c. Panorama of Jerusalem

Exclusive Exhibition Rights for the United Kingdom acquired by the Urbanora Exhibition Company

No. 1502.

NORTHERN ICE SPORTS.

Including the Principal Races of the "NORDISKA SPELEN," at Stockholm, Sweden, February 4th to 12th, 1905.

Photographs by Mr. F. ORMISTON-SMITH, by the courtesy of the GOVERNOR OF STOCKHOLM.

ORDER OF PICTURES.

1—Panoramic View of a Winter Landscape.
2—A Run with the Snow Shoe Club.
3—Tossing the Club Initiate.

4—World's Champions in Figure Skating at Adrotts Parken, Sweden.

5—Fancy Skating by W. F. Adams, Esq., of England.

6—Skating by Miss Harrison, of the London Figure-Skating Club (the winner of the Lady Championship).

7—Exhibition by Ulrich Salchow, of Sweden (the World's champion skater).

8—Skating Races for the World's Championship.

9—Skate Sailing Races at Stora Partan.

10—Ice Yachting at Stockholm.

11—Bob Sled Coasting Parties having a Run over Course.

12—Toboggans in Tow of Four-horse Sleigh.

13—Tobogganning Down a Steep and Bumpy Course.

14—Ski-Jumping Competition.

15—Sleigh Trotting Races—Coming Round the Curve.

16—Sleigh Racing—Exciting Finish down the Straight.

Total Length, 750 feet.　　　Price £17 10s.

Duration of Exhibit, 20 minutes.

NOTE.—This series is entirely distinct from our famous "International Winter Sports," to which it can be joined and both exhibited in consecutive order, thus making one of the most interesting, humorous, and exciting picture series ever photographed.

Duration of exhibiting entire series (Nos. 1240 & 1502), 30 minutes.

Total Length, 1,500 feet.　　Price £35.

Exclusive Rights acquired by the Urbanora Exhibition Company for the United Kingdom.

1505 A Visit to the "Steel Works."

Photographed by courtesy of the EARL OF DUDLEY'S Steel Works, Staffordshire.

ORDER OF PICTURES.

1—Unloading ore from railroad trucks at the Iron Works.

2—Carrying ore up incline railway to furnaces.

3—Dumping ore from barrows into furnace.

4—Top view of furnace during smelting progress.

5—Running molten metal into moulds (coloured).

6—Casting Pig-iron into bars (coloured).

7—Ladelling molten metal into crucibles (coloured).

8—General view of Iron Foundry (coloured).

9—Running off the metal after blasting operations. Molten metal running into 10 ton crucibles (coloured)

10—Engine drawing 10 tons of molten metal to steel works.

11—Another View of Engine and Ladle.

12—Hydraulic crane lifting crucible to top of Bessemer furnace.

13—Charging the blast through the furnace doors (coloured).

14—Tapping a charge of molten steel (coloured).

15—**The slag over-running the crucibles** (coloured).

16—**Pouring metal into moulds** (coloured).

17—**Emptying slag from crucibles** (coloured).

18—**Taking steel ingot from furnaces** (coloured).

19—**General view of Rolling Mills** (coloured).

20—**Rolling sheet steel.**

24—**Sawing steel into requisite lengths.**

22—**Hoisting a cargo of steel plates to railway truck.**

23—**Making chain cable for the British Navy** (coloured).

Total Length 450 feet.

SYNOPSIS OF SERIES.

The ore brought from all parts of the world is tipped into calcinating or drying stoves, to get the moisture out. It is then "blended" with the addition of a certain amount of "Flux." Next it is taken to the top of the blast furnace by means of water balance. Arrived on the top, it is tipped from barrows into the furnace. Here we see the iron run off from a blast furnace into sand moulds, which produces ingots of "pig iron." Next we see the mass being pounded by the steam hammer and finally the torging of the links. At the bottom of the furnace the "slag" is drawn off into small trucks. When the metal is thoroughly liquid it is drawn off and run into a "ladle." In this picture the amount of molten metal poured was about ten tons. An engine is coupled on to the ladle and away it goes as fast as possible to the Steel Works.

CONVERTING IRON INTO STEEL.

Next we see the engine with its load arriving at the Steel Works. The ladle is caught up by an electric crane (capable of lifting 50 tons) and taken on to the top stage of the steel furnaces, when the molten iron is turned into the steel retort. Next we see the steel furnace being fed with different chemicals. (These chemicals are used to drive out the impurities from the iron and so convert iron into steel. The chemicals used are also to put certain proportions of chemicals into the finished metal, which must be thereon analysed by the Chemist.) All the men wear very deep blue glasses to protect their eyes from the terrible glare. The door of the furnace is only allowed open just long enough to allow the men to put in the necessary ingredients. The Iron now having been converted into Steel all is ready for drawing off. We go round to the other side of the furnace and see a ladle here ready to receive the fluid. It then pours out in a terrific stream (15 tons was the amount poured the day the picture was taken and it occupied about five minutes). Next we see the "slag" running over the top of the ladle. This is brought about by "fluxing" the metal in the ladle. Next a plunger in the bottom of the ladle is withdrawn, thus allowing the molton metal to flow into gigantic moulds and so the steel is cast into ingots weighing each about a ton When cool the ingot is put into a heating furnace and we see it being withdrawn ready for the rolling process. The rolling being finished it but remains to cut the steel into suitable lengths for the market. After it is cold it is gathered into lots and taken by means of an electric travelling crane away to the railway trucks for distribution.

The picture finishes with a view of the smithy where link by link a length of heavy chain cable for the navy is forged by the blacksmiths.

NOTE:—All the interior pictures are coloured to suitably convey the glare and orange hue from the furnaces and liquid metal on their surroundings.

Off to the Hunt over the Downs

1509. Hunting the Red Deer,

WITH THE DEVON AND SOMERSET STAGHOUNDS.

Taken by kind permission of the Masters of the Hunt.

Photographs by Mr. H. M. Lomas.

1—Babyhood—Promising Young Puppies

2—The Devon and Somerset Pack.

3—Hounds "At Home"—Feeding Time in Kennel.

4—On the way to the Meet.

5—The Meet, in an old Somerset village.

6—Hounds and Riders Pass through Dunster.

7—A Hunting Morning—On the way to Exmoor.

8—Late Comers make up for lost time on the hard high road.

9—Meet on the open moor, near Dunkery Beacon.

10—Kennelling the Pack at Cloutsham—In the Barn.

11—Calling out the "Tufters" —About five couple of wise old hounds used to find the deer.

Babyhood of the Staghound

12—Going into the Woods to try for a Stag.

13—An old "Native" locating the Deer.

14—A Monarch of the Moor breaks out of the woods with his wives.

15—The Stag makes a Double and leaves his hinds.

Showing the intricacies of the Bioscope

16—Riding back for the Pack (*i.e.* all the hounds previously left kennelled in the barn.)

17—The Pack is released and taken to where the Stag crossed the hill.

18—Full Cry on the line of the Stag.

19—Away over the bracken.

20—The Stag makes for a river and gives a lively time.

21—He breaks through hounds and makes for the hill-tops again.

22—Good going over Lucott Moor.

23—The pace begins to tell and the stag makes for the wooded valleys.

24—Being hard pressed, takes to water.

25—Pursuit up stream.

26—At Bay—A dangerous customer.

27—At Close Quarters—Too close to be safe.

28—Away he Goes—Having baffled his pursuers he makes towards the coast.

29—View of the Hunters over the hills.

30—Porlock Vale and Hurlstone Point lie spread beneath—The stag has gone through the corners, down to the rocky coast below, and out to sea.

The Devon and Somerset Staghounds

31 — The Fishermen bring him in.

32—Landing the kill.

33—Breaking up the Stag.—Tit-bits for the hungry hounds.

34—Preparing for the homeward return of the pack.

35—Tired hounds bathing in the cool waters.

36—Blooding a novice.

37—Examining the dead stag's antlers and judging his age.

38—Carting stag home for venison.

39—Hunters return home.

40—A cool drink by the wayside.

Unkennelling the Pack.

Total Length 750 feet.

Duration of Exhibit, 15 *minutes.*

HUNTING THE RED DEER WITH THE DEVON AND SOMERSET STAGHOUNDS.

Away down in the out-of-the-world West of England, where rise the River Exe and Badgworthy Water, ere they make their ways North-South

On the Downs, Exmoor.

to the English and Bristol Channels, on a tract of beautiful yet desolate moorland, roam herds of wild red deer. No timid, tame little creatures these, but fine and powerful, wild and wily, are the four-footed inhabitants of this tract of country, once the Royal Forest of Exmoor. The stag, or full-grown red deer, is armed with large and heavy wide-spreading antlers, is large in body, and is almost double the weight of the park deer we are familiar with.

We first hear of stag-hunting over the forest in the reign of Queen Elizabeth, and nowadays there gather every year great numbers of well-known sportsmen from all over England, in fact, from all over the globe, to take part in this wild sport.

On the Scent—In Full Cry

To visit the puppies, a tumbling mass of youngsters, ere they grow up into sedate hounds, and are drafted into the pack, then later to visit the old hounds at feeding time, is an interesting sight.

Let us, by the aid of the Urbanora, follow in an ideal day's sport; see the big hounds being brought to the meeting place, see the crowds of riders as well as hundreds of people in carriages and on foot, coming in from the surrounding villages were they are staying, and note the beauty of these quaint villages and the glorious scenery through which we pass, till getting up amongst the hills we too arrive at the meet.

Pursued up Stream by the Pack.

Soon the Master arrives, and with the cry of "Hounds, please!" the pack is taken and temporarily kennelled in some adjacent farm building, then about five couple of wily old hounds are called out and taken off to try the woods where a good stag is reported to be lying. The riders have moved off to various points of vantage whence they can see what is happening, when suddenly a farmer near us sees something which excites him, something is moving in that distant wood; yes! there, out of the wood and over the sky-line, trot a fine stag and some hinds; then leaving them he crosses the meadows and makes for the hilltop.

Next the " tufters " (i.e., the first lot of hounds used to find the stag) come rushing out of cover full cry on his line. These must be stopped, so the huntsman and some others ride after them and stop them on the open hilltop, where the stag crossed whilst the Master gallops back to release the " pack " (i.e., the main body of hounds, left at the farm) with which he is soon back again, followed by a large crowd of riders, the horses all excitement at the sudden rush.

A few minutes more giving the Master and huntsmen just time to change on to fresh horses, then the pack is laid on to the line, and we are off. Up hill and down dale we go, with here and there a riderless horse, for although on top it is good going, the hillsides are very steep and the bottoms of the valleys soft and treacherous.

An argument in Mid-stream.

After some miles of hard going it looks as if our run were at an end, for there below us is our stag, beating up and down a big stream, the hounds close upon him; but he breaks away, and we once more make for the top, where he seems to have lost himself utterly and the huntsmen are baffled, when suddenly, just as it seemed hopeless, out he jumps from a clump of scrub, and makes for water once again. The hounds do not mean to be baffled this time, so close on him quickly, but with his great antlers he beats them off, and discretion being the better part of valour, he then makes off to the moor once more, in the direction of the coast.

Soon the cool evening breeze meets us, giving our tired horses new life, and there, below us, lies the blue Bristol Channel, shimmering in the late summer sun. There too goes a red speck, with white specks after it, through that golden cornfield. Those are the stag and hounds, making for the shore so riding as far as possible we at last tie up our horses, and scramble down the precipitous cliff, only to see the stag swimming out to sea.

Back again to our horses we scramble, and ride to Porlock Weir, to see the fishermen, news having been brought them, putting out to sea after the stag. An hour elapses ere the boat with the captured stag comes back ; he has had six years or more of good wild life, living as a king upon the wild moor, and has now given us a great run.

"Who whoop!" cries the huntsman, as he throws the stag's entrails to the hungry hounds, then gives the "slots" (feet) away as trophies, and marks a newcomer on the face with a piece of flesh, as a sign of his initiation to the sport.

Dragging the Stag from the Stream.

The day is over, our mounts are gruelled, and we start on our long ride homeward, taking it easily, and stopping to water the horses at a stream. Then on again, taking with us our faithful Bioscope which will have to be out many a day again, till at last, after a total of 1,200 miles over hill and down dale, we secure a representative series of pictures of this noble sport, to place before audiences the world over by "Urbanora."

The most exciting Stag Hunt series ever photographed.

FOR OTHER RECENT HUNTING SERIES
see description . . . .

1508 'A Fox Hunt with the Quorn Hounds'
1510 'An Otter Hunt on Exmoor.'
BOTH SPLENDID SERIES.

3300 ... BLACK DIAMONDS ;

Or, THE COLLIERS' DAILY LIFE.

Photographed in the Black Country (Midlands) by Messrs. MITCHELL
AND KENYON.

Coal is wanted by everybody, but very few persons know anything about the conditions under which it is mined. The mines of the United Kingdom have an output of 230 million tons per year, and a portion of this huge total is taken from pits more than 2,000 feet in depth. The procuring of this enormous quantity of coal entails great risk to life and limb every year, providing an alarming list of killed and injured. Sometimes men are entombed under circumstances so dangerous, that to reach them means almost certain death, yet rescue parties are ever ready to brave any danger. This series of Pictures has been arranged for the express purpose of representing the miner's life exactly as it is lived day by day. The scene showing an explosion, where men are at work 1,500 feet deep, only represents what actually happens with alarming frequency.

ORDER OF PICTURES.

1—"Good Morning." The miner leaving his home for the day's work.

2—Arrival at the Pit. Men going down in the cage.

3—The Pit Head. Hauling tubs of coal to different levels.

4—A Revolving Hauler passing tubs from one place to another.

5—Out of Darkness into Light. Coal coming up the shaft.

6—Sorting. Coal passing through a chute on to endless belt.

7—Pit Brow Girls at work on the belt.

8—At the Pit Mouth. Men and women at work—a most remarkable scene.

9—In the Pit 1,500 feet deep. A miner "holing" coal—coal "getting"—an explosion—men buried in *débris*—comrades to rescue.

(*This section is tinted to impart a subdued light on the scenes.*)

10—Coals for Everybody. Coal-laden trains leaving the Pit.

11—The Day's Work done. Men coming up the cage—examination of lamps, &c.

12—The Wage List. One man in a hurry has "come up" only partly dressed.

13—The Miner Returns. Hastening to welcome "Daddy."

14—The Collier's Back Garden. Washing day—a wet reception—speeding the parting guest (comic).

FINIS—A Warm and Cosy Fire. Showing the blazing coal in an open grate.

(*This last section is coloured to the natural glow and blaze of the fire.*)

Total length 675 feet.   Price £17 10s.

NOTE.—Supplied on condition that it is not exhibited or re-sold in England or the United States, where exclusive exhibition rights have been acquired by **Urbanora**.

THE TRAGEDY OF .. ᴄᴇ PORT ARTHUR.

The Greatest in History.

The following Pictures, which are absolutely the only authentic Animated Views of events connected with the Siege of Port Arthur, were secured by Mr. JOSEPH ROSENTHAL, the only War Correspondent in the Far East who was granted permission by the Japanese War Office to accompany the 3rd Imperial Army in its operations against Port Arthur.

General BARON NOGI, Commandant of the 3rd Division, which Invested and caused the Surrender of Port Arthur, granted our Mr. Rosenthal every facility to further his object on our behalf.

General Baron Nogi, Commander of the 3rd Imperial Japanese Army . . . . .

Without depreciating the hardships undergone by the Press War Correspondents in sending forth to their respective journals accounts of the progress of the Siege, this work may be successfully accomplished from comparatively safe distances, and positions, but in the securing of Bioscopic records of the events depicted in the following series, **Mr. Rosenthal** was compelled to enter the firing line and expose himself and his instrument to many dangers unnecessary to the regular Press Correspondent or the Press Artist with the hand camera, who can " snap his views " at long ranges by means of telephoto lenses, which are not as yet applicable to animated photography.

While experiencing many narrow escapes, Mr. Rosenthal nevertheless succeeded in securing one of the most unique picture series since the invention of animated photography

NOTE.—Every Russo-Japanese War Picture listed by us is absolutely genuine and should not be confounded with the disgraceful series of fakes, eminating principally from French sources, which have, by their exhibition, misled the public and cast a doubt as to authenticity of the results obtained at great risk and expense by the concientious Film Maker.

Q

The Exhibition of Faked Incidents of **SERIOUS EVENTS** should be discouraged alike by the **Exhibitor**, as well as the **Manager** engaging him, as it results in depreciating this wonderful means of enlightening the public.

The Siege and Surrender of Port Arthur.

The stupendous event of the siege and defence of Port Arthur, with its subsequent surrender, has thrilled the whole world. It is safe to say that no siege in ancient, mediæval or modern times has exceeded in intensity of earnestness either the spirit of the besieger or that of the defenders. For many months what it is safe to call the most scientific army in the world, without apparently any lack of resources, has used its best endeavours, regardless of the loss of life or treasure, to capture this much coveted fortress.

British Officers watching the final attack on Port Arthur.

On the other side there has been a determination in the defence which may have been equalled, but certainly has not been exceeded, by that of Todleben and the brave Russian soldiers in Sebastopol; not even by the brilliant General Williams and the garrison of Kars, nor even by the brave French defenders of Strasbourg, Metz and the other fortified cities in the Franco-German war. Probably, when we take into account the undaunted sacrifice of human life, the seige and defence of Port Arthur is unequalled in the world's history.

The public has been thrilled and is eager to learn all the details, to have faithful representations of what has happened during this most momentous event. Nothing can faithfully portray the succession of incidents in connection with the siege as the life motion pictures secured by Mr. ROSENTHAL, the War Correspondent of the **CHARLES URBAN TRADING Co., Ltd.**

THE LIVING HISTORY OF THE GREAT WAR.

For the convenience of exhibition, this Life Motion Picture record has been divided into three separate sections, viz :

No. 1—"The Russian Army in Manchuria"

No. 2—"The Siege of Port Arthur"

No. 3—"The Surrender of Port Arthur"

Watching the Shelling of Port Arthur.

1520 The Russian Army in Manchuria.

Photographed by Mr. GEORGE ROGERS, *by courtesy of* General KUROPATKIN.

ORDER OF PICTURES.

1.—**Panorama of the Ural Mountain District, Siberia.** Photographs from the front of a moving train of the Trans-Siberian Railway.

2—**Entraining of Reserves for Irkoutsk.**

3—**Arrival of General Kuropatkin at Irkoutsk** — being received by Generals R e n n e m k a m p f and Grekoff.

4—**Russian Infantry and Troop of Cossacks** crossing the frozen Lake Baikal.

5—**A Train of Troika Transports of Army Provisions and Ammunition** crossing Baikal over Ice.

6—**The Departure of the Ice-Crushing Steamer " Baikal "** from Baikal Station.

7—**Arrival of the Survivors of the Battle of Chemulpo** at Baikal Station.

8—**General view of Railway Station at Harbin** showing arrival of the 1st Regiment Siberian Sharpshooters.

9—**Arrival of General Kuropatkin and Staff** at Harbin Railway Station.

10—**General Kuropatkin Reviewing the Russian Troops at Harbin.**

" Loot."

11—Animated Street Scene of the Native District Mukden (since captured by the Japanese).

12—Extraordinary Feats of Horsemanship by Siberian Cossacks outside Harbin.

DESCRIPTIONS OF THE ABOVE SERIES will be noted under Subjects 3030, 3017, 3019, 3021, 3020, 3029, 3024, 3026, 3023, 3027, 3025. These Pictures are listed separately upon pages 91 to 105.

Total Length, 1,600 feet.   Price £40.

(Duration of exhibit, 30 minutes).

"THE SIEGE OF PORT ARTHUR,"

From February 8th, 1904, to January 2nd, 1905.

Showing Incidents during the Investment by the 3rd Imperial Japanese Army under Command of General Baron Nogi, in the Trenches and the Battlefields surrounding Port Arthur.

Photographed by our War Correspondent, Mr. JOSEPH ROSENTHAL.

Japanese Wounded at Dalny.

NOTE.—*The majority of Despatches reprinted herewith are Extracts from the " Daily Mail " Issues.*

DECISIVE DATES OF THE PORT ARTHUR SEIGE.

Landing of the Second Japanese Army at Pitsewo, May 5.
Port Arthur cut off, May 12.
Battle of Nanshan and capture of that position, May 26.
First sortie and repulse of the Russian fleet, June 23.
Second sortie and defeat of the Russian fleet, August 10.
First great assault fails, with Japanese loss of 14,000, August 20-4.
Second general assault on Metre Ridge and Antseshan fails, with terrible Japanese loss, September 19.
Bombardment with heavy guns begins, October 1.

Third great assault on the forts partially succeeds : Kuropatkin Fort captured, October 30.

Dockyard in Port Arthur shelled and destroyed by the Japanese, November 8.

Assault on 203 Metre Hill begins, November 25.

Metre Hill finally secured and Russian counter-attacks repulsed, December 4.

Peresviet put out of action by Japanese bombardment, December 5.

Poltava and Retvisan put out of action, December 6.

Pobieda and Pallada destroyed, December 8.

The Sevastopol, the last of the Russian battleships, leaves the harbour, and is ten times torpedoed, December 12-13.

One and a half tons of dynamite exploded under Fort North Kikwan, and the fort stormed by the Japanese, December 13.

Positions near Pigeon Bay captured by the Japanese, December 19-24.

Two tons of dynamite exploded under Fort Erhlungshan and fort stormed, December 28.

Mines exploded under Fort Songshu and fort captured, December 31.

Panlung West Fort and H fort stormed, January 1.

Surrender of Port Arthur, January 1, 9 p.m.

Formal Terms of Surrender arranged, January 3rd, 1905.

ORDER OF PICTURES.

1—**A Regiment of the 3rd Division Imperial Japanese Troops leaving Tokio for the Front**—A solid column of Troopers marching between lines of the native populace, who bid them farewell, and cheer them on their progress through the streets of the Mikado's capital.

2—**Army Transports passing through Dalny.**—Showing hundreds of Chinese two-wheeled carts, drawn by every specimen of mule or horse imaginable, passing through the main streets of the recent Russian settlement. The mode of transporting to the front of the vast Japanese army stores which were landed at Dalny has proven a most efficient one, although seemingly slow to the spectator; the ammunition carts being driven by Chinese, under Japanese escort.

Japanese Infantry awaiting Orders to Attack 203 Metre Hill.

3—**General Baron Oshima at Counsel with his Officers.**—A splendid portrai of the famous Japanese General discussing plans of compaign with his subordinates. (The picture was taken just outside of the General's tent, showing these officers at a table inside the tent with front flaps thrown back.)

4—Ammunition Transport proceeding through a Mountain Pass. Similar transport trains composed of two wheeled carts laden with Army stores, drawn by horses, could be noted for miles approaching the Camps from various directions over captured territory. The Japanese Army was thus supplied with a proficient quantity of ammunition and provisions during their investments of Port Arthur.

Japanese Trenches one mile from Port Arthur.

5—Troops Building Defences. The advance troops in making a likely stand against a skirmish of Russian outposts, hastily constructed defences by piling up sacks of sand, bales of forage, and Army stores which withstood the force of a Cavalry charge and gave some protection to the troops firing from the openings of the thus hastily created barricades.

6.—Advance of the Japanese Army. This picture conveys an excellent idea of the nature of the country in which the two opposing Armies operated. It shows a regiment of Infantry filing through the mountains in the proximity of 203 Metre Hill, which latter fort they captured after one of the hardest fought and most stubborn assaults in history.

General Baron Oshima in the Trenches watching the Shelling of Port Arthur.

7—Cleaning Guns after an Action. A group of Japanese soldiers cleaning their rifles was secured in the advance trenches after the first assault on 203 Metre Hill. The alternate expression of determination and laughter on the faces of these warriors convey a good idea of the resolute yet happy disposition of the Japanese soldier.

8.—Inspecting Rifles in the Advance Trenches. Previous to an action, all guns are tested and inspected. This picture was taken in a trench 100 yards from the Russian firing line at the base of 203 Metre Hill, and shows an officer inspecting every rifle most carefully.

9—Attack on the North Kikwan Fort. This picture was taken in a downpour of rain showing a detachment of troops storming the North Kikwan Fort after the same had been blown up on December 24th, 1904, by mines containing two tons of dynamite, which were planted under the fortress by the Japanese engineers tunnelling into the Hill side.

Japanese Long Range Naval Guns.

(*Press Notice.*)

STORMING OF NORTH KIKWAN.

WITH GENERAL NOGI'S HEADQUARTERS BEFORE PORT ARTHUR.
Wednesday, Dec. 21.

The principal attack on Fort North Kikwan was led in person by a general of division dressed in a new uniform, his breast covered with orders and medals. At the head of one battalion he swore, sword in hand, to capture the fort or die in the attempt.

It was going to certain death to attack in force in face of the Russian machine guns. The men consequently dribbled forward singly until the detachment had assembled under the shelter of the débris caused by the explosion.

North Kikwan Fort was rushed after five hours of fierce fighting at close range. Its garrison is estimated at 300 of whom few escaped, as the blasting operations had blocked the passage to the rear.

The Japanese who attacked wore grey jerseys and drawers over their dark uniforms, and carried only rifles, bandoliers, and hand-bombs. On their caps, tunics, and leggings their names had been written so as to be known even if they were blown to pieces, as happened in the assault on 203 Metre Hill.

The assailants well knew the fate which probably awaited them, but they faced it with unflinching courage.

On December 18, at the same moment that North Kikwan was blown up, a Russian shell struck 203 Metre Hill. A Japanese store of hand-grenades was destroyed, and the violent explosion which resulted caused considerable damage.

10—**Panoramic View of the principal Fortifications of Port Arthur.** This unique picture was secured on January 3rd, after the capitulation of Port Arthur (we show the picture at this stage in order that the public may, by its exhibition, gain an accurate idea of the " theatre of war " in which the following events transpired). The prominent hill in the foreground is crowned by West Erhlungshan Fort, then follows the grand ring of Russian defences assailed and captured by the Japanese between December 16th and January 1st.

This view also plainly shows the sapping operations and trenches made by the Japanese in their operations against the forts.

MILES AND MILES OF SAPPING

After the failure of the general attack, the Japanese showed they had no intention of imitating the Russians at Plevna. There was only one thing left to them then : to make such arrangements that their own men should be as well sheltered during their advance as the defenders behind their ramparts. Earth must combat earth. Not a step must be taken without shoving a wall of earth or sandbags in front of them which could stop the enemy's bullets. Bomb-proofs must be built on the way where the men could rest, when they had been relieved, and sleep overnight. Miles and miles of these saps would have to be dug sometimes through soft, alluvial soil, sometimes through shale rock, sometimes through rock made up of conglomerate of limestone and flint and quartz, so hard that it had to be chiselled out; it could not be helped; it was all in the day's work.

And they could not let their saps advance in straight lines against the forts : that would, of course, expose them to an enfilading fire. They had to dig them in zigzag lines, so as always to present a protecting wall against the enemy, and as in this case it was not a question of protecting their men against one fort only but from forts out to the left and out to the right as well, these saps or approaches had in most places to be dug in more windings and more parallel to their base than in ordinary cases.

1000 Men Transporting an 11-inch Siege Gun.

11—Field Gun in Action. Showing one of the field guns operated by a squad of Artillerymen firing round after round from the gun, which rebounds up an incline after each shot. This photograph was taken by Mr. Rosenthal during the assault on 203 Metre Hill.

MARKED JAPANESE SUCCESS.

*(From the "*DAILY MAIL*" Correspondent.)*

TOKIO, Monday, December 19.

Reliable despatches from the front state that the right wing of the army besieging Port Arthur seized on December 18 an important position a thousand yards south-east of 203 Metre Hill.

12—Transporting an 11-inch Siege Gun. Showing the manner in which these heavy Howitzer (17 ton) guns are transported from one position to another, sometimes requiring the united efforts of 1,000 troopers to move them. The gun carriages are mounted on comparatively small but very wide iron wheels to prevent them sinking into the soft ground owing to the tremendous weight of the gun.

11-inch Guns pouring 500lb. Shells into Port Arthur.

13—The Battery of 11-inch Guns pouring 500lb. Shells into Port Arthur. Showing four of these formidable Howitzers in action during the shelling of Erhlungshan and Songshushan Forts, the fall and capture of which were finally accomplished on December 28th and 31st. The taking of these forts led to the surrender of Port Arthur.

(Press Notice.)

GREAT FORT TAKEN.

Saturday, Dec. 31.

Fort Songshushan was captured by the Japanese at eleven o'clock this morning.

At ten o'clock the besiegers exploded mines, according to a pre-arranged plan, and blew up the parapet of the fort.

Two tremendous explosions took place, and the majority of the garrison were buried in the débris caused by them.

The left column of the right centre of the besieging army charged the fort, and occupied the whole of it by eleven o'clock. Practically the Japanese encountered no opposition. One of the Russian mines exploded, but did no damage to the attackers.

The remainder of the garrison effected their retreat from the fort to a height lying south of it.

Sunday, Jan. 1.

This morning the Japanese effected an entrance into the bomb-proof gorge of Fort Songshushan, and they gradually rescued all the Russians who had been entombed by the explosions.

Two officers and above 160 men were saved and made prisoners; they stated that 150 soldiers were killed by the falling débris.

The fall of Port Arthur is largely the result of the terrible high-angle fire from the heavy Japanese howitzers. These shot indifferently at the beginning of the siege, but after the capture of 203 Metre Hill their practice was wonderfnl.

Mode of Japanese Advance for Attack on 203 Metre Hill.

14—**Blowing up Erhlingshan Fort, December 28th, 1904.**—This picture was taken from the Japanese position (which is depicted in the previous view, showing *Siege Guns in action*), and is about one mile distant from Erhlungshan. The following Press extracts refer to this incident:—

(*Press Notice.*)

It is officially reported by the Army besieging Port Arthur that Fort Erhlungshan was captured at 7.30 p.m. on December 28.

WITH THE JAPANESE THIRD ARMY.

Friday, Dec. 30.

General Nogi's left centre at ten o'clock on the morning of December 28 exploded six mines containing two tons of dynamite under the front breastworks of Erhlungshan fort, this being the strongest fort on the east ridge.

The explosion killed many of the garrison, and a number surrendered.

The front part of the fort was immediately rushed, and trenches and passages were quickly constructed.

The inner and higher part of the fort was rushed at two in the afternoon, and was followed up by heavy hand-to-hand fighting inside. Ultimately the Russians were driven out at three o'clock on the morning of December 29. The Japanese casualties amounted to 1,000, and would have been much larger but for the fact that the troops were admirably supported by their heavy artillery.

The two vital forts of Port Arthur are Erhlungshan and Sungshushan, and they were strenuously defended. The forts of East Erhlungshan and Peyushan are rather subsidiary forts, and they are able to assist in the defence, but their fighting capacity is small.

Sungshushan is, therefore, virtually isolated. The saps in that direction are believed to be complete, and an explosion is imminent.

The survivors of Erhlungshan have taken refuge in Sungshushan.

HEADQUARTERS, JAPANESE THIRD ARMY, BEFORE PORT ARTHUR.

Thursday, December 29.

Of the Russian garrison of 500, one-third escaped. — Reuter's special.

15—**Erhlingshan Fort after the Capture.**—A panoramic view taken inside the fort, showing the general havoc wrought by the Japanese shell fire and the explosions of dynamite which demolished the fort and guns and entombing 160 Russians (all that remained of a garrison of 500 men). These were rescued by the Japanese and made prisoners. During the assault on the fort, part of the garrison sought protection in the underground shelters, the shattered entrances to which are plainly shown in this picture, and it is owing to these that the captured Russians owe their lives.

Inside the Erhlungshan Fort after Capture by the Japanese.

"TWO TONS OF DYNAMITE."

WITH GENERAL NOGI'S HEADQUARTERS BEFORE PORT ARTHUR.

Friday, December 30.

The garrison of Erhlung Fort numbered 500 men of the 26th Siberian Rifles. Half of them were killed by the explosion of the mines, which contained two tons of dynamite, or by the first rush of the storming party. The remainder fought gallantly for ten hours, and 150 of them escaped.

The retreating Russians set fire to the buildings to the rear of the fort. The capture of this work of colossal strength in one day is a brilliant feat of arms.

16—**Baron Oshima Examining Shells and Torpedoes.**—In many of the captured forts were found a large number of torpedoes, mines and shells which were stored in underground magazines, and thus avoided exploding during the assault on the fort. These are brought forth and laid out for the inspection of the General.

17—**Russian Prisoners Captured at Erhlungshan.**—The blowing up of the fortress caused these 160 Russian soldiers to become entombed in the underground shelters by the shattering and closing up of the entrances. These men were dug out and rescued by the victorious Japanese after they had stormed and captured the fort.

A most pathetic sight to see these men with grim set countenances filing by with an armed escort of Japanese.

Total length about 1050 feet. Special Price, £45.

Thus ends the Series of unique Pictures which portray the Principal Events that led to the Surrender of Port Arthur.

THE SURRENDER OF PORT ARTHUR.

Photographed by Our War Correspondent,

Mr. JOSEPH ROSENTHAL, attached to **General Nogi's Head-quarters, Third Imperial Japanese Army, Port Arthur.**

Reprint from "THE DAILY MAIL," January 3rd, 1905.

THE SURRENDER OF PORT ARTHUR. HOW GENERAL STOESSEL CAPI-TULATED. HISTORIC SCENES.

Port Arthur has fallen after a siege of 235 days, and General Stoessel yesterday surrendered to the Japanese.

The capture of the fortress was the direct result of the storming of Erhlungshan and Songshushan forts. The Japanese pressed their successes on January 1 to the utmost, and during the day succeeded in carrying Wantai Fort. By the evening the Russians were in a hopeless position, and General Stoessel sent a flag of truce into the Japanese lines, proposing surrender.

At dawn yesterday General Nogi sent a messenger into the fortress and arranged for the immediate conclusion of the surrender. The terms offered by the Japanese were accepted by Russians and, though not as yet officially published, are said to allow the garrison to march out with all the honours of war, after which the Russian troops are to return to Russia on their parole. They will not be permitted to serve again during the present war.

The news of the great victory was received in Japan with extraordinary jubilation. The effect upon St. Petersburg is described as stunning.

General Baron Nogi and Staff leaving the Chinese House after meeting General Stoessel.

ORDER OF PICTURES.

1—The Meeting between General Baron Nogi and General Stoessel, January 5th, 1905.—Panoramic View of the Chinese House in the Ruined Village of Swishiying, where the terms of surrender were completed.

2—Arrival of General Baron Nogi and Staff to arrange Terms of Surrender.

3—General Stoessel, Colonel Reiss, Lieutenant Maltchenko and Cossacks leaving after their meeting with General Baron Nogi.

4—General Baron Nogi leaving after arranging Terms for the Surrender of Port Arthur.

NOTE.—*The preceding four views are the principal incidents referred to in the following Despatch:—*

Reprint from " DAILY MAIL," by kind permission of the Editor.

HISTORIC SCENE. FULL DETAILS OF THE RIVAL GENERALS MEETING. TOUCHING CHIVALRY. GENERAL STOESSEL AND HIS HORSE.

From the " DAILY MAIL " War Correspondent, B. W. NORREGARD, with General Nogi's Army at Port Arthur.

Saturday, Jan. 7.

I have been permitted by the censors to send further and fuller details of the great meeting between Generals Nogi and Stoessel on January, a brief account of which I have already telegraphed. The place of the meeting was the now historic Plum Tree Cottage in Swishi ying village, where the terms of capitulation were arranged some days ago.

General Stoessel was the first to ride up on a beautiful grey Arab steed, attended by his chief of staff, Colonel Reiss, Captain Maltschenko-Lieutenant Nebelskoff, and seven Cossacks. He was received by Captain Tsunoda, of the Japanese general staff.

General Nogi rode up on a fiery bay waler with his chief of staff, General Ijichi, Colonel Watanabe, and Captains Yasuhara and Matsudaira. He was nearly an hour later than General Stoessel, owing to a mistake. The two generals and their staffs then proceed inside the house.

The single room inside was perfectly bare. Its walls were papered with Japanese newspapers. It contained a table and a few Vienna chairs.

The two generals shook hands, Nogi opening the conversation with the words, "I am proud to shake hands with the gallant defender of Port Arthur—with a soldier who has fought so gallantly for his country."

General Stoessel replied that he was grateful for the compliment, and that he was fortunate in having met the hero of the besieging Army. General Nogi then read a message from the Emperor of Japan ordering him to treat General Stoessel with every possible honour, and stated that because of this message the Russian officers had been permitted to retain their side-arms.

MUTUAL COMPLIMENTS.

General Stoessel expressed his deepest gratitude to the Emperor, and said that his Imperial message would exalt the honour of his name among all future generations. After this General Nogi handed to General Stoessel the Czar's reply to General Stoessel's inquiry as to whether the Russian officers had permission to give their parole. The Czar's reply was as follows:—

> "I allow all my officers either to profit by the privilege offered to them, of returning to Russia under an obligation not to take any further part in the present war, or to share the fate of the prisoners. I thank you and your brave garrison for your gallant defence.—NICHOLAS."

Then followed a conversation in which each general complimented the other on his soldiers' bravery. They went on from this to discuss the capture of the Songshushan Fort. General Stoessel said that the whole garrison was buried by the mines exploded under the fort, and praised the practice made by the Japanese artillery, especially the manner in which the whole of the long line of siege batteries instantly concentrated their fire upon the spot where the explosion had occurred.

He declared that the skill shown by the Japanese infantry in constructing entrenchments and doing engineers' work was above all praise.

Knowing that General Nogi had lost both his sons in the campaign and was childless, General Stossel, in moving terms, condoled with him. He praised their loyalty and devotion, and praised, too, the father who had made so mighty a sacrifice for his nation and Emperor. General Nogi received these words with a calm smile, and went on to say that one of his sons was killed at Nanshan and one on 203 Metre Hill.

He added, "These vital positions, admirably defended as they were by your troops, were not too dearly bought with the lives of my two sons."

The words deeply moved all who heard them.

General Stoessel's Gift.

Then General Stoessel asked General Nogi's permission to present him with his own horse as a small token of his esteem. General Nogi declined with thanks, as he said that all the property taken belonged to the Army and he had no right to accept anything. But he declared that the horse would be carefully tended and always treated with exceptional kindness.

General Nogi next asked General Stoessel to remain at Port Arthur until proper arrangements could be made to take him and his family to Russia. He promised to bury all the fallen Russians in one great tomb, and to erect a memorial to them in honour of their bravery.

General Stoessel asked that the town of Fort Arthur should be occupied by the Japanese without delay, as the unwounded regular troops had now been sent to Yahutsui Fort. It was difficult, he went on, to prevent the volunteers or civilians from committing acts of incendiarism. He apologised for two fires which occurred that day.

After lunch the group of officers and generals was photographed by the Japanese official Army photographer. Then General Stoessel had his horse led in and mounted it, showing General Nogi its good points.

The two generals separated at 1.10, after further mutual compliments, and General Stoessel rode back to Port Arthur. Both sides displayed the utmost cordiality and dignity, but dramatic incidents were altogether absent.

B. W. Norregaard.

General Stoessel leaving Port Arthur.

5—**Panorama of the New Town, Port Arthur.** This view was photographed during the entry of the first Japanese troops into Port Arthur, and distinctly shows the effect of the shelling of the Town. The civilians of Port Arthur who survived the siege are seen grouped along the sides of the main street watching the entry of the victors. The second view is a circular Panorama of the Japanese camp outside of Port Arthur, photographed the day after the surrender, showing a vast expanse of country literally covered with tents, camp kitchens, troops, horses, field guns, &c., ascribed here preparatory to the State entry of the 3rd Division into Port Arthur.

6—**Luncheon to the Entire Staff Officers of the 3ed Imperial Japanese Army.** To celebrate the victory, an elaborate luncheon was spread for the officers and troops, thousands of whom are seen partaking of the bountiful rations served in honour of the momentous event.

7—**Luncheon to the Troops of the Victorious Army.** This is a continuation of the previous picture, and shows the vast army of troops enjoying the feast spread for them in the open. All are well covered by fur overcoats, but owing to the intense cold (it being mid winter), the men are constantly on the move while eating in order to keep warm. Even the horses are provided with extra allowance of fodder which they apparently appreciate.

The officers mess is divided from those of the troops by a wide " street," in which was erected a triumphial arch, carrying the Japanese colours

8.—**Russian Prisoners leaving Port Arthur, January 8th.** For description of this picture see the following reprint of Reuters' Special.

HOW THE RUSSIAN TROOPS MARCHED OUT.

The Russian prisoners at Port Arthur are being steadily moved to Dalny, and details are given to-day of the march of 5,000 of them from Pigeon Bay to the nearest railway station on the Dalny line. There are signs of renewed activity on the Shaho, where the Japanese are expected to move as soon as weather conditions permit. Wireless messages, which may be from a Russian or Japanese cruiser, have been taken in by the British cruiser Mauritius.

PATHETIC SPECTACLE.

HEADQUARTERS OF THE THIRD JAPANESE ARMY OUTSIDE PORT ARTHUR.

Friday, Jan. 6.

Five thousand of the garrison of Port Arthur marched this afternoon from Pigeon Bay fifteen miles to Changlingtsu railway station. The first detachment of a thousand men arrived at Changlingtsu at three o'clock.

Other detachments followed, each with half-a-dozen transport wagons, and were taken to Dalny in special trains composed of open trucks. From that port they will embark immediately for Japan on transports which are waiting in readiness.

The long procession of the remnants of the gallant Russian garrison presented a pathetic spectacle. The first arrival at Changlingtsu were four droskies, which were drawn by sorry-looking horses, and which contained staff officers who had refused to give their parole not to take any further part in the war. The officers all wore their swords, as permitted under the terms of capitulation.

A few minutes later the first detachment arrived. The regimental officers marched with their men. Their heads were bowed and their faces were seamed with lines, the result of the mental and physical strain of their long resistance.

HUMILIATING POSITION.

As the Japanese soldiers desiring to get a nearer view crowded about them, their faces presented a curious study. All appeared to feel keenly their humiliating position. While some appeared resigned, others showed signs of resentment at being gazed upon with such curiosity.

The men looked well-fed, but their faces showed signs of the terrible physical strain which they had undergone. The officers were clean and well-clothed, but the men were clad in filthy sheepskin coats. They seemed resigned, and glad indeed that the end had come.

The horses drawing the Transport wagons were staggering with fatigue, although their loads were small. Tied to the carts or led by orderlies were many lean-looking pet dogs belonging to some of the officers.

In many cases the officers refused to wear their swords, and had them carried behind them by orderlies. They saluted the European correspondents, who were stationed among the Japanese troops, and appeared surprised and pleased to find that the prisoners, as they marched through the rear lines of the investing army and the ranks of the war-worn Japanese soldiery were treated with the greatest respect and kindliness, though they were regarded with much natural curiosity. They were given food, cigarettes, and beer, and I even saw Japanese soldiers voluntarily carrying the effects of the prisoners when they noticed that these were overcome with fatigue.—Reuter's Special.

Japanese Encampment outside Port Arthur.

9—**Transport of Prisoners' Baggage to Pigeon Bay.**—This picture is likewise described in same article.

10—**Departure of the First Train of Russian Prisoners for Dalny.**—Showing about 20 open trucks absolutely packed with Russians prisoners on their way to Japan, each truck being under guard of Japanese soldiers.

R

11—Arrival of General Stoessel, Madame Stoessel, and the Children at the Railway Head. This is one of the most pathetic pictures ever photographed, and as the photographic quality is excellent and personages depicted therein life size, an excellent portrait is had of every one passing our camera.

STOESSEL LEAVES PORT ARTHUR.

Tokio, Thursday, Jan. 12.

General Stoessel, accompanied by his family and Maojr-General Reiss, left Port Arthur to-day. Generals Fock and Smyrnoff and other officers joined them at Changlingtsu station, where they entrained for Dalny. They leave that port to-day on the Ogura Maru, bound for Nagasaki.

GENERAL STOESSEL IN JAPAN.

Naasgaki, Saturday, Jan. 14.

The Kamakura Maru arrived here early this morning, and at 3 p.m. General and Mme. Stoessel, two members of his personal staff and seven officers, two ladies, and six orphan children landed in three steam launches at the Inasa Jetty, where they were received by a guard of fifty police and several gendarme officers.

The general was attired in a grey military overcoat, and wore his sword. He looked well, and walked with a stately step, preceded by a few police officers and followed by his retinue.—Reuter's Special.

12—Train Bearing General Stoessel and paroled Officers and Soldiers leaving for Dalny. In this picture the train described in the following article is vividly shown :—

Reprint from "Pall Mall."

In a long article the correspondent of "The Times" with the Port Arthur army describes, as follows, some of the circumstances amid which General and Madame Stoessel made their final departure from Port Arthur :—

Then occurred a scene which those who witnessed it will never forget, and will ever remember with shame and disgust. Even third-class carriages are scarce on the Dalny-Port Arthur line ; one has to be content to make the journey in open trucks ; but on this occasion there was a saloon for Stoessel, with a few carriages for the women and children. Directly the General and his wife had entered the train one expected to see the women and children led forward and assisted into the remaining vacant seats ; but no, the crowd of generals and officers pushed forward and entered the carriages, pushing past the women and children without paying the slightest regard for them. Soon every single carriage was packed with these gentlemen, and the women and children were left on the platform sitting on their luggage.

The indignation of every foreigner present, and every Japanese, was instantly aroused by this last exhibition of callousness and brutality. "They treat their women like so many beasts," was the comment of one. Some of the station officials and Japanese officers intervened, and assisted the helpless ones into the most empty of the open trucks, which were already nearly full of the officers' servants, who, taking the cue from their masters, were not going to wait for the women and children to be seated first. Some of the women found seats in the trucks, intermingled with the dirty, common soldiers, and the luggage of the officers in the closed carriages. One beautiful widow, whose husband had been killed in the siege, whose very appearance one would have thought might have aroused a spark of dormant gallantry in the breast of one of the Tsar's warrior, was left wandering about, and would have missed the train had not General Nogi's A.D.C., Captain Matsuada, cleared out some of the soldiers and found room for her in a truck.

Then, with a last whistle, the train slowly moved off, carrying with it the true cause of Russia's downfall in the Far East, and leaving seated on the platform, to await for hours the arrival of the next train, the majority of the women and children. It was a miserable scene, and dissipated the last remaining feeling of regret for the misfortunes of the garrison.

Japanese Entry into Port Arthur (Mr. Rosenthal Bioscoping the event) January 13th 1905.

13.—**State Entry of the Japanese Army into Port Arthur, January 13th, 1905.** The procession is headed by the Japanese Military Band, which, after marching past the camera, is stationed to the right of General Nogi and Staff.

14.—**Entry of General Baron Nogi and Staff, accompanied by Foreign Military Attaches.** The General and escort take up their position in the main square of the New Town, Port Arthur, preparatory to the review of the entry of the victorious Army.

15.—**Review of the Entry of the Third Imperial Japanese Army into Port Arthur.** A grand picture of an historic scene.

THE JAPANESE ENTRY.

(From Our Own Correspondent.)

Tokio, Friday, Jan. 13.

At ten o'clock this morning was held the ceremony marking the entrance of the Japanese Army into Port Arthur.

R 2

One detachment of infantry and another of artillery, with a body of cavalry and engineers, assembled north of the fortress. The column marched to the sound of the bugle in extended formation through the Old and New Town, of Port Arthur presenting a fine martial spectacle.

As the regimental colours, tattered by shot and shell and stained with blood, were carried past the ranks, the faces of the men showed deep emotion.

The Russian and Chinese residents are now peacefully pursuing their occupations.

Total Length about 1,150 feet.
Special Price - - - £55.

Complete Series "Russian Army in Manchuria," "Siege of Port Arthur," and "Surrender of Port Arthur,"
Total Length 3,800 feet.   Price £140.

Duration of Exhibit about 1 hour 20 minutes.

Lantern Slides of the above will be supplied at 2s. each.

IMPORTANT NOTICE. — All Pictures of the "SIEGE AND SURRENDER OF PORT ARTHUR" are Copyrighted, and we will proceed against anyone infringing our rights.

The Resale or Exhibition of this series is Prohibited in the UNITED KINGDOM and the UNITED STATES OF AMERICA, for which Countries the URBANORA EXHIBITION COMPANY have acquired the Exclusive Exhibition Rights.

Re Private Urbanora Exhibit.

AT THE JAPANESE LEGATION, LONDON.

———◆———

"DAILY EXPRESS," *April 14th*, 1905.

War in Pictures--Port Arthur Siege on the Bioscope.

Within the next three weeks London will be gazing at bioscope pictures of the actual scenes at the taking of Port Arthur, the entry of the Japanese, the meeting of Generals Nogi and Stossel, the plunging of enormous shells, the capture of forts, and the departure of prisoners.

This marvel will become possible through the enterprise of the Urban Bioscope Company, whose "correspondent," Mr. Rosenthal, has sent home a complete series—the only one in existence—taken during the siege of the great fortress.

The pictures will be exhibited at eight special matinees at the Alhambra and then at the evening performances.

One set of films shows an attack on the formidable Urlung Fort at Port Arthur, with the heavy guns at work. Another shows the Japanese entering the same fort after its capture. The Russian dead are strewn around, and the devastation wrought by the heavy artillery is painfully manifest.

Several films show actual fighting, both artillery and infantry, and many contain details of the havoc worked by the deadly 11in. shells.

The meeting of Generals Nogi and Stoessel at Shiushiying is fully shown. Then there is the entry of the Japanese army—regiment after regiment of war-worn troops filing past into the captured fortress.

———————

" WINNING POST," *April 15th*, 1905.

The enterprise that has been awakened by the possibilities of modern photography is exemplified every day by the Urbanora management. Their latest achievement has been the taking of animated pictures of the siege and evacuation of Port Arthur. The chief condition upon which the Japanese Government permitted these pictures to be taken, was that they should in their entirety be shown to Viscount Hayashi and the personnel of the Japanese Embassy before being exhibited publicly. His Excellency has appointed Thursday evening, the 20th inst., for Mr. Urban's attendance, after which date no doubt the public will be able to form some opinion of the horrors of Port Arthur from an actual representation of events as they occurred.

———————

" MORNING ADVERTISER," *April 21st*, 1905.

New War Pictures.

A private exhibition of Urbanora pictures of the Japanese-Russian war was given on the bioscope at the Japanese Legation last night in the presence of Viscount Hayashi and about 40 members of the Legation, and friends.

The pictures which form this remarkable series have been taken by the war correspondents of the Charles Urban Trading Company, who, since the outbreak of hostilities, have been with the armies of Russia and Japan. Every outstanding incident of the war has thus been secured for a collection of animated pictures which **in point of historical interest and importance has no parallel in cinematography.**

The exhibition was given last night in fulfilment of a condition imposed by the Japanese military authorities that the pictures of the operations before Port Arthur and of the surrender of the fortress were not to be shown in public until they had been submitted privately to the Japanese minister and the personnel of the Legation,

"WEEKLY DISPATCH," *April 23rd*, 1905.

War by Picture.—How the Japanese Legation Greeted News of the Fall of Port Arthur.

The Japanese Legation in London has had a red-letter day in watching, by means of special biograph pictures, the progress of the Russo-Japanese war from the commencement of hostilities to the fall of Port Arthur.

The occasion was a private exhibition of Urbanora pictures of the war, taken by correspondents of the Charles Urban Trading Company, who have throughout the struggle accompanied the contending armies.

In all there were some forty members of the Japanese Legation present, and among the four Englishmen privileged to view the historic films was a representative of the "Weekly Dispatch.'

Viscount Hayashi, the Japanese Minister, was there, and on his knee nestled a tiny little Japanese boy, who took the liveliest interest in the pictures.

Calm and inperturbable Baron Hayashi watched the gallant deeds of his brave countrymen without showing any outward sign of enthusiasm, until a splendid series of pictures of a successful attack on the East Erhlung Fort was shown. Then, momentarily, his enthusiasm showed itself, and he cried aloud, "Bravo! Bravo," while the youngster sitting on his knee shyly looked up into his smiling face and whispered audibly, "When I grow up to be a big man I fight the Russians." The Ambassador's reply was merely an encouraging smile

Ah, the Brave Nogi

The Japanese ladies viewed the proceedings quite calmly until a magnificent picture of the arrival of General Baron Nogi to arrange terms with General Stoessel for the surrender of Port Arthur was shown; the historic meeting, however, then entirely broke down their reserve, and in shrill falsetto tones they cried "Ah, the brave Nogi."

As a fine Urbanora picture of the entry of the Japanese army into Port Arthur was shown on the sheet, Viscount Hayashi cried, "Brave men, brave men." His tiny charge clapped his hands delightedly and then, mindful of the disappointment and splendid defence of General Stoessel's troops, the youngster sadly said, "Poor, poor Russians." In all over forty-three pictures were shown.

So great was the difficulty in getting then out of the country that on one occasion a number of films were wrapped in cabbage heads to escape the vigilant watch kept by the censors of both armies.

JAPANESE LEGATION,

4, GROSVENOR GARDENS,

LONDON, S.W.

April 21st, 1905.

Messrs.

THE CHARLES URBAN TRADING COMPANY, Ltd.

Dear Sirs,

At the desire of Viscount Hayashi I have the pleasure to say that the War Pictures which you kindly displayed at this Legation last night very much interested the Viscount, as well as all his friends who were present. He further directs me to express to you his thanks for your courtesy and kindness in thus bringing those remarkable Pictures before his notice.

I am,

Yours faithfully,

(Signed) **C. KAIKÉ,**

Secretary.

RAILWAY SERIES.

1068 ... THE C.P.R. IMPERIAL LIMITED AT FULL SPEED
(*See* Canadian Series.)   **50 feet**

1078 ... SNOW BREAKING ON THE WANGERALP RAILWAY
(*See* Swiss Series.)   **150 feet**

1081 ... SCENES FROM A CAR ON THE REICHENBACH RAIL-WAY
(*See* Swiss Series.)   **150 feet**

1098 to 1227 ... CANADIAN PACIFIC RAILWAY PANO-RAMAS

For description see " Rocky Mountain " Series.

1127 ... THE JUNGFRAU ELECTRIC RAILWAY—Swiss
(*See* Swiss Series.)   **75 feet**

1133 ... THE PRESIDENTIAL TRAIN LEAVING THE ST. LAZARE STATION, PARIS
50 feet

1146 ... "WILL THE EXPRESS OVERTAKE THEM?"

A gang of trackmen are seen racing a hand-trolley within a few hundred yards in front of the approaching express train, the latter gradually gaining on the trolley, the men on which work their hardest to prevent a collision, by increasing the speed of their frail car.
Length 60 feet

1152 ... THREE C.P.R. TRAINS CROSSING THE SELKIRKS

This picture was obtained in three localities in the Rocky Mountains, each amidst most picturesque surroundings. First we note a C.P.R. passenger train rounding a curve and proceeding towards the camera at a high rate of speed—then follows a view of the " Imperial Express " thundering by, while the last section shows a heavy train drawn by two gigantic engines coming up a heavy grade of the Kicking-horse Pass. An excellent picture with fine smoke and steam effects.
100 feet

1259 ... TRANSPORT OF GIGANTIC 100 TON ARMOUR PLATE BY THE GREAT CENTRAL RAILWAY
A novel cargo.
100 feet

1345 RAILWAY ACCIDENT BY COLLISION

Showing an engine shunting trucks, colliding with another train in consequence of which the trucks are derailed and hurled down an embankment.
100 feet

1348 ... **RAILWAY COLLISION AND RESCUE OF WOUNDED**

This picture includes a splendid view of the same accident as in 1345, after which is shown the work of the Red Cross Society in rescuing and tending the wounded. Full of action throughout and of splendid photographic quality. **275 feet**

1349 ... **THE FIRST ELECTRIC TRAIN ON THE GREAT WESTERN RAILWAY**

Showing the first Electric Train leaving Paddington Station on one of the electrically equipped branch lines of the G.W.R. **50 feet**

1350 ... **AROUND THE PADDINGTON ENGINE YARD**

Scores of trains and switching engines constantly in view, some leaving the Station, others shunting, being turned on revolving platform, Trains arriving, being coaled, &c.

A typical picture of a busy corner of the Railway World.

175 feet

1358 ... **RAILROADING THROUGH THE PASS OF TIRNOVA, BULGARIA**

Tirnova is one of the most ruggedly picturesque spots on the Continent, lying amidst the mountain fastnesses of the Balkans. The town was formerly the seat of the Bulgarian Government, and is destined to become one of the places of pilgrimage of tourists who are constantly in search of experiences amidst novel surroundings. These they will find at Tirnova, hidden away in "savage Europe."

200 feet

1428 ... **THROUGH CONWAY ON THE NORTH WESTERN**

Panorama of the London and North-Western Line from Colwyn Bay to Conway.

This picture, taken from the front of a special train starting from the well-known holiday resort, Colwyn Bay, gives a unique experience of passing through a large junction station at full speed ; just as the train passes through the Junction, the "Llandudno Express" is seen coming to a stand in the Station. Leaving Llandudno on the right, the line takes us over the estuary of the River Conway, and a beautiful panoramic view of Conway Castle comes into the scene. This ancient castle, built by Edward I., still retains its mediæval walls and battlements, and the Conway Station, through which the special train passes, has been built in complete harmony with its historic surroundings. A beautiful picture of a beautiful place! **200 feet.**

1429 ... **FROM CONWAY TO ANGLESEY ON THE LONDON AND NORTH-WESTERN RAILWAY**

Another splendid panorama, being really a continuation of the last picture. Leaving Conway—the line runs a short distance through a rocky cutting—Penmaenmawr Hill suddenly comes into view, covered with its network of slate quarries, through Penmaenmawr Station and Tunnel, showing a view of the sea shore, with its busy holiday-makers at Llanfairfechan. Next the train dashes through Aber, the seat of Lord Penryhn, appearing in the woods on the right. Through Bangor Station the line takes us due west, crossing the Menai Straits to Anglesey by the famous Britannia Tubular Bridge, built by the Stephensons, the entrance to the bridge being guarded by two huge stone lions. Emerging from the bridge, a view of the beautiful Menai Straits on the right is given, showing the Suspension Bridge, built by Telford, 560 feet long and 100 feet above water level. On the left is Plas Newydd, the seat of the late Marquis of Anglesey.

175 feet

1430 ... PANORAMA OF THE NORTH-WESTERN RAILWAY THROUGH CONWAY FROM THE WEST

A magnificent panorama of Conway and its approaches photographed from the train passing in a reverse direction to that shown in the pictures. Quite a different aspect of the Town and the Castle is thus obtained which in many respects is more picturesque than the usual view with which many are familiar. **125 feet**

1431 ... THE "IRISH MAIL" PASSING THROUGH CONWAY

A striking picture of this world-renowned train travelling at the rate of 60 miles an hour, emerging from the tubular bridge and passing the camera at the speed indicated. The "Irish Mail" is preceded and followed at intervals by two express trains going in opposite directions. **75 feet**

1476 ... RAILWAY PANORAMA FROM FROM GLENBROOK TO MONKSTOWN, IRELAND

175 feet

1477 ... DITTO—MONKSTOWN TO DRAKE'S POOL

200 feet

1478 ... DITTO—DRAKE'S POOL TO CROSSHAVEN

For description, see "Ireland." **100 feet**

1495 ... THE NORTH-WESTERN SPECIAL OVERTAKING THE "SCOTCH EXPRESS" NEAR CREWE

Panoramic view of a portion of the Main four-track line of the London and North-Western Railway between Stafford and Crewe, showing one train passing and repassing another.

This picture was taken from an observation car attached behind the 2.0 p.m. Scotch Corridor Train from Euston to Aberdeen. The country traversed is famous as being the scene of many of Izaac Walton's angling reminisences. As the Scotch train dashes along it gradually overtakes and completely passes the Mid-day Mail Train from London, which in turn overtakes and repasses the train to Scotland. A picture full of life and interest. **100 feet**

TRAINED ANIMAL SERIES.

1033 ... TRAINED ELEPHANTS WORKING AT MACGREGOR'S TIMBER YARDS AND MILLS AT RANGOON

Their sagacity in pushing, pulling and stacking timber is remarkable. Within a week of being captured in the jungle, the elephants are sufficiently tame to do such light work as is indicated in a portion of this film. They seem to know the hour for discontinuing their arduous task, and it is said they have even refused to work after the steam whistle has been blown which marks the close of the day's labours. The remarkable degree of intelligence displayed by these huge creatures in their work must be seen to be understood.

200 feet

1056 ... CAPT. TAYLOR'S TRAINED ELEPHANTS, PONY, AND DOGS—Section 1

The trained elephants, poodles and pony of Capt. Taylor perform such astoundingly clever evolutions that reason, not instinct, must be conceded as the groundwork on which their education has been built up. In this film (Section 1) the elephant standing on inverted tubs holds a trace by rings at either end, and over this in a great variety of fashions, jump the pony, "Tommy," and his canine friends. Then we have the elephant's couch brought on in sections by the attendants, which the ponderous mammal fairly tumbles himself upside down on, and then on to his feet, which are extended high in mid air, the poodles mount by means of ladders and gangways until one dog stands on each upturned pedal extremity of their sagacious friend, who views their evolutions with critical but kindly interest. After the dogs come down the staircase the elephant resumes his normal posture on terra firma and appears to bow his acknowledgments to the applause which always greets this part of his performance.

300 feet

1057 ... CAPT. TAYLOR'S TRAINED ELEPHANTS, &c.— Section 2

This section opens with dogs and elephants skipping, and the zest with which the latter swings the rope to the poodles jumping would do credit to the most facile skipper in a bevy of schoolgirls. The elephants march majestically and also dance about, the dogs all the while running in and out and around the feet of their ponderous colleagues in absolute freedom from any fear of their being unwittingly trod upon, and when in the concluding part of this section the elephant marches round holding in his trunk a hoop through which the dogs jump, the high state of education to which this combination of intelligent animals have attained must be readily appreciated. Some fine balancing feats in mid-air by the elephant is especially noticeable in this section, which concludes by one of the elephants lifting by his trunk, as one would lift a market basket, the trainer, Captain Taylor, and in this fashion carrying him right out past the camera. **250 feet**

1058 ... CAPT. TAYLOR'S ELEPHANTS, &c.—Section 3.

Here we have the pony "Tommy" lying down while the elephants walk over him. The feat is repeated with the trainer as the lying down subject. Then we have elephants, pony, and poodles walking round with fore-paws on each others backs, similar in style to the game beloved by schoolboys. A brief dance, a la cake walk, by Capt. Taylor and one of his elephants is most amusing, and a splendid scene is fittingly concluded by the mammoth animal lifting Capt. Taylor up over its head until he stands on its shoulders, when he proudly marches off with him in this elevated position, while a jubilant poodle, on his hind feet, dances into the foreground as if to express his entire satisfaction with the manner in which he and his colleagues have gone through their marvellous entertainment.

175 feet

Nos. 1056-7-8 supplied in one continuous roll. Total length 725 feet.

1135 ... MAN'S BEST FRIEND—THE DOG

A fine series of pictures of the 1903 Kennel Club prize winners, including dogs of the following classes, viz. :— Mastiffs, Newfoundlands, Dalmatians, Pointers, Bloodhounds, Old English Sheep Dogs, Irish and Scotch Terriers, Great Danes, Greyhounds, Woolfhounds, Dachshounds, Poodles, Toy Spaniels, Collies, Chow Chows, &c., &c. A picture full of life and of excellent photographic quality.

125 feet

1257 ... ARRIVAL AND RELEASE OF 40,000 HOMING PIGEONS AT AMBERGATE

Showing the arrival of the "Pigeon Special," from which hundreds of baskets are unloaded. These are stacked along the station platform, and at a given signal the front flaps are raised and the pigeons released. Thousands take to flight without further invitation, the result being a pretty picture full of action. A magnificent subject. **150 feet**

1258 ... THE MONKEY AND THE ICE CREAM

An Italian boy rests his monkey on the ledge of an ice cream booth while he partakes of the cooling "mystery," occasionally giving the monkey a taste. A young lady who ordered an ice, turns her back to greet an acquaintance who had just arrived. The monkey seizing the opportunity, grabs the ice and causes the same to rapidly disappear. The theft is discovered and the picture terminates with a most humorous climax. Screamingly funny. **100 feet**

1293 ... RACE HORSES ARRIVING AT EPSOM

Showing the arrival and unvanning of the French Racer, Gouvernant, after its Channel trip. St. Amant and other horses are being exercised in the paddock. Fine quality. **75 feet**

A group of Prize Winners at Dog Show.

1374 ... LADIES KENNEL CLUB SHOW, BOTANICAL GARDENS

Fine dogs and beautiful toilets amidst charming surroundings. **225 feet**

1381 ... Tschernoff's Performing Ponies and Dogs.

One of the most interesting Trained Animal Exhibits before the Public, the intelligence of the Dogs and Ponies being almost human.

Scene 1.—Introduction. Pony lying down and Herr Tschernoff, bending forward, is kissed by the pony, while its two companions rise to an erect position on their hind legs.

Scene 2.—Two ponies with hind legs supported on pedestals back to back, while a wolf-hound stretches across the intervening space, front and back feet supported on the croupe of each pony, while another performs the figure 8 around and between the group.

Scene 3.—The entire troupe standing on their hind legs, with their front feet planted on the backs of one another.

Scene 4.—Eight fox terriers and a bull dog chase a cat over the roof of the stable. The cat takes refuge in the hay-loft and hides. The dogs chasing after, miss her, and emerge again from the left door, sliding down a plank to the ground, when they again jump to the roof and repeat the sliding act until the cat is captured by the bull-dog.

Scene 5.—Hoops are attached to the girth band of three ponies which progress around the ring, the dogs jumping through the hoops while a fox-terrier passes in and out between the fore feet of the pony.

Scene 6.—Pony is hitched to a gate. Master orders food. Same is brought, but drink delayed. While Master is gone to fetch same, pony slips his halter, eats the food from master's plate, goes to the dog-house, takes the dog by the back with its teeth, sets him on the table before the empty plate, and slips its head into the halter after opening a Book, on the pages of which is read, "*Dog eaten all.*"

Scene 7.—Three vases are placed on pedestals around the ring. The pony inserts its head and neck through the handles of each and carries them to the attendants.

Scene 8.—The most difficult of all. Pony hitched to cart driven by master, while six fox-terriers run in and out between the fore and hind legs of the pony; circulate through the spokes of the wheel, and keep their balance on the revolving hubs of the cart.

Total length 400 feet

1392 ... PERZINA'S TROUPE OF EDUCATED MONKEYS.

One of the cleverest troupes of monkeys ever placed before the public. *Their* trainer was finally induced to give us a "sitting" of his highly educated pets for life-motion purposes, and a more lively lot of subjects have never come within range of our cameras. Full of rollicking fun and of excellent photographic quality. **150 feet**

No. 1392. Perzina's Happy Family.

1393 ... PERZINA'S HAPPY FAMILY

Another view of Herr Perzina's Monkeys while being fed. "Mike," the clown, depends on his own "finds." which he extracts from his neighbour, which does not lend itself willingly to the hunting operations. **100 feet**

433 ... ELEPHANTS SHOOTING THE CHUTES

This unique picture was secured at Luna Park (Coney Island), and shows three elephants sliding down a steep incline into a pool, the waters of which they strike with a great splash. They reluctantly leave the cooling waters into which they so rapidly descended. A big hit. **125 feet**

1434 ... THE BEGGING HORSE

Another example of intelligence. A horse grazing in the fields is seen approaching the window of a farm-houso, and after raising the window sash with its nose, helps itself to sugar it had discovered there while looking through the glass. It is caught in the act. and after repeated closings of the window, it repeats the operation of opening same until its appetite has been appeased. **100 feet**

3033 ... THE BEAR CUBS AND THE WAR CORRESPONDENT

An excellent picture. (See Russian Series for description.)
150 feet

3048 ... "KUKU," THE COMICAL APE

This picture was secured in Port Said (Egypt), and shows an Arab with a trained monkey, who is put through all manners of tricks, including the imitating of a drunken man, balancing on a tamborine stood on edge, walking on its hands, &c. One of the most humorous monkey films ever taken. **150 feet**

HUNTING AND MISCELLANEOUS.

1508 ... THE BRAHAM MOOR FOX HUNT.

(Held in Yorkshire, near Arlington Hall.)

1—The Master of the Hunt, Colonel Lane Fox, the Huntsman and Hounds, on their way to the Meet.
2—Arrival at the Park Gates.
3—The Field make for Covert Side, and leave the Meeting Place.
4—The Juvenile Hunter and the Donkey.
5—Off to Covert—after the Hounds—over the Old Bridge.
6—Proceeding through the Fields towards where the Fox is expected to break Covert.
7—" Yaaai !" away goes a Fox, and Hounds lead the Field a pretty gallop across Country.
8—Riders taking a Hedge.
9—The Hounds in Full Cry.
10—The Field has to Ride Hard, if they wish to see the End of the Run.
11—Hounds and Riders.
12—" Tally Ho ! "—closing in on Master Fox.
13—The End of the Ron—the Kill in the Snow.
14—The Huntsman takes the Fox from the Hounds, to save His Brush and Mask.
15—The Carcase to the Hounds.
16—Trophies—giving away the Brush.

Our friends across the Channel tell us that we English say, " It is a fine day ; let us kill something ! " We certainly are out to kill something to-day, but it is the love of hard exercise and skill in outdoor sport, not a cruel wish merely to take life, that has brought this large gathering of sportsmen on horseback together.

We are in the heart of Merrie England, on our way to a Meet of Foxhounds in the Park, which lies spread out dotted about with grand old elm trees, before one of those "Ancestral Homes" of which we are so proud. Riders many and riders various arrive. There is My Lord ——— —, and the Honourable ——— on a beautiul blood horse; and now here comes the Master; the Huntsman, with his spick and span Pack, arrives; and there is Bill Bailey, a keen sportsman, but one whom I am afraid does a little poaching at times, in tattered coat, and mounted on his own stout shanks—all keen to see as much sport as possible. Surely this is the well-known note? "Hee-haw!" and an undeniable "moke," in beautiful condition, takes its place among the horses- The Master soon gives word, and the huntsman trots the pack through the park gates, over the old bridge, and off to the Home Wood, whither follow all the riders.

We have not long to wait, for a Fox breaks cover close to where the first whip is watching, and hounds are cheered out of cover on to his line, then away we go. It is a mild morning, although there was a fall of snow yesterday, and hounds go strong upon a hot scent, leading the field a swift race across the meadows and ploughed land, with their intervening fences and hedges. The pace and the stiff jumping are beginning to tell, the ranks of the foremost are thinning, and there ahead of us goes Mr. Fox, hounds closing rapidly on him. "Tally-ho!" there he goes! Then soon the cry is "Who-whoop!" for they have run into him right in the open, a seething mass of hounds, into which the huntsman, giving his horse to another, quickly dives, and emerges with the dead fox.

Most of the field is now up with us, and horses stand around, glad to be relieved of their riders' weight, and blowing out clouds of steam into the winter air, for the warm morning has given place to a chilly afternoon, and around us in this more exposed part the snow still lies.

"Keep your horses back, gentlemen." Yes, indeed, we will, for the hounds are having a stormy tussle over the carcase, whilst the trophies of the chase, the Brush and Mask, are given away, and so ends our day's Fox Hunting. A typical English day's sport amidst typical English scenery, with nobleman and farmer, the landlord and his tenantry, meeting together for the exhilarating exercise of a day's sport. **400 feet**

1510 ... OTTER HUNT IN THE EXMOOR COUNTRY

On the borders of the Exmoor Country so vividly described by Mr. Blackmore in "Lorna Doone," is the great Dunkery Beacon, the highest point of land in the South West of England. On the slopes of this young mountain, whose name recalls tales of beacon fires lit to warn the affrighted peasantry of more wild deeds and maraudings of those rascally Doones, up among the tall heather, so bleak in winter, so glorious in its mass of purple in autumn, are many bogs and "soft places," treacherous to the unwary horseman. Out from these glowing patches of green bog moss, trickle little silver streamlets, which joined by yet others, form themselves into small rivers in the deep valleys some miles below. These are the haunts of the wild Otter, where he lives in a wild land alone. Yet not always alone, for to-day, although the August sun has but recently risen, there are many people gathering at a little village of whitewashed and thatched cottages nestling among gnarled old walnut and other trees.

A hunting horn sounds in the distance, setting the village dogs barking with excitement, and soon round the corner of the lane there comes the Master with his pack of big Otter Hounds, and bevvy of shaggy, rough coated terriers, the latter yelping and straining at their leashes

Over the meadows we go first, Hounds trying the stream bit by bit, then into the woods, where in the shade of the old trees and mass of tall, tangled undergrowth, Hounds are almost hidden from our view. We have scrambled over many hedges, helping the ladies over at some times, at others ungallantly having to leave them in order that we might get the Bioscope's omnicient eye pointed upon the Hounds as they begin to whimper and feather on some faint scent.

Soon we leave the path and take to the water, wading in and out of cool pools, tripping and slipping on the boulders to the peril of the Bioscope. The hills have closed in on either side, fine old oak trees, rich in green, their trunks covered with green lichen, rise up around us, yet we have not found an Otter. But what is that? One old Hound hugging the bank gives a whimper, the others gather round, and the Terriers wishing to have their say, dash up and look important ; then there is a splash, a streak of shining grey flits across the water, and we are away full cry. Hounds giving tongue, Terriers barking, and some local country gentlemen loudly shouting, we race up stream. " Give the Hounds room, and don't yell," promptly cries the Master ; the whips take up their positions, cheering on the Hounds, and thus we go up the stream, till at last, in a clear deep pool, the sides of steep rock covered in rich green moss, among a tangled mass of dead tree trunks, Mrs. Otter gets away underground. Then the Terriers have their day working down into her underground refuge, and out she pops to lead us yet further up among the hills, when at last, surrounded and secured by Hounds, she is caught, not killed, for she has to go to a North Country Park to live quietly for the rest of her days.

A sack has been brought, and with bitter cries from those who hold it (for Mrs. Otter can, and does, use her teeth), she is safely " bagged," whilst the disgusted and bloodthirsty Terriers, tied up safely out of reach, bewail in their own undignified way, the fact that they have not been allowed to slay their foe.

The sun is now high over our heads, and with cheery " good-byes " to the Field, the Master and Whip walk their pack home, many miles over the hills, back to kennels once more, in time for their evening meal. **200 feet**

1511 ... SNARING RABBITS

In this picture, Mr. Bryant, a typical professional snarer, is seen at work. Choosing the runs across the fields where that troublesome, yet most edible rodent, the Rabbit, makes his way at night-time from the cornfield to the woods, he skilfully pegs down fine wire nooses. Coming round in the early morning, he visits them one by one, taking out the young thieves who have met in them an untimely end ; then meeting the farmer, who congratulates him upon his skill, they both return to the farm-house to sample a few young ones, fried, for breakfast. **60 feet**

1512 ... A FRENCH LOAF

Angel Pouchet and her little brother have been sent on an important errand, for has not " la Mere " given them five sous and told them to get some bread? Who should ask for it? Jacques can do that ; but Angel, " la petite," as a staid lady, thinks a mere boy should not have the glory of carrying it through the street. It is a question whether the bread should not carry " la petite," for it is taller than she is. A pretty picture this simple and happy family makes, as Madam, gets the good red wine, and " le Pere " saws great pieces off the loaf to the delight of the hungry and merry kiddies. **75 feet**

1513 ... A DIFFICULT SHAVE

Cold morning—Lost strop—Upset shaving water— Bother—Must be done—Ugh ! (Next remark is unprintable).———Ugh !——— Blunt—Anguish—(More unprintable remarks). Have you ever shaved with cold water and a blunt razor? Sticking plaster will be needed. Poor man ! Sorry for him, but can't help laughing.

60 feet

1514 ... REVERSING A SHAVE (or the Barbarous Behaviour of a Barber)

Shaving with a bad razor may be depressing, but when, as in this picture, you begin with a clean face, then the razor, going backwards, creates and leaves a coat of foam all over the face, which the brush, on being applied, licks off, finally leaving a growth of untidy dirty whiskers—well, that *would* be depressing. " What's the use of shaving ? What's the use or anyfink ? W'y, nuffink." **75 feet**

1515 ... NATURAL LAWS REVERSED

Captain Benediah Koffdrop had suffered serious reverses, and was reduced to living alone in a log cabin, but his " reverses " still continued ; water would rise from the ground to fill a tumbler, his hat and stick would reverse the usual ways of such things, and fall upwards to meet him ; flowers and papers rise from the ground and tidily collect themselves and come to him. Finally we see him " entering " them and himself in his " log " (cabin). He evidently knew how to take a " rise " out of them **75 feet**

1516 ... JOVIAL EXPRESSIONS

A genial countenance is here spread out before our view, rolling away in gentle and everchanging curves and creases in an absolutely killing manner. To anyone among an audience whose life is dull for want of smiles, this picture will come as a cheering and soul inspiring solace. An excellent study of expressions. **50 feet**

1517 ... FEEDING SEAGULLS FROM LONDON BRIDGE

One of the most beautiful scenes in the great Metropolis during hard winter weather, is here depicted. The graceful and swift grey seagulls are darting down upon their favorite food, sprats, catching them in the air as they are thrown up by the interested crowd of spectators. A delightful picture of the river and its bird life in winter, and showing in a remarkable manner the way in which these gulls turn, pounce, and dive in mid-air. **50 feet**

SPAIN.

1285 ... PANORAMA OF VALENCIA HARBOUR

General view of this important Seaport Town, renowned for its fruit shipping industry, and general picturesque aspect. **75 feet**

s

1286 ... BARCELONA (The Liverpool of Spain).

An interesting Series of 10 Pictures

1—The Harbour and Water Front
2—Panorama of the Shipping, &c
3—The Customs-house and Surroundings
4—Statue of Christopher Columbus
5—Yachting Club and Pleasure Craft
6—The Docks and Lighthouse
7—Panorama of Barcelona Heights
8—Life on the Rambla, St. Monica
9—Toy Booths on the Boulevards
10—Crowds of Holiday-makers in Streets

Total Length 275 feet

3035 ... PANORAMA OF THE ROADSTEAD OF SAN SEBASTIEN

A beautiful view of this famous Spanish Harbour and surrounding district. **100 feet**

3036 ... CIRCULAR PANORAMA OF SAN SEBASTIEN

St. Sebastien is one of the most picturesque sea-side resorts on the Spanish Coast. Its buildings, perched against the gradual rising of the surrounding heights; its sands and bathing machines, pavilions and bull-ring, all give prominence to this unique view. **75 feet**

3037 ... PANORAMA OF THE BAY OF STRAITS OF ST. JUAN

A splendid picture of an entrancing subject. **75 feet**

3040-1 ... THE BULL AND TIGER FIGHT AT SAN SEBASTIEN

(See "Sports.") **275 feet**

3042 ... THE SPANISH BULL FIGHT

(For description of above, see "Sports.") **300 feet**

FRANCE.

1000a ... THE BOIS DU BOLOGNE STATION—Arrival of Royal Train with King Edward and President Loubet
75 feet

1000b ... KING EDWARD ARRIVING AT BRITISH EMBASSY, PARIS
100 feet

1001 ... PRESIDENT LOUBET AND KING EDWARD AT VINCENNES
100 feet

1002 ... REVIEW OF THE ARMY OF FRANCE AT VINCENNES
275 feet

1002b ... ALGERIAN ZOUAVES AND FRENCH INFANTRY
150 feet

1003 ... LEAVING VINCENNES AFTER THE REVIEW
100 feet

1131 ... PRES. LOUBET DECORATING FRENCH OFFICERS

50 feet

1132 ... REVIEW OF THE ALGERIAN REGIMENT BY PRES. LOUBET

50 feet

1144 ... T.M. KING AND QUEEN OF ITALY'S VISIT TO PARIS

150 feet

1479 ... PANORAMA OF MARSEILLES SEA FRONT

Photographed during one of the recently numerous dock hand strikes when hundreds of sailing and steam vessels were idly berthed in the docks and along the water fronts. A regular forest of masts hulls and smokestacks forming in the foreground, while the prominent buildings along the front form a most picturesque setting. As interesting and varied a panorama as has ever been our good fortune to secure.

100 feet

3052 ... THE CARNIVAL PROCESSION IN NICE

This world famed festival has been done justice to in cinematography for the first time. Photographed in the square at Nice, which is formed by one of the most interesting groups of buildings in Southern France. The gorgeous floats and multitudes of masqueraders passing in one ever varying procession to which much humerous element is added by the antics of grotesque characters lends much to the highly interesting nature of this lively picture series.

Order of Pictures.

1 The Gold and Silver Chariot
2 The Infernal Regions
3 Grotesque and Comic Characters on horse and foot
4 Gendarme Cavalry (comic)
5 The Cake Walk by gigantic figures
6 The Apaches-Indians
7 Fireladdies at work in burning Building
8 The Reward of Beauty
9 The Riviera Express
10 Cavalcade of Masqueraders
11 Entrance of the Queen of the Carnival
12 The Palace of Music
13 Refuge of the Disappointed.
14 Car of the Lunatics
15 The Nice Carnival
16 Noah's Ark
17 School for Cats
18 The haunted Castle
19 Departure of the Carnival Queen

The wonderful scope of artistic decorations and construction of tableaux cars or floats supersedes everything previously attempted at Nice or elsewhere in this direction. A wonderful picture. **600 feet**

SPORTING AND MISCELLANEOUS.

(Received too late to classify under regular headings).

1503 ... LONG DISTANCE HORSEBACK RACE, STOCKHOLM

Showing the start of the military long distance horseback races, with views of the contestants passing the various stations and the winner reaching the goal at Stockholm. A splendid series of pictures.

125 feet

s 2

1504 ... AN ICEBREAKER PLOUGHING THROUGH A FROZEN RIVER

Many of the frozen rivers in Sweden are kept open to navigation in winter by means of the ice crushing steamers which crush the thick crust and keep the channel open. The picture shows the approach of an ice crusher at work, a view of the channel from the stern, and the landing of infantry on the ice in mid stream. Unique in every respect. **125 feet**

1506 ... BARNEY OLDFIELD DOING "A MILE A MINUTE' ON A RACING MOTOR

An exciting series of pictures taken at the Toronto Fair Grounds, showing Barney Oldfield, one of America's champion and fearless motorists doing 60 miles an hour. The clouds of dust raised by the terrific speed of the car as it skids around the curve of the track is most wonderfully depicted, also a splendid portrait of Mr. Oldfield and the car after the speed trial. **100 feet**

1507 .. TRIUMPHAL RECEPTION OF LOU SHOLES AT TORONTO

Lou Sholes won the Diamond Sculls at the Henley Regatta last year. He is a Canadian. Whole Toronto turned out in steamers, yachts or anything that floats, to greet the conquering hero on his return from England. This scene on the St. Lawrence river has never been surpassed for interest and action amidst picturesque surroundings. **75 feet**

1518 ... THE OXFORD AND CAMBRIDGE BOAT RACE, 1905

A wonderful series. The best yet secured. **300 feet**

1519 ... BOAT PRACTICE WITH THE LEANDER CREW

150 feet

1523 ... ARRIVAL OF THE NORTH-WESTERN SPECIAL AT AINTREE FOR THE GRAND NATIONAL RACE

75 feet

1524 ... THE GRAND NATIONAL RACE, MARCH 31st, 1905

The best and most exciting race picture ever photographed. **200 feet**

1525 ... SCOTLAND v. ENGLAND FOOTBALL MATCH

Crystal Palace, April 1st, 1905. **150 feet**

1527 ... THE FINAL FOOTBALL CUP MATCH—Aston Villa v. Newcastle United

Crystal Palace, April 15th, 1905. **450 feet**

1529 ... "UNIVERSAL PEACE" Allegorical

Showing Peace, beckoning the nations to shake hands and be friendly. The last group is Russia and Japan. A grand conception. **100 feet**

1530 ... ENGLAND AND AUSTRALIAN CRICKETERS
At the Crystal Palace, May 5th, 1905.

Order of Pictures.

1—**Mr. & Mrs. Clem Hill** entering the grounds, also Mr. Trumper (Australia.) in ordinary dress.

2—**Gentlemen of England.** Practice, batting and bowling at the nets.

3—**Portrait.** Dr. W. G. Grace.

4—**Groups surrounding Mr. Poidevin,** securing "autographs" from that player.

5—**Dr. Grace and W. Murdoch** (ex captain), coming towards camera, Mr. G. W. Beldam following up.

6—**Group.** W. G. Grace, talking to Jessop, also Murdoch, Beldam, &c., &c.

7—**Australian Batsmen.** Armstrong, Newlands, Trumper, and Duff, practice batting in front of Pavilion.

8—**Australian Bowlers.** Practice.

9—**Australian Team.** Complete with umpires entering field to play—Grace and Warner, first English bats also entering field.

10—**English Team** and Umpire entering field.

11—**General view of the Match.** Grace batting, scoring and changing ends.

Excellent portraits throughout. **Total Length, 350 feet**

1528 THE SCIENCE AND HUMOUR OF GOLF.

As played by Professional and Amateur Golfers.

This extensive series was secured during the Championship Golf Matches, between **Messrs. Varden, Toogood, Braid, White, Goudin, Herd and Ray**, showing the individual style of each player at the Rochford and the Londesborough Golf Links. Between the matches many humorous pictures (herewith included) were secured by depicting amateurs making the best of difficult positions, all of which add greatly to the general interest of the series.

Order of Pictures.

1—**Players leaving the Marquee,** showing **Varden, Goudin, Herd and Ray,** with Lord Londesbourough and Lord Westmoreland leaving for the first tee.

12—**The First Drive,** showing the style of driving by **Varden, Toogood, Braid, and White**—Crowds following the Players.

3—**Putting on the 2nd Green**—Watching the little ball disappear down the small hole.

4—**Spectators following the Players** over the course.

5—**Varden and Toogood driving**—Terrific strokes.

6—**The Ball in the Pond**—Showing half-a-dozen boys scrambling in the water for the mis-directed ball.

7—**Crossing a Picturesque Stream on the Course.**

8—**Caddies scramble across the Ditch.**

9—**Difficult "Putting" on the Green,**

10—**Amateur's Drive in the Ditch**—Driving a ball from the mud.

11—**A " boomerang " drive**—Showing an amateur driving a ball skyward, which according to the gaze of the spectators has changed its course in mid-air and fallen at back of the players.

12—**Bunkered in a Ditch**—Playing a ball from running water. Great splash and ducking of the caddy.

13—**A difficult approach from a Ditch.**

14—**A difference of Opinion**—Sheep fighting in a bunker.

15—**An Amateur's Trouble**—" Many a slip 'twixt the Tee and the Green."

16—**Amateur " Gardening "**—Shifting sand in a bunker

17—**Players negotiating a Stile.**

18—**" Up a Tree "**—With apologies to the Prime Minister, who played a similar stroke at Chatsworth.

19—**The small Caddies advice to the Fat Golfer.**

20—**The Fat Golfer's rise in Life**—Stroke from the summit of a bunker.

21—**Professionals Driving**—Showing **Varden, Goudin, Herd** and **Ray** at their best.

22—**Spectators following the Players**

23—**Herd putting**—A long shot in his characteristic style.

24—**Professional Play on the Green.**

25—**An awkward Stroke** from under a meshed Wire Fence.

26—**A " dry " subject in a Wet Spot**—Difficulties of an enthusiast.

27—**Caddies recovering a sunken Ball in a marsh.**

28—**End of the Game**—Caddies fight for the Winning Ball.

An Excellent series throughout.   **Total Length 900 feet**

FURTHER NEW UNIQUE . . .

Urban Films

will be announced in the JULY SUPPLEMENT.

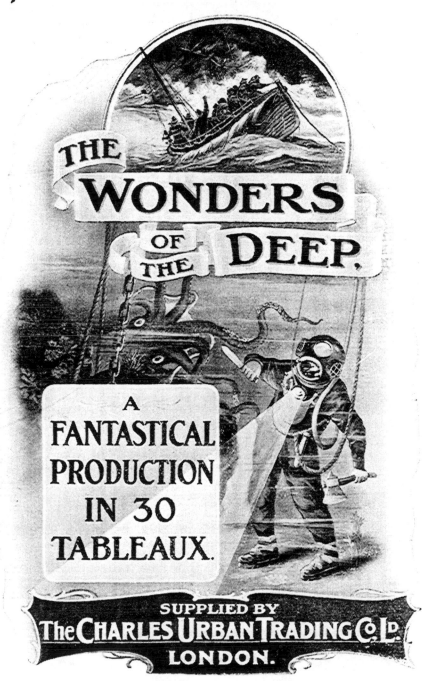
357

SPECTACULAR AND PANTOMIME.

No. 219 ## CINDERELLA:

A Grand Spectacular Production, illustrating every Scene of the popular Fairy Tale.

Supplemented by marvellous Tricks, Dissolving Scenic effects, Ballets, Marches, &c., in which over 35 people take part.

In 20 Tableaux, as follows:

SCENE.	SCENE.
1 Cinderella in her Kitchen	11 The Prince and Cinderella
2 The Fairy, Mice and Lackeys	12 Arrival at the Church
3 The Transformation of the Rat	13 The Wedding
4 The Pumpkin change to a Carriage	14 Cinderella's Sisters
5 The Ball at the King's Palace	15 The King, Queen and Lords
6 The Hour of Midnight	16 The Nuptial Cortege
7 The Bed Room of Cinderella	17 The Bride's Ballet
8 The Dance of the Clocks	18 The Celestial Spheres
9 The Prince and the Slipper	19 The Transformation
10 The Godmother of Cinderella	20 The Triumph of Cinderella

Total Length about 400 feet.

Price, complete £12. Superbly coloured, £24.

Amusing. Startling. Sensational. Marvellous. The Film for Holidays or any other time.

264 ## JOAN OF ARC.

An historical Bioscope production in 12 Scenes.

About 500 persons enacting the Scenes, all superbly costumed. The triumphal Orleans Procession; The Battle of Compiègne; The Coronation of Charles VII.; The Burning at Stake; The Château de Baudricourt; and the Apotheosis are pictures of great beauty, in the production of which nothing has been stinted.

SCENE.	SCENE.
1 The Village of Domremy, birthplace of Joan of Arc	8 Battle of Compiegne
2 The Forest of Domremy	9 Joan in Prison
3 Joan of Arc's House at Domremy	10 The Interrogation in Torture Chamber
4 Port of Vancouleurs	11 Joan at the Stake—Market Place at Rouen
5 Castle of Baudricourt	12 Apotheosis
6 Triumphal entry into Orleans	
7 Coronation of Charles VII. at Rheims	

Total Length about 800 feet.

Price - - £27. Coloured. £54.

298 A CHRISTMAS DREAM.

In 20 Scenes with Dissolving Effects, Tricks and Spectacular Tableaux,
Snow Scenes, Ballets, Night Effects and Marches.

SCENE.
1 The Children's Bed Room
2 The Dream
3 The Review of the Toys
4 The Celestial Messengers
5 Dolly's Ballet
6 On the Roofs of the City
7 The Guardian Angels
8 The Old Bell-Ringer
9 The Great Bell in the Steeple
10 The Midnight Service
11 The Procession of Lanterns

SCENE.
12 The Christmas Eve Supper
13 The Poor Man's Portion
14 The Merry Christmas Morn
15 The Presents
16 The Ice Country
17 The Snow Statue
18 The Delight of the Children
19 The Christmas Tree
20 Apotheosis, " Santa Claus in his
 Glory "

Total Length over 525 feet.

Price - - £18. Coloured, £36

337 RED RIDING HOOD.

A grand Spectacular Production in 12 Tableaux.

SCENE.
1 Kitchen of Mr. Plumcake
2 Main Street of the Village
3 & 4 In the Forest -- Dance of
 School Girls
5 & 6 The Merry Miller and the
 Mill

SCENE.
7 Grandmother's Cottage
8 The Wolf in Grandmother's Bed
9 Pursuit of the Wolf
10 Death of tne Wolf in Waterfall
11 Return to the Village
12 Apotheosis

Total Length 500 feet.

Price - - £18. Coloured, £36.

360 BLUE BEARD.

Fantastical Production in 12 Scenes.

SCENE.
1 The Betrothal of Blue Beard
2 Preparing the Wedding Breakfast
3 The Wedding Feast
4 Blue Beard departs on a Journey
5 The Forbidden Chamber
6 A Troubled Dream

SCENE.
7 Blue Beard condemns Fatima
8 On the Tower looking for help
9 At the Place of Execution
10 The Rescue of Fatima
11 Death of Blue Beard
12 Apotheosis, the Eight Wives
 come to Life

Total Length about 650 feet.

Price - - £20. Coloured £40,

399 # TRIP TO THE MOON.

An extraordinary Bioscope Series in 30 pictures.

SCENE.

1 The Scientific Congress at the Astronomic Club
2 Planning the Trip. Appointing the Explorers and Servants. Farewell
3 The Workshops : Constructing the Projectile
4 The Foundries. The Chimney-stacks. The casting of the Monster Gun
5 The Astronomers enter the Shell
6 Loading the Gun
7 The Monster Gun. March Past of the Gunners. Fire!! Saluting the Flag
8 The Flight through Space. Approaching the Moon
9 Landed right into the Eye !!!
10 Flight of the Shell into the Moon. Appearance of the Earth from the Moon
11 The plain of Craters. Volcanic Eruption
12 The Dream (the Bolies, the Great Bear, Phœbus, the Twin Stars Saturn)
13 The Snow Storm

SCENE.

14 40 Degrees below Zero. Desending a Lunar Crater
15 In the Interior of the Moon —the giant mushroom grot to
16 Encounter with the Selenites— Homoric Fight
17 Prisoners ! !
18 The Kingdom of the Moon. The Selenite Army
19 The Flight
20 Wild Pursuit
21 The Astronomers find the Shell again. Departure from the Moon
22 Vertical Drop into Space
23 Splashing into the open Sea
24 At the Bottom of the Ocean
25 The Rescue. Return to Port
26 Great Fete. Triumphal March Past
27 Crowning and Decorating the Heroes of the Trip
28 Procession of Marines and the Fire Brigade
29 Inauguration of the Commemorative Statute by the Mayor and Council
30 Public Rejoicings

Total length about 800 feet.   PRICE £25.   Coloured, £50.

430 # ROBINSON CRUSOE.

The Bioscope version of "Robinson Crusoe" is not a Pantomime or fantastical series, but **is a play** depicting incidents from the story to which lines it strictly adheres except in the "Apotheosis" (Scene 25), which is added to give a bright finish to the picture.

SCENE.

1 The Shipwreck
2 The Raft
3 Progress up the River
4 Three days after
5 The last Hope
6 The Signal of Distress
7 Constructing the Hut
8 The Cannibals
9 The War Dance
10 Rescue of Friday
11 Robinson's Flight
12 The Pursuit
13 The Attack on the Hut

SCENE

14 After the Battle
15 Building the Canoe
16 The Earthquake
17 Sailing around the Island
18 The Meeting
19 The Rescue
20 Robinson leaves the Island
21 The Quay at Southampton
22 Robinson's Return
23 Home, sweet Home
24 The increased Family
25 The Apotheosis

Total length about 850 feet.   PRICE £26.   Coloured, £52.

426

GULLIVER'S TRAVELS

In the Land of the Lilliputians and the Giants.

One of the most extraordinary productions ever conceived.

A great success. Startling and amusing effects.

Total length about 250 feet.   PRICE £7 10s.   Coloured £15.

483

WONDERS OF THE DEEP,

Or "KINGDOM OF THE FAIRIES."

A New Spectacular Bioscope Production in Thirty Tableaux.

SCENE
1 The Betrothal of Prince Bel-Azor
2 The Gifts of the Fairies
3 The Witch's Curse
4 The Boudoir of Princess Azurine
5 Abduction of the Princess by the Demons—the Chariot of Fire
6 The Top of the Tower—the Castle in Alarm
7 Flight through the Skies in the Chariot of Fire
8 The Armoury of the Castle
9 The Vision in the Haunted Castle
10 The Genius bestows upon the Prince the Armour
11 The Impenetrable Armour—the Prince Knighted
12 Embarkation on the Royal Gallery
13 Encountering a Tempest at Sea (NEW EFFECTS)—Thunder and Lightning and Torrents of Rain — The horizon overcast by angry clouds—The heaving seas, mountainous waves and rain produced by real water.
14 The Ship Wrecked on the Rocks
15 Sinking to the Ocean Bed—Real Fishes and Sea Monsters
16 The Prince rescued by the Mermaid Queen

SCENE
17 The Submarine Caves--Encounter with a Cuttle Fish
18 Review of the Habitues of the Deep—Father Neptune's Car
13 The Palace of the Lobsters
20 The Azure Grotto—the Flowers of the Sea
21 In Neptune's Empire — Great Submarine Spectacle
22 The Whale—the " Omnibus of the Deep
23 On Land Once More—the Entrance to the Cave
24 Escape from the Cavern—On the Edge of the Precipice
25 The Plunge of a Hundred Yards
26 The Castle of the Devil—the Witch in League
27 The Castle on Fire—Rescue of the Princess
28 The Death of the Witch—(Enclosed in a Cask and cast from the Cliffs into the Sea)
29 The Palace of the King –the Wedding Procession
30 Apotheosis— The Kingdom of the Fairies

The personnel of the various characters depicted in this stupendous production (rehearsals for which commenced in March) were engaged from 17 Parisian Theatres.

The Duration of Exhibit of this Film is about 20 minutes.

A continuance of marvellous surprises, startling visions. Full of humour, action and quick changes. Wonderful dissolving views. Introduction of new fire, element and cyclonic effects.

GORGEOUS   SCENES   AND   COSTUMES.

Total length, over 1,000 feet.   PRICE £35.   Coloured, £70,

527 *Special* ... **THE CONDEMNATION OF FAUST**

An extraordinary conception of a most fantastic subject, with diabolical trimmings, in 16 tableaux, inspired by the " Damnation of Faust," of Berlioz. Scenes, decorations, and tricks, by G. Melies.

SCENE.	SCENE.
1. Faust pays his debt	11. The Revels of Hades. (Great Fantastic Ballet.)
2. Entering the Infernal Regions	
3. On the borders of Hades	12. The Infernal Cascade. (New Trick with Apparition on Waterfall.)
4. The Cursed Rocks	
5. The Torrents and Waterfall	
6. Descent to the Infernal Cavern	13. Water Nymphs and Seven-headed Hydra
7. The Fantastic Grotto	
8. The Stalactite of Crystal	14. The Descent into Hell
9. The Devil's Cave	15. The Caldron
10. The Cavern of Ice	16. The Triumph of Mephistopheles

Total length over 500 feet. Length of Exhibition about 12 minutes. Price. £17 10s. Coloured, £32.

DESCRIPTION.

The picture commences with a scene immediately after the death of Marguerite. Mephistopheles, to whom Faust has sold his soul, does not give him much time before exacting payment. He compels Faust to mount with him a fiery steed, thus starting on the Infernal Regions. The picture represents an immense circle enclosed by perpendicular cliffs, through a fissure of which the horses and riders approach to the centre. Mephistophles dismounts, and pinning his prisoner by the arms violently pulls him from the saddle and pushes him towards the entrance to the cave. Here is seen a natural waterfall of great height, before which Mephistopheles and Faust arrive. Demons approach and welcome the return of " His Satanic Majesty " with the soul he has purchased, and which he will turn over to them for destruction. Mephistophles commands the water to cease running, thus showing the entrance to the cavern, into which the two disappear, the waterfall again pouring forth its volumes into the torrents below. Mephistophles and his captive now reach a sort of tunnel, which leads to further caverns and grottos. Here a struggle takes place between the two, Faust becoming fairly frightened, but he is soon overwhelmed and is dragged into the Fantastic grotto, through which they pass on their way to Satan's Empire. (In this scene many successive changes and dissolving effects are introduced, showing a grand array of brilliant and constantly varying scenes). The last effect is a marvellous grotto of Crystal Stalactites, which grotto is illuminated by the hovering flames. Finally arriving before the tunnel which leads to the " recreation grounds of his Satanic Majesty," they stop long enough to let Faust cool himself in the Ice Cave, before proceeding further. The latter's sadness gives way to signs of pleasure in witnessing the brilliancy represented by this magnificent cave of transparent ice. Here the feminine portion of the Lower Regions are commanded by the demons to put in an appearance. Then follows a fantastic dance, or ballet, ordered for Faust's benefit. Suddenly the dancers finish, and the ice walls are transformed to a great waterfall, through which are seen floating water nymphs, and the dreaded Hydra, a monster with seven heads, these being moved about in different directions to the great terror of Faust. In its turn the monster disappears, and the demons, carrying lighted torches, pass and repass through the falls. Then begins the battle between fire and water, fire finally triumphing over the water which ceases to flow. Mephistopheles catching Faust, winds his cloak about him, and they both sink to the Lower Depths through a vertical shaft sunk into the rocks. (Here is introduced another new effect to cinematography). Mephistopheles and Faust apparently go down in space, whilst the walls of the shaft roll upward, this producing a wonderful effect. Arriving at the bottom of the shaft Faust beholds a caldron, into which he is thrust. Great volumes of steam and flames issue therefrom, whilst demons and imps dance around the furnace. The last picture is the apotheosis, showing the triumph of Mephistopheles.

"FAUST."

A GRAND BIOSCOPIC PRODUCTION IN FIFTEEN TABLEAUX

Depicting the Principal Scenes from the famous Opera
founded on GOETHE'S MASTERFUL WORK.

Performed in Synchronism with the principal Airs from
Gounod's Opera, " Faust."

Scenes are reproductions of the Settings of the Grand Opera, Paris.

Scenes, Costumes, Ballets, Effects, and Stage Direction by

Mons. GEO. MELIES, PARIS.

No. 562 " Faust."   Scene II.—The Apparition.

ORDER OF PICTURES.

1—**The Laboratory of Dr. Faust.** Appearance of Mephistopheles.
2—**The Apparition of Marguerite.** Faust regains his youth—Sells his soul to Mephistopheles.
3—**The Kermis (Fair).** The Villagers Dance.
4—**The Fiery Wine.** Wagner and the Students.
5—**Meeting of Faust and Marguerite.**
6—**Marguerite's Garden.** Siebel's present—The Casket of Jewels.
7—**The Soldiers of Valentine.** The Review.
8—**The Duel.** Death of Valentine.
9—**The Night of Walpurgis.** The Witches Cave.
10—**The Souls of the Dead.** The Vision.
11—**Among the Ruins.** Ballet of the Queens of Beauty.
12—**The Church.** Marguerite at Prayer—Mephistopheles.
13—**The Prison.**—Death of Marguerite.
14—**Ascension of Marguerite's Soul to Heaven.**
15—**Apotheosis**—The Domain of Saints.

562-74 *Special —*

Length about 850 feet (Duration of Exhibit 18 minutes). **Price £32**

PRICE, artistically coloured, £60.

ARGUMENT.

In producing the Bioscopic Version of "Faust," we arranged that all action in the various scenes, including the marching, ballets, etc., were performed to synchronize with Orchestral Accompaniment, thus adding greatly to the effective success of the pictures. The operatic airs to which each scene is enacted are noted in the detailed description of each Tableau, which we will supply on application.

This is the first attempt of anyone at reproducing by Animated Photography such a stupendous work as the Grand Opera and in selecting the universally-known opera, "Faust," it is our belief that the reproduction of the Film by the Urban Bioscope will meet with great success with the Public, especially if accompanied by Orchestral Selections.

No. 562 "Faust." Scene IV.—The Fiery Wine.

Furthermore—for the Showman who caters to high-class audiences, but who has not the convenience of an Orchestra to render the selections—we will supply with list of selections for Piano and Organ accompaniment.

The story of "Faust and Marguerite," depicted by the Bioscope, tells its own tale (the story being familiar to all), the interest being greatly enhanced through magical scenic and dissolving effects being introduced by the Master of the Art, Mr. Melies (and only possible to reproduce by animated photography), the story of the play being perfectly enacted by well-known artists.

NOTE.—The foregoing subject, "FAUST" can be supplied separately, as it forms a complete story in itself; but should it be desired to add thereto No. 527-33, "Condemnation of Faust," (description in our Supplement No. 1) the combined series would create a great success as the most fantastical and diabolical production ever formed.

The **First** depicts the tale as universally known (with a few ingenious embellishments added).

The **Second** — a Fantasy created from the composition of Berlioz "**Damnation of Faust.**"

PRICE—No. 562 and 527 complete, total length 1350 feet = **£46**

     ,,   ,,   ,,   ,,   (**handsomely Coloured**)= **£90**

Combined Duration Exhibit about 30 minutes.

SYNOPSIS OF PICTURES.

With Title of the Musical Selections to Synchronise with Action depicted in this Bioscope Production.

1. ... THE LABORATORY OF DR. FAUST

Faust is seen sitting at his table, much out of humour owing to his inability to discover the secret enabling him to regain his youth. (AIR: "Hail to my last morning")—As a last resource the idea occurs to him to call upon His Infernal Majesty, which he sets into action, Mephistopheles suddenly appearing before him from a cloud of smoke. (AIR: "The sword at my belt, the feather in my hat.") — Mephistopheles promises the return of youth to Faust, provided he signs an agreement to consign his soul to Hades after his death. Faust refuses. Mephisto causes to appear before Faust an apparation of Marguerite.

No. 562 " Faust."   Scene V.—Faust and Marguerite.

2. ... APPARITION OF MARGUERITE

Which gradually appears on the window of Faust's laboratory. Marguerite is seen spinning at the wheel, and singing to the air " It was a King of Thule." Faust is charmed with the vision, and hastily conforms to the Devil's proposition. Mephisto gives him the enchanted liquor of fire ; Faust drinks it, and is gradually transformed to a handsome youth. (AIR: " Come to me youth.")

(This dissolving effect is produced without black background, and is a decided novelty.)

Faust, satisfied with himself, thanks Mephisto, who proposes going to the Neibourg village, in order to meet, at the fair held there, the living image seen in the vision, viz : Marguerite.

3. ... THE COUNTRY FAIR

To the right of an Inn, next to which are stationed big wine casks, are seen nobles, soldiers, students, country men and fair maidens singing and drinking. (AIR: " Introduction of the Kermesse.) Several old men arrive and drink with the students. (AIR: " Chorus of Old Men.") The boys and girls now start waltzing on the green. (AIR: " Waltz of Faust.") Wagner, standing on a chair, sings a gay song to the students ; sudden appearance of Mephisto, who pulls Wagner from the chair. (AIR: " The Golden Calf.") Mephisto drinks the health of the students but finds the wine not to his liking. Valentine, the brother of Marguerite, demands an explanation from Mephisto for his behaviour. (AIR: " Wherefrom comes the stranger none had ever before seen.") Mephisto seizes his hand, and from the life lines thereon predicts that Valentine will be killed in a duel.

4. ... THE FIERY WINE

Mephisto draws his sword, and plunges it into the end of the cask from which opening flows a stream of liquid fire. He catches a wine-glass full, which is seen brimming with flame. He drinks this fiery fluid. The students, surmising that this stranger is a demon, draw their swords ready to strike him down. Mephisto draws a magical ring on the ground around him, at which the swords of the students all fall broken to pieces. Wagner, however, reverses his sword, pointing the hilt of the sword, which is shaped like a cross, and the students pick up that portion of their broken swords and do likewise, Mephisto shrinking from these signs of the cross; he escapes amidst the tumult of the students, who rejoice in their victory.

5. ... THE MEETING OF FAUST AND MARGUERITE

Mephisto spies Marguerite on her way to the church, accompanied by her servant Martha. He calls Faust, who upon arriving greets the young girl and offers her his arm. (AIR: "Will you not allow me?") Marguerite refuses the offer. (AIR: "No Sir, I am not pretty.") Marguerite proceeds on her way, followed by Faust who is pushed along by Mephisto. The country people continue their waltz. (AIR: "Waltz of Faust.")

No. 562 "Faust." Scene VII.—Soldiers Review.

6. .. IN MARGUERITE'S GARDEN

The scene opens disclosing Siebel, a young page, who is in love with Marguerite, making a nosegay from flowers picked in her garden. (AIR: "Bring to her my love.") He places the nosegay on the ledge of Marguerite's window. Arrival of Faust and Mephisto. (AIR: "Salute pure House.") Mephisto sarcastically laughs upon seeing the flowers placed by Siebel, and hands Faust a casket full of jewels which he orders him to also place on the window ledge near the flowers. Upon hearing Marguerite open her window they both conceal themselves behind a tree. Marguerite appears breathing in the fresh morning air. (AIR: "I should like to know whom was this young man.") She snatches up the flowers left by Siebel. (AIR: "A nosegay from Siebel without any doubt.") She suddenly discovers the jewels, drops the nosegay, and clasps the necklace about her deck while gazing into a mirror to view the effect. (AIR: "I laugh in seeing me so pretty.") Mephisto steps forth from his place of concealment, pushing Faust towards Marguerite at the same time telling him that now is the time to make his declaration of love. The pleadings of Faust. (AIR: "Let me look at your pretty face.") Marguerite falls into the arms of Faust and while the two lovers embrace Mephisto, again concealed behind a bush, sings a triumphal song in accompaniment with the guitar. (AIR: "Don't open your door unless married.") He leaves the garden still laughing.

7 ... VALENTINE'S ARMY

The brother of Marguerite, at the head of his army, is seen returning from the wars. Here follows a grand review of the soldiers. (AIR: "The Soldiers' Chorus.")

8   THE DUEL AND DEATH OF VALENTINE

Faust is seen issuing from Marguerite's house at midnight. Marguerite is then seen on the balcony throwing him kisses. (Continuation of the "Soldiers' Chorus"; volume of music to gradually diminish.) Valentine suddenly arrives, and notes Faust leaving his sister's house. Here follows a deadly duel between Valentine and Faust, witnessed from the balcony by Marguerite. Mephisto issues from a shadow of the garden, and each time Faust is in danger he intercedes by taking part in the duel. As Mephisto's sword touches the swords of the others flashes of flame and clouds of smoke result from the contact. Valentine falls wounded, and Mephisto and Faust make their escape. (AIR: "The

No. 562 " Faust." Scene VIII.—Death of Valentine.

Duel.") Marguerite, rushing from the house, runs to the aid of her wounded brother calling for help, which is responded to by the crowds invading the garden. Marguerite pleads for her brother's pardon, this he refuses to give, and expires after launching forth curses upon her. (AIR: "Marguerite be reprobated.") The crowds kneel in sorrow.

9 ... THE NIGHT OF WALPURGIS

A splendid picture of the "Valley of the Rugged Mountains," with grotto in the foreground. Through the opening is seen the moon illuminating the mountains in the background. The moonlight also penetrates the grotto by means of which is noted a deep and black abyss.

10 ... THE SOULS OF THE DEAD

Here phantoms and witches congregate in the grotto. Forming a circle they dance around flaming braziers. Arrival of Mephisto, who orders the phantoms to disperse. He explains the nature of the grotto to Faust, finally showing him a vision of Marguerite in the mouth of the abyss. Faust, who has so cruelly deserted Marguerite whom he had betrayed, kneels before the apparition pleading her pardon. The vision vanishes. To console him, Mephisto promises Faust to take him direct to his kingdom, where he will show him the Queen of Beautys who is much prettier than Marguerite. (*Excellent dissolving effects.*)

T

11 ... BALLET OF THE QUEENS OF BEAUTY

The foregoing scene gradually dissolves, until there appear splendid ruins. Around a long table filled with golden dishes and fruit, are congregated the souls of the departed. Faust and Mephisto occupy the top of a grand staircase. Entrance of Greek and Egyptian dancers. Cleopatra and Helena, Queens of Egypt and Greece appear and salute their master Mephisto. Their slaves dance about them. Entrance of the corps de ballet.

No. 562 " Faust."   Scene XI.—The Ballet.

Dances. (AIR: " Ballet of Faust.") The dances are concluded by a grand tableau. Faust, thoroughly enraptured by so magnificent a spectacle, is suddenly recalled to reality by Mephisto who leads Marguerite to him.

12 ... THE CHURCH

Arrival of nobles, ladies, pages, soldiers, and nuns all entering the church (*Here should be introduced subdued organ selections*). Arrival of Marguerite, who kneels before the shrine asking pardon for her sin. Apparition of Mephisto, who gradually takes form from a pillar of the the church. He interrupts Marguerite's prayers. (AIR: "No, you will not pray.") Marguerite is frightened hearing the voice of Mephistopheles. (AIR: " Remember the past.") As Mephisto approaches her she falls swooning to the floor. The demon disappears as mysteriously as he previously appeared. The congregation, hearing a noise rush out to Marguerite, and administer to her comforts.

No. 562 " Faust."   Scene XII.—Marguerite at Prayer.

13 ... THE PRISON—DEATH OF MARGUERITE

After all this persecution Marguerite loses her mind. She has killed her child, for which act she is imprisoned (This view depicts

Marguerite lying on a pallet of straw in a vaulted prison cell). Faust, accompanied by Mephisto. called to see her. She does not recognise Faust at first, and can only recall the circumstances of their first meeting. (AIR : "Will you not allow me.") Marguerite, becoming blind to her surroundings, has a vision of heaven, and a longing to join the angels, to whom she offers her pleadings. (AIR : "Pure Angels") Faust just catches her in his arms as she falls over dead. Mephisto hastily seizes Faust

No. 562 " Faust." Scene XIII.—Death of Marguerite.

over whom he throws his cloak, and they both disappear into a rush of fire issuing from the ground.

14 ... THE HEAVENLY REGIONS

The pillars of the prison here dissolve into clouds, from which issue two angels, who carry Marguerite's soul into space, while the body of Marguerite is still seen in the original position on the ground of the prison. (Continuation of the air : " Pure Angels.")

15 ... APOTHEOSIS

The apparition of Marguerite supported by two angels, is seen rising to the centre of the picture. The clouds vanishing, leaving an unobscured view of the surroundings. (AIR: "Apotheosis of Faust.") At the pinnacle of the group are seen the saints, sitting upon clouds below them likewise supported, are the angels and archangels, and the martyrs kneeling around the body of Marguerite. GRAND FINALE.

NOTE.—We are the exclusive Agents for—

Melies' Star Films,

For the United Kingdom and the British Colonies. . . . .

T 2

662 THE WANDERING JEW

In Four Scenes.

1 ... THE SHORES OF THE DEAD SEA

Isaac Laquedem, the wandering Jew, comes in sight, driven by an irresistable power, which never allows him to halt in his wanderings— He is condemned to walk during all eternity without rest, for having refused a cup of water to Christ as he hung upon the Cross. He is worn out with fatigue, and falls upon his knees, but a voice from Heaven which follows him always compels him to continue his journey. "Forward! Forward!" These fateful words make the poor wretch tremble. He rises, but fatigue overpowers him, and he falls to earth again to snatch a moments sleep.

2 ... THE VISION

At this moment his brain is haunted by a fearful dream, he sees in the sky a vague vision—It is Christ who advances to the top of the mount, carrying his cross, and followed by the holy women, his guards, and the crowds. Christ falls, and in his dream Isaac Laquedem sees himself again (who has been but a shoemaker in his youth), refusing Christ the water for which He had asked, and answering him with a sneer. "Forward!" The vision passes. The wandering Jew rises —He revolts against the Divine Power, but is obliged to resume his march in spite of himself.

3 ... THE ACCURSED ROCKS

The scene changes—Isaac Laquedem, travelling continually arrives at rocky country. There he again wishes to rest, but Satan appears, snatching the staff from the old man's hand, belabours him with all his might, and suddenly disappears. At the same moment the voice from Heaven orders the wandering Jew to start again, and the vision of an angel appears in the sky, who with an imperious gesture compels the unhappy man to resume his travels.

4 ... THE ELEMENTS UNCHAINED

The wandering Jew pursues his eternal journey in the midst of a frightful storm; he is assailed by waterspouts, lightning flashes blind him, the winds howl with rage, but he goes on—on—always on, while the centuries roll past. **200 feet**

A splendid subject for Sacred Concerts or Sunday Entertainments.

PRICE £5 5s. Artistically Coloured (greatly enhancing the effects) £10 10s.

JULES VERNE OUTDONE.

"WHIRLING THE WORLDS."

Adventurous Voyage of the "Exploring Club" by Train, Motor-car, Air-ship, and Submarine.

The most Fantastic Picture Series ever conceived.

Invented and arranged by Mr. GEO. MELIES,

No. 641-59.   Order of Pictures.

Scene 1. ... MEETING OF THE GEOGRAPHICAL SOCIETY

The interior of the magnificent rooms of the Geographical Society, where a meeting has been called for the purpose of discussing a bold suggestion for an extraordinary voyage to be made by some of its members. The Engineer, who conceived the idea gives

a practical demonstration and full explanation of his plans before the assembled members, who finally vote for the adoption of his plans, and issue an authorisation for the construction of the engines, airships, motor car, balloon and submarine boat. Votes are then cast (*amidst great enthusiasm*) as to the personelle of the voyagers, of whom twelve are selected, it is finally agreed that the wives of the President, as well as the Engineer, are to accompany them on their journey.

Scene 1.—The Meeting of the "Explorers' Club."

Scene 2 ... THE MECHANICAL CONSTRUCTION WORKS

Showing the interior of a vast machine shop, with whirling fly-wheels and ponderous machines, steam hammers and cranes, in full operation. The Engineer is very busy in supervising the construction of the engines to be utilised for the extraordinary trip. A servant arrives with lunch, but the Engineer, in his excitement, upsets both servant and lunch. Next we have the arrival of the members of the expedition, bent on an inspection tour, the Engineer showing them in consecutive order the now almost finished train and steam locomotive of his own invention; the airship, automobile, submarine, ice-chest, and hundreds of other accessories which will be required for the trip.

Scene 3 ... INTERIOR VIEW OF THE FOUNDRIES

Showing the foundry where large sections of the machines are cast. The President's wife, who is rather inquisitive, gets too close to the cauldron during the casting, and is almost suffocated by the smoke and steam. She faints, and a rush is made for water. A workman who happens to arrive with a large pail of water, pours it over her. The lady comes to, and surveying herself after the bath, becomes indignant at her

Scene 2.—View of the Construction Works.

dress being spoilt thereby, and repays the kindness of the workman by slapping his face. Eventually quietness is regained.

Scene 4 ... THE RAILWAY STATION, PARIS

All preparations for the trip having been completed, members of the club are ready to commence their voyage, making their way towards the express train in waiting. We see some of the friends who are accompanying the voyagers as far as Switzerland, purchasing their tickets at the booking office. Servants with packages, boxes, trunks and so forth are pushing through the crowd. Baggage trollies come into collision with hurrying passengers, amidst general confusion. All finally board the train, which slowly leaves the station.

Scene 5. ... THE SNOW-COVERED MOUNTAINS OF SWITZER-LAND

The train having crossed the frontier, is seen progressing over the snow-covered mountains from a distance, gradually growing larger as it rounds the curves, until it passes at full speed across the bridge and water-fall in the foreground. In its climb up the mountain the train is again seen winding its way towards the far distance, growing smaller and smaller as it recedes from view.

Scene 6 — INTERIOR OF RAILWAY CARRIAGE

This view depicts a full sized railway carriage of several compartments (*the wheels are rotating at great speed, the background, telegraph poles, wires, bridges and so forth passing in the opposite direction, conveying the idea of terrific progress made by the train, as seen from the carriage window*). Upon its arrival at the Jungfrau the train comes to a stop, the porters throw open the doors of the three compartments, and the travellers descend.

Scene 7 ... JUNGFRAU RAILWAY STATION

The exterior of the railway station at the base of this great mountain. The advent of the "Exploration Club" having been heralded throughout the country, the travellers are received by the inhabitants amidst much cheering and general welcome. Arrival of the special train bearing the automobile and submarine and ice chest.

Scene 8 ... START FOR THE MOTOR CAR TRIP

Here we see the porters unloading the Automobile and pushing same to the outside of the station, where the fourteen members of the expedition receive the good wishes of the crowds assembled. The motor car, which is of special design and constructed to run at a speed of 500 miles an hour, is certainly a most wonderful creation, especially when equipped with its tremendous high power lanterns and great horn. There is seating capacity for all, while the luggage

Scene 8--Start of the Automobile.

is strapped to the roof of the car. After the valet takes his place at the back of the car, the Engineer who acts as driver, mounts his seat, pulls the levers and the car starts gradually on its adventurous trip.

Scene 9 ... CRASHING THROUGH THE RIGI INN

In the foreground of the picture is noted a portion of the Swiss Country Hotel, stationed near the curve of the road leading up to the Mountain. The Hotel keeper and his servants notice the approaching motor car and realising that it cannot negotiate the curve at their speed, make frantic motions and efforts to warn the drivers, so as to prevent an accident. As expected, the motor car crashes with terrific force through the walls of the Inn, which it penetrates, leaving in its wake a great cloud of dust, and a hole in the wall through which it had disappeared. *(The action of this scene takes place amidst picturesque surroundings, there being a snowstorm raging at the time. The aforesaid Inn is built of real bricks and mortar, therefore the effect of the rushing car breaking through the brick wall, scattering the latter in all directions, is most realistic).*

Scene 10 ... THE INTERRUPTED TABLE D'HOTE

The dining saloon of the hotel, showing twenty-four persons seated at a large table enjoying their luncheon. Suddenly the motor-car crashes through the wall dashing across the room over the entire length of the table, upsetting everything in its path. The guests, thoroughly astonished and alarmed, scatter in all directions, the servant dropping and smashing a big pile of plates. The driver of the automobile coolly requests the people not to disturb themselves on his account, and continues his journey by driving the car through the opposite wall.

Scene 10.—The Interrupted Table d'Hote.

Scene 11 ... 500 MILES AN HOUR—THE ACCIDENT

The driver, not at all affected by the last mishap, increases his speed, and proceeds over the mountain at a wonderful pace. The snow storm increases, the motor car bumping over hillocks and rough portions of the roads in its progress up the mountain. (*The scenery in the background shoots by at terrific speed*). The members of the expedition finally arriving at the summit of the Rigi, from which a magnificent panorama of the surrounding scenery is had. Owing to the momentum gained in their ascent, the driver is unable to stop the car in time to prevent the same leaping from the summit, which happens, the car and its passengers dropping over the precipice, a distance of 2,000 feet. The car is seen rebounding from rock to rock in its rapid descent, and finally disappears into space.

Scene 12 ... ALPINE GUIDES TO THE RESCUE

Next we see the base of the precipice, showing the car, passengers and luggage striking the rocks and snow with terrific force. The passengers and baggage, as well as fragments of the car, scatter in all directions (*the latter having been entirely demolished in its descent*). A number of Alpine guides, who happen to be in the vicinity, run to the aid of the unfortunate travellers, whom they extricate from the wreck.

Scene 13 ... IN THE HOSPITAL

We next see our travellers taken to a ward in the hospital, where various operations are performed. They remain in the hospital for five weeks, during which time they all recover, and apparently are no the least discouraged, so they set off once more to continue their journey

Scene 14. ... **THE SPECIAL TRAIN**

This picture shows the exterior of the Hospital to the entrance of which the *Special Exploration Train* has been brought. The Engineer's wife, who during her detention at at the hospital, has grown extremely stout, finds it necessary for her fellow travellers to almost force her through the door of the carriage, which is somewhat too narrow to admit so corpulent a person. The

Scene 11.—Going at 500 miles an hour.

passengers finally get aboard and the train departs.

Scene 15 ... **FULL SPEED OVER THE MOUNTAIN SUMMIT**

The engineer, or former driver of the motor car, heads the train in the direction of the summit of the Jungfrau. In its journey up the mountain the speed of the train is much accelerated, and gaining a tremendous momentum when reaching the summit, bounds from the top of the mountain into the air, being supported by the airships which are attached to the train forming part of its cargo, thus the entire equipment is seen launched into space.

Scene 16 ... **THROUGH THE CLOUDS**

Encouraged by the apparent success of this mechanical combination, and the unique launching forth of a full train load of travellers and baggage, the engineer increases the steam pressure, thus gaining greater speed, and the entire train, with its trail of black smoke, is seen dashing through the clouds.

Scene 17 ... **PASSING THE PLANETS**

Night arrives, and the train going at full speed passes the planets, stars, and other bodies of the celestial sphere, the latter all being passed at a tremendous pace, glittering as this unique train dashes by in its progress.

Scene 18 ... **THE SUNRISE**

The clouds disperse as the sun rises at dawn. The sun awakens and we see the jovial and gigantic face of the sun still yawning, the whole being surrounded by the rays which gradually increase in brilliancy.

Scene 19 ... A DISAGREEABLE PILL

The train arriving at full speed shoots its entire length into the yawning mouth of the sun. The latter, after a series of comic grimaces pours forth volumes of smoke and fire the result of the indigestion, caused by the swallowing of an unexpected train.

Scene 14.—Boarding the Special Train.

Scene 20 ... COLLISION WITH THE SUN

The fantastic scenery of the sun. The train is smashed to bits by the impact. The locomotive with its tender and the carriages all in a heap, present an undescribable chaos ; the catastrophe has caused a series of eruptions on the sun ; the same producing a most startling effect.

Scene 21 ... THE WRECK OF THE TRAIN

Most realistic scene of the wreck of the train. Our travellers not much injured crawl from under the wreckage and all having been accounted for in spite of this extraordinary adventure they congratulate one another. The Engineer has escaped with a black eye and the others with a few scratches. Their garments however are all torn. The Engineer enthusiastic over the novelty of the surrounding scenery induces his fellow travellers to investigate this unknown world.

Scene 22 ... AURORA BOREALIS

The explorers admire the splendid aurora and its beautiful effects upon the surrounding scenery, which is composed of crystals of wonderful shapes and sizes.

Scene 23 ... THE ERUPTIONS ON THE SUN

Suddenly while our explorers are full of admiration they commence to become affected by the heat of the rising sun. The surface begins to throw off steam and smoke, flames shoot out of the crevases and the heat becomes unbearable.

Scene 24 ... A COLD REFUGE

The temperature being constantly on the increase, the atmosphere becomes suffocating. The explorers are discarding their remaining clothing, perspiration steaming off their brows. They believe that certain death with terrible torture will put a finish to their undertaking. Suddenly the Engineer remembers the icebox which fortunately has not suffered in the recent wreck. The same is brought forward and everybody climbs in, the Engineer awaiting to enter last, but as he opens the door for the purpose he is confronted by the curious spectacle of seeing his companions frozen into a solid block of ice, and all huddled together in the most grotesque positions, the tremendous cold temperature of the ice box having frozen them all as soon as they entered.

Scene 25 ... RESCUED FROM AN ICY GRAVE

The resourceful engineer knows that he has not a minute to spare and in spite of much suffering of heat, he runs to the wreck and fetches therefrom a bale of straw, which he sets fire to around the ice box, the heat of the burning straw with the heat of the sun, thaws the ice and his companions are saved. He convinces them that they must leave the sun if they wish to save their lives and endeavour to return to earth.

Scene 26 ... THE SUBMARINE BOAT

The travellers find their way back to the wreck, and amidst the debris, discover the submarine boat, which marvellously has not been been seriously damaged, they all get inside of the boat which is still fastened to the top of the railway truck.

Scene 27 ... THE JUMPING OFF PLACE OF THE SUN

Scene 15.—Leaving the Earth.

The engineer having got up steam, gets the screws to work. The air resistance against the rapidly revolving screws, propels the carriage and supports the boat towards the edge of the sun. The truck is steered against a projecting rock, and the momentum tearing the fastenings, the submarine is launched into space.

Scene 28 ... LAUNCH INTO SPACE

The engineer had foreseen the likelihood of such predicaments and thus forestalls all accidents. The moment the boat leaves the sun and falls into space the closed parachute attached to the upper decks opens, thus allowing the submarine to make a gradual descent.

Scene 29 ... STRIKING THE SEA

The speed of the descending boat increases as it nears the Earth, upon reaching which it drops into the sea with a splash. The waves part and swallow the submarine and its passengers, all sinking into the deep.

Scene 16.—Proceeding through the Clouds.

Scene 30 ... THE BOTTOM OF THE SEA

The boat, with all screws working, makes rapid progress through the water, and by means of a large searchlight, the surroundings become illuminated, bringing to view the many inhabitants of the sea.

Scene 31 ... THE INTERIOR OF THE SUBMARINE

The explorers are now wondering where good fortune has brought them after all their escapades. The engineer is of opinion that they are near some shore. A lively discussion ensues, as the others believe they are still in the middle of the ocean. In order to convince his companions, the engineer opens one of the panels of a porthole, and through it they see a lot of fishes and other aquatic evidence of being near shore somewhere. After proceeding farther, the search-light reveals proximity of land, with this assurance they are all pleased.

Scene 32 ... FIRE ON BOARD SHIP

Yet another incident is in store for them. The firemen we see in the engine-room greasing the machinery. The steam-pipe bursts, and fire breaks out. General consternation. The voyagers are seen endeavouring to put out the fire with pails of water.

Scene 19—Arriving at Sunrise

Scene 33 ... THE EXPLOSION

Suddenly a terrific explosion takes place; the boiler having burst, and the submarine is blown through the waters.

Scene 34...CAST ON SHORE

A sea-port, showing sailors following their various occupations, which are interrupted by the explosion of the submarine taking place about a hundred yards from the shore. A portion of the submarine falls in their midst; the sailors rush to this strange wreck, and are much surprised to see our travellers emerge unscathed from this remaining portion of the sub-

Scene 21—The Railway Wreck

marine boat. The travellers recount their experiences to the sailors who flock about them.

Scene 35 ... THE EXPLORERS' RETURN AND RECEPTION

The whole of the world has by this time been informed of their extraordinary experiences, and upon their return the Geographical Society gives a splendid reception in their honour. The engineer is carried on the shoulders of four sailors who accompany the travellers home, and others carry with pride the screw of the submarine, which is to be retained by him as a souvenir of the daring adventure. The travellers, after having received their welcome and recovered from their emotions, hasten to change their clothes

Scene 27—Plunging from the Sun.

to conform to the occasion, and arrive attired in gala dress at the Geographical Institute, where they give an official account of their

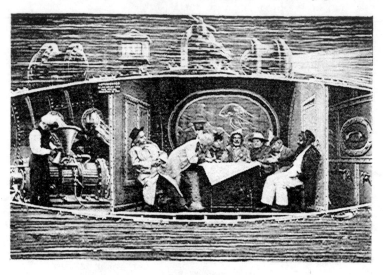

voyage to the assemblage, which is graced by the presence of generals, admirals, ministers, deputies, scientists, &c., who arrive in procession, making a fine spectacle as they mount the grand staircase leading to the Audience Hall of the Institute where the crowd awaits them.

Scene 31—Interior of Submarine.

The members of the "Exploration Club," all of whom have returned safe and sound, are made heroes of, but they treat their experiences as though of everyday occurrence, and pay but little attention to the celebration held in their honour. They proceed with their studies, and are now planning another trip to other worlds by means of even more extraordinary methods of locomotion than those which they have only recently brought into successful use.

Total Length - - - Over 1,200 feet.

(Duration of Exhibit, about 25 minutes).

Price £40.   Artistically Coloured £80.

Set of 20 Photographs mounted (7 by 4½ inches) of the most important Scenes for Advertising purposes **£1 0 0**

Set ditto, hand coloured, price **2 10 0**

NOTICE.

BEWARE OF ALL STAR FILMS offered in Great Britain, except through us (who are the exclusive Agents for Mr. G. MELIES). These are either Smuggled or Pirated Copies. We will injunct against any one using such spurious duplicates.

669   # THE BEGGAR MAIDEN.

The Deserving Poor and the Good Samaritan.

(In Seven Scenes.)

1 ... POVERTY

In a miserable attic a poor woman is lying on a bed of sickness. Near her, her husband a poor workman and their little daughter Marie are occupied in preparing her medicine. The roof is broken, and the snow is falling through ; hopeless misery has its grip on the unfortunate family, there remains neither wood nor coal to light a fire. Into this scene of desolation comes a baliff to seize their wretched furniture. In spite of the prayers of the unfortunate people, the baliff does his duty and leaves, though not untouched by so much misfortune.

The poverty stricken father, without any resources, begs his daughter to go to the neighbouring town to beg at the church door, perhaps some charitable souls will help them with alms. Little Marie, stout of heart, kisses her father, and sets out courageously in spite of the snow flakes whirling in the darkness. She starts, hoping to bring back some money which she would beg from the congregation leaving the church.

2 ... THE FROZEN COUNTRY

The snow covers the landscape, the poor child, shivering in her rags, hurries towards the town, she is benumbed with cold, and the snow lashing her face, blinds her, and makes her lose her way ; but she finds it again, and continues with the energy of despair.

3 ... SUNDAY CHURCH SERVICE (Picturesque scene representing the porch of a big Church).

The steps of the Church are covered with professional beggars who wait for the devout worshippers to come out, since they are almost always generous on this day. Little Marie comes to take her place among them, but the others drive her away, threatening her with their sticks and crutches. The poor child overcome with fatigue, goes and sits down at the foot of a lamp post. Soon out come the worshippers who give their alms to the professional beggars, footmen and grooms carry the umbrellas and cloaks for the ladies. Poor little Marie holds out her hand timidly but is roughly refused by all, their patience having been worn out by the solicitations of the other beggars. One gentleman whom she follows in despair bullys her, and strikes her violently. She falls on her knees bleeding.

4 ... THE COOK SHOP (Magnificent Scene.)

On the right is the street fading away into the night. The lighted windows throw a bright reflection on the snow. In the foreground on the left is the cook's fireplace, in which the fire burns gaily. The servants are plucking and roasting the fowls. Clamorous groups come to get for their midnight meal, the fattest possible, and buy the birds.

The poor little beggar comes in her turn, but she stops outside, her nose glued against the window of the shop shivering with cold. and devouring with her eyes all these good things which awake tortures in her empty stomach.

5 .. ON THE BRIDGES (Paris at night, on the left the outline of the Palais de Justice Silhouetted against the sky. bright with the first rays of dawn. In the distance are the bridges over the Seine, lighted up with gas lamps, and reflected in the water).

Marie, driven from every place comes to the bridge overcome with fatigue and falling asleep. Belated passers-by, blinded with snow pay no attention to the poor girl.

Not having strength to go any further, she lies down on the parapet and goes to sleep. A rag picker comes along, who, having picked up the papers scattered on the bridge, hits against the body of the poor girl. He turns his lantern towards her, and throws a bright ray on the unfortunate sleeper. The brave man, terrified awakens her, and scolds her for sleeping thus in the falling snow at the risk of getting ill. He advises her to hurry home, and touched by her distress, he shares with her a small piece of bread, and wraps the child up in a coat. Being very poor himself he could do no more, and he watches sadly the poor girl who goes away thanking him. The rag picker wipes away a tear and continues his wanderings.

6 ... THE GOOD SAMARITAN

Now Marie hurrying home has passed the gates of the town. The country stretches white with snow as far as eye can see, the growing dawn vaguely lighting the way. The snow storm increases in severity, the poor girl dazzled by the snow flakes whirling around her, and frozen with cold, which she has bravely endured all night, unable to go any further falls fainting in the road. The pitiless snow gently covers her. An old gentlemen and his daughter returning by motor, rather late after an evenings enjoyment in Paris, narrowly avoid running over Marie, lying in the snow on the road. They stop the motor, jump out and lift the poor girl into the car. After wrapping her well in his fur-coat, the gentleman learns the girls story and hurries back to the City, where he orders a great quantity of food and fuel to be brought to the home of Marie's parents.

7 ... THE HAPPY HOUR

This scene shows the interior of the poor man's garret, where he and his wife are anxiously awaiting the return of Marie. While in despair at her prolonged absence they see a vision of an angel who promises their daughter's safe return and speedy relief to their wants, no sooner does the angel's vision fade from view, than the door is burst open and Marie followed by the good Samaritan and his daughter enter and greet the now bewildering parents. Then follows a procession of butchers and bakers, confectioners, coal merchants, clothiers, &c., &c., all bearing great burdens of provisions which were ordered by the old gentleman. These are deposited in the room and while the poor couple and their daughter overwhelm the philantropist with thanks, in walks the Bailiff, who renews his demands for payment of the rent. He is promptly paid and kicked out amidst rejoicings of the entire gathering. Thus are the deserving poor finally awarded.

A grand picture of Pathos and Humour with a Moral.

Length 600 feet.   Price £20.   Coloured £40.

Choicest "Star" Films

(COPYRIGHTED).

PRICE £1 15s. NET per Single Length of 20 Metres.

(About 65 feet). Longer Lengths in proportion.

Colouring extra 35s, net per Length of 20 Metres.

No	TITLE	LENGTH
26	A TERRIBLE NIGHT	
70	THE VANISHING LADY	1
78	THE DEVIL'S CASTLE	3
96	THE HAUNTED CASTLE	1
118	LABORATORY OF MEPHISTOPHELES ...	3
122	THE BEWITCHED INN	2
126	THE CHARCOAL MAN'S RECEPTION ..	1
127	THE PRIVATE DINNER	1
129	WHILE UNDER A HYPNOTIST'S INFLUENCE	1
130	AN IRRITABLE MODEL	2
140	DEVILISH MAGIC	2
147	DIVERS AT WORK ON A WRECK UNDER THE SEA	1
149	A NOVICE AT X RAYS	1
150	DEFENDING THE FORT	1
153	BLACK MAGIC	1
155	THE FAMOUS BOX TRICK	1
156	PYGMALION AND GALATEA	1
159	ADVENTURES OF WILLIAM TELL ...	1
160	THE ASTRONOMER'S DREAM	3
164	THE CAVE OF THE DEMONS	1
165	THE ARTIST'S DREAM	1
166	THE PAINTER'S STUDIO	1
167	THE FOUR TROUBLESOME HEADS ...	1
168	THE TRIPLE LADY	1
169	TEMPTATION OF ST. ANTHONY ...	1
170	THE BEGGAR'S DREAM	1
171	A DINNER UNDER DIFFICULTIES ...	1
172	FANTASTICAL ILLUSIONS	1
175	ROBBING CLEOPATRA'S TOMB ...	2

MÉLIÈS
STAR FILM

PARIS—NEW-YORK

Facsimile of Trade Mark on beginning each Film.

U

u 2

514	THE ENCHANTER	3
517	COMICAL CONJURING	3
520	THE MAGIC LANTERN, or the Bioscope in the Toy Shop	5
525	THE DREAM OF THE BALLET MASTER	$2\frac{1}{2}$
534	WHAT BEFELL THE TURKISH EXECUTIONER ...	$2\frac{1}{4}$
536	THE "APACHES" (Parisian Hooligans)	$2\frac{1}{4}$
538	PIERROT AND THE MOON	$2\frac{3}{4}$
540	"TIT FOR TAT"—The Head in a Case	2
542	A JUGGLING CONTEST BETWEEN TWO MAGICIANS	3
545	EVERY MAN HIS OWN CIGAR LIGHTER ...	1
546	THE INVISIBLE SYLVIA	$1\frac{1}{2}$
547	THE ENCHANTED TRUNK	$3\frac{1}{2}$
550	SHORT LIVED APPARITIONS	2
552	THE KING OF THE MACKEREL FISHERS	2
554	THE DREAM OF THE CLOCK MAKER	$2\frac{1}{2}$
556	IMPERCEPTIBLE TRANSFORMATIONS	2
558	A MIRACLE OF THE INQUISITION	$2\frac{1}{4}$
560	BENVENUTO CELLINO, OR THE CURIOUS ELOPEMENT	$2\frac{3}{4}$
575	THE MERRY PROPHET OF RUSSIA...	3
578	THE CHINESE JUGGLER	3
581	THE WONDERFUL LIVING FAN (Fine)	4
585	COOKERY BEWITCHED (Acrobatic)	$4\frac{1}{4}$
589	THE DEVIL'S PLANK „	2
591	THE IMPOSSIBLE DINNER (Burlesque)	2
593	THE MERMAID	$3\frac{1}{2}$
596	THE DRUNKARD'S MISHAPS	$2\frac{1}{2}$
598	THE FISHER'S GUARDIAN ANGEL	5
603	PRACTICAL JOKE ON A YOKEL	$3\frac{1}{4}$
626	ANIMATED COSTUMES	$2\frac{1}{2}$
628	BILL BAILEY'S DINNER	$4\frac{1}{4}$
632	THE MAGIC FRAME	2
634	THE MAGICAL ROSE TREE	3
637	THE ENCHANTED CUPBOARD	$2\frac{1}{2}$
639	MARRIAGE BY CORRESPONDENCE	2
662	THE WANDERING JEW	3
665	CASCADE OF FIRE	3
668	GROTTO OF SURPRISES	$1\frac{3}{4}$

NEW SUBJECTS CONSTANTLY IN PREPARATION.

These will be noted in our Supplementary Lists.

"G.A.S." FILM SUBJECTS.

3500 ... **LET ME DREAM AGAIN**

A humorous facial expression picture, with surprising climax. An elderly beau flirting with maiden at masquerade ball, wakes, and finds himself in bed bestowing unexpected caresses upon his "old missus." **75 feet**

3501 ... **GRANDMA THREADING HER NEEDLE**

Succeeds after many attempts, whilst the cat contentedly washes by her side. Excellent photographic quality. **50 feet**

3502 ... **SCANDAL OVER THE TEA CUPS**

A famous subject. Two maiden ladies at afternoon tea relate shocking secrets of society with mingled horror and pleasure depicted by their expressions. **75 feet**

3503 ... **THE POLITICAL DISCUSSION**

Two ardent politicians of rival views discuss with much earnestness and heat the situation as set forth in their favourite newspapers. **50 feet**

3504 ... **A GAME OF NAP**

The excitement and surprises of the game vividly depicted by a couple of old sports. **50 feet**

3505 ... **GAME OF CARDS**

Similar to preceding film, but with more incident. **125 feet**

3506 ... **GOOD STORIES**

Told by two jolly good fellows. Most amusing expressions. **100 feet**

3507 ... **THE LAST BOTTLE AT THE CLUB**

Two old club cronies at a late hour are remarkably mellow and affectionate. **50 feet**

3508 ... **TWO OLD BOYS AT THE MUSIC HALL**

From their position in a stage box the two elderly Johnnies fully appreciate the dancing of a serio-comic behind the footlights. **75 feet**

3509 ... **WHISKEY OR BULLETS**

A very fine facial study, with a surprise at the end. **50 feet**

3510 ... **THE MONOCLE—"ME AND JOE CHAMBERLAIN"**

A roguish fellow sitting by a large sketch of Mr. Chamberlain attempts to emulate the Statesman, as far as the eye-piece is concerned, at any rate. **50 feet**

3511 ... THE LITTLE DOCTOR

Children playing at "doctors," with the kitten in a cradle as patient. When the medicine is administered a magnified view of the kitten's head is shown, the manner in which the little animal receives its dose (of milk) from a spoon being most amusing.

100 feet

3512 ... THE SICK KITTEN

A shorter version of the above. **50 feet**

3513 ... AT LAST ! THAT AWFUL TOOTH

A gentleman suffering with toothache, and having tried numerous remedies in vain is making frantic efforts to pull out the offending member with a piece of string. He at last succeeds, and in his delight seizes a large reading glass to view the tooth. A circular picture showing the magnified tooth as it appears through the reading glass makes a laughable finish. **50 feet**

3514 ... THAT AWFUL CIGAR. " I'll smoke it if it kills me."

An amusing picture of the effect produced by a smoker's efforts to make the best of a very bad cigar. **100 feet**

3515 ... PA'S COMMENTS ON THE MORNING NEWS

A breakfast table study of a demonstrative citizen who reads his paper and makes visual comments on the pleasing and painful uews therein. **75 feet**

3516 ... A PHOTOGRAPH TAKEN FROM OUR AREA WINDOW

What do we see ? Nothing but feet and legs, but oh! what a variety. **100 feet**

3517 ... GRANDMA'S READING CLASS

A most successful film. Grandma is sewing, and her little grandson amuses himself by viewing the surrounding objects through her large reading glass. Circular and magnified views are shown of the objects he beholds, viz.: the **works of his watch,** the **canary in its cage,** his **grandma's eye,** the **cat's head, etc.**

100 feet

3518 ... AS SEEN THROUGH A TELESCOPE

An inquisitive old man by the roadside sees a young couple leading a bicycle in the distance. As the couple pause to tie a refractory shoe lace the old man raises his teleseope to participate in the ceremony. A circular and enlarged view of the shoe tying appears on the screen ; but the old gentleman's pleasure is sadly marred, for the young man has observed the operation with the telescope and on arriving at his side bonnets him so severely that his camp stool collapses and deposits him in the dust. **75 feet**

3519 ... THE VALENTINE

The mingled emotions of the old maid as she receives a valentine are graphically expressed, and her final horror on discovering that she is the victim of a saucy joke is very laughable.

50 feet

3520 ... A BAD CIGAR

Another version of the smoker's attempt to grapple with a cigar unworthy of the name. **50 feet**

3521 ... THE HOUSE THAT JACK BUILT

A reversing film. Very interesting. A tiresome boy shakes down the house laboriously· built by his sister, then gleefully pokes and shakes the pile of bricks which mysteriously rebuild themselves as he proceeds. **50 feet**

3523 ... MARY JANE'S MISHAP

This film shows the kitchen operations of Mary Jane the servant in early morning. Her laughable efforts to clean boots, light the fire, &c., are exhibited, and magnified views of her facial expressions are interspersed. She is clearly detected in putting paraffin on the kitchen fire to promote a blaze ; but her success is not great, for an explosion occurs and projects Mary Jane up the chimney. She is next seen emerging from the chimney pot on the house top. and her scattered remains fall to earth. As a final warning to future Mary Janes a visit is paid to the cemetery where an old lady endeavours to improve the occasion by exhibiting the unhappy slavey's grave to other slaveys. But the gathering is scattered, for Mary Jane's ghost rises from the tomb in search of her paraffin can, and having secured this desired article she retires again to her final resting place, the domestic cat being the sole remaining witness. **260 feet**

3524 ... AFTER DARK, OR THE POLICEMAN AND HIS LANTERN

A most successful film. Amusing and very original. The police leave the station on their night beat. Then follows a series of views as seen by the lantern rays of one of the force. Interest is kept up by beggar boys, drunken swells, latch-key troubles, and burgling episodes are presented. **225 feet**

3525 ... " LETTIE LIMELIGHT IN HER LAIR "

This laughable film shows a young actress (not so very young) in her dressing-room preparing for her performance. The art of make-up is revealed on a very clear scale, and the final abandon of the lady who removes her wig with joy during the perusal of a "masher's" note is not the least amusing part of this glimpse behind the scene. **200 feet**

3526 ... A SHAVE AND BRUSH UP

A man's face reflected in a mirror as he carries out these amusing though trying operations. **50 feet**

3527 ... THE DULL RAZOR

Shaving under difficulties. "There is something not altogether displeasing in the misfortune of others." **50 feet**

3528 ... THE BILL POSTER'S REVENGE

The bill sticker displays three full length posters of different subjects. A rival during his absence reverses the sheets bearing the legs of the subjects with ludicrous results. **50 feet**

3529 ... IN THE GREEN ROOM

A pantomime artist makes up for the part of "giant" in the dressing room. He leaves for the stage—height 10 feet 6. **100 feet**

3530 ... THE COMEDIAN AND THE FLY-PAPER

Mr. Mat Melrose, the Crystal Palace dancer, shows how troublesome a fly-paper becomes when it once gets possession of a fellow. **75 feet**

3531 ... THE ADRIAN TROUPE OF CYCLISTS

Performing evolutions in their " Tea Cup " track, smallest in the world. **150 feet**

3532 ... " CIRCLING THE CIRC "

The same four artists as above, in further feats. **65 feet**

3533 ... THE CAKE WALK

The best picture of this crazy dance. Performed by the Melrose Trio of the Crystal Palace, London. **75 feet**

3534 .. THE DONKEY SERPENTINE DANCER

A comedian and his donkey on the Music Hall stage essay a Serpentine Dance with more agility than art. **75 feet**

3535 ... TOMMY AND HIS HARRIET ON BANK HOLIDAY

A tall soldier and his girl indulge in an amusing dance on the grass much to the amusement of the other holiday makers in the boat-swings. **50 feet**

3539 THE MOUSE IN THE ART SCHOOL

Young lady art students are sketching a tiny sailor boy when a mouse disturbs their work. Magnified view of mouse's head protruding from hole. Gallant tiny sailor slays mouse, and art students left adoring the hero. **50 feet**

3537 ... THE MONK'S RUSE FOR A LUNCH

A monk induces a tourist to share luncheons. The tourist's lunch having been demolished by the monk, the former demands the production of the latter's basket for sharing purposes. It transpires in the end that the wily monk's basket contains only a little dog. **100 feet**

3538 ... PANTOMIME GIRLS HAVING A LARK

A theatrical performance having been given on a gentleman's yacht, the ballat girls in stage costume and tights got possession of a small boat and made for the beach. A comedian joined the party and the return from shore was productive of some lively fun. **50 feet**

3539 ... THE MARCH OF THE AMAZONS

A pantomime ballet. Sixteen Amazons perform interesting marching and dancing evolutions. **75 feet**

3540 ... TOPSY-TURVY DANCE BY THREE QUAKER MAIDENS

This is a laughable sell, for although the Quakeresses apparently retire behind a flag and dance with their feet and legs in the air, the attendants accidentally drop the flag and show " how it is done." **125 feet**

3541 ... TAMBOURINE DANCING QUARTETTE

A good dancing film by qualified dancers and high-kicking damsels. **135 feet**

3542 ... PANTOMIME SCENE

A dance on ship's deck. Hornpipe. &c. **125 feet**

3543 ... THE UNFORTUNATE EGG MERCHANT

75 feet

3544 ... TOO MUCH OF A GOOD THING

A happy father is presented with his first born by the old nurse. His joy is modified shortly after when a second infant is produced; but when a third is proudly brought forth and offered to the bewildered parent he decides that the thing must end and promptly rushes for the family doctor and ejects him from the house. **50 feet**

3546 ... THE NURSERY RHYMES

This is a long film depicting all the incidents of the nursery rhymes in the manner beloved of children who readily recognise the favourites of their nursery teaching the old favourites introduced are : (1) "Jack and Jill" (2) ' Old Woman who lived in a Shoe " (3) "Sing a Song o'Sixpence " (4) Old Mother Hubbard " (5) "Goosey Goosey " (6) " Cat and the Fiddle," &c. Each Story introduced by a title. Exhibited with great success at the children's entertainments at the Shaftesbury Theatre and elsewhere. **600 feet**

3547 ... BALLOON INFLATION

Various stages of the interesting operation of filling a balloon with gas. **125 feet**

3548 ... THE LONDON TO BRIGHTON "GLOBE WALK"

A fine film and the only successful one depicting the famous 52 mile rolling globe "walk " of Mdlle. Florence. Taken at different parts of the journey. **125 feet**

3549 ... THE YOKEL'S LUNCHEON (Reversing)

Devouring spoonsfull of pudding which action when reversed produces most ludicious results **75 feet**

3550 ... THE MONK'S MACCARONI FEAST (Reversing)

125 feet

3551 ... "DOROTHY'S DREAM"

This is an exceptionally interesting series of pictures for the Pantomime season and exhibits for children, as it combines the principal scenes of seven of the best known fairy tales all reproduced successfully with intervening space and title. The picture commences with a handsome drawing room, which a pretty little girl enters, carrying a book of Fairy Tales. She seats herself in a comfortable arm chair before a spacious fireplace, and after paging over the leaves of the book, falls asleep and dreams of the different tales treated in the book. The good Fairy appears, gradually taking shape from a nebulous mist floating in the air; she waves her magic wand over the little dreamer, and causes to pass, in review, visions of the principal scenes of the fairy tales : " **Dick Whittington**" "**Robinson Crusoe,**" " **The Forty Thieves,**" " **Cinderella,**" " **Aladdin and the Wonderful Lamp,**" " **Blue Beard,**" and " **Red Riding Hood** "

The good fairy having accomplished her object, vanishes, by gradually dissolving again into space.

The maid now enters the room in search of the child found sleeping in the chair. The latter wakes up and hardly realizes her surroundings, rubs her eyes to make certain that she is not really amongst the scenes of her dreams. Of these she tells the maid, who then leads the little girl from the room.

One of the neatest and cleanest Fairy Tale Series ever produced by Bioscope. Excellent Photographic Quality.

Total Length 600 feet

3452 ... **JOHN BULL'S HEARTH** (Fiscal Policy Skit)

185 feet

3553 ... **THE FREE TRADE BENCH**

John Bull crowded off by Foreign Invaders. **50 feet**

3554 ... **LONDON WAIFS' EXCURSION TO BRIGHTON**

Thousands of slum children rushing from the Fresh Air Fund Excursion Train as it arrives at Brighton. An animated scene. Excellent quality **100 feet**

3555 ... **WAIFS ON BRIGHTON BEACH**

This picture shows the waifs up to all sorts of mischief and play —some bathing, others building sand castles, &c. **50 feet**

3556 ... **LONDON WAIFS' (BOYS' AND GIRLS') RACES**

A continuation of the preceding series, showing spirited Races of Boys and Girls, with an award of prizes to the winners. **50 feet**

3557 ... **THE BABY AND THE APE**

Baby put into the perambulator by its mother, who supplies it with a nursing bottle, and thus leaves it in full content of itself. An Ape, which happened to have escaped from a Menagerie, spies the baby from the top of the garden wall. It stealthily makes its way towards the perambulator, and steals the bottle from the baby. We next see him enjoying the contents, while the baby is bewailing the loss of its food—large tears rolling down its cheeks, and looking otherwise most disconsolate. **150 feet**

WILLIAMSON'S FILMS.

HUMOROUS AND PATHETIC SUBJECTS.

4004 ... **WASHING THE SWEEP**

75 feet

4005 ... **WINNING THE GLOVES**

65 feet

4006 ... **THE FORBIDDEN LOVER**

65 feet

4011 ... **THE CLOWN BARBER**

70 feet

4020 ... **COURTSHIP UNDER DIFFICULTIES**

67 feet

4123 ... **ATTACK ON A CHINA MISSION**)Bluejackets to the Rescue

The scene opens with the outer gate of the premises; a Chinaman with flourishing sword approaches and tries the gate. Finding it fastened, he calls the others who come rushing up; one leaps over the gate, and the combined attack results in forcing it open; nine Boxers in Chinese costume of varied character now swarm in, stopping occasionally to fire in the direction of the house.

The second scene shows the front of the house—the missionary walking in front with a young lady; wife and child are seated a little further off. At the first alarm, the missionary drops his book and sends the young lady into the house to fetch rifle and pistols; he then rushes to his wife and child, and sees them safely into the house; takes cover behind some bushes, discharges his revolver at the Boxers advancing in different directions, kills one. then picks up rifle and discharges it at another; his ammunition exhausted, he comes to close quarters with another boxer armed with a sword, and, after an exciting fight, is overcome, and left presumably killed. Meanwhile, others of the attacking party have closed round the young lady and followed her, retreating into the house.

Missionary's wife now appears waving handkerchief on the balcony; the scene changes and shows a party of bluejackets advancing from the distance, leaping over a fence, coming through the gate, kneeling and firing in fours, and running forward to the rescue, under command of a mounted officer

The fourth scene is a continuation of the second. The Boxers are dragging the young lady out of the house, which they have set on fire, at the moment the bluejackets appear; a struggle takes place with the Boxers; mounted officer rides up and carries off the young lady out of the melee.

The missionary's wife now rushes out of the house pointing to the balcony, where she has left her child; a bluejacket has secured it, but his passage down the stairs being blocked, three sailors mount on each other's shoulders and land the child safely in the mother's arms.

The struggle with the Boxers continues, but they are finally overcome and taken prisoners.

This sensational subject is full of interest and excitement from start to finish, and is everywhere received with great applause.

230 feet

4142 .. **A BIG SWALLOW**

65 feet

4143 ... **THE MAGIC EXTINGUISHER**

110 feet

4144 ... **THE ELIXIR OF LIFE**

90 feet

4145 ... **STOP THIEF !**

115 feet

4149 ... **OVER THE GARDEN WALL**

65 feet

4150 ... **THE MARVELLOUS HAIR RESTORER**

104 feet

4152 ... **ARE YOU THERE ?**

75 feet

4153 ... **THE PUZZLED BATHER AND HIS ANIMATED CLOTHES**

80 feet

4155 ... **TEASING GRANDPA**

92 feet

4166 ... **PING-PONG (An Amusing Burlesque of this Popular Pastime)**

90 feet

4172 ... **THE SOLDIER'S RETURN**

A bit of real life. There is no suggestion of acting in the picture, and the setting is perfectly natural. In four scenes.

Scene one, shows a portion of a row of poor cottages—one occupied, another empty. Soldier walks in with his kit bag on his shoulder, tries the door, peeps in the window—the cottage is evidently deserted; a woman comes out of the next cottage and says something to him—no doubt with reference to the late occupant, which appears to upset the soldier a good deal; a blocksmith walks up, claims acquaintance, and is warmly greeted; the soldier hands his bag to the woman next door to look after, and walks away.

The next scene shows the outside of workhouse; soldier enters, presents a paper to the gate porter, who looks at it and points out the direction in which he is to go.

The next scene shows the door of the women's ward; soldier walks in knocks at the door, which is opened by a nurse who looks at his paper and goes in again, soldier waiting outside; after a short interval an old lady in workhouse garb appears, evidently the mother of the soldier, as they warmly embrace—a pathetic picture, true to life. The soldier indicates that he has come to fetch her home, and motions to her to go and change her clothes; he helps her up the steps, and walks to and fro while the old lady is dressing. After a short time she comes out again dressed in her own clothes—the soldier takes her arm and walks away with her; they only get a few steps, however, before they are called back by the other old inmates, who have followed the old lady, to shake hands, congratulate her and wish her good-bye.

Another short scene shows them walking out of the gate. The last scene shows the outside of the cottages again—but what a change! The windows cleaned, clean curtains up, flowers in the window, a bird in a cage hanging up by the door, the old woman sitting by the door sewing, while her son in his shirt sleeves is planting some flowers in the little slip of garden in front—he stops to light his pipe, and asks if that will do; the old woman nods approval, and he resumes his work. He looks up again later and says something to her, then goes into the cottage and brings out a cup of tea and hands it to his mother; and the picture closes just as she is drinking the tea.   **185 feet**

4175 ... A WORKMAN'S PARADISE

A puzzling picture. *Scene:* Buildings in course of erection; workman slouces in and beckons the hod which glides in without his help; he points out where it is to stop, calls the bricks, which are seen to sort themselves out, and jump up into the hod; the workman walks off, the hod following; the scene then changes, and shows the brick-layer on the scaffold; the labourer, by some mysterious agency, comes up head first and lands on the platform, the hod full of bricks following him; the same thing is repeated with a hod full of mortar. The brick-layer is then seen laying the bricks; one by one the bricks rise into his hand, and the mortar jumps up on to the trowel, until three courses of bricks are laid. Very amusing, interesting and puzzling.

170 feet

4182 ... THOSE TROUBLESOME BOYS

102 feet

4200 ... CLOSE QUARTERS : "With a Notion of the Motion of the Ocean "

4204 ... THE ACROBATIC TRAMPS

104 feet

4205 ... INSECTORIUM (Fight between Spider and Centipedes)

90 feet

4207 ... FIGHTING HIS BATTLES OVER AGAIN (Scene in a Canteen in Barracks)

145 feet

4209 ... THE LITTLE MATCH SELLER

200 feet

4234 ... THE DESERTER

Scene I.—Inside of barrack room. Soldier polishing accoutrements; comrade enters with telegram: "Father worse, come at once if you wish to see him alive." Officer enters; Soldier shows telegram and asks for leave; Officer finds fault with different things, swears in dumb show, and knocks things about, "No, you cannot have leave." and marches off. Soldier and comrade consult, thinks he can just slip away and get to his father's cottage and back in time for next parade. Another comrade, evidently a bit of a sneak, and probably having a grudge against the soldier, witnesses the departure and informs against him.

Scene II.—Soldier seen climbing over wall and running off.

Scene III.—A country pathway; soldier rushing down, evidently pursued; turns off into a harvest field, dropping his cap in the field. Two horsemen now seen coming over the brow of the hill and down the pathway; find the soldier's cap; one dismounts, examines it, remounts, and gallop off.

Scene IV.—Harvest field; harvesters' dinner time, lighting fire and preparing meal. A child comes rushing up and points out soldier dodging amongst the sheaves and coming toward them; the harvesters take in the situation at once, and hide him amongst the sheaves behind them just as the pursuing horsemen are seen approaching; one of the horsemen questions the harvesters; one of them points away in the distance evidently putting them off the scent. As soon as the horsemen are out of sight they uncover the fugitive, whom they find in a terribly exhausted state; they furnish him with some old clothing as a disguise; he starts away in a direction opposite to that of the patrol.

Scene V.—Interior of cottage bedroom. Father of the soldier in bed, mother and brother attending him on one side, while a young woman who is evidently something more than a sister to him is watching on the other side. It is evidently a death-bed scene. The soldier now stumbles into the room, met by the young woman, who exclaims at his appearance; the situation on both sides is quickly explained, the soldier kneels by the bedside, and is rejoiced to find that his father recognises him, and feebly passes his hand to him. At this moment the patrol enters, having traced the fugitive to the cottage. They prepare to secure their prisoner, but are stopped by the young woman. The soldiers perceive the solemn nature of the scene, and at a word from the deserter silently pass out again.

Scene VI.— Outside cottage. The patrol walking up and down. Soldier and the young woman evidently deeply distressed now come out together; after an affecting leave-taking the soldier calls the patrol, and holds out his hands to be handcuffed. His comrades, however, spare him this indignity, and they walk away together. We have no doubt that they will see that a proper account of the circumstances is laid before the Colonel, and that the punishment, inevitable though it be, will be mitigated thereby.

Scene VII.—Orderly Room. Colonel seated at table; enter Orderly Room Sergeant with official letter. Colonel opens it; enter Captain who took part in Scene I., salutes, and seats himself beside Colonel; the latter discusses the charge with the Captain, then orders prisoner and escort before him. Prisoner is asked what he has to say in answer to the charge; produces the telegram. Colonel tells the Captain the man ought to have had leave as requested. Who reported this? Informer is brought in, and escort dismissed. Informer questioned; then Colonel goes up to prisoner, pats him on the shoulder, tears up the charge, and dismisses him; then turning to the informer, admonishes him, and dismisses him also. Scene finishes with Colonel and Captain in animated converse, the latter apparently also being admonished.

Scene VIII.—Outside of Orderly Room. Prisoner's comrades hanging about; when the escort comes out they gather round anxiously enquiring as to result. Directly afterwards their discharged comrade appears, and is loudly cheered; closely following him comes the informer, who is severely hustled, and the last scene shows him being doused in a horse-trough, the hero of the story coming to his rescue. **520 feet**

4232 ... **THE WRONG POISON**

160 feet

4239 ... **AN EVIL-DOER'S SAD END**

125 feet

4240 .. **" BOYS WILL BE BOYS "**

290 feet

4241 ... **JUGGINS' MOTOR ; or, why he now offers it " for Sale so Cheap "**

Very funny, **125 feet**

THE STOWAWAY

A TEMPERANCE STORY, WITH A MORAL

SCENE 1.—THE INTERIOR OF A MISERABLE GARRET

Untidy woman with head on table apparently asleep: enter ragged little urchin with papers on his arm; looks at his mother and disconsolately seats himself on a box; the mother rouses herself, staggers towards him and asks him for his money; hands him a bottle and orders him to go and fetch her some drink; the boy refuses; the woman clutches the boy, drags him round the room, and throws him in a corner. Overcome with her rage she drops into the chair again and falls into a drunken sleep. The boy now rouses himself, and after some show of grief and hesitation evidently makes up his mind to run away and leave her. He puts on an old coat and boots and prepares to depart. It occurs to him to leave a note for his mother. Looking round for a piece of paper he sees the torn wall paper and tears a piece from that and laboriously writes on it his message to his mother. At the door he again turns and looks longingly towards his mother and goes back and adds something to the paper he has written. After he

has gone, the mother rouses and calls him ; goes to the door and calls
again : she begins to think he must have left her and sees the paper,
picks it up in a feverish way, and reads excitedly :—

　　"dear mother ı hav gone to sea i will cum back wen you gives
up the drink　　Jim
　　pleas god look after mother."

The woman is at first staggered a bit, but breaks out into a
frenzied rage, in the midst of which a clergyman appears at the door ;
he is about to retire upon seeing her condition, but is called in by the
woman ; she endeavours to explain her trouble, but is evidently so
incoherent that he can make nothing of it until she gives him the
paper to read.　The clergyman tries to comfort her, and takes out his
Bible to read to her.　After reading a little she starts up, and, snatching the Bible, asks, "Where does it say that?"　He points to the
passage, which she reads, and apparently considers for a moment, then
asks if it is possible that she can be forgiven, and if he thinks she can
be a good woman again.　The woman, now thoroughly repentant,
listens patiently to the clergyman's advice.

SCENE 2—THE SHIPPING DOCK

We now follow the boy and see him hanging around a wharf;
being driven off by one of the men; and finally when no one appears
to be looking, slipping up a gangway on to a ship just about to sail.
He is seen by an old sailor who, however, does not inform against
him.　The same old sailor is afterwards seen by the clergyman who
gets from him the name of the vessel and its destination.

SCENE 3.—THE CLERGYMAN'S HOME

We next see the clergyman visiting the woman again ; she is
now tidy and is busy sewing ; she expresses her joy at hearing about
her boy, and asks the clergyman to write to him for her.

SCENE 4.—IN THE SHIP'S HOLD

We again follow the boy and see him seated amongst boxes and
barrels in the hold of the ship ; hearing someone approach he hides,
but is discovered by the sailor who comes to look for a box.

SCENE 5.—THE SHIP'S DECK

We next see him being pushed up the hatchway on to the deck
where the sailor thrashes him with a rope's end.　At this moment the
little four-year-old son of the captain runs up and bangs into the old
sailor with his little fists, then puts his arms round the boy to protect
him ; the captain now comes up, and after finding out what it is all
about walks off with the stowaway.

SCENE 6.—THE MOTHER'S LODGINGS

We return to the mother for a brief period, and find her in better
lodging, apparently doing dressmaking and with a young woman
working for her.　The clergyman enters and asks if she has any
news of her boy ; she shows a letter from him ; the clergyman reads
and expresses his satisfaction ; looks round approvingly, enquires
about her business, &c., and departs.

SCENE 7.—THE SHIP'S FORECASTLE

We now see the stowaway among some other sailors on board the
ship dressed in a jersey and trousers.　Old sailor is handing round
drinks and offers the boy some ; he refuses ; old sailor tries to make
him drink it—he will never make a sailor if he does not; but the
captain who has been looking on, intervenes and takes the boy away.

SCENE 8.—IN PORT

In the next scene the ship is evidently in port again ; the captain is seen talking to a naval officer, and the boy is called forward ; after some conversation together, it is evidently decidently decided that the boy shall go with the naval officer, no doubt to be sent to a training ship ; just before he leaves his little friend, the captain's son runs up to say good-bye.

SCENE 9.—THE RE-UNION

Our last scene shows the mother in apparently good circumstances with all the evidences of a good dressmaker's business in progress ; two young women at work ; one at a sewing machine ; dresses and materials, fashion plates, &c., strewn about. Once more the clergyman enters with some news, which apparently excites the mother : " Is he coming home ? Will he be long ? " Then evidently suspecting that he is at the door, she rushes towards it, but the clergyman asks her to calm herself, and he will bring the boy. When the boy, now a smart lad dressed in naval dress, enters with the clergyman, he does so with some hesitation, uncertain as to his reception, surprised at the altered surroundings ; but seeing his mother's arms stretched towards him he rushes up to her, and they are clasped together in a long embrace ; the young women looking on with some astonishment, while the clergyman's attitude suggests his great satisfaction and thankfulness for the reformation of the woman and the reunion with her child. **Total Length 550 feet**

4249 ... " THE GREAT SEA SERPENT "

Mr. MacDoodle, arrayed in true nautical fashion, and with a big telescope, is out for a trip on the " Brighton Queen " with some friends. He has fallen asleep, and some wag has taken the opportunity to insert a worm at the big end of his telescope. When Mr. MacDoodle wakes up, and proceeds to take observations, he becomes very excited, much to the amusement of his friends, and our picture shows what marvels he sees through his telescope. He innocently asks them to look for themselves, and some of them do. An officer on the vessel has a look, and at once points out to Mr. MacDoodle that he has been " had." Then the little man assumes a fighting attitude, and some of his friends are upset. **135 feet**

4251 ... " OH! WHAT A SURPRISE "

Shows what mischief-makers boys are, and how easily as jealous woman is deceived. **90 feet**

4266 ... AN INTERESTING STORY

So interesting that the reader forgets everything else ; pours his coffee into his hat ; falls over the maid cleaning the tiles outside ; walks into a skipping rope ; tumbles against a donkey in a fish cart, politely raises his hat and apologises ; stumbles against another pedestrian ; finally is run over by a steam roller ; some cyclists finding him flat on the road use their pumps and pump him up again ; they put him on his legs, find his hat and book for him, and off he goes again still reading. Very laughable. **235 feet**

4267 ... GABRIEL GRUB—How the surly sexton learnt Goodwill towards Men. After Mr. Wardle's story in " Pickwick " Papers by Charles Dickens.

Gabriel Grub was an ill-conditioned, cross-grained old sexton and grave digger who on Christmas Eve delighted to dig a grave, preparing as he said a nice Christmas Box for someone, instead of joining in

w

the joy and gladness of Christmas time. His special aversion was to see anyone, especially children happy. The tradition was that Grub was carried off by demons on that Christmas Eve, but our version shows that it was only a temporary abduction ; for although the goblins take him down into his own grave that he had been digging—down, down amid fire and smoke, they show him some pictures of the manner in which others enjoy their Christmas. They pull him about and kick him and make him drink some liquid fire ; but there is some room to suspect that the contents of the black bottle had something to do with it after all. At any rate Gabriel Grub found himself asleep next morning covered with snow, and racked with pain and stiffness where the goblins had been kicking him ; or was it cold and rheumatism ? Gabriel Grub however has learnt a lesson and is a changed man. After shaking himself to get rid of the snow, and straigthening his limbs he realises that it is Christmas morning—he hears the church bells ringing, and sinks upon his knees in a humble and devout attitude.

A final scene is shown where Gabriel Grub in his changed character appears among some children who are playing ''blind man's buff ; '- at first they run away from him in alarm, but he is laden with toys and soon wins the confidence of the youngest. They soon recover from their alarm and each one with some token of his goodwill towards them starts skipping around him till finally the surly Gabriel Grub is himself a happy child again skipping with the rest.

We suggest an imitation of church bells ringing as an accompaniment to the second church-yard scene. **400 feet**

4269 ... THE OLD CHORISTER—A pathetic story adapted for musical effects

Scene I.—A Country Lane ; a feeble old man who is in the restlessness of old age has wandered to his native village is seen walking (Church bells ringing in the distance) he stops and listens ; memories of his young days crowd upon him, and stopping to rest on a mile-stone he sees himself once more a choir boy singing in the village church (bells gradually fade away and boy's voice is heard singing as visions of choristers appears) two lines of "I know that my Redeemer liveth," *Handel* (suggested) voice fades away as vision fades and bells again heard ; the old man rises and listening again to the bells walks off in the direction of the sound.

Scene II.—Another country scene showing church on a hill in the background.

(Bells still ringing but sounding nearer) ; old man is on his way to the Church.

Scene III.—The Vestry Door.

Choir boys playing round waiting for door to open (bells ringing now very loudly as they are supposed to be immediately overhead) verger opens the door and the boys troop in (bells now stop ringing and one bell tolls) ; the old man comes in and hangs round the door watching the choristers go in ; the clergyman now enters and seeing the old man stops to speak to him ; the old man tells him that he used to sing in the choir in his young days, and the clergyman eventually persuades the old man to sit once more in his old place, and the two enter together ; the verger then closes the door and this scene fades away. (When the verger appears at the door the bell should cease and the organ be heard, gradually fading as the door closes.)

Scene IV.—Church interior showing chancel and organist sitting at the organ.

Choristers march in singing " Onward Christian Soldiers " (*Sullivan*). NOTE.—If boys' and men's voices are available with organ accompaniment there is just time for one verse to be sung from the opening of this scene to the dramatic part where the boys and men leave off singing in the excitement. In the procession the old man and the clergyman come last, the clergyman leads the old man to a seat in the choir stalls and himself takes a seat behind. The old man in a feeble way is trying to sing with the others but his mind wanders, his book drops from his hand, and looking towards the altar he fancies he sees an angel beckoning him he wanders from his place towards the vision holding out his hands ; he is closely followed by the clergyman and a verger also goes to his assistance ; they are just in time to catch him as he falls ; a glass of water is brought and put to his lips, he revives slightly and again holds out his hands as he sees an angel above him holding a crown—the old man has found his rest at last. **225 feet**

4271 ... THE TRAMP'S REVENGE

A tramp has just emerged from a back-garden door and is examining the contents of a sack which he is carrying when a policeman comes up, looks over his shoulder, enquires what he has there, where he got it, &c. ; he then orders him off, handling him a bit roughly, the tramp looking after him with a menancing scowl. Another scene shows Mary Jane shaking a mat outside the back door ; seeing her favourite policeman she beckons him, he comes forward and after a little persuasion walks in to get some proffered refreshment, no doubt ; he divests himself of his overcoat and helmet and leaves them on the low wall outside. The tramp, who has been watching, now comes on vowing vengeance, probably thinking of reporting the circumstance to the inspector. However, seeing the coat and helmet, a new idea strikes him ; he quickly stows these two articles in his sack and runs off. Our next scene shows him on a country road where considering himself now safe from pursuit he stops to consider what to do with the policeman's garments ; he is about to throw them over a hedge when he hears a motor-car coming, he has another happy thought, quickly dons the coat and helmet and stands in the roadway waving his arms to stop the car, which now approaches at top speed. The car pulls up and the newly-made policeman declares that they are travelling above the speed limit, and proceeds to take the number ; the driver remonstrates, but offers a "tip." which our friend readily accepts, and the car drives off. Highly delighted at the success of his ruse he nevertheless realises the danger of keeping it up, promptly throws the coat and helmet over the fence as he first intended, and begins to retrace his steps. He has not gone far when he sees the policeman coming his way, so he turns back assuming as much as possible a look of injured innocence. The policeman rushes on without coat and hat and asks him if he has seen anyone with a policeman's coat running along this way. Yes, he replies, pointing to a bend in the road, and off the policeman runs, leaving the tramp doubled up with laughter at his successful revenge.

210 feet

4272 ... AN AFFAIR OF HONOUR, à la Francais

Two gentlemen sitting outside a café drinking, one is reading a paper and a discussion ensues, followed by a violent quarrel, ending in the exchange of cards and an appointment for the following morning. The resulting duel follows the usual lines except that everybody gets shot except the two principals, who now considering honour satisfied, shake hands and walk away very good friends. **215 feet**

w 2

A SELECTION OF THE CHOICEST

LUMIERE FILM SUBJECTS.

Length of each Film is 50 feet. PRICE 25s. each, net.

Perforated to Standard American Gauge.

NOTE.—In ordering Films of this Series please specify " LUMIERE No.——"

MISCELLANEOUS.

4 Ostriches in the Jardin des Plantes, Paris

8 Arrival of a train at Villefranche Station

12 Niggers bathing

16 Boxing match

21 Feeding Swans

40 Demolishing a wall

41 Pussy's Breakfast

53 Japanese Juggler

56 Japanese Wrestlers

54 Feeding a Lion at the Zoo

95 Feeding the Tigers

64 Peasants burning Weeds

73 A friendly game of Nap

89 Family at Dinner

277 Baths of Diana, Milan. High Diving

475 "Ball of Sable," peasants in national costume

620 Departure of a Steamer on Lake Leman

627 A heavy load — a team of horses dragging a waggon load of stone up a steep hill

653 Arrival of a train at La Ciotât, France

770 Transport of a Turret by a 60-horse team

929 Stonemasons at work

1008 Parade of automobiles decorated with flowers. The Departure

1009 Parade of automobiles. The Return

1017 The "Grand Prix" of Paris. Vehicles and crowds

1018 The return. Place de l'Etoile

1019 In the Bois de Boulogne

1020 In the Champs-Elysees

1034 Oil wells at Baku

1121 M. Santos Dumont's steerable balloon. I. Bringing out the balloon

1122 M. Santos Dumont's steerable balloon. II. The balloon and its motor

1128 Automobile Parade at Nice

1134 A Swiss trooper

JUVENILE SUBJECTS.

49 Boy and Dog

50 Street Arabs playing at marbles

67 Baby's first steps

69 Baby and Goldfish

82 Children quarrelling

88 Baby's Tea

94 Children playing with a cat and dog

654 Children's Dessert

658 Children Romping

659 Childrens Ring Dance

767 Children on the Sands

958 Children Playing

959 Pussy and Babies at Dinner

1099 Parade of Baby carriages

1100 Little girl and her Cat

GYMNASTS AND EQUILIBRISTS.

CLOWNS.

460 The Air Balloon. Two clowns "head" an air balloon imitating football

461 The Hats I. — Hat tricks by clowns

462 The Hats II. — Hat tricks by clowns

463 Hat and Balancing tricks

464 Dangerous jumping. Clown turning somersaults over several men

440 A Bareback rider

668 Juggling with balls

758 Japanese acrobats

THE KREMOS (Equilibrists)

986 Boxing Cats

987 Educated Dogs. Serpentine Dance

988 Educated Dogs. Leaping

989 Educated Dogs. Exercise with Barrel

1040 Dangerous jumping

1041 Dangerous double jumping

1042 Dangerous jumping by two

1043 Dangerous long jumping

1044 The Pyramid

1045 The little Wrestlers

1048 Educated Cat. Working windlass

1050 Educated Dogs. Balancing in various postures without moving

FIRE BRIGADE SERIES.

76 Engines leaving Station, gallop through street, followed by crowd

77 Preparing to play on Fire

79 Life Saving. Escaping from the fire by means of canvas chute

710 I Engine galloping through street followed by crowd

711 II A second engine, then the escapes arrive at the fire, and the firemen commence operations

723 The alarm. Engines leaving the Station

724 Life saving exercise; Firemen mounting escape

778 Fire engine passing through a Paris street, followed by crowds

779 Fire engine returning to station

780 Fire in a court which is filled with smoke. The firemen erect the escape and a person descends

1348 Fireman mounting the escapes

1349 Hose exercise. Firemen drawing up in a line play on the fire

SPANISH BULL FIGHT.

1107 Entrance of the Troop of Bullfighters

1108 Entrance of the Troop of Matadors, &c., and commencement of the fight

1109 Picadors I.

1110 Picadors II.

1111 Mantle throwing

1112 Mantles and banderilles

1113 Mantles and banderilles II.

1114 Attack

1115 Death of the Bull

1116 Removal of the Bull

THE PASSION PLAY.

COMIC SUBJECTS.

MILITARY SUBJECTS,

6th BATTALION of ALPINE CHAUSSEURS.

MILITARY SUBJECTS—*continued,*

799 Square against cavalry, and deformation
800 Muster
801 Boxing Exercise
802 Ascent of the summit of the Diable
803 Descent from the summit of the Diable
804 Mountain Artillery—Placing gun in position and firing
805 Mountain — Artillery loading mules
806 A battery in the mountains (ascending)
807 A battery in the mountains (descending)

ALPINE GUARDS IN THE ALPS.

1242 Parade of the battalion I. foot soldiers
1243 Parade of the battalion II. infantry
1244 Parade of a battalion of mountain artillery
1245 Parade of a battalion of mountain artillery—Striking tents

1246 Parade of a battalion of mountain artillery—Opening a road
1248 Parade of a battalion of mountain artillery—Piling arms, and rest
1251 The alarm —at the sound of the bugle the soldiers spring from their beds to take their posts
1252 A battery in the mountains
1253 In Indian file on the glacier —I. Mounting
1254 In Indian file on the glacier —II. Descending
1255 In Indian file on the glacier with snowshoes—I. mounting
1256 In Indian file on the glacier with snowshoes—II. Descending
1257 Descending across the rocks I.
1258 Descending across the rocks II.
1259 Transport of cannon on soldiers' backs
1260 Soldiers sliding down a snow-covered hill.

ITALIAN MILITARY.

297 Carbiniers
398 Infantry
1071 Artillery :—A difficult passage
1072 Artillery :— Halt in a ravine.

1132 Horse slipping on a steep incline
1347 A Carousal: Evolution of troops at a Fete in honour of Prince Amédée

TURKEY,

414 Parade of Turkish Infantry
415 Turkish Artillery

MARINE SUBJECTS.

9 Boat leaving Harbour (La Ciotat,) in rough weather
45 Children Shrimping
52 Rough sea

87 Rochers de la Vierge (Biarritz) Rough Sea
838 The call to Arms on Board Ship
842 Sailors racing on foot

MARINE SUBJECTS—*continued.*

1039 The bows of a transatlantic liner in rough weather

1096 Rough weather in Port

1233 Departure of Senior boats for the Shore

1235 Collecting linen on board the " Couronne "

1236 Boxing lesson on board the " Bouvines "

1237 Sailors returning on board

1238 Sailors embarking in boats

1241 Scene taken from a whaler's boat

IRONCLADS of the French Squadron at VILLEFRANCE.

196 The Ironclad, " Le Magenta ',

195 The Ironclad, " Le Brennus ',

809 The Ironclad, " Le Formidable "

810 The Ironclad " Le Courbet "

811 The Ironclad " Le Carnot "

ON BOARD THE " FORMIDABLE."

813 Sailors dropping from the beams into their boats

814 Departure of the Senior boats

818 Cutlass Exercise

821 Scrubbing the deck

823 Drying the deck

824 Collecting Sailors' linen

828 March past of Naval Artillery

DANCING SUBJECTS.

655 Italy : Tarantélla Dance

765 Serpentine dance

845 La Jota

846 Boleras Robadas (together)

850 Boleras Robadas (two)

852 Bolero de medio passo (together)

854 "El Ole de la Cura."

1089 Italy : Saltarello Romana Dance

1090 Italy : Tarantéll at Sorents

1092 Scotch Dance. (The Matta Trio)

1123 La Feria Sevillanos

1124 La Feria Quadro Flamenco

1190 La Bourboule — Local dance executed by a wedding party on leaving the Church

1226 Maillane : La farandole. The Bridge dance

1292 Annamite Dance

THE CAKE WALK at the NOUVEAU CIRQUE.

1350 Negroes

1351 Negro children

1353 The Eltres, Cake Walk champions

1354 Final

RAILWAY AND STEAMSHIP PANORAMAS.

295 Venice — Panorama of the Grand Canal, taken from a boat

296 Venice — Panorama of St. Mark's Square

383 Egypt—On the the Railway

384 Egypt : Panorama—On the Benha Railway

385 Egypt : Panorama—On the Tauch Railway

386-393 Panorama of the Banks of the Nile

399 Jaffa to Jerusalem Railway· Panorama on the line

RAILWAY AND STEAMSHIP PANORAMAS—*continued.*

400 Jaffa to Jerusalem Railway. Panorama on the line (hills)

408 Leaving Jerusalem by Railway

416 Constantinople : Panorama of the Golden Horn hills

417 Constantinople : Panorama of the Banks of the Bosphorous

436 American warship San Francisco at Villefranche

630 ZerLatt: Panorama taken from the Viege to Zermatt Railway

694 Panorama of Autéuil

931 Passing through a railway tunnel

992 Panorama seen while ascending the Eiffel Tower

993 Panorama from the Bellevue Funicular Railway I.

994 Panorama from the Bellevue Funicular Railway II.

997 Panorama from a captive balloon

1098 The Aix-les-Bains Funicular railway at Mont Revard

1135 Montreux — Panorama taken from a tramway

1193 Dinard—Panorama taken when leaving the Harbour

1210 Panorama of the Cauterets line 1.

1211 Panorama of the Cauterets line II

1212 Panorama of the Cauterets line III. The Tunnel

1230 Nice—Panorama on the Beaulieu to Monaco—line I

1231 Nice—Panorama on the Beaulieu to Monaco—line II

1232 Nice—Panorama on the Beaulieu to Monaco—line III

1381 Panorama of Algiers Harbour

1382 Panorama of Algiers Harbour continuation of preceding

1383 Leaving Government Square Algiers

1384 Algiers to Coleah line—The Algiers

1384 Algiers to Coleah line—The great ravine

1385 Algiers to Coleah line Ponte Pescade Tunnel

FOREIGN STREET SCENES, &c.

1204 Chamonix—The Mauvais Pas

1206 Chamonix—The Mer de Glace —Ascent

1207 Chamonix—The Mer de Glace —Descent, (Tourists climbing)

1208 Chamonix—Arrival of excursion carriages

1209 Chamonix—The Village

1213 Cauterets—Pass 1

1214 Cauterets—Pass II

1216 Pau—The Terrace

1217 Pau—The Market Place

1218 Biarratz—A street

1219 Biarritz—The Old Gate

1220 Biarritz—The Beach

1221 Biarritz—Beach and the Establishment

1222 Arles— Leaving St. Throphime

1223 Arles — Farandoleurs in the arena

ALGERIA AND TUNIS.

198 Algiers —Donkeys

199 Algiers—Arab Market

200 Algiers —Government Square

201 Algiers—Bab-Azoun Street

202 Algiers—Unloading vessels

203 Tlemcen—Rue Mascara

204 Tlemcen—Rue Sidi-Bou-Médine

205 Tlemcen—Rue de France

ALGERIA AND TUNIS—*continued.*

207 Tunis—The Market
208 Tunis—-The Fish Market
209 Tunis—The Vegetable Market
210 Tunis—Street and gate of Bab-el-Kadra
211 Tunis—Gate of France
212 Tunis—-El-Halfaouine Street
213 Tunis—Sidi-ben-Arous Street
214 Tunis --Place Bab-Souika

215 Tunis—Souk-el-Bey.
216 Souza Coal Market (with camels)
217 The stop at the station
296 Tunis—The boy and his escort
1386 Biskra—Native children pick-up coins
1387 Biskra—A native wedding

INDO=CHINA.

1262 March Past of Marine Infantry
1263 Review of Troops
1264 The Tirailleurs (Sharpshooters)
1266 Annamite Tirailleurs I.
1267 Annamite Tirailleurs II.
1269 Annamite Reapers
1271 Annamite Funeral
1272 Flower fete
1274 Annamite children gathering sapeques before the ladies' Pagoda
1276 Leaving the brickfields of Meffre and Bourgoin, at Hanoi
1277 Unloading a brick kiln

1280 The Dragon Procession at Cholon I.
1281 The Dragon Procession at Cholon II.
1282 The Dragon Procession at Cholon III.
1288 Regatta boat races (rowers seated)
1289 Regatta boat rowers (standing)
1295 Parade of elephants at Phom-Penh
1297 Leaving the Œug-Kor-Wat jetty in ox carts
1298 Traversing the Nuages Pass (Annam) in sedan chairs

MARTINIQUE.

1388 Fort-deFrance—Women basket carriers
1389 Fort-de-France—The Market

1390 Fort de France—Negro children at play

ITALY.

276 Genoa—Via Carlo Alberto
280 Naples—Via Marine
281 Naples—Via Roma
429 Rome—Repetta Bridge

430 Venice—St Mark's Square
431 Naples—A Street
432 Naples—Santa Lucia

BELGIUM.

526 Brussels—Boulevard Anspach
527 Brussels—La Bourse
528 Brussels—Palace de Brouck-ère

529 Brussels—Grande Palace
530 Brussels—Sainte-Gudule
531 Antwerp—Arriving in a Boat

ASIATIC TURKEY.

394 Jaffa—Arrival of a train
395 Jaffa—Market I
396 Jaffa—Market II
397 Jaffa—Market III
401 Jerusalem—Jaffa Gate (East Side)
402 Jerusalem—Jaffa Gate (West Side)
403 Jerusalem—The Holy Sepulchre
404 Jerusalem — The way of Sorrows
405 Jerusalem—Way of Sorrows and intranceto
406 Jerusalem—A Street
407 Jerusalem—Camel Caravan
409 Bethlehem—A Square (showing beggars)
410 Beyrot—Cannon Square
411 Beyrout — Souk - Abou- el - Nassarh
412 Damascus—A Square
413 Damascus—Soue-el-Fakhra

EGYPT.

359 Alexandria—Embarking
360 Place Méhemet-Ali, Alexandria
361 Arrival of Ramleh train
362 Cairo — The Khedive and Escort
363 Cairo — Procession of the Sacred Carpet
364 Cairo—Bedouins with camels leaving the Custom House
365 Cairo—Kasr-el-Nil Bridge
366 Cairo—Camels leaving Kasr-el-Nil Bridge
367 Cairo—Donkeys leaving Kasr--el-Nil-Bridge
368 Kasr-el-Nil
369 Cairo—A funeral procession
370 Cairo—Citadel Square
371 Cairo—Government Square
372 Cairo—Opera Square
373 Cairo -- Soliman Pacha Square
374 Cairo—Sayeda-Zenab Street
375 Cairo—Ataba-el-Khaira Street
376 Cairo—Sharia-el-Nahazin
377 Cairo—Laht-el-Rab Street
378 The Nile Dam
379 Life under the palm trees
380 Village of Sahkarah — Donkey rides
381 The Pyramids (General Views)
382 Descent of the Great Pyramid

NORTH AMERICA.

319 New York—Broadway
320 New York—Arrival of a train at Bathing Place
321 New York—Brooklyn Bridge
322 New York—The Metropolitan
323 New York — Broadway and Wall Street
324 New York – Passengers descending from Brooklyn Bridge
326 New York — Broadway and Road Street
327 New York—Skaters in Central Park
328 New York — Broadway and Union Square
329 New York—Whitehall Street
330 Brooklyn—Fulton Street
331 Boston—Washington Street
332 Boston—Market Street
333 Boston—Commercial Street
334 Boston—Atlantic Avenue
335 Boston—Fremont Row

NORTH AMERICA—*continued.*

336 Chicago—Police on Parade
337 Chicago—Michigan Avenue
338 Chicago—Great Wheel
339 Niagara—The Falls
340 Niagara—The Rapids
341 Executive Mansion

342 March Past of the Colombia District Artillery
343 March Past of the James Blain Republican Club
344 March Past of the Colombia District National Guard

MEXICO.

346 Transport of the block of Independence
348 The President Walking
349 Bayonet exercise
350 Cowboys lassoing a wild horse
351 Indians meal
353 Mexican dance

354 Lassoing buffaloes for work
355 Indian market on the Viga Canal
356 Mexican on restive horse
357 Cowboys bathing horses
358 Spanish street dance

JAPAN.

733 Japanese Dinner
734 Family meal
736 Unloading a vessel (Japanese coolies)
738 A Street in Tokio
739 Shintoist Procession
740 Japanese Dancers
741 Ainos at Yeso I
742 Ainos at Yeso II
743 Coolies at Saigon
975 A Scene at the Japanese Theatre
976 Japanese Actors — Dancing man
977 Japanese Actors — Performance with a wig

978 Japanese Actors — Sword Dance
979 Female Dances—Fan Dance
980 Congreation leaving Shintoist Temple
981 A Street in Tokyo
982 A Street in Tokyo
913 An Avenue in Tokyo
984 A Public Square in Tokyo
1022 Harousame Dance
1026 Japanese Singer
1027 Japanese lady at her Toilet
1028 Returning from the Races
1029 Reaping rice
1030 Handmill for irrigation of ricefields

NEW FILM SUBJECTS . . .

Which are constantly being received from all countries will be fully described in our Supplementary Lists, issued frequently.

In Preparation

AN EXTENSIVE CATALOGUE of the most perfect and Up=to=date Models of   .

Cameras, Projectors, Printers

And all Appliances pertaining to ANIMATED PHOTOGRAPHY.

Copy sent post free on application.

. . INDEX . .